A BRIDGE OF DREAMS

◆ A BRIDGE OF DREAMS ◆

THE STORY OF PARAMANANDA,
A MODERN MYSTIC,
AND HIS IDEAL OF ALL-CONQUERING LOVE

———————◆———————

SARA ANN LEVINSKY

INNER TRADITIONS ✦ LINDISFARNE PRESS

Published by The Lindisfarne Press
Box 127, West Stockbridge, MA 01266

Distributed by Inner Traditions International
377 Park Avenue South
New York, New York 10006

ISBN 0-89281-063-7
Library of Congress Catalog Card Number: 83-82698

Printed in the United States of America

For my father, Irving Levinsky,
who practices the truly universal religion: selflessness,
and
for my mother, Leah Lintz Levinsky,
whose mother-in-law once asserted to me,
"Your mother is not a human being; she's an angel."

The knower of the Atman does not identify himself with his body. He rests within it, as if within a carriage. If people provide him with comforts and luxuries, he enjoys them and plays with them like a child. He bears no outward mark of a holy man. He remains quite unattached to the things of this world.

He may wear costly clothing, or none. He may be dressed in deer or tiger skin or clothed in pure knowledge. He may seem like a madman, or like a child, or sometimes like an unclean spirit. Thus, he wanders the earth.

The man of contemplation walks alone. He lives desireless amidst the objects of desire. The Atman is his eternal satisfaction. He sees the Atman present in all things.

Sometimes he appears to be a fool, sometimes a wise man. Sometimes he seems splendid as a king, sometimes feeble-minded. Sometimes he is calm and silent. Sometimes he draws men to him, as a python attracts its prey. Sometimes people honor him greatly, sometimes they insult him. Sometimes they ignore him. That is how the illumined soul lives, always absorbed in the highest bliss.

—SRI SANKARACHARYA

Crest Jewel of Discrimination
translated by Swami Prabhavananda
and Christopher Isherwood

CONTENTS

List of Illustrations

Hiking at Ananda Ashrama, 1925.

Group photograph, Ananda Ashrama.

Planting in orchard, Ananda Ashrama, 1924.

Paramananda with his brother Bibhu Charan's family. Dacca, 1928.

Temple of the Universal Spirit, Ananda Ashrama, 1929.

Interior of Temple.

Cohasset ashrama, "House on the Rock," August, 1929.

On the "High Rock," Cohasset ashrama, c. 1929.

Swami Paramananda. c. 1929.

Ojai, California, 1927.

Cloister patio, June, 1926.

FOLLOWING PAGE 480

Gayatri Devi and Paramananda. Ananda Ashrama, December, 1927.

Sister Devamata. c. 1928.

Sister Daya. September, 1929.

Paramananda. New Year's Day, 1927.

Aboard ship, en route to India, December, 1932.

Outdoor class at Dacca Ananda Ashrama, 1931.

Group photograph. Dacca, 1935.

Chapel of the Vedanta Centre, 420 Beacon Street, Boston, 1939.

Boulder tossed down by flood, Ananda Ashrama, January, 1934.

Group photograph. Ananda Ashrama, c. 1937.

Paramananda with Cincinnati students. July, 1933.

Last picture taken of Paramananda, with Miss Sherwood
at her 80th birthday party, June 5, 1940, Ananda Ashrama.

Swami Paramananda. Cohasset ashrama, 1939.

Introduction

Before he was known as Paramananda, they called him Basanta — Springtime — and how that name fits him! Every word, every action of his seems to radiate the joy, the freshness, the youthfulness of a spring morning. His life's work, too, marks the springtime of Western enthusiasm for the wisdom of India, a blossoming of which we are only now beginning to reap the fruits. Springtime is pregnant with possibilities, and Sara Ann Levinsky catches this air of promise in the pages of Paramananda's biography. No one will be able to read this book without sensing a touch of spring.

Let me make a confession. Confronted by the sheer bulk of the voluminous manuscript, I secretly hoped that by merely skimming through it I could glean material enough to write an introduction. I'm pretty good at skimming through books. But there is no skimming through this one. In no time I was captivated. The freshness of spring is not only in the story of Swami Paramananda's life, but also in the way that story is told here. I like the early spring when things are still plain, almost stark. And I find that quality in the unassuming voice of the narrative sections, refreshingly interspersed with Swami Paramananda's own poems of fervent devotion. As I went on reading, it became more and more difficult to put this book down.

What moved me most deeply was Swami Paramananda's childlike spirit. This may well be his highest achievement. If childlikeness is not an achievement, it is merely retardation. Jesus does not invite us to remain, but to become, like children. Spring is always too short. Childhood is too short for us to become the children we are meant to be. A lifetime is barely long enough for a task like that. But here is a man who accomplished that task. "Every hour that passes grows younger." This is how the poet Rilke captured the spirit of early spring. And St. Paul wrote words which Swami Paramananda could have made his own: "Even though outwardly we wear out, inwardly we grow younger day by day" (2 Cor. 4:16). He was never younger than on his last day when he walked out the door with a dancing step. Who could have suspected that he was not to cross that threshold again?

He blazed a trail. Historically, we may put it that way. And yet, the towering image of a pioneer falls short of conveying Swami Paramananda's true greatness. To his contemporaries he seemed at times like a babe in the woods because he was a child venturing out on a spring morning, his eyes shining with the delight of discovery. But with the wisdom of the child, he found a surer path than many of the noisy trail blazers among his contemporaries. In the prophetic words of Isaiah: "A little child shall lead them" (Is. 11:6).

You have to have worked on a farm to get the full impact of that passage in Isaiah. I, for one, have barely managed to make two calves walk together. It seemed difficult enough without adding a lion. But Swami Paramananda shared Isaiah's vision of the Peaceable Kingdom and that included the wolf, the lamb, the leopard, the cow, the bear, and all the rest of us. Nothing would satisfy him but to "put an end to the intense strife between the different religions." Little children reach for the stars. But the officials of those different religions were not in a mood to "lie down together." It was a cold springtime.

In 1937, a Parliament of Religions was held in Calcutta. It was the occasion of Swami Paramananda's last visit to his native India. Delegates from all over the world were present. Rabindranath Tagore attended, Charles Lindbergh came from America, and some liberal professors from Europe spoke from a Christian perspective. Yet, not one of the Christian churches of the West sent a delegate. The closest to an official representative of the Christian world was the head of the local Y.M.C.A. If this seems hard to believe, less than half a century later, we owe it to children who reached for the stars. We owe it in greater measure than we may realize to Swami Paramananda, in whose heart-warming presence "prejudice melted away."

He proved to be a Christ figure, more Christian than those Christians who narrow-mindedly opposed him out of sectarian prejudice. He was catholic, if that means "all-embracing," yet harassed by officials of Catholic Boston. Sri Ramakrishna had experienced profound mystical communion with Christ. His disciple, Swami Vivekananda, visited America in 1893-97 and here, inspired by the so-called "active" Christian orders, conceived the ideal of the Ramakrishna Mission, combining God-realization and active service to the human family. Paramananda, the third in this succession of great teachers, had but one goal in life: to become "an open channel for God's love." As one seeker who met him exclaimed: "For the first time I have seen Christ's teaching exemplified in a living character."

Only days before his death, Swami Paramananda startled his intimate disciple with the question, "Have I been a good shepherd?" — "The good shepherd lays down his life for his sheep" (Jn. 10:11). Many times, Swami Paramananda had to lay down his life. Confronted by prejudice, slander, suspicion, he chose not to defend himself, but to trust in the power of truth. "It is no easy thing to begin a new work," he wrote, "especially in a strange country." His biographer aptly calls it "planting flowers in a hail storm." But in his heart of hearts he knew it was springtime, and he went on planting.

The first ones in the world to plant gardens were women. In a male-dominated society Swami Paramananda stood up for the rights of women long before that had become a trend. But more than that, he cultivated womanly virtues in himself. Steeped in devotion to the Great Mother, he did not found his communities as an architect lays foundations for a building. Rather, he planted them, and he knew the labor pains of mothering. This gives his biography an added timeliness today.

Equal rights for women was not a matter for debate; it was an axiom for Swami Paramananda. He stood firm on this point, even when he met with opposition from his own order. In this he proved himself a faithful disciple of his master. Swami Vivekananda had put his own service under the motto, "Women and the poor." He was convinced "there is no chance for the welfare of the world, unless the condition of women is improved." And he compared a society in which men have all the power to a bird trying to fly on one wing. Swami Paramananda may have had all the charm of a child, but in upholding these principles he showed all the fire of a radical.

Springtime is a season for planting, but it is also a season for burning. Last year's dry leaves and husks are consumed in the fires of spring. Again he quoted his beloved teacher Vivekananda: "The world is burning in misery." And, fighting fire with fire, he let his own burning conviction blaze: "We cannot think one thing — peace, and prepare for another — war. It will not, it cannot work!" What would he say to us today?

He does still speak. It has been my privilege to feel the fire of Swami Paramananda's spirit still burning brightly in the Ashramas he started. His chosen disciple, Srimata Gayatri Devi, a great Mother, keeps the fire fervent and the light clear. "Paramananda strove to create not an organization, but an atmosphere. He wanted to so charge the Vedanta Centre with peace and holiness, that people could directly benefit just by entering the place." And what a privilege it is to breathe that atmosphere, as of a garden in May. This book will extend that privilege to many who cannot travel to one of the Ashramas. It is a timely book, for we need places to refresh our hearts. And we need what healthier generations had on their bookshelves: *Lives of the Saints*. They must be saints for now; catholic saints, who belong to all traditions, like Swami Paramananda. I trust that his biography will keep alive not only the memory of a springtime, but the power of spring in our hearts.

BROTHER DAVID STEINDL-RAST, O.S.B.
Monk of Mt. Saviour Benedictine Monastery

Selected List of Characters

The following alphabetical lists are intended to provide distinguishing features to help the reader remember the various members of Swami Paramananda's community and the many swamis with Sanskrit names.

SWAMIS OF THE RAMAKRISHNA ORDER

ABHEDANANDA. Direct disciple of Sri Ramakrishna; head of the New York Vedanta Society when Paramananda was assistant.

AKHANDANANDA. Direct disciple of Sri Ramakrishna; head of ashrama in Murshidabad, India. President of the Ramakrishna Math and Mission from 1934 until 1937.

AKHILANANDA. Disciple of Swami Brahmananda; came to America in 1926 to assist Paramananda; founder of Vedanta Society of Providence, Rhode Island.

ASHOKANANDA. Head of the San Francisco Vedanta Society from 1931.

BODHANANDA. Disciple of Swami Vivekananda; briefly assistant to Swami Abhedananda in New York, then head of the Pittsburgh Vedanta Society; head of the New York Vedanta Society after 1912.

BRAHMANANDA. Regarded as second only to Vivekananda among the direct disciples of Sri Ramakrishna; President of the Ramakrishna Math and Mission from 1901 until 1922.

NIKHILANANDA. Founder of New York City's second Vedanta center, the Ramakrishna Vivekananda Center of New York, in 1933.

PRABHAVANANDA. Disciple of Swami Brahmananda; came to America in 1924; founder of Vedanta Societies in Portland and Hollywood.

PRAKASHANANDA. Disciple of Swami Vivekananda; came to America in 1906; head of the San Francisco Vedanta Society 1915-1926.

PREMANANDA. Direct disciple of Sri Ramakrishna; manager of the Belur Math.

RAMAKRISHNANANDA. Direct disciple of Sri Ramakrishna; founder of the Madras Math; Paramananda's mentor.

SARADANANDA. Direct disciple of Sri Ramakrishna; lectured in America from 1896 until 1898; Secretary of the Ramakrishna Mission from its founding until his passing in 1927.

SHIVANANDA. Direct disciple of Sri Ramakrishna; President of the Ramakrishna Math and Mission from 1922 until 1934.

TRIGUNATITA. Direct disciple of Sri Ramakrishna; head of the San Francisco Vedanta Society from 1902 until his death from a bomb explosion in 1915.

TURIYANANDA. Direct disciple of Sri Ramakrishna; lectured in America, especially in California, from 1899 until 1902.

VIJAYANANDA. Disciple of Swami Brahmananda; founder of Vedanta Society of Buenos Aires.

VIRAJANANDA. Disciple of Swami Vivekananda; beloved friend of Paramananda; President of Ramakrishna Math and Mission from 1938 until 1951.

VIVEKANANDA. Foremost disciple of Sri Ramakrishna; founder of the Ramakrishna Math and Mission; first swami to teach in America; guru of Paramananda.

THE VEDANTA CENTRE-ANANDA ASHRAMA COMMUNITY

ACHALA (Edna Massman) (1888-1960). Stenographer from Indiana who joined the Vedanta Centre in 1918, and became Paramananda's secretary.

AMALA (Camille Christians) (1900-1977). Los Angeles Vedanta student who moved to the Boston Centre in 1919, the youngest American sister.

CONCORDE BRODEUR. Talented French-Canadian who joined Ananda Ashrama in 1925.

DAYA (Georgina Jones Walton) (1882-1955). Daughter of a U.S. senator, she met Paramananda in Los Angeles in 1919, and became his platform assistant.

DEVAMATA (Laura Glenn) (1867-1942). Paramananda's first disciple and first platform assistant, the senior sister of the community.

GALENE PHILADELPHEUS. Greek social worker who lived at Boston Vedanta Centre from 1920 until 1929.

GAYATRI DEVI (1906-). First Indian woman to join the community, she was brought from India by Paramananda in 1926, to be trained as one of his assistants.

GEORGE WEIGAND (1890-1967). Versatile foreman of the Pasadena Ice Company who joined Ananda Ashrama in 1924, and became head of the brotherhood.

HILDA JOHANIGMANN (-1954). German Vedanta student from Cincinnati, who lived in the community periodically from 1920.

JESSIE TRUEWORTHY. California miniaturist who lived in the community periodically from 1928.

JOHN QUICK (-1950). Former prize-fighter who joined Ananda Ashrama in 1938.

LILLIAN ENGSTRAND (1888-1978). Head nurse of Boston's Floating Hospital for Children, who moved into the Vedanta Centre in 1926.

MANGALA (Margarite Morgan). California Vedanta student who moved to the Vedanta Centre in 1921, and alternately lived in the community and with her mother in Monterey.

PHILIP REIHL (-1965). Ananda Ashrama student who joined the community after his wife was killed in the New Year's flood of 1934.

SATYA PRANA (Eliza Kissam) (1866-1948). Taciturn New York Vedanta Society member who became the second member of the community in 1912.

SEVA (Mae Gladwell) (1875-1964). Former Mormon who heard Paramananda lecture in Los Angeles, and joined the Boston work in 1917. One of the pioneers of Ananda Ashrama, she planted the gardens, kept the bees, and was Mother of the Community House.

SHANTA (Mary Lacy Staib) (1890-1950). Quiet and practical student from Louisville who joined the Boston community in 1921, Paramananda's "Kentucky Wonder."

VIMALA (Alice Affsprung) (1891-1968). Dainty musician from Cincinnati who often visited the Boston Centre and permanently joined the Ananda Ashrama community in 1925.

NOTE

There is no invented dialogue in this biography. Complete conversations which are quoted were actually recorded by members of Swami Paramananda's community, who valued their teacher's utterances enough to remember and record them verbatim.

Sources have been quoted exactly as written, without correcting the occasional mistakes make by Swami Paramananda and others for whom English was not the native language.

1

Youth In The Indian Village

THE TROPICAL MIDDAY SUN beat down upon the courtyard surrounded on four sides by thatched-roofed, mud-walled dwellings. In one corner, squash, coconuts, bananas, and betel nuts from the recent harvest were piled high. Some of it had been grown on Ananda Mohan's own land, but most had been brought there by the local peasants, his share as manager of the estate. The position, as well as the land, had come to him as dowry for his first wife. The bride's father, a wealthy landowner, had considered himself fortunate to procure a son-in-law of such high status. Everyone had said that Ananda Mohan Guha Thakurta would become a rich man, but instead he invited his two brothers to Banaripara to share his good fortune, and divided his property with them. They and their families occupied the cottages on the north and west sides of the courtyard; after the produce had gone to feed so many mouths, Ananda Mohan had little left to sell for cash. His first wife had died after bearing three children. He married again, a gentle young woman named Brahmamoyee Basu. She added eight more voices to the childish shouts and cries which ever filled the courtyard.

But at this hour of the afternoon siesta, a hush hung over the homestead. Everyone was sleeping, except Suresh, Ananda Mohan's eight-year-old son. Silently, he stole out of the room which he shared with his brothers and sisters, crossed the courtyard, and left behind the slumbering dwellings. He continued to tiptoe, past the estate office and over the bamboo bridge which spanned the moat separating the family enclosure from the rest of the village. Then he broke into a run, through the mango grove and the lichi orchard, between two lotus-covered pools, and around the edge of the rice paddies. When he reached the fields which skirted the village, his playmates were already flying their homemade kites in the cloudless sky. Gleefully he joined them.

Only a few minutes had passed before one of the boys gave out a yell. Watching his kite rise, he had spotted a bunch of ripe dates at the top of a tall palm tree. Immediately, the kites were down and abandoned in favor of the new adventure. The boys gathered at the foot of the tree, craning their necks and squinting their eyes to inspect the proposed quarry. Palm trees were hard to climb; they were exceptionally high, and provided no footing. Automatically, all eyes fell on Suresh. He was the tallest, fleetest, and most agile. Besides, there was no feat he would not dare.

Suresh smiled, and in an instant, he sprang up onto the trunk and began to climb. His friends watched as he worked his way up, reached the top, picked the precious dates, and tossed them down. The boys caught them and devoured them hungrily. They did not see Suresh lower himself onto a withered stem. It broke with his weight, and Suresh plunged into a muddy ditch at the base of the tree. The others ran to him, startled. Suresh sat up and smiled. He assured them he was unhurt, but he held his left arm and winced as he rose.

His main concern was his muddy clothes, a tell-tale sign of his truancy. With his right hand, he took them off, washed them in a nearby pond, and spread them in the sun to dry. In half an hour he was dressed again. He picked up his kite to resume his play when, suddenly, he heard shouts coming from the direction of the village. His mother and aunts were running toward him, having heard of the accident. They took him to the local doctor, who pronounced the arm broken.

The incident is strangely symbolic. Paramananda was forever ascending the heights and tossing down the fruits to others, who were so intent on enjoying them, they rarely noticed the price he paid.

———————◆———————

Paramananda was born Suresh Chandra Guha Thakurta on February 5, 1884, in the village of Banaripara, in what is now Bangladesh. The youngest son of a prestigious family, he was endowed with that rare combination of good looks and good humor, intelligence and affability which easily wins hearts. Congenial, gentle, and affectionate, the boy became everyone's favorite.

Most of all, Suresh was cherished by his father. The delight of Ananda Mohan's old age, the boy became his constant companion. The venerable patriarch's heart swelled with pride when Suresh, even at the age of five, charmed large gatherings with his singing of holy songs.

A respected figure in the village, Ananda Mohan was widely known as a progressive and as a champion for women's education, a legacy he was to pass on to his sons. He established a girls' school in Barisal district, one of the first in East Bengal. Not only did he break through the confines of village society by sending his sons to the city for a university education, but he married his second eldest son to a woman doctor, an even rarer phenomenon in India than it was in America at that time.

Independent and strong-minded, Ananda Mohan had managed to remain free from both the camps that were dividing India in the nineteenth century. On the one hand, the mainstream of society had become stagnated by superstitions, caste restrictions, and the suppression of women. On the other hand, zealous reformers, impressed by the economic superiority of the West, were not content merely to chop off the dead or diseased limbs, but sought to pull the tree out by its roots and plant in its stead the sapling of Western materialism and a Protestantized version of Hinduism. Ananda Mohan had little use for the caste dictates of whom he should and should not associate with. He was friendly toward Moslems and threw open the hospitality of his home to the oft-despised Christian missionaries, who were technically "out-castes." At the same time, he had a deep respect for Hinduism and refused to join the Brahmo-Samaj (a casteless, unritualistic reform movement) or other reform groups of the day.

———————◆•◗———————

Suresh was only nine years old when he saw his mother's life languish away. Stricken with cancer, Brahmamoyee gradually had to relinquish her many duties as matron of the large household. Suresh watched her suffer the slow and painful ravages of the disease until she died, in her early forties.

The men in the family naturally undertook the austerities of mourning, and Suresh clamored to join them. Like them, he wanted to sleep on a straw pallet, eat only unsalted rice and plain vegetables, shave his head, and spend long hours in prayer and meditation. His relatives, however, were convinced that he was too young.

Aunts, older cousins, and sisters-in-law automatically took up the task of rearing Brahmamoyee's children; the extended family system spares the children parental deprivation. But seeing his mother's life slip away at that early age marked Suresh on a deeper level. He recognized that her death was not a unique event; death was the shared fate of all humanity. From that time on, he identified the world with one adjective: transitory. In a notebook of his teenage years, we find, copied in his youthful scrawl, a verse from the *Iliad*:

> Beauty and youth; in vain to these you trust,
> When youth and beauty shall be laid in dust.

And, in another excerpt of slightly more mature script, from *Gray's Elegy*:

> The boast of heraldry, the pomp of power
> And all that beauty, all that wealth e'er gave,
> Await alike the inevitable hour;
> The paths of glory lead but to the grave.

The pursuits and ambitions which captivate most men had lost their power to tempt him, even before they had begun.

In the wake of his second wife's death, Ananda Mohan, now over sixty years of age, began to withdraw from public and social activities, and to devote himself to the inner life, to sacred study and contemplation. According to the ancient Indian concept of the four stages of life, a person becomes successively a student, a householder, a hermit, and a renunciate, each phase having its own particular goal and ideals. Having fulfilled his duty to his family and community, Ananda Mohan embarked upon the path to God-realization.

Suresh's encounter with death did not leave him morose; on the contrary, perhaps only those who experience how ephemeral life is truly know how to play. Cheerfulness was Suresh's intrinsic quality. Once he was reading when someone asked him, "Why are you smiling? Is it so very funny?" Suresh replied, "I am not smiling. My face is made that way." He plunged again into his round of games and sports, swimming and fishing. Dexterous, agile, and enthusiastic, he became an adept athlete. When he was only twelve years old, the tall and slender youth was invited to join an adult soccer team, and at the age of fifteen, he was elected captain of a boys' athletic club.

His family looked on with pride. They had high expectations for the future of this boy who seemed to excel in everything he tried. He would go to the university in Calcutta, and the finest families in the district would offer generous dowries to acquire him as a son-in-law. His successful career, in whatever field he chose, would in turn bolster the family's flagging fortunes. For, with Ananda Mohan's retirement and the family's intermittent sojourns in the city, the agricultural yield of their land was becoming less and less adequate. His eldest son by his second marriage, Bibhu Charan, was a hard-working but physically frail law student. A bout of typhoid at the age of fifteen had permanently deranged the mind of the middle son, Dinesh. Suresh, with his unusual gifts and endowments, was to be the shining star of the clan.

Young Suresh, however, was fired not with ambitions, but with ideals. He longed, as he put it, to "do something worthwhile" with his life, a goal very different from the family's notion of success. He was fascinated by the *sadhus*, or wandering holy men, who would beg alms at their door wearing tattered loin cloths and rosaries, carrying their only possessions, a water-pot and begging bag. His family, faithful to the tradition of Hindu piety and their own generous nature, extended unlimited hospitality to these mendicants. They fed them and gave them a place to spend the night, while Suresh observed their renunciation and detachment with obvious admiration. One morning, several hours after the latest visiting *sadhu* had taken his leave, they noticed that Suresh was missing. Soon neighbors reported that they had seen him leave the village with the holy man. He was fourteen years old. The frantic family pursued him and, much against his will, brought him home. His normally even-tempered brother, Bibhu Charan, was thoroughly unsettled. He slapped the boy for his mischief, for he felt that Suresh's motivation went deeper than merely a child's quest for adventure.

Fun-loving and carefree, Suresh had no interest in education; his quick-witted and intuitive mind found the formalities of the village school irksome and its method of learning by rote tedious. Finally, he appealed to his father for freedom. Ananda Mohan, ever ready to indulge the boy, agreed. Confident, however, that Suresh would outgrow his playful indifference, he arranged for tutors to give him private lessons at home, an acceptable prerequisite for college, which alone could fit a man for worldly success in nineteenth-century Bengal.

Among his peers Suresh was known for his fearlessness. One day as the boys were walking home from a soccer match, they spotted a cobra in their path. The other boys stopped dead in their tracks, but Suresh laughingly picked the cobra up by its tail, swirled it around his head, and tossed it into the adjoining field.

Although Suresh loved sports, he disliked competition, or rather that competitive spirit which turns the will to win into the drive to beat. A congenital lover of harmony, Suresh was ever the peacemaker. Once, he tried desperately to pacify a friend who was lashing out furiously at an older man. The boy ignored Suresh's pleas and lunged forward to attack his adversary. Suresh threw himself between them and took the boy's punch, a blow so hard that it knocked him unconscious.

Those who knew him during those early years remember principally Suresh's affectionate nature. "He loved me very much," was their uniform recollection. He would hold his younger sisters, nephews, and nieces on his lap, hugging and petting them, or he would carry the youngest ones on his hip as he walked through the village. With the oft-neglected young women who had married into the family, he would play cards or sing or share fantasies. He was never too busy to take a younger relative to the annual fair or to a cricket match in a neighboring village. Although his playmates teased him for it, Suresh particularly enjoyed the companionship of elderly people, whom he admired for their "mellowness, sweetness, and ripeness." No one remembers ever seeing him angry or out-of-sorts.

———————◆•●———————

When Suresh was sixteen years old, his father began to go blind. Having given up his worldly preoccupations, Ananda Mohan spent his time in prayer and meditation, but his failing eyesight prevented him from delving into the sacred writings. Suresh became his father's eyes. Each evening he sang devotional songs for him and read to him from the scriptures and other holy books. Suresh became keenly interested in the expositions and admonitions he read aloud in his father's books. Particularly compelling was a collection of "Sayings of Sri Ramakrishna," the much-revered saint who had passed away only fourteen years before.

Ramakrishna had been a simple, unlettered priest of the temple of the Divine Mother at Dakshineswar, near Calcutta. Not satisfied with the mere formalities of worship, he threw himself into a maddened quest to know and experience God directly. He made his whole life a one-pointed thrust toward the Divine, eschewing even natural human needs, such as sleep, and relations with his wife. After he finally attained his goal, he undertook, one by one, the prescribed practices of the different sects of Hinduism and of Christianity and Islam, and through each he attained the same state of exalted consciousness. These experiments convinced him that all religions are equally valid paths to the same goal of union with the Divine.

During the last years of his life, people began to flock to Dakshineswar to see the holy man and to hear his teaching. Among his group of dedicated disciples, several young university students were willing to give up all to follow the precepts of their teacher. After Ramakrishna's passing, these became the nucleus of the monastic order founded in his name by his chief disciple, Narendra, known to the world as Swami Vivekananda.

Ramakrishna's message was simple and straightforward: the purpose of human life is to experience the reality of God, within one's own soul and permeating the entire universe; to fail to undertake this quest is to squander the great opportunity of human birth; any person can attain this state of God-consciousness if he is willing to break the hypnotic spell of material acquisitiveness and sexual desire; the most suitable means for realizing God in this age is the path of love and devotion.

The teachings and the example of Sri Ramakrishna fell on Suresh's soul like seed on fertile ground. Decades later he was to testify of Sri Ramakrishna: "He tried to instill into the hearts of men that not only was 'Seek ye first the Kingdom of God' practical and possible, but it was the only thing to do; and he proved it by his own life."

For Suresh, that quest for God quickly became "the only thing to do." One of Sri Ramakrishna's sayings which particularly impressed him was: "The butter that is churned in the early morning is best. That which is churned after sunrise is not so good." After all, he pondered, why should he fritter away the prime of his life on a vain pursuit of money and pleasure, and give only the remnant of his energy and dedication toward realizing God? Ananda Mohan could not discern the effect the nightly reading was having on his beloved son.

During this same period, Suresh spent much of his time with older friends who were closely associated with the Ramakrishna Math (monastery) and its nucleus of ardent young swamis. They introduced him to Swami Nityananda, who had been given the vows of renunciation by Swami Vivekananda. Nityananda often visited a village across the canal from Banaripara, and Suresh became his avid student. The boy yearned to make a pilgrimage to the new headquarters of the Math at Belur, three miles north of Calcutta, but his family protested that he was too young for such a journey.

Then one night he had an experience which catapulted him out of his normal consciousness. It was a glimpse of the beatific vision, as if the veil which shrouds Reality had been lifted and he could see existence as it really is, scintillating with consciousness, permeated with God. Later he was to write:

Thy love's lightning struck me;
I was dazed and motionless.
The fear of death, like a dark shadow, hung over me;
But Thy lightning danced and glowed
      and in its flash I found life again.
For this new gift I am more wholly Thine
      than I am mine.

How long the vision lasted, or what exactly took place, Suresh
never divulged. Throughout his life he was extremely reticent
about his mystical experiences. But the aftermath of the experience was obvious for all to see. For ten or twelve days, he
staggered around like a drunken youth, abstracted, changed in
manner and mien. The world for him was no longer a playground but a prison, barring him from that beatific realm he had
glimpsed. His family naturally were dismayed and bewildered.
They could not understand how the boy who had loved to
fondle children on his lap could suddenly grow so cold and
indifferent to family, friends, and all that had been dear to him.

Once more he pleaded to be allowed to visit the Ramakrishna
Math. His father was wary. Only a month before Swami Vivekananda had returned from his second triumphal visit to the
West, where his exposition of Vedanta philosophy had drawn
crowds of avid students. Now all of India was aroused by
Vivekananda's very presence on the subcontinent. Ananda
Mohan would have preferred to keep his son away from the
gravitational pull of this luminary, but he had no reasonable
grounds for refusing. A group of older men from the village was
planning to journey to Belur for the birthday celebration of Sri
Ramakrishna. Their departure would coincide with Suresh's sev-
enteenth birthday. Reluctantly, Ananda Mohan consented for
his son to join the party.

The pilgrims reached the Belur Math a couple of days before
Sri Ramakrishna's birthday, 1901. The grounds were crowded
with people, bustling with preparations for the approaching

festival. It was expected to be the biggest celebration in the Order's short history.

The monks had acquired this property only two years before. Prior to that they had occupied a series of rented houses commensurate with their meager finances and uncertain status. Shortly after the formation of the Order in 1886, the same year that their Master, Sri Ramakrishna, had passed out of the body, some of the young renunciates had moved into a dilapidated dwelling, partly in ruins and rumored to be haunted. There, against the opposition of their families and most of Ramakrishna's householder disciples, and with almost no financial or moral support, they plunged into a rigorous life of spiritual discipline and practice: meditation, prayer, night-long vigils, study of Eastern and Western scriptures and philosophy, devotional singing, and frequent fasting (as much from lack of funds as desire for austerity). Narendra, the future Swami Vivekananda, had been designated by Sri Ramakrishna as their leader; he guided them with a demanding zeal matched only by their own ardor.

But the incipient Order was so loosely held together that its permanence was questionable. It is doubtful that all sixteen of Ramakrishna's monastic disciples ever lived in the monastery simultaneously; several rarely lived there at all. Some travelled with the Holy Mother, Ramakrishna's widowed consort; others preferred to undertake their practices in the holy city of Vrindavan or some Himalayan retreat; still others simply resided independently in Calcutta. By the late 1880's, most of the young *sannyasins* (monks) had embarked upon the life of wandering traditional to India's holy men.

Then, in 1893, Vivekananda sailed for America to represent Hinduism at the Parliament of Religions. This event, more than any other, consolidated the fledgling Order. With his towering spirituality, brilliant intellect, and commanding personality, Vivekananda was hailed as the hero of the convention, and in the lecture tour which followed, thousands of Americans flocked to hear India's ancient teachings from his lips. When he returned home in 1897, he was a national hero. His countrymen felt he had redeemed India's fallen glory before the World. His Order was catapulted into national prominence; his monastic brothers returned to the Math at his call or undertook preaching or philanthropic work with his approval.

The monasticism which Vivekananda envisioned after his visit to the West was entirely new to his motherland. For thousands of years the life of renunciation in India had been synonymous with contemplation, seclusion, and austerity. The *sannyasin* cultivated his own inner development, and benefited society indirectly through his prayer and meditation, as in the great contemplative orders of the West. He might preach the truths of religion as he wandered from place to place, yet his concerns were exclusively with man's spiritual welfare. Vivekananda, having long been moved by the dire physical plight of India's masses, now declared that the ideal of the monk must be twofold: God-realization and active service to mankind. He called for an organized, residential community of monks who would minister to the physical and educational, as well as the spiritual, needs of the people.

It was a revolutionary concept in a land which resisted even minor reforms. At first even his own brotherhood was reluctant to give up the life of solitary meditation for this active involvement in social welfare. The orthodox Hindu society, which Vivekananda had already offended by violating the proscription against a *sannyasin* crossing the ocean, was aghast. Nevertheless, the tide of popular approbation was with him, and the new Order surged forward. Branches were founded in Madras, Dacca, and Almora; charitable dispensaries were started in Murshidabad and Benaras; and three periodicals began circulation. Eighteen more men, their spirits quickened by the message of Ramakrishna and the accomplishments of Vivekananda, renounced the world and joined the original disciples.

In January, 1899, the monks moved into their permanent monastery, located on seven acres of land on the bank of the Ganges at Belur. Swami Vivekananda left for his second visit to the West in June of that year and returned to take up residence at the Math on January 24, 1901.

This was the state of affairs when the pilgrims from Banaripara, a month later, entered the Belur Math grounds amidst all of the excitement of Sri Ramakrishna's birthday preparations. In accordance with the ideals of Vivekananda, the occasion was to be celebrated by the feeding of thousands of the poor and devotees. Giant cauldrons of rice and pulse were bubbling over large outdoor fires. In the cooking huts, piles of fried bread and sweetmeats almost touched the ceilings. Huge earthen jars containing hundreds of gallons of water had been implanted in the ground. Into these were being thrown pounds of rock candy, which would dissolve by the following day so that lemons could be squeezed into it, making *sarvat*, the Indian version of lemonade.

Confounded, Suresh made his way to the main building of the Math. He entered the courtyard, and there beheld, under a mango tree, reclining on a camp cot, Swami Vivekananda himself. As Suresh, years later, described it:

> I found myself face to face with a being quite different than anyone I had ever seen before, or even imagined in my vivid consciousness. He looked at me with his big, luminous eyes, which seemed to speak volumes without a single word. I was not formally introduced to the great master, but as my eyes met his lustrous spiritual gaze, I know the feeling which swept me from head to foot was indelible.

"One touch, one glance, can make a whole life change," Vivekananda had once declared. Now his gaze was stirring Suresh's depths, as the rays of the rising sun awaken the natural world. Haltingly, yet as if drawn by a magnet, the boy approached the awesome swami. Kneeling before him, he touched the teacher's feet, the customary Indian sign of respect. Vivekananda surveyed the lad with interest, and, in a voice of tender concern, asked him many questions about himself.

The boy's faculties were no match for this towering presence which had staggered the great intellects and personalities of both East and West. Ramakrishna himself had paid homage to Vivekananda's spiritual genius. Now it swept Suresh's soul like a tidal wave, propelling his destiny along in its mighty current.

In meeting Vivekananda, Suresh came face to face with that reality he had barely glimpsed in his vision. He would later describe him as "love and wisdom incarnate in flesh." Through that day and those that followed, whenever Vivekananda was in view, Suresh hovered nearby, devouring every word and scene. "Have you not," he queried years later, "sometimes seen a face so transcendently, benignly beautiful that you cannot turn your eyes away from it? If you have not, I will not argue about it, for I myself have seen such a countenance."

Once Swami Vivekananda was sitting on the verandah of the main building, surrounded by the other monks. They sat facing the Ganges, which flowed by the monastery. Suddenly a boat came into view bearing huge quantities of provisions for the coming celebration. It docked opposite the main building and out stepped a mammoth, imposing-looking man, who was later identified as Swami Sadananda, Vivekananda's first disciple. As Suresh described the scene thirty years later: "He was wearing a white turban and his face was covered with a full beard. There was great commotion and excitement as he approached and prostrated before Swamiji [Vivekananda]. Such a contrast! Swamiji seemed so fine, so transparent, a being altogether of another world, and this one who came and saluted him, remaining at his feet like an abject slave, was so powerful and huge in stature."

In his life, Suresh would witness much splendor and grandeur, but no sight ever impressed itself as deeply on his mind as this simple scene of devotion and surrender. It struck him that greatness consists not in how high a man can raise himself, but in how low he can humble himself.

On the day of the festival itself, Suresh was assigned the task of pouring the *sarvat* into clay cups for the thirsty pilgrims. Hoards of people thronged the Math grounds. Swami Vivekananda, who was prohibited by his doctors from mingling with the throng, surveyed the crowds from a distance and asked different ones to guess their number. "Some made exaggerated comments that there might be forty or fifty thousand," Suresh recalled. "But Swamiji made a very modest estimate that it was probably not more than ten thousand. As far as my opinion was concerned, I thought the whole world was there. Swamiji always expressed great aversion to exaggeration and self-glorification. Not only would he not blow his own trumpet, but he disliked it very much if anybody else tried to do it for him. It was truth — truth in its nakedness and entirety — that was his great passion."

During that first visit, Suresh had the opportunity to hear Swami Vivekananda sing at informal musical gatherings.

As I listened to Swamiji in the act of singing, one thing impressed me greatly. Although he possessed perfect technique and a great gift of musical talent, he was never given to display of frills, which is so often the customary mannerism with accomplished musicians in India. He himself was lost in the pathos, the depth of devotion, and that was one moment when all his listeners lost themselves. Seeing Swamiji in the act of devotional song, and listening to his beautiful, melodious voice, it was easy for me to visualize how the great Master, Sri Ramakrishna, completely lost his physical consciousness. It was, as it were, a call to the soul, rousing the very depth of a man's being. I am afraid that no words I may use can possibly convey the magnitude and ecstasy which Swamiji brought forth through his songs and devotional bearing.

Too soon the party from Banaripara was ready to return home. Suresh looked at the pile of holy pictures he had collected for his room, and realized that he had lost interest in the pictures, lost interest in his room, lost interest in returning home altogether. During the two-hundred-mile journey back, that glance from Swami Vivekananda's eyes was constantly before him.

When he returned to Banaripara, Suresh tried to settle back into his family milieu, but he felt suffocated by his old life, with its trivial concerns and petty values. His ideal, the ideal he had experienced in his vision, the ideal he had seen embodied in Vivekananda, loomed large before him, and he longed to forsake all to pursue it. Nothing had ever so fired his imagination, so challenged him. Vivekananda had declared: "If you want to rob, rob the king's treasury. If you want to hunt, hunt rhinoceros. What will you gain by robbing beggars and hunting ants? So if you want to love, love God."

As Suresh himself would later describe this awakening:

> When wholehearted and one-pointed love for the Ideal awakens, it comes like a flood and washes off everything — ignorance, narrowness, fear, doubt, selfishness, and leaves what! The Ideal. The Ideal alone is left shining in the heart. Then it becomes easy to renounce everything that is earthly, because nothing has any value except the Beloved. He is the Eternal, the Permanent, the Unchanging; all other things are transitory and changing. He is the Effulgent Spirit; everything else is perishable matter.

Suresh knew he must renounce the world and join the holy Order. With naive frankness he announced his decision to his father and Bibhu Charan, expecting them to rejoice with him. Instead, they reacted with consternation and firm opposition. How could he consider throwing away the privileges and opportunities which awaited him, to become a penniless mendicant! The very suggestion was unthinkable. They tried coaxing him and scolding him, but to no avail. Finally, in desperation they set a watch over him to prevent his leaving secretly.

It is a story as old as that of Bernadone of Assisi disowning his son Francis as mad because the young man preferred rebuilding the Lord's church to inheriting his father's textile business. Such good and pious parents give religion a respected place in their lives, somewhere between their families and their bank accounts. But they consider the person who tries literally to follow the teachings of Jesus, Buddha, or other great saviours an "extremist," as if these teachings were not to be lived, but only revered.

The family was united in their bitter opposition. Ananda Mohan had disentangled himself from most of his earthly ties, but his attachment to his youngest son was stronger than ever. To see Suresh relinquish the brilliant future they had all anticipated for one of his calibre seemed a shameful waste.

The days dragged on. Suresh yearned to return to Belur, to kneel once more at the feet of that colossal spirit whose eyes filled his dreams and waking hours. But Ananda Mohan was intransigent in his refusal, and Suresh could not bring himself to hurt his father, whom he loved and esteemed. The boy had been the sunshine of the household, and now they all felt as though they were living through an untimely and unsettling eclipse. His aunts murmured that in a day or two he would return to normal and give up these outlandish ideas; Ananda Mohan maintained a stoic silence; and when Suresh's two younger sisters taunted and teased him for his odd behavior, Bibhu Charan sternly silenced them, for he did not take the matter lightly.

Since his childhood, Suresh had been unable to witness other people's unhappiness without taking it upon himself to dispel their gloom with a song or a smile. Now he watched his family's misery with a sense of impotence. Love was tearing him in two directions. He loved his family and cherished their love for him, but in Vivekananda he had seen love assume entirely

new proportions, unbounded by delineations of who was one's
"own." He who had known only the village pond had suddenly
glimpsed the ocean. He longed to plunge into it, to bathe in the
depths of that love which frees, rather than binds, for he sensed
that he, too, could connect with its inexhaustible source.

One night, the servant who was assigned to guard him fell
asleep. Bibhu Charan's young wife Charuprabha, to whom alone
Suresh had revealed his innermost feelings, unbolted the door,
and Suresh stole out of the house. He made his way along canals
and through jungle, following the beckoning of that haunting
gaze straight to the Ramakrishna Monastery at Belur.

When he reached the Math, Suresh was overcome with joy
and relief. He immediately went to the main building and requested admission to the Order. He was abashed when one of
the monks looked him up and down and replied that he was too
young. The lad was only seventeen years old, legally a minor. If
his family did not approve his entry (as they most decidedly
would not), they could make trouble for the Order, and even
sue the monastery. The Math, ever in financial straits, could not
afford to lose such a suit. They had just been involved in legal
proceedings upon which the economic future of the organization had hinged. The Hindu orthodoxy of Calcutta, always up in
arms at the new Order's liberal ways, had persuaded the local
Municipality to tax the Math premises on the ground that it was
not a genuine religious establishment, but rather a personal garden house of Vivekananda. The case had been decided in the
Math's favor by the Calcutta High Court less than a month
before. Greatly relieved, the monks were wary of any new controversy or bad publicity, such as might result from the group's
accepting a minor.

Suresh stood crestfallen as the older swamis of the Order
became engaged in a heated discussion over the question of his
admittance. Some, impressed by his sincerity and obvious calibre,
firmly maintained that he should be allowed to stay. Others

argued that he was too young, and that the possible repercussions were too hazardous. They told him to go home and resume his studies and that later on, if his feelings persisted, there would be plenty of time to join the Order. The boy made no reply, but watched the debate in mute anguish. Finally the swamis took the matter to their leader.

After hearing all the arguments, Vivekananda turned to Suresh. His piercing glance met the lad's pleading eyes. Tenderly he asked him: "Khoka [little one], can you sing?" In a quivering voice, Suresh sang to the Divine Mother:

> I recognize nothing, I know nothing, I understand nothing,
>   I only know I want You.
> Consciously and unconsciously,
>   being pulled by my heart's attraction,
>   I am running toward You.
> Here before me is this boundless, expansive,
>   limitless space,
> And I see nothing, only I hear a gentle,
>   tender voice calling.
> I only know, and know for certain, that I have a Mother.
> I possess no other knowledge.
> I recognize nothing, I know nothing, I understand nothing.
> I only want You.

The voice melted into silence. Vivekananda gazed intently at Suresh. Then, turning to his brothers, he announced: "The boy shall stay. I will take full responsibility."

2

With Swami Vivekananda

THE GUHA THAKURTA FAMILY was not about to surrender their treasure so easily. They knew Suresh had gone to the Belur Math, and they sent Bibhu Charan to bring him home. Face to face with Swami Vivekananda, the neophyte lawyer pleaded the family's case: The boy was too young to take such a momentous step, and his father, aged and blind, depended on him. Besides, this was no ordinary runaway. He was a lad of exceptional gifts, with too promising a future to waste.

Vivekananda stared at this man who dared to equate waste with renunciation. Then, in the booming voice which had shaken audiences from America to India, he retorted: "What do you want your brother to be? A doctor? A lawyer? A great man of the world? He will be far greater than any of those."

Bibhu Charan returned to Banaripara alone.

Vivekananda initiated Suresh into *brahmacharya*, the preliminary stage of renunciation. He shaved his head except for a single, symbolic lock at the crown, and gave him a white cloth, the signs of a *brahmacharin*. He also transmitted to him a *mantram*, or empowered phrase incorporating one of the names of God. The *Ishtam*, or particular aspect of the Divine, so designated, would become the disciple's lifelong ideal, whom he would worship and to whom he would direct his devotion.

Vivekananda gave Suresh a double *Ishtam*: Divine Mother and
Sri Ramakrishna.

After this initiation, Vivekananda departed for a tour of East
Bengal. He left his youngest disciple to the training and care of
the President of the Math, Swami Brahmananda, a soul considered second only to Vivekananda among the spiritual sons of Sri
Ramakrishna.

Swami Brahmananda was immediately impressed by the lithe
and charming youth. Noticing how Suresh moved about the
monastery, always with a smile on his face and a song on his lips,
he would call him, "Basanta Kokhile" [spring-bird], or simply
"Basanta" [spring]. And he would affectionately quote Sankaracharya's verse: "A saint is like the spring; wherever he goes he
carries the song of birds and the fragrance of flowers." Quickly
"Basanta" became the boy's new name. Once, when Swami
Brahmananda was paternally stroking Basanta's head, another
older monk jokingly asked whether he was trying to steal Vivekananda's disciple. Brahmananda smiled at the radiant boy and
said, "Well, at least I can be your *upa-guru* (demi-guru), can't I?"

In great contrast to Basanta's first visit, the monastery was
now free of all pilgrims and visitors. The actual residents consisted
of only twelve or fifteen monks, "whose divine lives and character poured forth upon my own life," Basanta recalled, "streams
of love such as are not to be found in the world of mortals."

Only a short time passed before Swami Brahmananda decided that Basanta should be sent out of Bengal, away from the
harassment and emotional pull of his family. Four years before,
one of Sri Ramakrishna's disciples, Swami Ramakrishnananda,
had founded a branch of the Math in Madras, a thousand miles
south of Calcutta. To that monastery Brahmananda now thought
of sending Basanta.

The suggestion stirred up a commotion. All of the young
men and even some of the older swamis thought that Basanta
should not be subjected to the severe discipline of Swami

Ramakrishnananda. In private some of them even tried to persuade the youth not to go. But the more they elucidated the rigors of Swami Ramakrishnananda's training, the more determined Basanta became to fling himself into the challenge.

On his first nights at the Belur monastery, when he was permitted to sleep on the hard floor, a great thrill of spiritual exaltation had swept over him. "It was in a sense as if I were actually nearer to heaven, a taste of joy." It reminded him of the period after his mother's death, when his relatives had prohibited him from fully executing the austerities of mourning. "Now I felt that I was having the full measure of what once I considered a real taste of heavenly bliss."

Basanta's heart was burning with renunciation. The prospect of a life of austerity under the stern tutelage of Swami Ramakrishnananda filled him with eager anticipation. Also, Swami Ramakrishnananda was known as the Order's greatest exponent of the devotional path, a perfect mentor for Basanta's loving nature, which required direction and proper expression. As the young novice left Belur, Swami Brahmananda said to him: "Stay with Swami Ramakrishnananda for three years and everything will be done. Your character will be fully formed in every way. Nothing more will be necessary."

The train journey south had its own trials and temptations, as if the boy's resolution was to be tested at every juncture. At Brahmananda's urging, Basanta stopped at Puri to make a pilgrimage to the ancient Temple of Jaganath. As he approached the holy temple, he suddenly noticed his aunt and a cousin, who, by some freak of fate or play of providence, happened to be making the pilgrimage at the same time. He tried to avoid them in the crowd, but they recognized him, fought their way toward him, and seized him. With frenzied agitation, they demanded that he return home with them. Basanta stood there amidst the bustling throng of pilgrims and refused to budge. His aunt harangued and derided him, but he would not move a

step. Finally they had to let go of the boy. He proceeded straight
to the temple and disappeared through its cavernous doors.

Swami Brahmananda had arranged for Basanta to spend his
stay at Puri at the home of Balaram Bose, a famous householder
disciple of Sri Ramakrishna. Balaram had passed on, and the
house was now presided over by his widow and their son,
Ramakrishna Basu. Fascinated by Basanta, Balaram's widow
showered on him kindness and warmth, and urged him to extend his visit.

Decades later Basanta was to write:

> One strange experience I had to undergo everywhere was
> that even involuntarily my presence aroused great tender-
> ness. The mother of Ramakrishna Basu was kindness itself
> towards me. She used to sit by me, and insisted on my
> eating, just like my own mother. All insisted on my prolong-
> ing my visit there. Here again I experienced a peculiar
> struggle. Had I left home and bonds of family, only to be
> once more entangled through human affection?

Spurning any delay, he proceeded to Madras. It was a long
and tedious rail journey, for the through route had not yet been
completed. Finding his way to the Math, a dusty and weary
Basanta was met at the door by the imposing figure of Swami
Ramakrishnananda.

Swami Ramakrishnananda was a man of astounding single-
ness: in heart, mind, and purpose. The principles he believed,
he lived; and what he lived, he lived wholeheartedly. Massive
and stocky in build, he was like a spiritual monolith. Not the
least trace of duplicity ever entered his character. Brilliant but
guileless, astute but ingenuous, he lived and spoke with a
directness which sometimes must have endeared him only to
God. His spiritual peers revered him, his students feared him,
and the general public steered clear of this teacher who insisted
on feeding them Truth without condiments.

Ramakrishnananda (or Sashi, as he was originally called)

was raised in an orthodox Hindu family. When he began to question the traditional beliefs during his university days, he joined the reformist Brahmo Samaj. Intellectual and scholarly by temperament, he revelled in the study of mathematics, Sanskrit, philosophy, and English, until, at the age of twenty, his meeting with Sri Ramakrishna deflected his energy and enthusiasm from the mind to the heart. Throwing his books into the Ganges, he became the most ardent devotee among Ramakrishna's young followers. When the Master fell ill with cancer, Sashi gave up college and devoted himself fulltime to caring for his teacher. While the other young disciples spent hours in meditation and other spiritual practices, Sashi attended on Sri Ramakrishna day and night, heedless of his own needs and of sleep itself.

After Sri Ramakrishna's passing in 1886, Sashi directed the same wholehearted devotion to the worship of the Master through his picture and relics. His towering intellect had no qualms about this seemingly primitive form of religion, for Hindu philosophy holds that God, the formless and absolute, can manifest through form for the comprehension of the finite human mind. As Sri Ramakrishna used to say: "God is both with and without form. Just think of a shoreless ocean, an infinite expanse of water. Only here and there you see blocks of ice formed by intense cold. The water and the ice are of one substance. Similarly, under the cooling influence of the devotee's love, the Infinite congeals into the finite, the Divine takes form."

Sashi was not one to dally with a vague abstraction termed "God." He knew that just as the components of material existence are real for man, occupying his mind and heart at all hours, so the Divine too must become real for man. An invisible, unqualified Absolute may pacify the philosophers, but it can rarely grip man's mind or displace the powerful hold of the senses over his affections. To transform one's being, God must become a concrete, living presence in the devotee's daily life. Accordingly, Sashi set up a shrine with the picture and relics of the Master.

There he offered flowers and cooked food, and, when the weather was suffocatingly hot, he spent hours fanning the sacred image, lost to the consciousness of his own sweating body. He served the shrine not as a formal and mechanical ritual, but as loving and intimate ministrations to the living Presence.

Once a cynical, young intellectual asked him if he really felt that ritualistic worship was the highest form of adoring God. Ramakrishnananda answered: "To see God everywhere is the highest worship. Meditation is the next best. Prayer and repetition of the Divine Name are lower than that. External worship is the lowest." Why, then, did he spend so much energy in external worship, the young man rejoined. Ramakrishnananda replied: "The worship is not at all an external affair. It is almost wholly internal. Real worship is not done until devotion overflows from the heart and tears roll down from the eyes. A true devotee takes God's name with every breath — and offers flowers, leaves, and water to God without any selfish motive, saying, "O Divine Mother, worship and prayer are nothing but opportune moments to call on you.' "

The shrine which Sashi set up became the stable center of the fledgling Order's first makeshift monastery. And Sashi himself, ever dedicated to service — service of God, guru, and the devotees — became, as Vivekananda said, "the main pillar of the Math. Without him, life in the monastery would have been impossible." While the other young brothers spent themselves in practicing meditation and other disciplines, Sashi attended to their physical requirements, sometimes feeding them forcibly. And when the others, one by one, were seized by wanderlust and left on pilgrimage, Sashi alone stood sentinel, maintaining the shrine and the Math amidst their comings and goings. When the time came for their leader to assign them monastic names, Narendra wished to choose for himself the name of their beloved Master, but he realized that Sashi, with his supreme devotion, deserved it more. Thus, Sashi became Swami Ramakrishnananda—"One who enjoys the bliss of Ramakrishna."

On Vivekananda's triumphal return from America in 1897, he passed through Madras, the cosmopolitan center of South India. The residents there were stirred with enthusiasm by Vivekananda's message, and asked him to send one of his brother disciples to carry on his teaching. It was a challenging situation, for Madras, swept up in Westernism and materialism, was at the same time the stronghold of Hindu orthodoxy. Vivekananda immediately thought of Ramakrishnananda, devoutly orthodox, yet an intellectual match for the most scientific and sophisticated. As soon as Vivekananda reached Calcutta, he asked his spiritual brother to extend his service of the Master by heading the public work at Madras. Everyone who had witnessed Ramakrishnananda's life of secluded worship for more than a decade expected him to refuse. They underestimated how completely service had displaced every vestige of self in him. When the next steamer sailed for South India, Ramakrishnananda was on it.

———————————◆◆———————————

He established the Madras Math on the Triplicane beach, on the ground floor of the "ice house," a building with exceptionally thick walls which had been constructed by an American company to store ice. It was several steps below the ground, and although the thick walls made it cool, it was dank and dark.

Ramakrishnananda lived there alone for most of the first four years. It was a strenuous life. In addition to scrupulously maintaining the shrine and carrying on the housekeeping and cooking, he taught classes in different parts of the sprawling city, with no convenient means of getting from one to the other. Sometimes he would return to the Math after an exhausting day of classes and lectures to find that there was no food for the evening meal. The people of Madras, complacent in their orthodoxy or contemptuous in their intellectual skepticism, were hard to arouse to religious truths which demanded a loftier tenor of living. Nor did Ramakrishnananda have the personality or the charisma necessary to maintain the enthusiasm aroused by Vivekananda's visit. A spiritual purist, it never occurred to him to embellish the teaching to make it more appealing. Thus, financial contributions to the Math were meager, and although many of the classes were well-attended, at other times the teacher himself was the only one present. On such occasions, he delivered his lecture anyway, saying afterwards that he taught these classes as a service to the Lord, and human attendance or lack of it was irrelevant to him. One notes that his own prestige or popularity was even more irrelevant to him.

<hr />

When Basanta knocked on the heavy metal door of the ice house, it was opened by a massive, bearded figure. Basanta introduced himself as the *brahmacharin* (novice) sent from Belur. Swami Ramakrishnananda looked hard at the serious, shaven-headed youth before him. Then he abruptly asked: "How did you wear your hair when you first came to the monastery?"

Basanta had inured himself for the unexpected; nevertheless, he was startled by the question. He described his wavy locks and traced with his forefinger the faint line down the middle of his scalp where his part had been. The swami broke into a broad smile. He moved to one side of the threshold, and Basanta stepped into his new life.

Much later the swami revealed that he had dreamed of his Master, Sri Ramakrishna, and this same boy, but with thick, wavy hair parted in the middle. Sri Ramakrishna had said to him in the dream: "I am giving you this boy. He is my child. The only difference is that you came earlier, and he came later."

According to Swami Ramakrishnananda, the arrival of the vital young *brahmacharin* brought fresh life to him and to the monastery. "There was nothing in it when Basanta came," he said. "But as soon as he arrived, things began to pour in. There is no doubt he is a pet child of Lakshmi [the Goddess of Fortune]. I had nothing to tell the time. The first offering brought was a clock. Then a gentleman gave us some cots, another gentleman some chairs, and soon the place was quite well fitted out."

Basanta immediately joined in the daily routine the swami had established. They rose at 5 A.M., performed their morning ablutions, opened the shrine, made the morning offering, cleaned the shrine room, and then had a cup of tea. Afterwards, they polished the vessels for worship and cut the vegetables for the main offering, while the Swami discoursed on some holy text. Punctually at 11 o'clock, Ramakrishnananda began to perform the worship, which was over by 12:30. Then they ate the food which came from the shrine (their only real meal of the day) and took their midday rest. In the afternoon, for two hours they chanted in Sanskrit and translated one of India's great epics or scriptures. It was from Ramakrishnananda that Basanta learned his polished Sanskrit and impeccable English. In the evenings, or sometimes during the day, the swami went out to give classes or lectures. Several evenings a week the classes were held at the Math.

As the days and weeks passed, Swami Ramakrishnananda scrutinized this lad who had been entrusted to him by Sri Ramakrishna himself. He stood poised to administer the corrections and rebukes for which he was famous, but, as if in confirmation of the dream, the boy's actions, manner, and attitude were above reproach. Whatever he was asked to do, he did with great care and sensitivity, and never had to be told anything a second time, often not even a first time. He maintained a tranquil disposition which never wavered, and showered affection on everyone who entered the Math. A decade later Ramakrishnananda was to assert: "Paramananda lived with me for six years, and I was never able to find a single fault in him." One can be sure he looked.

As Sri Ramakrishna had termed certain of his direct disciples *nitya-mukta*, ever-free, so Swami Ramakrishnananda now declared that Basanta, this later child of Ramakrishna, was also entirely free of ego, born into the world without the triple bondage of lust, anger, and greed. One day the teacher said to the abashed youth: "I wish I had brought to my Master, Sri Ramakrishna, the purity you have brought with you."

It was a staggering evaluation by a teacher who was not easily pleased or impressed. Every other *brahmacharin* who ever lived under his direction testified to his uncompromising standards, demanding expectations, and stern method of training. When one young novice broke down in tears after a severe scolding, Ramakrishnananda explained to him, "A blacksmith first puts a lump of iron into the fire, and when it becomes red hot, then he puts it on the anvil and beats it into shape. . . . You are all like that unformed lump, and it is for your good that you are put to the forge and beaten to shape on the anvil by such scoldings." And the novice, who went on to become a swami, admitted: "Indeed, his method was that of the sledgehammer blow of the blacksmith. Many came, but few could stand his test."

Basanta alone passed it with flying colors, completely unscathed, lauded and spared at every turn. And it galled him terribly. Was this the life of stringent renunciation about which he had been warned and for which he had rushed to Madras? He was prepared to go days without food and nights without sleep, to suffer humiliation and chastisements, to muster heroic reserves of fortitude and will. Instead, all he received was loving admiration and encouragement. To be sure, Swami Ramakrishnananda was constantly instructing him, warning him of pitfalls, admonishing him to hold to the highest ideals. But the mortifications by which Basanta longed to prove himself were emphatically withheld from him.

In his zeal to renounce the world, Basanta severed all ties with his family, not even corresponding with them. Charushila, a niece of his own age and his childhood playmate, wrote to him, "That you who were so tender, like a flower, should so suddenly become like a rock, unfeeling! What has possessed you?" Swami Ramakrishnananda circumvented Basanta's resolve by writing to Bibhu Charan about his brother's welfare.

One day Swami Ramakrishnananda noticed some red marks on the youth's arm caused by the coarse straw mat which he spread on the floor for his bed. The swami immediately ran to the bazaar and returned with a cot, a quilt, and some soft pillows. That night Basanta slept more uncomfortably than if he had lain on a bed of nails. Tossing and turning, he fretted that he had had enough pampering in his life. Why had the siren of indulgence and ease pursued him even into the monastery, even into this renowned bastion of austerity? It was against his nature to fight; instead he resolved to slip away quietly, just as he had run away from his village home. He would find a place in the jungle where he could practice austerities unhampered. This decided, he dozed off.

Suddenly he was awakened by the quick touch of Ramakrishnananda's hand on his face and arm. "You are still here," the swami exclaimed, relieved. "I just dreamed that you had run away. Promise me that you'll never go without telling me."

Startled, Basanta sat up. He admitted that he had planned to leave, and reluctantly made the promise. But how could he be content when he was prevented from practicing the disciplines necessary for his development?

Then, by the light of a kerosene lamp, Swami Ramakrishnananda disclosed the secrets of Basanta's soul which had been revealed to him: that he was really one of Sri Ramakrishna's *antaranga*, his inner circle, born later in order to carry on the work further in time; that he was born for the West, and would serve the Master there; that, like certain other great souls, he would be able to give up his body at will, at the time of his own choosing. Thus, not only did he not need austerities, but they could actually harm him by putting undue strain on his delicate constitution. It would be better service to the Divine to take care of his physical instrument, for it was destined to accomplish great works. "Your body was not meant for such things," he said as he left Basanta's room.

The young *brahmacharin* had promised not to run away, but his spirit still rebelled at the situation. The more he grew to love his intractable teacher, the harder the conflict became, for Swami Ramakrishnananda insisted on keeping all the roughest tasks of the monastery for himself. Months passed, but this contention between them remained largely unresolved.

One day in early October, 1901, Swami Ramakrishnananda received a letter from Swami Brahmananda instructing Basanta to return to Belur. His family, provoked by his persistence in the new life, was threatening to sue the Ramakrishna Mission for admitting a minor. Brahmananda felt that the only solution was for Basanta to go to his village home at Banaripara and work out some understanding with them.

Soon after Basanta reached the Belur Math, Swami Brahmananda fell ill. The young *brahmacharin* was assigned to attend him. As the President of the Order lay in bed, his body racked with fever, he found Basanta's massage soothing and cooling, and he was impressed by how the boy intuitively fulfilled all his needs, before they were even verbalized. The visit to Banaripara was forgotten.

Swami Vivekananda was then in residence at the Math. The diabetes and asthma which had pursued him around the world had caught up with his fatigued body. His days of extensive traveling were over for good. Now he devoted himself to teaching and training personally the monks who would carry his message to the world.

For Basanta, this cherished interlude was the only chance he ever had to live in close contact with his renowned guru. As he described that period in his memoirs:

It was the winter of 1901 when the great Swami Vivekananda
was still in the flesh, moving about at the Belur Math like
a living flame, charged with visions and aspirations which
seemed then utterly impossible of human attainment.
Swami Vivekananda was surrounded by his illumined
guru-bhais (spiritual brothers) such as the Swamis Brahma-
nandaji, Premanandaji, Shivanandaji, Saradanandaji, and
others whose one objective was to glorify the Master. . . .

Basanta watched his guru closely, imbibing the unspoken
lessons that can come only from association with a great soul.
Although Swami Vivekananda is usually characterized as a fiery,
dynamic warrior, Basanta was most struck by the tender side of
his guru's nature. Again and again he witnessed in the great
swami "gentleness almost like that in the heart of a young girl."
One day, as they sat on the bathing *ghats* [steps leading down to
the Ganges], a rough-hewn boat pulled up to the river bank. A
teenage boy, thin and in rags, alighted from the boat. Vivekananda, gazing intently, called the boy over to him and tenderly
asked him questions about where he came from and the conditions there. As the boy described the plight of his native village,
where food was scarce and disease rampant, Basanta saw the
great teacher's eyes fill with tears. And Basanta realized the "lion
of Vedanta" had the heart of a lamb.
   Once Vivekananda had been away from the Math for a few
days. When he returned, he noticed his young disciple and was
so full of loving enquiry that he sat with Basanta for over an
hour, engrossed in conversation. He made the youthful *brahmacharin* feel that he was conversing with a delightful playmate
his own age, as in later years Paramananda's own followers likewise remarked on his faculty for making all feel as though they
were his equals. Thirty years later Basanta was to recall: "He was
so graciously understanding that he quite made me forget any
difference in age or wisdom." And again:

I cannot begin to convey merely through words what my experience was with Swami Vivekananda. We imagine a great man as someone we cannot approach. Swami Vivekananda, however, was the simplest of people. It would have amazed you! His interior was like a child, gentle and mellow, and that was the real Swami Vivekananda. A great, loving heart! Sometimes reading from his books, you do not get quite the picture. I have seen him weeping. I have seen this great soul weeping, when he thought no one saw him, for the suffering poor of India. His heart was heavy with sadness because there was so much suffering in humanity. It is this, not intellectuality, that makes people great, and it was this which left an indelible impression on my mind, that cannot be wiped out.

After his return from the West, Vivekananda was most punctilious about cleanliness and neatness in his monks. The matted-haired, unkempt *sannyasin* would find no place at the Belur Math. One day Vivekananda lined up his disciples and was sternly upbraiding them for carelessness in good grooming. When he noticed one man with long, dirty fingernails, he pulled Basanta out of the line, held up the novice's immaculate hands, and shouted, "Look! Look at this boy's hands! Look at them!" Basanta, of course, was mortified.

In Madras, Basanta had begun to practice strict vegetarianism, as is the custom in South India. That November, for the first time, the Belur Math observed *Kali Puja*, the festival of the Divine Mother in Her terrible, death-dealing aspect. The ritually offered meal included goat meat, which afterwards was distributed among the members of the monastery, seated in long rows in the dining hall. When Basanta's turn came, he silently shook his head to the server. Out of the corner of his eye, Vivekananda noticed this refusal of the sacred *prasad*. With a forceful gesture, he flung a piece of meat from his own portion onto Basanta's plate. Trembling, Basanta ate it. And he learned the lesson: that while certain diets were beneficial for the aspirant, rigidity in any matter could become an attachment, and thus one more fetter for the soul. The highest was to accept "food what chance may bring," as Vivekananda put it.

From his guru Vivekananda, Basanta learned what was to become the ruling gospel of his life. One morning the august swami was sitting on the monastery verandah overlooking the holy Ganges. He was surrounded by a small group of his disciples and fellow swamis. As if plummeting to the depths of his own soul, Vivekananda began to sing a Bengali composition he had written:

> Listen, friend, I will speak my heart to thee,
> I have found in my life this truth supreme —
> Buffeted by waves, in this whirl of life,
> One ferry alone takes us over the sea.
> Forms of worship, control of breath,
> Science, philosophy, systems one and all,
> Renunciation, possession, and the like,
> All these are but delusions of the mind; —
> Love, love alone is the only Treasure. . . .
> "Give," "give all" — whoever asks return
> His ocean full of gifts dwindles to a drop.

All were still for several long moments, wrapped in the song's spell. In the enchanted hush, one refrain reverberated through Basanta's tremulous being: "Love, love alone is the only Treasure." This theme would echo through the rest of his life, growing louder with the years, until it drowned out every other voice within him.

Early one morning near the close of November, Swami Vivekananda was sitting with Swami Premananda on the long, arched verandah outside the Math dining room, drinking tea. The guru called Basanta to him and asked, "Khoka, can you beg for me?" The boy assented instantly; he did not know that this was one of the tests preliminary to receiving *sannyas*, the final vows of renunciation. Vivekananda then told him to put on a ragged cloth and go from house to house, silently, giving no hint of who he was or from where he came. He should stand at the gate and wait for alms. If the people gave him nothing, he should pass on; if they deposited something in his proffered bag, he should accept it, whatever it was. But he was not to speak a word.

When Basanta had changed to a tattered loincloth, he came back to Vivekananda, who exclaimed, "You do not know how happy it makes me to see you like that. How well it becomes you!"

Basanta turned to go, but Vivekananda called, "Wait! I will give you your first alms." He ran to the storeroom, took a little rice and some raw vegetables, and dropped them into the begging bag. Then he sent the boy off.

It was meant as a test of humility and forbearance: to ingratiate oneself, to beg, to expose oneself to taunts and scorn, and not to utter a redeeming word of excuse or explanation; to strip oneself of possessions, rank, and identity, and to put oneself completely at the mercy of other people's charity or lack of it. Basanta revelled in the challenge. For tests such as this he had longed all during those painfully easy months in Madras.

At the first house the residents scolded him for leaving his parents. At another, a group of gentlemen lectured him against begging. At several others, the women of the house lamented over him, saying: "You are too young and delicate to take up such a life." At still another house they would not take him seriously, and accused him of play acting. Only once did Basanta make a reply, and that was by a mute gesture of refusal when someone wanted to give him money.

He returned to the Math about noon, and emptied his bag before Swami Vivekananda. The swami was overjoyed. He called Swami Premananda and told him to use a little of it each day for the offering in the shrine. "There is no holier offering," he said, "than this pure food begged by a pure soul. Sri Ramakrishna was especially fond of such food." Then he asked Basanta if he could cook. "Yes," the boy replied. With his fearlessness and inherent faith, Basanta's confidence always preceded his accomplishments, rather than being the result of them.

Vivekananda waited for Basanta to prepare his midday meal until two o'clock, long after everyone else at the Math had finished eating. When at last he partook of it, he exclaimed that he had never tasted sweeter food. He told the boy to give some to each member of the monastery. "Food begged by a pure heart must purify whoever eats it," he said. Then he fed Basanta from his own plate, one of the most intimate gestures a guru can make to a disciple. Basanta exulted in his guru's love. Later, when he himself had charge of disciples, he would say: "Appreciation for a soul is like sunlight for a flower. Only a shallow nature is spoiled by praise."

This period at Belur also had its tests and challenges for the aspiring novice. One day a swami berated Basanta for something he had not done. The boy, trained in the ideal that one who truly trusts in God must not defend himself, kept silent. The older monk grew sterner in his rebuke. Still Basanta said nothing. Finally the swami exclaimed sharply, "What is the matter with you? Are you deaf and dumb that you do not speak?" That evening, when Basanta was washing the dust from his feet before going to the Shrine, the swami approached him and told him tenderly that he knew all the time he was not at fault, only he had wanted to test his endurance.

A few days later news came to the monastery that the husband of Basanta's eldest sister was lying dangerously ill at his home in Calcutta. A short time afterward, he died. He had been a man of exceptional qualities, and his death was a tremendous loss to the Guha Thakurta family. It underscored the necessity of Basanta's prompt visit to his village home. When he left the Math, Swami Brahmananda told him to reach some definite agreement with his father about his vocation before returning.

One can imagine the inner and outer conflicts which besieged Basanta upon his arrival at Banaripara: on one side the distress and importunings of his family, bolstered by his own love for them and concern for their happiness; on the other, his spiritual ardor and zeal of renunciation, which a few years later he would voice in a letter:

> I've offered my life to God. Can you expect me to take it back? When a person has renounced the world, he has vomited the world out of his system. How foolish, how wretched, he would be to taste that filthy stuff again. Renunciation means giving up never to take back.
>
> What good is there in sense-enjoyments? It brings only misery and darkness. I should never like to run after such pleasure even if I do not get a single glimpse of spirituality by my whole lifelong struggle. At least self-control will make me more independent. Never mind whether I realize God or not in this life, but there is no reason why I should live a life of slavery or live in the world and beget children, and create more and more bondage around me. No, I mustn't. I know the world is bad. Why should I be tempted again by that? No, by no means shall I go back.

Particularly agonizing must have been the sight of his blind, aged father, who mourned and missed the youngest son who used to sing and read to him. What could Basanta offer him for all those unread pages, for all those songless nights? He had nothing to share except his own spiritual yearnings, which he poured out to Ananda Mohan in such a compelling stream that the old man was momentarily carried along in its current. After Suresh's disappearance, when Swami Nityananda had come from the neighboring village to console the anxious family, he had told them: "Do not worry. The boy will not perish. He will become a spiritual gem of the world." Ananda Mohan was familiar with the Hindu belief that if one man attains liberation, he becomes the redeemer of his entire family. Thus, one night during Basanta's stay with his family, Ananda Mohan took his son's head into his hands, blessed him in his chosen vocation, and called him *kula-pavaka*, the purifier of the clan.

While Basanta was in Banaripara, Swami Vivekananda had summoned Swami Ramakrishnananda to Belur to confer with him on some important matters. Shortly after his arrival, Vivekananda asked him: "What has become of that young *brahmacharin* whose body shone with such light?"

Ramakrishnananda, who corresponded with Basanta, replied, "He is with his family."

"What is he doing there so long?" Vivekananda rejoined. Ramakrishnananda wrote this to Basanta.

Basanta had been away a month, and was yearning to return to the monastery, but he shrank from inflicting the pain which his departure would cause his father and the whole family. The letter provided a compelling reason for terminating his visit. When he took leave of his father, both their hearts were heavy, their eyes filled with tears, and their minds weighted with a sense of finality.

A few months later, Basanta had a dream in which he saw himself carrying his aged father in his arms across an ocean. Although the ocean seemed very deep, the water never went above Basanta's knees. Soon after, he received news that Ananda Mohan had died.

One day, shortly after his return to Belur, Basanta was sitting near the banyan tree behind the monastery. Suddenly Vivekananda walked up to him and abruptly asked, "Would you like to become a *sannyasin*?"

The normally poised youth was astonished and overwhelmed, for he was still only seventeen years old and had been serving as a novice for less than a year, while other, older *brahmacharins* had been in the Order three or four years. He could not have known what Vivekananda himself knew: that if he returned to Madras without receiving the rites of *sannyas* (final renunciation) from his guru, he would never receive them from his hand. For a long time the thirty-eight-year-old leader had been having premonitions of his imminent death. He did not wish to leave any unfinished business in the matter of Basanta's soul.

However startled he was, for Basanta it was a rhetorical question. If the guru thought he was ready for *sannyas*, no self-abasing claims of unworthiness could have made him resist. Without faltering, he answered, "Yes."

The ceremony took place on the auspicious full-moon day of January 2, 1902. His head had been shaved, except for a small lock of hair at the crown, and he had dyed a cloth in the ochre, or *gerua*, color which symbolizes the fire of renunciation. The day before, a *brahmin* priest had performed his funeral rites, representing his death to the world and his rebirth in God. Henceforth, his family was to be the whole human race, whom he was to serve without any motives of personal gain or partiality. Basanta sat between Swami Vivekananda and Swami Ramakrishnananda, before the sacrificial fire which they had lit. They poured oblations upon it as symbols of Basanta's past, which must be consumed so that the new life of selfless consecration may emerge. Vivekananda then tied the ochre cloth around Basanta's loins, and gave him his new name: "Paramananda" —one who has attained the bliss of the Supreme. Finally, the guru cut off the remaining lock of hair, signifying the severing of all worldly ties.

After the ceremony, Vivekananda prepared to depart for Benares, and he wanted to take with him the new *sannyasin*, whom he still affectionately called "Basanta." But Swami Ramakrishnananda, who was returning to Madras, begged to be allowed to take the boy with him. Vivekananda waived his claim, and the young Swami Paramananda prepared to head for the South once more.

Shortly before his departure, Vivekananda was sitting in his second-floor room when Basanta walked past on the verandah.

Vivekananda called him, and, gazing at him, began to intone the verse from Sankaracharya, a play on Basanta's name: "*Santa mahanto, Nirasanti santo basantavat locahitam charanta.*" "He is serene; he is great; his goodness abides, like the season spring; he brings benefit to all men." Thirty years later Swami Paramananda would recall, "Whether it was a conscious benediction, or whether it was the tenderness of love that he felt for me, I take it with bowed head, because it lives today just as real, just as true as then."

Swamis Ramakrishnananda and Paramananda reached Madras in the middle of January, 1902. On the night of July 4, as Ramakrishnananda sat in meditation, he heard the familiar voice of Vivekananda calling: "Sashi, Sashi, I have spat out the body." Soon after, they received official word that Swami Vivekananda was gone. He had passed on like a true yogi, while seated in meditation, on the fourth of July.

The two men were first stunned, then plunged into sorrow. Vivekananda had been the light of their lives. At his behest Ramakrishnananda had given up his secluded life of devotion in the Calcutta monastery for the active public life of Madras. He regarded Vivekananda with the same adoration and reverence he felt for the Master himself.

As for Paramananda, he rarely spoke of his guru, but he silently determined to make his whole life and character reflect that of his great preceptor. Years later he would say of Vivekananda: "We do not honor a great soul by speaking words of praise of him, but by making our lives like his."

How well he succeeded, or how naturally he was disposed to resemble his guru in the first place, was attested to by Vivekananda's close disciple, Sister Nivedita. This Anglo-Irish schoolteacher had given up everything to serve Vivekananda's cause in India; she travelled with him extensively, and enjoyed the privilege of close, daily contact with him for long periods. After his passing, she embarked on a lecture tour which, in December,

1902, brought her to Madras. She stayed at the Math, where Paramananda was appointed to look after her needs. Sister Nivedita was struck by the young swami's resemblance to their guru, and began calling him "Baby Swamiji." ("Swamiji" always refers to Vivekananda among members of the Order.) To the people of Madras Paramananda was generally known as "Kunchu Vivekananda" (the little Vivekananda).

The likeness which they sensed was certainly not based on physical appearance. Vivekananda was stocky and powerfully built, while Paramananda was tall, slender, and delicately framed. But the young swami apparently resembled his guru in his breadth of spirit, in his boldness, and in his spontaneity, which took little account of convention and rigid formalities. Many years later, when Paramananda was smarting with disappointment because one of his spiritual brothers would not recognize the right of his female assistant to address an assembly on the same platform with other religious leaders, he wistfully remarked, "Swamiji would have understood."

3

The Madras Math

In the monastery at Madras, Paramananda the mystic and his
creed evolved. The zealous novice who entered in 1901 emerged
five and a half years later committed to an ideology he would
adhere to and promulgate for the rest of his life. The mature
embellishments, the finishing touches, would be rendered in
far-flung corners of the globe, but Paramananda's basic values
never wavered from those that Swami Ramakrishnananda incul-
cated in him in the Madras hermitage. The character of the
beloved mentor, his devotion, simplicity, surrender, and child-
heartedness, struck a responsive chord in the young monk's soul,
and became the leitmotif of Paramananda's future teaching.

Paramananda's remaining four and a half years at Madras
were a direct preparation for the roles he would be called upon
to play in the West. He continued studying English, Sanskrit,
and Vedanta philosophy under the tutelege of Ramakrishnananda. The teacher's thorough skill and Paramananda's own
intuitive comprehension made some of the Americans who knew
him for thirty years assume that he had been educated at Oxford or Cambridge, rather than in the basement monastery of
Madras. During those latter years in South India, Paramananda
also got his first taste of public speaking, and when Ramakrishnananda was away on his frequent lecture tours, the young swami

was periodically in charge of the Math. It was his inner training, however, which best fitted him for his destiny as a spiritual guide for seeking souls.

———————◆◆◆———————

Paramananda revered and loved his mentor, who watched over him constantly with brooding protection, but in the months following their return from Belur, the conflict over the young monk's practicing austerities grew worse. Fired with his recent vow of *sannyas*, Paramananda's spirit was restless with longing for greater renunciation. But Ramakrishnananda remained adamant in his unwillingness to let Basanta practice the least austerity. "You do not need it," he would say. "Leave that for boys of coarser fiber." He refused to let the boy work in the kitchen, overheated by an open hearth fire, and continued to keep all the roughest tasks for himself.

Finally, in silent protest, Basanta shut himself up in his room, and would not come out or eat for twenty-four hours. He spent the time writing his first article, on (appropriately enough) "Freedom," which was later published in the Order's Bengali magazine, the *Udbodhan*:

> Even an ordinary bird, which we think has no power of discrimination and which we, capturing from the wild forest, put carefully in a cage made of gold, has its full awareness of freedom. The bird considers its golden habitation a dreadful bondage, and the best of food offered, unavailable in the woods, altogether undesirable . . . .

The composition reflects Basanta's preoccupation with conquering the senses, which was the ruling passion of his spiritual life during that early stage:

> Why does man work so hard? It is purely to fulfill his desires, and desires born of the senses are the cause of his various states of suffering, sorrow and misery. The senses

are the cause of his bondage. Then the only means to gain
freedom is by conquering the senses. . . .

To serve the senses in human life is simply an act of
cowardice. Oh brother, what an illusion you have that you
consider yourself brave and advance to kill your enemies
with shield and sword! It is simply foolishness on the part
of one who, being incapable of conquering the enemies
within the body, proceeds to conquer the enemies outside.
Conquer the self, then you will see that the whole world
would submit to you of its own accord. . . . Strike the
enemies inside with the sharp sword of discrimination,
and endure their counter-attacks patiently; do not be
dispirited. Do not trust the senses at all, for a moment
even, until you are able to bring them under your control.
What fear do you have once you gain freedom? Then you
will be eternally content and you will bring contentment
to hundreds and hundreds of other men and women.

The unspoken conflict between the youth and his teacher
surfaced again and again in a multitude of ways. One day at the
Students' Home founded by Ramakrishnananda, Paramananda
noticed one of the indigent boys shivering for lack of a wrapper.
Joyous for some small opportunity for sacrifice, Paramananda
gave him his woolen shawl, the only one he owned. On the next
chilly, rainy day, Ramakrishnananda noticed Paramananda going
about with only a thin shirt on. He asked where his shawl was,
but Paramananda tried to evade the question, answering, "I am
not cold." The older swami persisted until Paramananda admitted that he had given it away to someone who needed it more.
Immediately Ramakrishnananda wrote to the Belur Math asking
Swami Premananda to send the best ochre-colored shawl he
could find in Calcutta. When it arrived, he presented it to Paramananda, whose desire for self-abnegation had been foiled again.

Although their daily schedule included two hours of study,
the young Paramananda, in his indrawn frame of mind, yearned

to spend all his spare time delving into the sacred books and mystical teachings. Ramakrishnananda himself had been a scholastic prodigy until one day at the Dakshineswar Temple. He was studying Persian in order to read the Sufi poets in the original when Sri Ramakrishna called him, but he was so absorbed in his book that he did not hear the Master's voice. After the third call, he finally came running. Sri Ramakrishna said to him, "If you forget your duties for the sake of study, you will lose your devotion." A word was enough for the young aspirant. He took his books and threw them into the Ganges. From that day on he shared his Master's attitude that the acquisition of intellectual knowledge could be a subtle sidetrack on the path to God, and that scholarly learning led more often to pride than to wisdom. Thus, despite Paramananda's earnest entreaties, he insisted that the young monk did not need recourse to books. He maintained that Paramananda had come fully equipped from birth with the necessary spiritual knowledge, and that further education and studies would only fill his mind with superfluities which would have to be cleared out again for Divine truth to find a place. "You are greatly fortunate that your brain is not filled with such rubbish," he would say. And Paramananda was left frustrated and unhappy.

Ramakrishnananda's refusal to give in on the issue of austerities was not due to his indulgence of his beloved charge. On the contrary, the greatest indulgence would have been to let him have his own way. But Ramakrishnananda knew what Paramananda had not yet learned, that the truest renunciation is the renunciation of one's own will. God cannot fill a soul until it is completely empty of self, including one's own opinions, views, and ideals, however noble these may be. Conquering one's will is even more difficult than conquering one's senses. Forgoing his ardent desire for austerity turned out to be Basanta's chief austerity, designed to make him surrender the control of his own life, which saints must necessarily yield to God. It was not an easy test for a boy who had always had everything he wanted, and the struggle dragged on for more than two years. Finally, however, he conceded. "I came to know that the life of the Spirit lies deeper than the outer act," recalled Paramananda years later. "It lies in profound surrender to God and inward renunciation."

> Once I was a rebel and abhorred all subjection,
>   even unto Thee;
> My haughty heart would not bend.
> Now I smile to think with what whole-souled surrender
>   I lie at Thy blessed feet.
> Verily Thou art a transformer!

Of course, this was not his only struggle. During that formative period, the young monk was grappling, trying to find his balance between gentleness and weakness, between steadfastness and obstinancy, between surrender to God's will and surrender to man's whim. Particularly compelling for the innately tender youth was the question of strength. Swami Brahmananda once said to Basanta, "You are too tender. You are like a flower. You must become like a rock if you would endure." Aiming his sights at perfection itself, Basanta fought to exterminate every vestige of selfishness from within himself. "Unselfishness has always been my ideal," he wrote a few years later. "Whether I have ever been able to follow it successfully or not, I will struggle so long as the life remains in the body. . . . Oh, how I wish to serve Him and His children. But it is not possible to do unless we are thoroughly unselfish."

The driving force behind Basanta's life became his impassioned quest for the Divine. "Find God at any cost," he wrote. "Hold Him with all your might of thought and prayer. Keep Him with you always. Without Him there is nothing worth having."

The Madras years created Paramananda the mystic, just as later periods would shape him as a teacher and a leader. Without that deep inner grounding, he would have been just another lecturer or organization man, the clerical collar notwithstanding. Sri Ramakrishna, first and foremost, had been a God-intoxicated lover of the Divine. His spiritual heirs, whatever their particular leanings, were rooted in the mystical ideal of intimacy with and absorption in God. Even Vivekananda, with his driving concern for social welfare, had exclaimed: "Stick to God! Who cares what comes to the body or to anything else. Through the terrors of evil, say—my God, my love! Through the pangs of death, say—my God, my love!"

Five and a half years of intensive inner life—meditation, worship, constant and attentive ministrations to the living Presence —under the direction of one who sometimes went into ecstasy before the altar—all fanned the young Paramananda's spark of devotion into a blazing love of God. As he once poured forth in a letter:

> "Divine Mother is the goal. Ah! She is the only place of rest and peace. Pray to Her, pray to Her. Think of Her and Her alone. She is the real protection. She is the source of all happiness and bliss. Let us dive deep in the ocean of Her Divine love and be mad" . . . "Jai Ma Anandamai!" "All Blissful Mother, victory to Thee!" . . . Pray to Her: "O Mother! Give me true love at Thy feet. I do not want anything else. Take everything else from me, only give me pure love at Thy feet." Pray day and night, and weep for pure devotion and pure love. . . . Be absorbed in this grand worship.

Even as he fixed his gaze more and more on God, Basanta brooked no distinction between love for God and love for man. In his second published article, "Love," Paramananda, echoing the refrain he had learned from his guru, defined the true lover as one who, seeing God dwelling everywhere, loves all men and women as the children of that One. Nor was this simply a pious proclamation on his part, for the article is a scathing condemna-

tion of those religionists who preach love for all men but do not
translate it into actions. He reproached Christians who quote,
"Turn the other cheek; love everyone," but who in fact love only
a handful of people from their own society who have the same
views as they do. He censured Buddhists who proclaim *ahimsa*
(non-violence) as the highest virtue, but who "will not hesitate
to kill homeless foreigners whose opinions differ from theirs";
and the various sects of Hinduism who despise and compete
with each other.

The standard he promulgated (and obviously took quite
seriously for himself) is a lofty one: "To love all created beings
equally is love. . . . To injure no one with one's body, mind, or
speech is non-violence. To torture another by the use of one's
corporeal strength is violence. To contemplate harm towards
another is mental violence. To speak harshly to anyone or to say
something that will hurt the person is verbal violence. . . .
And unless one is free of violence, one cannot occupy the place
of a lover."

Aside from its theme, the article is noteworthy for what it
reveals of the young Paramananda's own nature: his intensity of
feeling, his idealism, his absolute insistence that one's actions
must be true to one's words, and his recurrent preoccupation
with freedom. A salient point of the article is that everyone must
be given the freedom to follow his or her own path, for even if
there is some fallacy in that viewpoint, since God dwells in him
or her as surely as in us, He will correct the error. The article also
defines his attitude toward human love. At no time did the
naturally affectionate young monk shy away from loving people.
Rather, he was determined to expand his love to encompass
everyone, for love that picks and chooses is based on self-interest
and is no love at all.

Thus, from the very beginning of his spiritual striving,
Paramananda championed the theme that was to become the
crux of his own life and teachings: "Love! Thou art my God."

Twenty-five years later Swami Paramananda enunciated a set of
resolutions which summed up his method for self-transformation.
Most likely, this was the program he himself had adhered to
during his formative years. They open: "I shall begin this day
with the resolution that I may in every way make myself an open
channel for God's love to manifest through me."

How was this to be accomplished? By firm commitment and
strict mental control:

> First of all, I shall with all my might make my thoughts free
> of all other elements that are not pure and unalloyed love.
> This task I know in my heart of hearts is most difficult,
> as there are people, places and occasions which may pro-
> voke unloving thoughts, but I shall cling with all my might
> to this principle, reminding myself forcibly that:
> Love is greater than hate.
> Love is greater than doubt,
> Love is greater than fear,
> Love is greater than anger.
> Love is greater than impatience,
> Love is greater than self-pity,
> Love is greater than all morbid feelings.
> Love is greater than depression,
> Love is greater than all the afflictions of body and mind.
> I shall therefore with solemn resolution try to shut out
> all other thoughts, images and impressions which provoke
> anything but love in my heart.

From his use of phrases such as, "with all my might," and
"reminding myself forcibly," it is clear that Paramananda himself
found this program rigorous. To unconditionally love everyone,
at all times, became the driving aspiration of his life. Whenever
he seemed to have mastered it, his fate would deal him an even
more difficult challenge to test him. Nevertheless, he never wavered in his yearning to make himself "an open channel for God's
love to manifest through me."

Paramananda had ample opportunity to practice this love
and tolerance as the Madras Math became more and more a
vital center of activity. Other young *brahmacharins* and swamis
of the Order came to apprentice themselves to Swami Ramakrishnananda, and many gentlemen of Madras began to frequent the monastery. They came with their troubles or doubts
or questions, choosing the hours between six and eight o'clock
in the morning, on their way to work, for their visits. Whereas
the monks had previously risen at five o'clock and, after attending to the shrine, had spent the early hours in secluded contemplation, they now had to rise at four in order to have some
quiet time before the public arrived. Paramananda made it his
practice to rise even earlier.

He was particularly popular with these lay devotees. Swami
Ramakrishnananda talked of his luminous assistant to everyone
he met, and many came to see him, surprised to find such a
youthful *sannyasin* when, from Ramakrishnananda's description,
they had expected a mature sage. Two of these men used to
come every afternoon and ask to see "that Beaming Intelligence,"
the name they had given Basanta before they knew his own.

Already his radiant smile had become his trademark. His
name "Paramananda" meant "supreme bliss," and he seemed to
live up to it without effort. His natural mirth bubbled up through
the young monk's grave earnestness, for he believed that cheerfulness was as essential to spirituality as any of the cardinal virtues.

Later he recalled, "I was relieved when I read in Sri Ramakrishna's teachings, and heard Swamiji say, that cheerfulness
was very desirable. It had been a doctrine with me and I feared it
might be a lack in me somewhere. There were times in the
monastery when I might have been morbid. I was much alone.
Of course, I read and meditated a great deal. But it is not natural
for me to be morbid. I am naturally buoyant."

Swami Ramakrishnananda, with all his brilliant intellect and
intense spirituality, had a keen sense of humor. During his youth-

ful days with the other disciples of Sri Ramakrishna, he would amuse the others by reading Mark Twain's books aloud, dramatizing them to the hilarity of all present. At Madras, he encouraged the young Paramananda to be cheerful not only when he felt like it, but always, for depression opened one up to lower tendencies, was an expression of self-centeredness, and denied the all-blissful Divine presence within. Once Paramananda was looking dejected. Ramakrishnananda asked him, "Why is that cloud on your face? I have never before seen you like this. You are always buoyant and cheerful." Paramananda explained that he had received some bad news. Ramakrishnananda replied, "A child of God should not be sad. Don't ever let me see a frown on your face again. It hides the smile of Divine Mother."

A devotee of Sri Ramakrishna from the village of Vayambadi, a few hours' journey from Madras, used to invite Paramananda to his village. It was there, in the small temple this man had built, that Paramananda gave his first public discourse on the spiritual life. He told Swami Ramakrishnananda afterwards that he had almost fainted from shyness. But the villagers loved it, and prevailed upon him to come back again and again, always making it an occasion for general feasting and rejoicing. Swami Ramakrishnananda, fearing the effect of the heavy food and continuous festivities on Basanta's frail constitution, finally had to limit these visits. "I was afraid they would kill him with their enthusiasm and devotion," he said.

The Madras monastery also became a popular halting place for members and devotees of the Order passing through the South. In 1903, Swami Trigunatita, a disciple of Sri Ramakrishna who was on his way to America to preach Vedanta in San Francisco, stopped at the Math for a fortnight's visit. Swami Ramakrishnananda was away on a lecture tour, so the care of this honored guest fell on Paramananda. As there were no extra beds in the monastery, Paramananda gave his own to Swami Trigunatita. When the older swami realized this one night as he was about to retire, he lay down on the floor and refused to take the cot. Paramananda threatened to put him on it by force, which made everyone present laugh, for Swami Trigunatita was a massive hulk of a man, weighing over two hundred pounds. Suddenly, however, Paramananda stooped, lifted him, and laid him on the bed. Everyone was astounded, except Swami Ramakrishnananda, who, hearing of it later, simply remarked that he always knew Paramananda combined the gentleness and delicacy of a woman with the strength and firmness of a man.

Swami Trigunatita took a special liking to Paramananda. Once, after tasting a cool drink which the younger swami had served him, he asked, "What do you put into whatever you prepare to give it such a special flavor? Your devotion has certainly awakened in you the divine instinct, so that all you do has a special fragrance." After Trigunatita reached San Francisco, several times he wrote urging Paramananda to join him as his assistant. But it was not yet time.

In 1904, Paramananda's health started to decline. He completely lost his appetite, and daily grew thinner and weaker. Swami Ramakrishnananda attributed the condition to his spiritual ardor and extreme self-denial. He commissioned a devotee to procure a daily supply of eggs, which was no mean task in that strictly vegetarian Brahmin district, and himself combed the bazaar and exhausted his ingenuity trying to find dishes to tempt the young monk's waning appetite. Paramananda, however, felt utterly unable to partake of a normal amount of food. A devoted friend, hoping that a change of climate would help, carried him off to Tanjore for three weeks, then another devotee took him to the hill station of Ootacamond. These trips somewhat revived Paramananda's strength, but his return to the devitalizing heat of Madras again weakened him.

Swami Ramakrishnananda, gravely solicitous over Paramananda's continued loss of weight, finally decided to take him back to Bengal. The medical expert in Calcutta, as if substantiating Ramakrishnananda's diagnosis, reported that there was nothing organically wrong with the young swami; he was simply run down and needed complete rest and nourishing food.

But the rainy season had descended, and Bengal was rife with disease. Paramananda, his power of resistance low, fell prey to typhoid fever. Those who loved him watched helplessly as his condition rapidly deteriorated. There seemed little chance of saving him. Finally, when the danger was greatest, he had the sensation of leaving his body and passing over to another realm. He felt joy in the experience, but suddenly he saw Swami Premananda, the manager of the Belur Math, approach Sri Ramakrishna and beg the Master to return the boy's life so that he could render service to the world. The next thing Paramananda knew, he was back on his bed, and the fever had broken. Gradually, he regained his health. The experience, however, left him with the conviction that his new-found life was not his own, but had been entrusted to him to carry out some higher purpose. Swami Ramakrishnananda fostered this feeling. He often told him, "You have come into this world for the happiness of many and for the good of many."

Swami Brahmananda sent Paramananda to convalesce at the home of Navagopal Ghose, a devout disciple of Sri Ramakrishna who lived across the river from Calcutta, and was always anxious to render any service to the Order. Navagopal's large and luxurious house was also the meeting place for his eldest son's pleasure-loving friends. They would gather there every night to smoke, play cards, and listen to music. When the ardent, shaven-headed swami moved into the house, both he and these young men, who were about his own age, felt a peculiar embarrassment. The presence of a monk in their midst cramped the young cardplayers' style considerably.

Paramananda, despite his own religious fervor, was never

one to condemn or condescend. He asked to join them in a game
of cards. The young men were astounded, but they dealt him a
hand. They were even more astounded when he won. In later
years his associates were to complain that they could never win a
game from him in anything—tennis, ping-pong, bridge. As the
modern manuals for yogis promise, once he had mastered the
art of concentration, he succeeded in whatever he tried.

So the convalescing young renunciate became a part of their
nightly game. The young men wondered about the religious
viewpoint that was wide enough to include card playing, and
they began to ask him about it. Paramananda shared his philosophy with them, and gradually the card game gave way more and
more to religious discussion. Finally the cards were abandoned
altogether, and the soirees became classes in which the swami
expounded Vedantic scriptures to his eager and enthusiastic
listeners. Navagopal himself exclaimed again and again: "What
have you done to these boys? You have succeeded in doing in a
few days what I have been trying to do for years. You must
certainly be full of electricity!" This was Paramananda's first experience as a teacher.

A younger son of that family eventually joined the Ramakrishna Order, becoming Swami Ambikananda. He is known in
India as the composer of two famous hymns to Sri Ramakrishna
and his consort, Holy Mother. In later years he also composed a
song in tribute to Paramananda, the swami who had restored
harmony to his boyhood household:

> Who are you, stealing our hearts
> With your smiling face, and radiating beauty?
> You are tender with love,
> And you are dedicated to a holy mission.

Soon Paramananda returned to Madras, where Swami Ramakrishnananda was intent on putting the finishing touches to his
training. He felt strongly and repeated often that Paramananda's

destiny lay in teaching Vedanta in the West. To go from a contemplative life in rural India to public work in fast-paced and technological Christian America would be a major adjustment. He had to be prepared, inwardly and outwardly, for the role.

In order to teach Vedanta philosophy to Americans, an understanding of and appreciation for their own religion was crucial. Universality was, of course, a keynote of Sri Ramakrishna's teaching. He himself had practiced many different religious paths, and his followers not only tolerated other religions, but actively drew upon their inspiration and wisdom. The original young band of disciples had been fused into a brotherhood on Christmas Eve, after Vivekananda had told them the story of Jesus' life. Throughout Vivekananda's travels in the West he always carried with him two books, the Bhagavad Gita and the *Imitation of Christ.*

Swami Ramakrishnananda had a particularly deep feeling for Christianity; Sri Ramakrishna used to say that in a previous incarnation Sashi (Swami Ramakrishnananda) had been a disciple of Jesus. Once, after Ramakrishnananda, Paramananda, and an orthodox Hindu friend had finished dining at the home of a student, they took a walk to the nearby Church of St. Thomas. Christianity in India, with its aggressive missionary approach, was viewed with animosity by most orthodox Hindus, who considered Ramakrishnananda one of their most orthodox exponents. The friend was thus somewhat surprised when Swami Ramakrishnananda asked to enter the church, and he was utterly shocked and horrified when Ramakrishnananda walked straight up to the altar, knelt before it in a Christian posture, and began praying.

Under Swami Ramakrishnananda's tutelage, Paramananda developed a love for and appreciation of Jesus and what he stood for, which would cause him later to write:

> If we are not kind, tender, loving and forgiving towards all, we have no share in the religion we profess. Jesus the Christ taught this through His life, through His self-

abnegation and His all-embracing love, a love which was
not confined merely to those who followed Him and loved
Him and were related to Him. . . . The man who forgives
most, who loves most, is a true Christian. He has reached the
Christ-Ideal, and also he has reached the universal spirit.

In June, 1906, Swami Abhedananda, another disciple of Sri
Ramakrishna, returned to India after nine years of leading the
Vedanta Society in New York City. A brilliant scholar, an energetic organizer, and a lucid speaker, Swami Abhedananda was
the most active and best known Oriental in the United States
from 1897 through the first decade of the twentieth century.
During his youth in the monastery, his unstinting practice of
austerities had earned for him the title, "the great ascetic." A
stunningly handsome man, with a patrician bearing and a serious,
aloof personality, he used his thorough knowledge of science,
logic, and Eastern and Western philosophy to prove skillfully the
relevance of Vedanta for the modern age. Greatly devoted to
Ramakrishna and Vivekananda, and zealous to propagate the
Vedantic teachings, he toured North America from Alaska to
Mexico, lectured in the Northeast, Midwest, Far West, and South,
published scores of pamphlets and books compiled from his
lectures, and founded short-lived centers in Brooklyn, Washington, D.C., and (later) Pittsburgh, San Francisco, Los Angeles,
Denver, London, and Paris. He was an independent figure, determined to succeed despite clashes with Vivekananda's American followers and eventual dissociation with the Belur Math
itself. In the twenty-four years he would spend in America, this
1906 trip was his sole visit back to India.

Swami Ramakrishnananda and Paramananda met Swami
Abhedananda's boat in Colombo, Ceylon, and accompanied
him to Calcutta. The people of India accorded the returning
swami a welcome second only to the one they had given Vivekananda nine years before. He had successfully carried on the

work of the greatly beloved leader, re-establishing India's respect-ability before the world. The journey from Colombo to Calcutta was like a royal progress. Triumphal arches were erected, rose petals were scattered along their way, torchlight processions ac-companied them, and in one place the enthusiastic young men unharnessed the horses from their carriage and drew it themselves. In Colombo, Madras, Bangalore, Mysore, Calcutta, and dozens of smaller cities, public meetings were held, attended by thousands.

It was Paramananda's first tour through India, and the fan-fare might easily have entranced him. But a devotee in Bangalore reported an incident which shows the real trend of the young monk's mind. One afternoon during that city's triumphal recep-tion of the swamis, Paramananda felt the need of rest and asked to stay quietly in their quarters. This devotee, a physician, re-mained with him. After talking for a while, Paramananda began to sing holy songs. In the middle of one of them, he passed into a state of higher consciousness and remained there for some time. When he returned, his face, according to the doctor, was shining with a light such as he had never seen on any other face. The swami just went on singing, without saying a word.

Swami Abhedananda constantly reiterated his need for more workers in America. Somewhere along the line, it was agreed that Paramananda would accompany him back to New York as his assistant. They stayed in Bengal for almost four weeks, which gave Paramananda a chance to bid good-bye to all those he knew and loved there. As he took his leave from "M.," the famous recorder of *The Gospel of Sri Ramakrishna*, Paramananda said, "I go to America not to teach, but to learn." He himself could not have realized how much he would be called upon to learn there. When they left Calcutta on October 5, he made his final farewell to Swami Ramakrishnananda, who stayed behind and shortly after returned to the South.

They continued, amidst much pomp and fanfare, across the subcontinent, through Benares, Agra, Almora, Ahmedabad, and on to Bombay. On November 10, 1906, Swamis Abhedananda and Paramananda departed from India on the English steamer, the *S.S. Marmora*. They stopped for two weeks in London, where Swami Vivekananda had spent much time and energy starting a Vedanta society. The organization had fallen apart with the defection of its local leader, E.T. Sturdy. Vivekananda used to address Sturdy as "Blessed and Beloved"; his betrayal, accompanied as it was by a scathing condemnation of the swami, had hurt Vivekananda deeply. Now Abhedananda tried to arouse renewed interest in Vedanta, and promised to come back soon and start a new center.

The *Marmora* docked in New York harbor two days before Christmas, 1906. As Swami Abhedananda, a seasoned traveller, made preparations for landing, his young assistant stood at the rail gazing at the tall buildings and mechanized civilization of his new home. For Paramananda, the idyllic days in the Bengali village and the South Indian hermitage were over forever.

4

New York Tempest

THE NEW YORK VEDANTA SOCIETY was a veritable lions' den, and Paramananda a most naive and unsuspecting Daniel. Two other assistant swamis had preceded him. One returned to India with broken health in January, 1906. The other, Swami Bodhananda, had arrived in New York in the summer of 1906. In January, 1907, only four weeks after Swami Abhedananda's return to New York, a disagreement between the two of them led Bodhananda to move to Pittsburgh to head a new center. In 1910, Swami Abhedananda himself parted ways from the Vedanta Society and retreated to the Connecticut Ashram which legally stood in his name, after which the Society practically disbanded for two years. In short, during that period in the New York Vedanta Society, dissension constantly prevailed—among the members, between the members and the swamis, and between the swamis themselves. It was a far cry from the loving nest of Madras.

Even Vivekananda had had trouble with this first-born child of his American enterprise. He had "founded" the New York Vedanta Society in 1894, during his first visit to America. That meant that he had enlisted a president, vice-president, secretary, and treasurer, and later two committees to handle the financial affairs, manage the details of his lectures and classes, and take care of the printing and distribution of his books and pamphlets. But he did not consider this an "organization." When an interviewer in 1896 asked him whether he had made disciples in each of the American cities he had visited, Vivekananda replied: "Yes, disciples. But not organizations. That is no part of my work. Of these [organizations] there are enough. . . . Organizations need men to manage them; they must seek power, money, influence. Often they struggle for domination, and even fight." And in a letter of 1895 speaking about the nature of the New York Vedanta Society, he wrote: "We have no organization, nor want to build any. . . . The Theosophists' methods can never be ours, for the very simple reason that they are an organized sect. We are not." Indeed, the Vedanta Society, which he considered a "cooperative work," rather than an organization, had no membership roll, no dues, no formal delineations.

Years later Swami Abhedananda described Vivekananda's dislike of organization:

> I know that when Swami Vivekananda started the work, he did not believe in organization. In fact, when he invited me to go to London and gave me the charge of his work, he did not organize. And where is the London Society today? It has gone to pieces. Then he started a Society in New York. He did not organize; in fact, he could not organize. He did not put his force in that line at all. He said that wherever there is organization, that is the seed of discord and inharmony.

Swami Abhedananda, on the other hand, firmly believed that organization was necessary and desirable. In 1897, Vivekananda returned to India and Abhedananda came to America to take over the New York work. In 1898, Abhedananda incorporated the Vedanta Society under the laws of the State of New York. In March, 1900, while Vivekananda was in San Francisco, the Board of Trustees opened a membership roll and established dues of $12 per year, or $250 for a life membership. Nonmembers would be charged 25 cents for the Tuesday evening classes.

Vivekananda observed these developments with detachment. He realized that organization was probably inevitable in the West, and he resigned himself to it. But his close and devoted followers in the New York Society, Mrs. Sara Bull and Miss Josephine MacLeod (both of whom, along with Sister Nivedita, had travelled with Vivekananda in India and had received daily private instruction from him) and Mr. Francis Leggett, who was president of the Society, reacted with indignation. They vehemently disapproved of the turn the Vedanta Society was taking and wrote to Vivekananda in California, demanding his intervention.

The controversy went deeper than the matter of organization. The real question was: who controlled the Vedanta Society? On the one hand, the swamis of the Ramakrishna Order came at the invitation of the American people and were considered their guests. The foreign chapters belonged not to the parent organization in India, but to the local members who sponsored them. Thus, Vivekananda's American disciples had a reasonable basis for claiming hegemony in the Society. Besides, their financial contributions kept the work going. But Swami Abhedananda had been empowered by his spiritual brother Vivekananda to be more than a functionary. He was the teacher and spiritual leader of the group, and had his own claim to authority, a claim he did not take lightly.

On April 12, 1900, Swami Abhedananda wrote to Mrs. Bull, who lived in Cambridge, Massachusetts, accusing her of turning Mr. Leggett against him (after three years of their working together harmoniously in Mrs. Bull's absence) and trying to sabotage his leadership of the Vedanta Society. He said that some of the original Vedanta students had warned him about her "plans and ideas" but only the current quarrel had convinced him of her undermining intentions. "You have tried your best to crush my work and drive me out of New York," he wrote, "and to bring a breach between me and my friends. . . . You may not call me spiritual. But I am not going to be guided by your or Mr. Leggett's standard of spirituality." He claimed that Mrs. Bull had made Swami Saradananda, another direct disciple of Sri Rama-krishna who had lectured in America from 1896 to 1898, "a tool" in her hands, and was unsuccessfully trying to do the same with the recently arrived Swami Turiyananda. To Mr. Leggett, he wrote: "I wish you would resign and leave us alone and would not quarrel with us any further."

The fatigued and beleaguered Vivekananda treated this conflict with characteristic detachment. He refused to get involved, and wrote to Josephine MacLeod: "You understand why I do not want to meddle with Abhedananda. Who am I to meddle with anyone, Joe? I have long given up my place as a leader — I have no right to raise my voice." And two days later, after receiving yet another note from Miss MacLeod: "If John or Jack does not obey you, am I to be hanged for it? What do I know about this Vedanta Society? Did I start it? Had I any hand in it? . . . These things get complicated sometimes, in spite of ourselves. Let them take their shape."

They did. Mr. Leggett resigned the presidency, and the Leggetts, Miss MacLeod, and Mrs. Bull went off to Europe. The newly enrolled membership elected in his place one of Abheda-nanda's own disciples, Dr. Hershell C. Parker, a professor at Columbia University. And, to settle the real question, Swami Abhedananda amended the Society's bylaws, giving the Swami-in-charge some measure of control.

Such disharmony among its followers may appear to reflect poorly upon a philosophy which aims to promote inner peace. This deduction, however, would be like discrediting medical surgery because its patients usually look and feel worse when they are rolled out of the operating room than when they went in. Inner peace is a goal which can be attained only after a long and pains-taking process of working with oneself. True peace is achieved not by repressing the negative elements in one's personality, but by recognizing, accepting and transcending them. This process of spiritual purification is often compared to lighting a fire under a pot. Ultimately, the boiling will sterilize the contents of the pot, but the first result will seem like just the opposite: all the impurities will boil to the surface, becoming more visible, so that they can be skimmed off. Thus, spiritual aspirants sometimes act more turbulently than other people, for while the aim is peace, the process is struggle.

This is particularly true in a system like Vedanta, which insists on the freedom of the individual and free self-expression. Indeed, the early followers of Vedanta in America were, for the most part, unwieldy individualists and freethinkers, attracted by Vedanta's undogmatic philosophy and universal tolerance. Having rebelled against the established churches and institutions, they ironically found themselves grouped together by their common interest and desire to learn from a teacher. Therefore, they were unlikely candidates for a harmonious association, and Vivekananda's prophecy about organization forming the seed of discord was amply fulfilled.

In 1900, the upheavals in the New York Vedanta Society had divided it into two factions. The "old students," who had joined during Vivekananda's first visit to America, still cherished the simple life of their original small circle. But Swami Abhedananda's drive to expand the work had drawn in many new students who had a different temperament and approach. As one of Swami Abhedananda's earnest young disciples (a Westerner who later became Swami Atulananda) wrote in *With the Swamis in America*:

The Swami became popular and his work increased. He was a very busy man, lecturing, holding classes, giving private instructions and writing books on Vedanta. The Society flourished, the intellectual world was attracted. . . . What had begun in a private, unostentatious manner, developed into a public movement. . . .

The old students did not like the change so much. . . . With larger classes and many strangers dropping in, the atmosphere changed. Perhaps it was not quite reasonable to expect that things would go on exactly on the old footing. Anyhow, the Swami felt that he was called to reach out beyond his little circle, that his message had to go forth to all quarters, that the success of his work necessitated his meeting with the intellectual and well-to-do people of New York; that Vedanta was not for the few, but for the many. (pp. 26-29, 39)

At that stage Swami Turiyananda, another direct disciple of Sri Ramakrishna, arrived in New York, fresh from India:

"Fresh from India" was in itself a recommendation in the sight of the old students. "We do not want a westernized Swami; business and lecturing we have enough in America, we want a simple, meditative man"—was their attitude.

Right or wrong, this was the state of affairs. Swami Abhedananda, always strong and positive, followed his own counsel. He wanted to spread Vedanta, he had to follow his own plan. And he flourished. . . . He was called to other cities to lecture. He was loved, admired and applauded wherever he went.

Swami Turiyananda was deputed by Swamiji [Vivekananda] to assist Swami Abhedananda in the New York work. This he did in his own quiet way. . . . Many of the old students rallied around him, he got a little following of his own. . . . He represented India as the old students pictured her—the land of simplicity, of meditation and of spirituality. Gentle, cheerful, meditative, little concerned about the things of this world, he made a deep impression on the minds of those who took Vedanta most seriously — not as a philosophy to satisfy the intellect alone, but also as a practical guidance in their spiritual life.

And so we had two Swamis of different temperament, attracting the different students. . . . (pp. 27-29)

One thing was clear. Swami Turiyananda did not care much for public work, organization and all that. He was for the few, not for big crowds. His work was with the individual — character-building. He seemed to be of the opinion that with organization the spiritual work is apt to suffer. "Lectures," he used to say, "are to reach the public, but the real work can be done only through close personal contact. . . . We must each follow our own way. Swami Abhedananda will reach many people through his lectures. But that is not my way." (p. 39)

Unfortunately for the old students, Swami Turiyananda soon left New York for Montclair, New Jersey, and then California. But their preferences, and grievances, lingered, and the stage was set, in December, 1906, for a re-enactment of the same drama, with a thoroughly unrehearsed protagonist.

———————◆———————

The hour of Abhedananda's and Paramananda's docking in New York conflicted with the regular Sunday morning service at the Vedanta Society. Consequently, only Laura Glenn, a prominent follower from Vivekananda's time, and two others met the *Marmora*. As Miss Glenn later described it:

When the steamer came alongside the pier, [Swami Paramananda] was nowhere to be seen. We were busy with the luggage when he took his place silently among us. . . . He was calm and perfectly at ease and he maintained the same quietness and simplicity when an hour later he faced a large portion of the congregation, who had lingered at the Society after the Service in the hope of seeing the arriving travelers.

In the beginning, the new young swami was met with genuine appreciation. Swami Abhedananda wrote to Swami Ramakrishnananda: "Basanta is an excellent boy. Having seen him for eight months I like him very much. I shall do my best to foster the good qualities which he has in him. His future is really very bright. After all, his character has been shaped in your hands. Can your power fail?" To this Ramakrishnananda wrote in reply: "The boy is pure by nature; so I take no credit for that."

Laura Glenn, recalling Paramananda's advent, which coincided with Christmas week, wrote: "He seemed to come as the spirit of Christmastide itself. As he moved through the halls there was always a murmur of song on his lips, and the unvarying brightness of his mood and bearing filled the house with joyousness."

Ironically, this very approbation sowed the seeds for the young swami's undoing in New York. One Monday in March, Paramananda spent several hours with Josephine MacLeod, who wrote enthusiastically to Sara Bull: "He is the youngest of Swamiji's disciples and *full* of Swamiji. The beauty, love and character of our Beloved. . . . My heart is full of the joy of Swamiji. This fine young child—fearless—sweet—strong."

In April, Mrs. Bull invited Paramananda to be her guest at her home in Cambridge. The widow of the famous Norwegian violinist Ole Bull, she presided over one of the most prestigious salons in that intellectual center, frequented by such notables as William James, Julia Ward Howe, Irving Babbitt, and the young Gertrude Stein. Paramananda stayed with her for three weeks and impressed her so deeply that in letters to friends in India she compared him to Sukadeva, the youthful sage of ancient India, whose calm and dispassion were so great that he could carry a goblet full to the brim around the king's palace, crowded with dancing girls, courtiers, and festivities, without spilling a drop. Mrs. Bull predicted that Paramananda had a great work to do in the West, and urged him to establish a center in Boston.

This friendship was bound to arouse Swami Abhedananda, who suspected Mrs. Bull of trying to undermine his leadership of the New York Vedanta Society. According to Swami Sarada-nanda (in a letter to Mrs. Bull), Swami Bodhananda, the previous assistant, had left New York because "Swami Abhedananda brought him to task for visiting a few old friends of Swamiji and for other trifling reasons." Given Swami Abhedananda's distrust of Mrs. Bull and the acclaim which Paramananda effortlessly won from Vivekananda's devotees, it is not surprising that the young swami returned to New York to face a tense confrontation.

A few days after his return, Paramananda wrote Mrs. Bull a brief note, addressing her as "Granny," the name that many of her Vedanta friends used:

> My dear Granny,
>
> I find it better to leave the society at once. So I am coming back to you this evening, Friday, by the Fall River boat and am wiring you to that effect. I hope that it will not put you to any inconvenience. I know, my dear Granny, that you will be glad to take care of me until I can make further plans. I will explain everything to you personally.
> With deep love and regards,
>
> > Yours affly,
> > Paramananda

He did not take the Fall River boat that evening. While it was his nature to respond to any "fight or flight" challenge by quietly slipping away, this time something made him suddenly choose a third alternative. He stayed and endured. Ironically, the ensuing ordeal would be the making of him, and the undoing of the New York Vedanta Society.

A conflict of issues, temperaments, and personalities polar-

ized the Vedanta Society behind the two swamis. By temperament Abhedananda and Paramananda were diametrically opposed. As the historian Carl Thomas Jackson described Swami
Abhedananda: "A forbidding sense of dignity kept a distance
between the man and other people. Although enjoying a fanatical devotion from a few disciples and a considerable popular
success as a lecturer, there was no such widespread outpouring
of appreciation and love toward him as one finds from the followers of Vivekananda or (later) of Swami Paramananda." One
of Swami Abhedananda's own disciples, Swami Atulananda,
wrote of him:

> One would think that we became very intimate with the
> Swami. But in reality, it was not so. He liked us, he loved
> us, but yet there was something in him which kept him a
> little aloof. He was always steeped in his own thoughts. He
> was very kind, and would answer any of our questions,
> and remove any of our difficulties—but intimacy, he would
> have none.

Paramananda, on the other hand, was warm, affectionate,
quick to form not only friendships, but deep relationships with
his students. Once, when asked the secret of the affection he
both gave and inspired in others, he replied, "people seem to
feel kinship for me. I love them and they love me. It is not a
thing of calculation." Paramananda watched over the welfare of
his students with almost motherly solicitude. Thus, he would be
troubled by the depression of one elderly gentleman, and would
take it upon himself to dispel it. Or a woman member would
report that the young swami was so intuitively responsive to
their needs that shortly after she had suffered a serious accident
in her apartment and while her sister was beside herself without
any means of contacting help, Paramananda suddenly showed
up at their door, asking, "Do you need me?"

Indeed, the two swamis, one with the public flair and the other with the personal touch, might have harmoniously complemented each other. As Josephine MacLeod wrote in March, "I like him [Swami Abhedananda] for what he is doing, not for what he lacks, and the new Swami will carry the love and warmth to give life to it all." But those who for years had bristled at Abhedananda's leadership, leapt at the new alternative, and Abhedananda's endeavors to expand the movement created a gap in New York which they were more than happy to fill.

At the end of January, 1907, Swami Abhedananda had gone to Pittsburgh for the inauguration of the new center. He had left Paramananda to take charge of the classes in New York, and when he was not able to come back for the Sunday morning lecture, Paramananda had found himself giving his first public address in America. In June, Abhedananda left for England to establish a new Vedanta Society in London, and did not return until September. Again in 1908, he spent seven months working in London and Paris. When he was in New York, Swami Abhedananda preferred to lecture at large rented auditoriums rather than at the Vedanta Society house, with its limited seating capacity. Consequently, Paramananda was given charge of the regular Sunday morning lectures at the Society beginning May 26, 1907. By autumn he was also conducting the two midweek classes and giving private counselling to those who requested it on Wednesday afternoons. The official circular announced: "The Vedanta Society reopened its Sunday Service and Classes on September 15th, with Swami Paramananda in charge."

The "old students" were delighted. Since the departure of Turiyananda, they had been waiting for just such a swami—simple, meditative, unbusinesslike, emphasizing the growth of the individual rather than the growth of the movement. They rallied around Paramananda, who was too naive to suspect a split or to calculate his behavior in order to prevent one.

Foremost among these students was Laura Franklin Glenn. Forty years old, a woman of brilliant intellect and culture, she had been born in Cincinnati of a prominent family, descended on her mother's side from Benjamin Franklin. After graduating from Vassar, for ten years she lived in Europe, studying at the Paris Sorbonne and other European academies. Religious and idealistic by nature, she tried a period as a lay sister in an Episcopal convent. In 1896, she heard Swami Vivekananda speak in New York and began regularly to attend his classes and lectures while he was in the city. From that time on she frequented the Vedanta Society, but her life continued to lack the direction and purpose for which she longed. Thirty years later she wrote of what happened next:

> I had fled from the hurried life of New York to the calmer atmosphere of Boston and was spending my days in seclusion and silence. One afternoon, as I sat alone in my living room, troubling over my aimless future, suddenly two figures stood before me. The face of one shone with a super-earthly smile, which seemed to shed an effulgence over his whole being. In quiet tones he spoke these words: 'Do not grieve. You have work to do for me.' Then both figures vanished, but the sense of their presence lingered for many days.
>
> In the early spring of 1902, I returned to New York and soon after became a member of the Vedanta Society, being put in charge of the Publishing Department. At that time books came out in rapid succession. My hours were very full and I was in frequent consultation with the head of the work [Swami Abhedananda]. One late afternoon he called me to his private study to talk over a new publication. As I entered the room, my eyes fell upon a photograph hanging over the mantel. I stood still, transfixed. It was the figure I had seen in Boston. I walked quickly across to the fireplace and asked, almost abruptly: "Of

whom is this a picture?" The head of the work replied quietly: "It is my Master, Sri Ramakrishna."*

From then on, Sri Ramakrishna became the object of her meditation and her love. A year and a half later she entered upon a course of intensive spiritual training under the supervision of Swami Abhedananda. This included hatha yoga postures, breathing exercises, and meditation. The meditation, however, caused her real grievance, because Swami Abhedananda, not taking into account her natural devotion to Sri Ramakrishna, had instead given her what she termed a "dry and mechanical" object for meditation. The problem was soon resolved, but it was not until Swami Paramananda appeared on the scene that she felt she had found a true guide for her particular path. She recognized him immediately, for he was the second figure who had appeared in her fateful vision.

On March 19, 1907, Swami Paramananda initiated Laura Glenn and gave her the name "Devamata" (Mother of the Gods). Thus, she became his first disciple.

Swami Abhedananda's supporters naturally felt that such alliances encroached upon Abhedananda's status as leader of the group. They reacted with indignation and resentment against both the disloyalty of the "old students" and the usurpation of the new swami. Regarding Paramananda's faculty for winning hearts, which had made him a general favorite at Banaripara, Belur, and Madras, as a deliberate ploy to wrest the hegemony of the Society away from its recognized leader, they unabashedly accused the young swami of arrogance and power drives. According to Jackson, the only religiously unaffiliated historian to

---

*Like most followers of Vedanta, Miss Glenn told her mystical experiences to no one save her guru. Shortly before her death, however, she realized that testimony of the revelations of a Divine being should be preserved, even though the seer herself might as well be forgotten. Thus, she recorded her experiences.

deal with the Vedanta movement:

> "The crisis seems to have been precipitated by the arrival
> of Swami Paramananda. . . . Given dissatisfaction with
> Abhedananda's leadership, Paramananda offered an alter-
> native. An amiable person of warm personality, who in
> later years won a tremendous devotion from his followers,
> it was understandable that he soon developed a following
> in the New York Society."

Sister Shivani (Mrs. Mary LePage), Swami Abhedananda's
disciple and advocate, recounted the events of 1907 and 1908 in
her biography of her teacher, *An Apostle of Monism*. The tone of
her diatribes against Paramananda gives some indication of what
the young swami had to endure during those years. Again, to
quote Jackson:

> Sister Shivani attempts throughout these events to make
> Swami Paramananda, who she says was "vain and arrogant"
> and who "felt he could carry on on his own and displace
> the older Swami," a major cause of Abhedananda's trou-
> bles. She suggests that he insinuated himself into control
> by playing upon some weaker members of the Society. This
> may be quickly discounted as partisan polemics, in which
> the book abounds—such an action being completely out
> of keeping with all other evidences of the character of
> Paramananda. His role seems to have been that of the
> unknowing victim of an explosive situation, a matter of
> circumstance rather than premeditation.

Five years of painstaking training under Swami Ramakrishnananda had prepared Basanta for the mystic way, not for the
streets of New York. While the ideals of most youths are quickly
consumed in the fires of the "real world," Basanta's ideals had
been carefully fired in the kiln of the Madras monastery and had
emerged from the heat well-baked and permanent. The call of
the Divine madman Sri Ramakrishna, the roar of the uncompro-

Sri Ramakrishna

Ananda Mohan Guha Thakurta, Paramananda's father.

Swami Vivekananda

Paramananda in his native village after becoming a swami.

Paramananda as a sannyasin, c. 1902.

Swami Ramakrishnananda

Group at Belur Math, c. 1901. Paramananda, rear row, seventh from right; Second row: Swami Virajananda, second from left; Swami Brahmananda, third from left; Swami Sadananda, third from right.

Swami Abhedananda seated in center, Paramananda to his right, Swami Ramakrishnananda to his left. India, 1906.

At the Greenacre Conference on Comparative Religion, Maine, c. 1909.

Paramananda and Mr. Stone. Milton, Massachusetts, 1909.

mising Vivekananda, and the daily example and admonitions of the quixotic Ramakrishnananda had effectively drowned out whatever the voice of worldly wisdom might have whispered in Basanta's ear. Unsophisticated and ingenuous, it never occurred to him to calculate the effect of his actions or to temper his spontaneity with shrewdness. Indeed, having been taught to wrestle with the internal antagonist, in the form of ego and desire, he had never suspected an external one.

Ignorant of the ways of the world, the skills of the spirit, born of his devotion to the Divine Mother, gave Paramananda the strength and detachment to face this trying period. As he wrote at the time:

> Those who take refuge at Her blessed feet need never worry under any circumstances. Even when dangers come from all sides like thick clouds, if we do not forget Her, and patiently bear everything, then we find that it is true that She can make most impossible things possible for the protection of Her devoted children. There is no other power which can make us suffer. She is the only power in this universe.

The split which was dividing the Society was not based merely on the distinction between old and new students. More accurately, it was an issue of different paths. Some students had chosen the path of *bhakti*, or devotion to a personal God, which Sri Ramakrishna had extolled as the safest path for this age. This entails forming an intimate relationship with God through prayer, repetition of the Divine name, song, ritual, and constant thought of the Beloved, as practiced and taught by Swami Ramakrishnananda. Most of the New York students, however, having been drawn from intellectual circles, had embarked upon the path of *jnana*, or knowledge, which endeavors to discriminate between what is real (the Divine Self) and what is unreal (everything else). God is conceived of as *Brahman*, the Absolute, beyond name and form, and man's true self as the *Atman*, essentially one with God. It is a more difficult path, for the *Atman*, or Higher Self, is commonly confused with one's lower, ego self. The result, instead of a lofty transcendence, is a magnified egotism which is the opposite of spirituality. The two paths have been defined as the difference between "I am Thine," and "I am Thee."

Swami Abhedananda, a brilliant intellectual with wide academic interests, leaned toward the path of *jnana*, and under his tutelage the *jnanis* formed the majority of the Vedanta Society. Vedanta accepts the validity of all paths, but warns against the intermingling of aspirants on different paths. Sri Ramakrishna had specifically advised his devotional disciples to avoid the influence of those practicing the path of knowledge, for discussions between them could serve only to disorient the former and annoy the latter. The situation which developed at the New York Society was a perfect example. Mrs. Mary LePage, an ardent *jnani*, reveals in her book the tone which prevailed among them:

> All the *jnanins* had stormy lives. They took life without gloves, crashed their problems and made the clearing. . . . They may have been willful, these *jnanins*, and stubborn, too prideful at times perhaps, but they were no weaklings. . . . Only the *jnanin* student could keep pace with the rapid realignments of principle and sentiment as Swami Abhedananda directed us toward ordination and the continence of pure study. . . . The *Bhakta* students, those who insisted upon the path of devotion and worship, were the ones who mostly provided material for the intensive training that went on within the Society's inner precincts, those who worshipped in form and ceremony and insisted upon a certain catering to ritual and observances. Among the *Jnanins* nothing so incited to resistance as some obstinate triviality forcing itself into their austerity of thought after a long and hard-earned capitulation to an inclusive and universal tenet almost realized.

Mrs. LePage also relates an incident which illustrates the

friction then prevailing. She was cleaning and preparing the Society's library for Swami Abhedananda's weekly reception of callers. When she had finished, Miss Glenn, an ardent *bhakta*, rearranged the Swami's chair so his back would not be to the altar, in accordance with the principle that an altar must be treated like a living presence.

"He never sits with his back to Sri Ramakrishna's picture," she explained.

Mrs. LePage protested: "But the sun will be in his eyes and he cannot see his visitor."

Miss Glenn turned the chair again, saying, "Well, put it this way."

"Yes," came Mrs. LePage, "and then the visitor cannot see the Swami. After all, is God only on the altar? I supposed He was everywhere."

Miss Glenn, who was her senior both by age and by tenure in the Society, insisted that the altar must be respected, and then left. As soon as she was out the door, the indomitable Mrs. LePage restored the original arrangement.

Inevitably, the *bhaktas* claimed as their champion the devotionally inclined Paramananda, who must have been appalled when the Society occupied its new quarters at 135 West 80th Street in April, 1907, without first "installing the Lord" there and setting aside a room for His worship. Paramananda himself took the initiative and established a shrine room where, while he did not attempt the elaborate rituals of India, he daily practiced a simple devotion, offering flowers, fruits, and prayers to the "living Presence."

When Swami Ramakrishnananda heard about the non-devotional stance of the New York Society he wrote indignantly to Paramananda:

> "Vedanta without devotion is no Vedanta at all. One who thinks of egotism as Brahman, will never be able to do any good to himself. And, for such a person, it is altogether

impossible to do good to others. This egotism, anger, jealousy, and envy are coming from a lower nature."

While the *bhaktas* gratefully acclaimed Paramananda's inward bent and mystical tenor, their adulation doubtlessly irritated those who felt that he was too contemplative, "too dreamily mystical," as Mary LePage put it. As a matter of fact, these members, who had initially been won over by Abhedananda's incisive logic and widely gathered fund of knowledge, felt that Paramananda was inexcusably lacking in education and dialectic skills. According to Mrs. LePage, Swami Abhedananda arranged for Paramananda "a definite and advanced education at Columbia University." The very suggestion was untenable to Paramananda. His nature recoiled from formal education, and his training under Ramakrishnananda had repudiated the need for the accumulation of information which the scriptures call *apara vidya* (secondary knowledge, as opposed to *para vidya*, knowledge of the One). Sri Ramakrishna himself had derided those who spend their time and energy acquiring intellectual knowledge rather than direct experience of God. "Man has come here to eat mangos," he declared, "not to count the number of trees, branches, and leaves in the mango orchard." When Paramananda refused to enroll at Columbia, some members of the New York Society attributed it to vanity and arrogance.

To add to the strain of the situation, Paramananda, like other monks of the Order before and after him, did not agree with Swami Abhedananda's methods and techniques of propagating Vedanta. This disparity over the issue of methods eventually, in 1923 after his return to India, caused Abhedananda to separate himself from the Ramakrishna Math and Mission and to found his own organization, which he called the "Ramakrishna Vedanta Math." But in 1907, their paths had just begun to diverge, and Paramananda, wholly unsuspecting, was caught in the rift. When he declined to go along with the prevailing method of operation at the Vedanta Society, he added more fuel to the accusations that he was an uncooperative subordinate. Swami Abhedananda wrote plaintively to Ramakrishnananda: "I wish I could get two or three monks who would follow me faithfully and would act according to my way of thinking."

True to his resolution of love, Paramananda never uttered a critical word about Swami Abhedananda or the New York Vedanta Society, either during the conflict or throughout the rest of his life. He directed his energy not to overcoming his adversaries, but to maintaining evenmindedness within himself, repeatedly reminding himself that trials were a blessing, meant for his greater growth. In his letters of that year, he wrote:

> In every man's life there come moments of weariness and struggle, when everything appears gloomy and hard. But know that no true character was ever formed without passing through these stages. So we must be bold and patient. This world is no lovely flower garden, as some foolish people regard it. It is full of thorns, and we must be very, very careful as we walk in it. . . .
>
> Misery and difficulties come at times to strengthen our character. They are like examinations. We must prepare and pass them. Know that they are very good for the formation of character. The more we meet with difficulties, the more we remember our Mother for protection. . . .
>
> He is a true hero who can stand firmly on his own feet even when the whole world acts against him. That is the test of life. In order to mould a perfect character we need many things. We must go through both good and bad, happiness and misery, pleasure and pain. And when we can remain undisturbed both in happiness and misery, then we have reached perfection.

Paramananda's life in New York was a confounding combination of adversity and adulation. A devotee invited him to visit her home on the Hudson and afterwards wrote: "My home seems even more radiant since you have honored it with your presence. We are truly blessed in knowing you and I feel that a man of God has been in our midst." Other letters of appreciation came frequently, such as:

> Everything is so changed and I owe it all to you. I have learned to be the same in pleasure and pain and to realize that I am nothing by myself, but that Divine Mother can help us to do the impossible thing. . . . I am more than grateful to you, dear Swami, and bless the day that brought you to me.

Paramananda was aware of the dangers of such outpourings of praise, which followed him all his life. He wrote at that time:

> All glory must go to Him. Offer all the honor, respect and love you receive from people at His Divine feet. This is the secret.
>
> I am no great man, but I am always a simple, innocent boy. . . . I do not want to deceive anyone by claiming myself as very great. I would rather die instead of making a great fuss.
>
> As far as I and my abilities are concerned, it is the same feeling I still hold and in same position I stand, to say sincerely that I have no power or anything of my own, but everything you noticed in me came directly from Him. As the days pass, so I find this feeling firmly rooted in me. How can I help seeing it? All the lecturing and talking and the praise and adoration that come before me, make me convinced every day of that wonderful Power.

Most people are like crustaceans: they wear their skeletons on the outside—a hard shell of pretensions and defenses. But pierce through that crust and they are soft and vulnerable. Paramananda had the true structure of a human being; he wore his skeleton at his center. Externally he was soft, gentle, completely unguarded. The world could, and often did, bruise him, but nothing could penetrate the adamantine faith at his core. He was the flower with the pistil of rock, and strength had become his rallying cry:

> We must live here boldly, have purity and strength of character, then face everything fearlessly, all the difficulties and dangers. Whom to fear? We are the children of Divine Mother; our Mother is the Ruler of the universe, the whole world belongs to us. Have that kind of life-giving faith.

In March, the Vedanta Society had purchased 370 acres of land in the foothills of the Berkshires, near West Cornwall, Connecticut, to serve as an ashram, or retreat. There Paramananda spent the summer of 1907 with a small group of students. It was the type of life he loved: enjoying nature, teaching informally, meditating under the trees. At one point he observed a sixteen-day period of silence. Miss Glenn (Devamata) was spending the summer in the Catskills, preparing for publication the notes which Miss S.E. Waldo had taken of Vivekananda's talks at Thousand Island Park and which were to become the book *Inspired Talks*. Paramananda wrote to her frequently, candidly revealing his childlikeness:

> I stay out of doors sometimes and walk alone in the woods, lie down on the rocks and sometimes think, think deeply; all harmless and innocent thoughts cross my mind. Sometimes I think as if I am a baby lion, maybe motherless, still must not be afraid of other animals. My own experience tells me that strength only is religion, strength is truth.

"I am after all," he writes in another letter, "only a little boy, but an innocent boy. What Mother wants me to do I do not understand but I know I am Her child. I am sure She will guide me and protect me. That is all I want. Let the whole world stand against me; I do not care. I am a soldier, a faithful, true soldier. It is a very hard battle; but no great work was ever performed without the supreme sacrifice."

———————•◆•———————

This period was a turning point in Devamata's life. She felt impelled to commit herself completely to the cause of Vedanta, to renounce all and follow this "pure, holy child," her new-found teacher. But her aged father, a staunch Episcopalian, warned her that if she became any more involved in the Eastern cult, he would disinherit her. Moreover, she was a bastion of the New York Vedanta Society, giving afternoon meditation classes, as well as heading the crucially important publication department. Her taking formal discipleship from this embattled new teacher caused Abhedananda's fiercest proponents to rage against her. "It was a moment of grave crisis with me" she wrote, "and the Swami [Paramananda] sought to sustain me in every way possible. His frequent words, stirring and vital because they came from one who lived them, carried me over the difficult places and made the darkest hours bright with the satisfaction of conquest."

She formed the habit of copying the instructive portions of Paramananda's letters into a notebook. One day during meditation it occurred to her that these letters could be compiled as a book, which would reach and inspire many souls. She wrote nothing of her plan to Paramananda, but when she returned to New York in September, she laid the manuscript in his hands. "His child-like pleasure was delightful to see. There was no vanity in it, no thought that he was to have something in print; only deep joy that what he had done so lovingly for one might prove a help and blessing to many."

The book, entitled *The Path of Devotion*, came out in November, less than a year after Paramananda's landing in America. It met with immediate success. Critics compared it to the works of Thomas à Kempis and Brother Lawrence, and to other devotional classics, great in their simplicity. A Christian clergyman in

Cleveland, Ohio saw a review of the book in the *Cleveland Plain Dealer*, sent for it, and after reading it, wrote:

> In most of my books are to be found marked passages, to which I can turn for comfort or inspiration, but when I read "The Path of Devotion," I felt that I could mark the book in but two places — at the beginning and at the end. Every sentence is alive with Divine Fire, every word is illuminated.

To understand the relationship between Paramananda and Devamata, one must understand that the guru-disciple relationship in India is more intimate than even the bond between parent and child. The guru does not give instruction like a university professor; he imparts his very being, his life, his spiritual potency to the disciple, who in turn serves his guru with wholehearted devotion. Just as Western romantics feel that marriages are made in heaven, so Eastern mystics declare that the relationship between guru and disciple is so sacred that it is not wrought by chance. Rather it is ordained by an inner bond which re-establishes itself in life after life. To those souls who entrusted themselves to his guidance, Paramananda was indeed a paragon of love and tenderness. Thus, he could write to Devamata:

"Your letter of Sunday has given me very great joy and very deep feeling of tenderness which I do not know how to put into words. Day and night prayers go to the Divine Mother for your welfare and protection and your wisdom. And love from the very core of my heart always flows towards you."

Although he was surrendered and stoic about his own fate, he often doted like an anxious parent over the tribulations of his spiritual children:

> Let us fully depend on Her and say sincerely, "Let Thy will be done." I remember this, but still sometimes comes a little sense of anxiety in my mind. This is the nature of intense love. A mother may not care for herself very much

but can never help feeling anxious about her child. So my heart feels at times very full.

To be sure, while Eliza Kissam (who was to be given the name Satya Prana) and perhaps others became his disciples at this time, the relationship between Paramananda and Devamata was a special one. Sri Ramakrishna had taught that to escape the snare of lust a man should look upon all women as mother. This was a natural relationship for Paramananda and Devamata, for indeed she was old enough to be his mother. Thus, he always addressed his letters to her as "Mother, dear," and signed himself, "Your son." Devamata was his indefatigable supporter and advocate, always on hand with the practical skill, the experienced know-how, the faithful encouragement. She nursed him when he was sick, attended on his mundane needs, and bolstered his faith in himself by her own unwavering confidence in him.

In a sense, Devamata created Paramananda the teacher by her faith and adoration. As Vivekananda explained, "The disciple must have intense faith in the Guru, and so also must the Guru in the disciple; without that the disciple's progress is impossible. Through the Guru's love and trust, the inspiration comes to the disciple, and also through the disciple's one-pointed devotion and faith, Guru gets more and more spiritual power."

Paramananda recognized her service on all levels, and he was appropriately grateful. He showed her life-long respect, and, although he was the master and she the disciple, he never failed to stand up when she entered the room. When Devamata was facing disinheritance, Paramananda wrote to her, quite the reverse of what the public has come to expect of Indian gurus and their American followers: "I hope, through Divine Mother's grace, that you shall have no difficulty in any way. You must remember always that anything I have to call my own is also for your use; if at any time you find the need of money, you shall only have to send me a word and at once you shall have all that I have."

Again, upon receiving news that she had recovered from a dangerous illness, he could write with characteristic spontaneity:

> Oh! such a joy in my heart. Your cable came this morning right after breakfast. The news made me so full of joy that I hardly could control myself. First of all I came to my room and threw myself before the altar and bathed the feet of Mother Divine with tears of gratitude and love and devotion. It is something very deep and inexpressible. You know, Mother dear, what earnest and eager prayers I constantly offered at Her Divine feet for thy protection. . . . When I rose before the altar, I said (chanted in Sanskrit) with great, great feeling of gratitude that "never Thy devotees suffer, Mother." Then also I danced like a boy of five years.

The relationship between them must be seen in its proper context, for, incomprehensible to outsiders, spiritual directors and their especially apt disciples have always shared a bond whose intimacy is easy to misinterpret. The fact is that, finding a rare kinship on the soul level, they leave bodies far behind. Great lovers of God must necessarily be great lovers of man, and it is not surprising that François de Sales should have shown such tenderness to his disciple Jeanne de Chantal, or that Claire should have cherished Francis of Assisi as she did.

Devamata's open espousal of Paramananda as her guru brought upon her the calumny of Abhedananda's supporters. This grieved Paramananda deeply: "There comes at times a pang in my heart when I think I have been the outward cause of most of the suffering you had to undergo. Then again I think that everything is done through Her will."

Suddenly, at the very end of 1907, Paramananda thought of a way to remove Devamata from the field of battle. He arranged for her to go to India to study under Swami Ramakrishnananda. It was a sacrifice on his part, for as the crisis came to a head it left him bereft of his strongest human supporter.

At the Belur Math itself, the senior swamis' understanding
of the New York situation depended entirely on partisan reports
they received in the mail. A letter written by Swami Saradananda,
author of the authoritative life of Sri Ramakrishna, to Josephine
MacLeod on June 27, 1907, conveys their disapproval of the
reported behavior of both Swamis Paramananda and Bodhananda, while at the same time revealing their own misgivings
about Swami Abhedananda:

> We have great faith in Bodhananda—but we cannot say
> that with equal certainty of Paramananda. He is still quite
> young and has not been tried as yet. I do not like his
> showing so much temper to the Swami Abhedananda
> and it seems to me that both of them are ignoring what is
> really due to Swami Abhedananda, in their wild and young
> enthusiasm. The Swami Abhedananda has the habit of
> thinking himself Swamiji's [Vivekananda's] equal from the
> very beginning and yet Swamiji called him to the work,
> knowing full well his faults and merits. They forgot too
> that Swamiji will remain Swamiji, in spite of everything
> and everybody. . . . However, we have not written them
> anything by which they might think that we too hold the
> same opinion of Swami Abhedananda, but just waiting to
> see what shape things take by all these disputes.

Naturally Swami Ramakrishnananda, who had never found
a single fault in Paramananda, was shocked and dismayed by the
reports of his misbehavior. But his faith in Paramananda stood
firm. He had known him too well, had seen into his spirit too
deeply, to be shaken by even the most scathing declamations.
He declared that the accusations were false, the products of a
warped perception. "If I saw him do it with my own eyes," he
exclaimed, "I would say my eyes have deceived me." And he
wrote to Paramananda, "Everything is happening through the
Lord's will. Only an egoless, supreme devotee can feel this to be
true, and you are such a devotee."

At the General Meeting of the New York Vedanta Society held in January, 1908, Swami Abhedananda offered to resign in favor of the junior swami. He called on the membership to vote for their choice. Win or lose, it was bound to be a humiliating experience for Paramananda, publicly implying as it did that he desired to displace the senior swami. According to Mary LePage's account, only Eliza Kissam and five or six of the other older students stood up for Paramananda. On January 29, confident that his leadership of the Society had been confirmed, Abhedananda sailed for England again, leaving Paramananda to find his balance. The young swami confided in a letter to Devamata, "Often depression comes, but we must try to remain quiet and steady."

Throughout the entire turbulent period in New York, indeed throughout his life, Paramananda never defended himself nor justified his actions. This is a discipline taught by all religions, and it invariably adds to the inner strength of the accused and, unwittingly, to the irritation of the accuser. It is a practice not easily appreciated in the West, where revenge is considered justified, self-defense manly, and non-resistance cowardly. But it is exactly what Jesus meant by, "Whosoever shall smite thee on thy right cheek, turn to him the other also." Not to defend oneself when accused is a supreme test of humility, endurance, and reliance on God. As Paramananda wrote to Devamata:

> Take everything calmly and act wisely. Fighting, quarreling and all such things are very unworthy. When we hold such thoughts and try to defend ourselves by fighting or disputing with our opponents we . . . forget the protecting hands of our All Blissful Mother. Do not forget for a moment that we are all Her children, good or bad, all Her children. If She does not protect, there is no other power that can save us and when She protects, there is no power that can do any harm to us.

During this period, Paramananda had one of the few mystical experiences that he ever divulged. While in meditation, he felt that his subtle body was expanding in size, until it assumed colossal proportions, like one of the huge reclining Buddhas one sees in Ceylon. This Buddha-body seemed to rise, and hovered over the city of New York like a protecting presence. Afterwards, Paramananda interpreted this experience as symbolic of his role in America: a silent, sustaining presence, brooding over the land.

Meanwhile, Miss Waldo, a dedicated disciple of Vivekananda, suggested that harmony might be restored if Paramananda relocated in Germany. Theodore Springmann, an earnest Vedanta student there, wrote to Paramananda, inviting him to stay in the Springmann home and offering to send him to a leading university to learn German language and philosophy and help establish a widespread Vedanta movement there. Paramananda and Miss Waldo both relayed the proposition to Swami Ramakrishnananda. Ramakrishnananda replied that to learn a new language well enough to teach philosophy in it would be wasting a lot of time, and that Germany was too caught up in scholastic learning to be ripe for the true Vedanta teaching. Instead, he advised Paramananda to stay in New York:

> Make a great effort to live in such a way that you will be able to work harmoniously with others. Sri Sri Guru Maharaj [Ramakrishna] used to say: "There cannot be a form without some alloy." There is some imperfection in every human being. . . . With sweet words and a sweet manner, you must try to do your utmost to overlook the faults of the blamers and the blamed. . . .
>
> A true Knower regards dishonor as nectar and honor as poison. How many hardships had to be endured by Sri Sri Guru Maharaj and by Sri Sri Swamiji [Vivekananda]! How many times they bore insults . . . That is why Sri Sri Guru Maharaj has said: "Endurance is the primary virtue in this world. He who endures survives, he who does not endure is destroyed."

Swami Ramakrishnananda invited Paramananda to Madras for a rest, which must have been tempting for the young monk, whose spirit yearned for the quiet life of mystical communion he had known there. Every evening as he withdrew his mind in meditation, the roar of the New York streets faded away and "unmistakably I heard the vesper chimes and bells in far off India." Yet a binding sense of obligation to persevere in his guru's mission kept him at his American post. Grappling with this temptation, he uttered his cry of agony and surrender:

> O! Mother, Your name is so sweet. Give me intense love and faith in Thy name. Mother, O, Mother, take me on Thy lap, I don't want to stay here. This is not my home. You are my home. O let me come to Thee. Ah! Jai Guru. Your work must be done. Let me do it truly and faithfully with *unselfishness and purity.* "Let Thy will be done." Give us strength and give us light and may we say truly and sincerely, "Let Thy will be done."

Several years before, in Montclair, New Jersey, Swami Saradananda and Swami Turiyananda had taught a group of fascinated Vedanta students. It was a beautiful country town, about an hour's train ride from New York, and both the swamis found their stay there a pleasant interlude, a wholesome change from the scene in New York. Now, in 1908, this amiable group invited Paramananda to visit Montclair. The admiration and affection they quickly felt for the young swami was amply reciprocated, and he began to spend some time in their midst, commuting to New York for lectures and duties.

It was a refreshing break for him, emotionally and physically. His health had been fitful since his arrival in America. Coming from tropical India to New York in midwinter had played havoc on his delicate constitution. The pace of American life and the demands of a busy organization, added to his innate heedlessness of the needs of the body, combined to afflict him with recurrent maladies during his first years in the West. Ramakrishnananda, hearing of it from Devamata, admonished him in every letter to take better care of his physical instrument:

> You are having to work very hard. You are very young. . . . Be very careful about your health. The bodies of all beings are a veritable abode of the Lord. . . . That is why negligence towards the body is lack of loving attention towards God's abode, and therefore towards Him. That is why you should take particular care of the body. . . . Do not forget that it is as wrong to torture one's body as to torture other people's bodies. The work is neither yours nor mine, it is His. You are His instrument, do as He makes you do.

On May 30, 1908, Swami Abhedananda wrote to Ramakrishnananda from London: "Basanta is no longer a novice as before, he has become a good worker. Do not be anxious for him. He is so energetic that instead of getting tired with the work of the New York Society he has opened another centre at Montclair. He was so eager to take full charge of work that I had to come here leaving him there. . . . Please write to Basanta asking him to stay in New York. He is very faithful to you."

Late that spring, at the end of the official lecture season, the Executive Board of the Vedanta Society issued a formal note of thanks to Swami Paramananda: "Not only has Swami Paramananda conducted the work efficiently, but he has shown the Spirit of true Love and Devotion in all that he has undertaken."

Not everyone agreed. In midsummer, some of the New York students wrote to Abhedananda demanding his return. They maintained that the success of the work was in jeopardy. Paramananda could not or would not operate on the large scale for which Abhedananda aimed, and which was essential for the financial base of an already overextended work. Many of those who were attracted by Abhedananda's erudite presentation stopped attending the lectures, and Paramananda, staunchly opposing organization, took no interest in membership or fund-raising drives. The Society was in serious financial difficulties. Its membership dues were insufficient to maintain the headquarters, and the publication of the monthly magazine had to be suspended for lack of funds.

Swami Abhedananda returned to New York on August 21. After a brief rest at the Connecticut ashrama, he embarked on a lecture tour of Chicago, Denver, and other western cities. During the months that followed, more new members joined the Vedanta Society than in any period since Vedanta had come to America.

On September 26, the Executive Board of the Vedanta Society voted on a compromise which they hoped would satisfy all parties. Swami Paramananda was to give the Sunday morning lectures at the Society, and the Tuesday evening classes; Swami Abhedananda was to give the Sunday afternoon lectures at Duryea's Hall, which seated five hundred, and the Thursday evening classes. Paramananda was with Mrs. Bull when he was notified of the decision.

Less than three months later, the tensions of two years finally erupted. Exactly what precipitated the crisis remains obscure. To the end of his life, Paramananda never talked about his trials in New York, even to his closest disciples. But the climax came during the first week of December, 1908. Swami Abhedananda told Paramananda to leave New York.

The young monk left quietly for Boston, where Mrs. Bull was again urging him to found a center. He wrote to Devamata in India: "This is just a line to tell you I am going to Boston and I leave New York on Friday. Pray to the Mother that this new venture which I am undertaking may be Her own work. May I feel that alone."

When the news reached India, Swamis Ramakrishnananda and Brahmananda reacted with indignation and distress. Ramakrishnananda wrote: "That you tried to work by being harmonious with him—we know that well. You have done supremely well. You have shown great respect to Sri Sri Guru Maharaj's disciple. . . . Fear not, the victory is yours. Sri Ramakrishna is always with you. It is He that talks through you to save the souls of all from ignorance."

Swami Brahmananda, the President of the Order, declared: "Basanta has never written a word in all this against anyone. I believe that he is in the right." According to Swami Saradananda, both he and Swami Brahmananda had misgivings about Paramananda's shift to Boston. "But Abhedananda was recklessly insistent, & the lad himself had high hopes," Sister Nivedita recounted after hearing the story from Saradananda. "So they yielded, being indeed practically without option!"

Brahmananda immediately sent permission for Paramananda to work independently in Boston. "I never would have dreamed that he would treat you in such a manner," wrote Brahmananda. "Be that as it may, he treated three others in the same manner. You should start working independently from now on. Do not be afraid, Sri Guru Maharaj will protect you and be your support. . . . We are truly sad. However, you must stand on your own feet and do the work of Sri Sri Guru Maharaj."

In those days long before air mail, these reassuring letters did not reach Paramananda until two months after his departure from New York. In the meantime, he was bolstered by his own faith. He had before him the task of pioneering a Vedanta work in the city which Vivekananda had called the most difficult and most worthwhile place in America. It was a formidable challenge even for his independent nature. From India he could expect moral support, but no financial or practical help. Severed from his connections in New York, he was completely on his own. He was twenty-four years old.

5

Boston Beginnings

BOSTON IN 1909 was a melee of warring religious factions. An influx of Catholic immigrants was inundating the city. As the Protestants were retreating into the suburbs, leaving behind them diminished congregations and empty churches, the Protestant leadership was retaliating by sending their missionaries to work among the Catholic immigrants and convert them to their own camp. Meanwhile, among the Protestant denominations themselves rivalry, distrust, and condescension were the order of the day. The Boston bluebloods were divided into Episcopalians (who sneered at Unitarianism as "a religionless religion") and Unitarians (who scorned the Episcopalians' rituals, such as "kneeling in that ingratiating way"). Moreover, both looked down upon the Presbyterians and Baptists, not to speak of the Jews (whom the *Boston Herald* matter-of-factly referred to as "an alien race"). All of the above groups were united in their distrust of the burgeoning new sect, Christian Science, which had its Mother Church on the very soil of Boston. It was, they inveighed, "a Westernized version of Hinduism," and was only slightly more acceptable than New Thought, another experimental cult which had its birth in Boston. In 1909, the "Hub of the Universe" boasted four branches of the Church of the Higher Life (New Thought), three Swedenborgian churches, three established

Spiritualist groups, and a branch of the Theosophical Society — all within a three-mile radius of the Boston Common, where the Puritan Fathers had hanged Quaker Mary Dyer for preaching heresy.

In February, 1909, just about the same time that Paramananda started lecturing publicly in Boston, a local Protestant minister was giving a series of lectures in his church on "Religious Lunacies." As quoted in the *Boston Globe*, he ridiculed New Thought, labeled Krishna Worship "filthy idiocy," and denounced Theosophy (a system which combines Indian and Western esotericism) as "anti-Christian." "To think," he exclaimed, "that there are people in Boston, descendants of the Pilgrims, some of them, I've no doubt, who turn their backs on all that has made the world great and good, and grovel in the worship of Mahomet!"

This was the arena into which Paramananda stepped after his devastating experience in New York. It was rather like being cast from a turbulent pond into the vast ocean. He had but one connection in Boston, Mrs. Ole Bull, a tie that was soon to snap.

When Paramananda arrived on December 22, 1908, he went directly to Mrs. Bull's house at 168 Brattle Street in Cambridge. Sister Nivedita was also there, delighted to see her "Baby Swamiji" again. The other house guests were Dr. Jagadis Chandra Bose, the famous Indian botanist who was to be knighted for his revolutionary experiments in plant sensitivity, and Mrs. Bose.

It was a joyful reunion. Paramananda felt at home in this house where Vivekananda and Saradananda had also stayed and lectured, at home with Mrs. Bull and Nivedita, both faithful, devoted disciples of his beloved guru. They celebrated Christmas Eve with an eclectic service attended by several Hindu students from Harvard and some of their Christian professors. Sister Nivedita read the story of the nativity from St. Luke, as well as the astonishingly similar story of the birth of Krishna. Paramananda chanted Vedic texts in Sanskrit and sang Bengali hymns to the Divine Mother, while other guests sang Christmas carols. At the conclusion of the service Sister Nivedita handed the swami a porcelain shell filled with Ganges water and asked him to bless everyone present with it. He hesitated for a moment, glancing at the Christian professors and at Dr. and Mr. Bose, who belonged to the unritualistic Brahmo Samaj. But to his surprise everyone sat with bowed head or knelt before him as he sprinkled the holy water on their heads. This experience of his first Christmas in Boston moved him deeply.

Immediately after the holiday, Mrs. Bull, Nivedita, and Paramananda sat down to discuss the proposed Vedanta work in Boston. For the first time, the young swami ran up against what Abhedananada had stigmatized as Mrs. Bull's "plans and ideas." An energetic organizer, for years Sara Bull had managed her famous husband's concert tours. Now she mapped out a detailed plan for a Vedanta Society, which included Nivedita's pet interests, Indian national politics and academic study. Methodically she explained her strategy to the swami.

Paramananda was stunned. He had thought that, like Vivekananda and Saradanada, he could lecture and teach without any organization. "I came here as a wandering *Sannyasin*," he told a Boston audience years later. "I did not expect to settle down and have an established work."

And again:

> When I first came to Boston, I did not dream of establishing a permanent work here; I came because I had something in my heart, the same thing which had brought me all the way from India: an earnest desire to share with others the message of love, unity, and tolerance which lies at the root of all Vedanta teaching.

Paramananda had envisioned this new endeavor as an organic growth, in which his role would be not architect or builder, but gardener. He believed that if he planted the living seed of Vedanta in fertile soil, that is, in a few souls who were spiritually ready, and if he nurtured and cared for it with his own dedication, then the work would grow in its own way, without blueprints or human calculation. He did not want to impose a man-made Vedanta organization on Boston. He wanted to see it grow naturally, the true product of its own soil and climate, ever responsive to the sunlight of Divine guidance. This meant, of course, that no center would spring up as a building is erected in a matter of weeks or months, but the work, in whatever form, would grow slowly, like a tree, gradually adding to its girth with every passing season. It was a poetic vision, but Paramananda cherished it throughout his life.

Nivedita was urging him to study Buddhism, to mix with scholars and Cambridge's academic elite. Paramananda, suspicious of book learning, declined to confuse intellectual pursuits with the spiritual quest. Still, Mrs. Bull's sponsorship meant not only financial support, but a whole network of connections and introductions to Boston's most distinguished citizens. To proceed without her would be a steep, uphill climb; to go along with her would be to move in the wrong direction. Instantly he made his decision. He quietly informed them that he was not the man to carry out their program.

Now it was Mrs. Bull's turn to be incredulous. Had she brought him from New York and carefully worked out this strategy only to have it rejected by this impractical young Indian? Apparently she had mistaken Paramananda's gentleness for docility. Impressed by his depth of spirit, she had underestimated his spirit of independence.

Mrs. Bull was irked. "If you cannot adapt to the Western way of doing things," she upbraided him, "you might as well go back to India."

He replied in soft, measured tones: "I feel I came here by Divine direction, and I will leave by the same direction."

The interview was over. Paramananda was to try it his way, alone. He had unlimited independence—and very little else.

Although he claimed to move by Divine guidance, his rejection of what was to be their joint Vedanta venture seemed like stubborn inability to compromise. History, however, soon vindicated his choice. Just two years after they parted ways, Mrs. Bull died of pernicious anemia, at the age of sixty. In her will she bequeathed most of her $500,000 fortune to the Vedanta movement (ostensibly in India, where she had been supporting their relief work for years). But her daughter Olea was not content with her share of her mother's legacy. She contested the will, claiming her mother was of "unsound and disordered mind" and under "undue influence." She named several persons who, she maintained, were involved in a psychical conspiracy to snatch Mrs. Bull's fortune. Among them were Sister Nivedita and Dr. J.C. Bose.

The case developed into a major scandal. Maids and butlers offered lurid accounts of the goings on at 168 Brattle Street, how Indian swamis were received there, how their mistress kept a dimly lit meditation room decorated with "pictures of fat swamis," where she and her friends burned incense and sat in a suspicious hush which the servants called "seances."

The result was that Mrs. Bull's will was overturned. Her entire fortune was allocated to Olea, who died on the very day the case was closed.

Had Paramananda compromised to gain Mrs. Bull's sponsorship, not only would he have been abruptly deprived of his financial support, but his alliance with her would have dragged him into the scandal, implicated him as one of the "conspirators," and besmeared his reputation, as Sister Nivedita's was. To exert "undue influence" on a dying wealthy woman was a charge sufficient to estrange every sensible dowager in Boston. It could have been the death knell for his incipient work. As it was, however, Paramananda's severance from Mrs. Bull spared him completely. Although Mrs. Bull subsidized his personal maintenance during the early months of 1909, he took no help from her in establishing a center. By autumn, after her return from Norway, she became

entirely dissatisfied with his method of proceeding. By the last year
of her life their paths had irrevocably parted. During all the weeks
and months of testimony, his name was never mentioned.

The case is also noteworthy for what it reveals of the temper
of the times: that associating with swamis, burning incense, and
practicing yoga and meditation was enough to judge a person as
mentally unsound in New England in 1911.

These future developments could have been no consolation
to Paramananda as, trunk and all, he set forth from Mrs. Bull's
house, with no place to go. The temperature that day was 18° F.
An unknown young foreigner in a strange city, Paramananda
embarked on his great experiment, to prove that without plans,
organization, or funding, and with God's help and guidance
alone, he could succeed in Boston. He knew no one else in the
city, except some Hindu students even more destitute than he.
Leaving his trunk at the express office, he asked them to put him
up until he could find his own place. They lived in a shabby
lodginghouse on Appleton Street, and while they readily agreed
to help him, all they could offer was a cot in the public parlor.
The place was unclean, and the bathroom, used by many people,
was messy and unsanitary. Paramananda was by temperament
fastidious and by training meticulous. The situation grated on
his sensibilities, for his penchant for austerity inclined toward
bare simplicity, but never squalor.

After three days of combing the frigid city clasping a newspaper listing of "rooms to let," he found an inexpensive room at 94
St. Botolph Street. It was clean and decent, making him wonder
why the rent was so reasonable. His first night there he found out.
The room was so cold that he could hardly sleep. In the morning,
when he went to wash at the pitcher and basin provided, he had
to break through a quarter-inch layer of ice to get to the water.

He had brought with him from New York one letter of introduction to Mrs. George Gibson. Eager to begin his new venture, he called on her. When the door was opened, he took one look at the somber faces in the hallway, and realized he was intruding. A death had just occurred in the family. Leaving the letter and his card, he withdrew at once.

The life of austerity for which he had yearned was finally being granted to him, and in ways he least expected.

Paramananda specialized in knowing how to wait. A few days later he received an invitation from Mrs. Gibson to lunch with her. She was an ardent Swedenborgian, and a large class for the study of Swedenborg's writings met almost daily at her house. After the luncheon, she invited Paramananda to stay and address the class. Then he was urged to return the following morning and give another talk.

This second talk set off a chain reaction. A woman in the audience, Mrs. Tibbets, asked the swami to give a lecture in her home. She was leaving town, and the next day, Wednesday, January 6, was the only available day. They quickly sent out cards, and forty-five people came.

It was the right group. Instantly impressed by Paramananda's message and manner, they asked the swami to teach a regular Wednesday afternoon class for the study of the Bhagavad Gita; Mrs. Gibson offered to hold a Tuesday morning meeting in her house; Mrs. Tibbets suggested a Friday morning course in concentration and meditation; and Mrs. Briggs organized another class in Waltham, a nearby town, for Tuesday afternoons. The next day another gathering was held at Mrs. Bull's house. "The meeting this afternoon had about 30 people," Nivedita wrote to Mrs. Bull, who had gone to New York. "Swami was grand!" These meetings introduced Paramananda to more people, and eventually other invitations were extended, until his schedule was quite full, indeed, whirling.

According to Indian philosophy, spiritual truth is not taught by words, it is transmitted by association. The most valuable thing that a man of wisdom has to give other human beings is himself. By his silent example he imparts to them not facts to placate their intellects, but the rudiments of how to live. As one Jewish Hasid declared: "I came to my Master not to listen to erudite discourses, but to watch him lace his shoes."

The process may be even more subtle than that. By his mere presence a true man of God exerts an influence which those who are attuned can receive. They are uplifted by it. "By your very being," Paramananda once said, "you can give an impetus to someone, even in a streetcar." One devotee in New York attested to this, writing to Paramananda: "Your presence in the room without a word would be an inspiration and a help to live the spiritual life." In this transmission-by-association the teacher does not keep himself in grand seclusion or lofty remoteness; he comes to where the people are and mingles with them, whether it be by the banks of the Ganges, amidst the fishing boats of Galilee, or in the drawing rooms of Boston.

Paramananda's diary of that period records an endless round of engagements, visits, soirees, and personal interviews. On Friday he would set up an altar and conduct an informal service at Miss Wentworth's house. On Saturday he would visit Mrs. Briggs in Waltham and meet some of her friends. On Monday he would make contact with the Cambridge Theosophical Society, and then call on Mrs. Gibson. On Wednesday he would give the afternoon class at Mrs. Tibbets, then stay to dine with her and her husband. And two or three times a week he would drop in on "the boys," the Indian students who lived on Appleton Street, and who must have provided a relaxing break for the young swami after hours of hobnobbing over high tea.

"I came to Boston about Christmas time, 1908," Paramananda recounted years later. "I had no plans, but I was ready and willing to do anything that came to me to do. I went where I was invited,

I slept and ate wherever I happened to be; my life was wholly planless; and that is the way the Centre started. My purpose was not to proselytize or to establish a church. The message I brought, it seemed to me, had a tremendous human appeal, and I gave it wherever an opportunity presented itself. At first it was not easy. There was opposition and a great deal of misunderstanding."

As with the card parties at Navogopal's house, social gatherings with the swami inevitably, if imperceptibly, became infiltrated with spiritual content. Conversations would turn to India, then to Sri Ramakrishna and Vivekananda. Mrs. Gibson invited Paramananda to spend several days in her home. The first evening ended with a few hands of bridge, the second evening with a period of meditation, and the morning of the third day began with meditation before breakfast. He did not dictate norms of behavior to his hosts, but tried to infuse even the most prosaic pastimes with the air of sanctity which he cultivated and carried. Thus, when they spent evenings putting together jigsaw puzzles or playing at fortune-telling, he was an amiable participant. Yet he always kept before him Sri Ramakrishna's admonition that a person may enter into the world, but he should never let the world enter into him, just as a boat may be in the water, but the water should never be in the boat.

Despite some limited patronage, Paramananda's financial situation was always strained. When he was invited to dine at the homes of his students, he was fed sumptuously. But on the frequent days in between, all he could afford for a meal was "one egg and buttered toast" called across the half partition of a dairy lunch. He wrote a humorous account of his scant diet to Devamata, who was still in Madras. When she shared the letter with Swami Ramakrishnananda, he did not find it at all amusing. Growing gravely solicitous, he told her, "Write to Paramananda that he must eat enough. If he lacks for money, we will send it from here." Devamata was struck by the depth of Ramakrishnananda's love for his protégé, for, as she put it, "the Monastery was none too prosperous at that time, and ampler meals in Boston would mean poorer ones in Madras."

In fact, financial help flowed in the opposite direction. Swami Vivekananda had originally come to America seeking aid for India's impoverished millions. Realizing that the dehumanizing cycle of poverty could only be broken by a massive influx of money and resources, he had hoped that, as India shared its spiritual treasure with the West, the West would share its material treasure with India. It did not work out that way. While a few devoted disciples, such as Mrs. Bull and Miss Josephine MacLeod, generously gave of their wealth, Christian antagonists warned the American public of the mercenary motives of "Hindoo Swamis." Thousands flocked to hear Vivekananda, eager for his teachings, but they clutched their pocketbooks and offered in return nothing but applause.

One Sunday afternoon in New York, Paramananda and a group of students were serenaded from their window by some strolling black singers. They dropped a coin to encourage them, and after some time the swami was about to throw down another. Suddenly he exclaimed, "No, that will buy a meal for two hungry mouths in India. Let's start an Indian Fund with it." They took a candy box, cut a slit in the top, printed on it, "For the hungry of India," and placed it where people could drop in their loose change. That was the beginning of his lifelong effort for India relief. From then on, whatever the ups and downs of his own wavering fortunes, he managed to set aside regular sums which he sent to India for flood or famine relief or to meet the expenses at the Belur Math and its many social-service branches. Even in those straitened early days in Boston, by pulling his belt a little tighter he was able to save money to send to Swami Ramakrishnananda for badly needed building repairs at the Madras Math.

While some grateful followers eventually offered contributions for India or the Vedanta work, even once the Vedanta Centre was founded, the average Sunday collection during those early years ranged between three and four dollars, and the total monthly receipts rarely exceeded eighty dollars. Nevertheless, Paramananda gained the reputation of never asking for money. Years later he declared:

> I have asked nothing from you, because through my spiritual blessings I have learned that there is greater joy in giving. We [the Vedanta Centre] need material help. I do not deny that. Especially in the Occident we need material help at every turn. That was one of the greatest problems I had to solve in connection with this work, and also I felt the immensity of my task because I had no confidence in my own powers. All I felt was that I was called to do something and I wanted to do it with all my heart and soul. Yet in spite of that inner yearning and zeal to give what I had to give, I could not deny the facts of cold winters and rigid material conditions. It is not here as in India where a monk is recognized by his garb and does not have to worry about how he is going to eat, what he is going to wear, or where he is going to sleep. It was my faith that laid the foundation for this work.

Critics delight in pointing out that most of the followers of Vedanta were women, and many of the women were wealthy. The inference, of course, sometimes implied, sometimes boldly stated, is that infatuated women were attracted more by the personal magnetism of the swamis than by the profundity of their teachings, and that the swamis courted their money and their adulation.

A pamphlet published by the Christian Literature Society in 1897, entitled, "Swami Vivekananda and his Guru," describes in great detail the colors and fabrics of Swami Vivekananda's exotic robes and turbans, alleging that women devotees were more attracted by what he wore than what he was. And one

1912 article entitled "The Heathen Invasion of America " (and reprinted in the *Literary Digest* as "Strange Gods of American Women") charged:

> Eve is eating the apple again. Yoga, that Eastern philosophy the emblem of which is the coiled serpent, is being widely disseminated here. And before a charm that seemingly they cannot resist, thousands of converts are yielding to the temptation to embrace its teachings of strange mysteries. . . . Although the Swami's following includes some men of learning and college professors who wish to investigate a science brought from the roof of the world, most of its recruits are among women. . . . The descent from Christianity to heathenism is by such easy stages that the novice scarcely realizes she is led.

Paramananda was too handsome to escape these innuendos, which have accosted almost every Oriental teacher before or since. A 1910 *Boston Traveler* article on him pointedly referred to "his desk, which was littered with dainty notes, covered with feminine writing." During his first years in Boston, risqué rumors and gossip added to the atmosphere of derision that the new Vedanta preacher had to face.

The fact is: the majority of Vedantists were women. So were the majority of Baptists. It is a truism that the bulwark of almost all American churches has been women, often accompanied on Sunday mornings by their husbands out of a sense of family obligation or social propriety (factors which would not induce disinterested husbands to join Vedanta as well). And many of the women followers of Vedanta have come from the upper classes, although not nearly as many as vociferous critics have alleged. It is a fact of human nature that if, among a dozen people, there is one heiress, she will get all the attention and publicity, and the eleven other housewives and stenographers will be summarily ignored. Among Vivekananda's disciples, for example, it is true that Mrs. Bull and Miss MacLeod had money and social standing, but Sister Nivedita and Christine Greenstidel were middle-class schoolteachers.

Still, compared with Protestant and Catholic churches, Vedanta had a disproportionate number of upper-middle-class women followers. The reason, however, is the same that accounts for the surge of interest in Eastern mysticism of the 1960s and '70s. Just as the affluent young people of that era, unencumbered by the demands of earning a livelihood and dissatisfied with the superfluities of material abundance, had the time and mental leisure to consider "ultimate questions" and to pursue their answers through a plethora of philosophies and practices, so the same factors operated in the beginning of the century for those who had time and leisure, namely upper-middle-class women. Many of those who first evinced interest in Paramananda had already investigated and experimented with other "avant garde" philosophies. They had ample time and opportunity to attend lectures and classes, and sufficient social independence to eschew the traditional churches. Some, doubtlessly, were merely flirting with the exotic, impelled by boredom or daring. But these found little in Paramananda to titillate them. He studiously avoided sensationalism, dressed in Western clothes, and downplayed all Oriental trappings of ceremony and ornamentation.

On January 24, 1909, Swami Paramananda, on his own initiative, started giving public lectures in Boston. He hired a two-hundred-seat hall on Huntington Avenue, and placed a two-line listing in the Church page of the local newspapers: "VEDANTA PHILOSOPHY. Lecture, 'The Need of Religion' by Swami Paramananda of India. Sunday, 4 p.m. Huntington-Chambers Hall 510." He also had some circulars printed with equally modest phrasing.

The day of that first lecture it rained hard. Only fifty people attended. The second Sunday the hall was "pretty full." The third and fourth Sundays the hall was full, and many people were turned away for lack of room. Mrs. Bull, who attended the first lecture, afterwards clasped Paramananda's hand warmly and remarked, "You have an unusually pleasant way of presenting the teaching. Another might say the same thing, yet he would antagonize."

She spoke from experience, for she had watched her guru, Vivekananda, thunder his message, heedless of the reaction. He aroused the fierce opposition of churchmen and missionaries, who hounded him through every city of his American lecture tour. Perhaps this was inevitable, for the presentation of Vedanta to Western audiences was a direct threat to the vested interests of the Christian missionary establishment, which rallied its moral and financial support around its promise to save the poor heathen from the darkness and superstition of idol worship. The descriptions of burning widows, of Hindu families exposing their infant daughters to death rather than having to pay their dowries twelve or thirteen years hence, and of other barbaric practices supposedly endorsed by their primitive pagan religion inspired tremendous enthusiasm for foreign missions in the 18th, 19th, and early 20th centuries. In 1909, there were 19,875 Protestant missionaries abroad, as well as a significant number of Catholic missionaries, and the churches of America were spending more than $20,000,000 annually to support them.

Nothing could have more potently undermined that enterprise than to hear a Hindu monk expound the profound philosophy and the elevated concept of God which had formed the basis of his religion for thousands of years. The audiences which flocked to hear Vivekananda walked away incredulous at Christian presumption in wanting to teach religion to such as he. And nothing could have irked the Christian ministry more than to see the disillusioned heirs of "the one true religion" seeking out a "heathen" to learn of God. It was no wonder that the Christian establishment stood poised to defend its missionaries and its claim to exclusive truth against the threat of an enlightened and enlightening Hinduism.

While Vivekananda was a born warrior, rallying to a good fight, a spirited debate, Paramananda was an inveterate lover of harmony. The boy who had been knocked unconscious in his efforts to prevent a brawl grew up into the man who took as his motto "not to strike any discordant note." The ire of the American clergy had originally been aroused by Vivekananda's denunciations of the Christian missionary thrust in India. The "warrior-prophet" had declared that if the Christian West really sought to help India, they would do better to send industrial instructors than religious missionaries. Abhedananda had reiterated that challenge. Paramananda, on the other hand, defied no opponents, incited no controversies, made no unfavorable comparisons between Vedanta and any other creed. His nature and his method exuded gentleness: "Let us not find fault, but work silently, unheard, unseen, helping those around us in their tasks, lightening their burdens and doing evil to no man."

Rather than engaging in conflict with the conservative Christian establishment, adding one more front to the city's sectarian battles, Paramananda began his Boston work so quietly that those who might have opposed him scarcely noticed his presence. Those Protestant ministers who were willing to meet him, he won over by his graciousness and gentility of manner. One of these was the eminent Dr. William Norman Guthrie, rector of the historic St. Marks-on-the-Bouwerie Episcopal Church in New York City. Dr. Guthrie, who became the swami's lifelong friend, described his presentation as follows:

> His was rather a musical voluntary than a constructed discourse. No mystification ever. No pretense. No conscious assumption. No effort to convert, overbear, or even persuade. Merely spontaneous outpouring of poetic yearning, sympathy, joy, purely rational and aesthetic in appeal, without controversy or awareness of possible opposition.

Through the years it was often said of Paramananda that his

tread was so silent that no one ever heard him enter a room
(giving rise to fanciful speculation that he floated above the floor
rather than walked on it). Be that as it may, he surely entered
Boston so silently that witch-hunters, sensation-mongers, and
the press were barely alerted to his coming. Advertisements of
his lectures were confined to two-line press notices in the lower
right-hand corner of the newspaper "Church Directories," sand-
wiched between a YMCA club gathering and a Spiritualist
meeting, under the heading "Miscellaneous." He eschewed
attention-getting devices and dressed inconspicuously, much to
the disappointment of those who were fascinated by full Oriental regalia. Dr. Guthrie describes Paramananda's guest appearances: "We loved to have him duly vested and turbaned (he
preferred a cassock suit—just very neat clericals, but undistinctive,
unpicturesque) and he humored us as his hosts." When any
explosive confrontation did erupt, Paramananda bowed out
quietly. Thus, when Guthrie's superior, Bishop William T. Man-
ning, objected in print to "heathens" addressing the congregation at St. Mark's, and even attempted to oust the liberal rector,
Paramananda declined to make any more public visits to the
church, despite Guthrie's repeated and undaunted invitations.

Of course, such reticent methods are not conducive to attracting large numbers of people. Paramananda had, after all,
come to Boston to spread Vedanta, not to be a light under a
bushel. But, as lights go, his way was to be a lantern, not a neon
sign. Attracting multitudes of followers seemed to him not only
beside the point, but spiritually dangerous. "In spiritual work it
is not numbers that count," he said. "Dynamic spiritual power
does not seem to manifest in the same way when there are a
great many people." And again:

> Our work may not seem to grow rapidly, but we do not
> ask to grow in numbers, although we are happy to see
> many come with yearning spirit. All we ask is to serve
> those who come humbly and lovingly—not by binding

them to any special set of ideas, but by broadening their views and breaking down all barriers of difference. . . . The size of our work may be small, but the Ideal which it embodies is not small. Ideals, however, are not realized through big organizations; their realization comes in individual human hearts full of sympathy and tolerance.

From one of Vivekananda's published letters, he had copied the injunction: "Calm and silent and steady work and no newspaper humbug, no name making, you must always remember." Paramananda always remembered.

There was another reason for Paramananda's moving quietly and slowly in the beginning of his Boston endeavor. Vivekananda had written of the city: "Boston of course is the great field for everything, but the Boston people as quickly take hold of anything as give it up." Paramananda often spoke of straw fires, which are easily lighted and rapidly blaze up, but as quickly burn themselves out, compared to log fires, which take a long time to catch, but then burn long and steadily. The spiritual fire which Paramananda tried to kindle in Boston took a long time to catch; even at the tenth anniversary of the Boston Vedanta Centre the swami said: "We may not have accomplished much as yet; but we hope to do more in the future." When it finally took, however, it burned brightly, and seventy-five years later it is still burning.

Early in March, 1909, after giving six public lectures at the Huntington-Chambers Hall, Paramananda received an urgent request from the New York Vedanta Society to come there and conduct the public observance of Sri Ramakrishna's Birthday. Swami Abhedananda was in London again, and the Sunday lectures were suspended during his absence, but they were loath to bypass Sri Ramakrishna's birthday. Paramananda agreed to go.

At this time, some of his more enthusiastic Boston students took steps to create an organized Centre. They called a meeting and decided on officers and ways and means, including a membership roll, dues, etc. During the two weeks that Paramananda was in New York, they rented a larger hall for the public meetings and engaged from another organization the use of two rooms for the classes and the sale of literature.

It proved a cataclysm for the budding work. Those who had instigated the move obviously thought it would be a happy surprise for the swami. Instead, he was distressed by this violation of his ideals, concocted by man's ambitions rather than by God's guidance. Paramananda was willing to organize to a limited extent when the growth of the work required it, but these steps seemed to him premature, precisely the forced expansion which he had shunned. As he put it: "Impatience, planning, or other human effort is not characteristic of a true devotee. The Lord is our Guide and we must get all our support from Him."

The people who had taken these initiatives must have been disappointed at the swami's lack of gratitude for their efforts. They were eager to see the cause they had adopted succeed, and the swami's recalcitrance seemed like one more obstacle in an already difficult enterprise. Whether they chose to abandon the venture, or whether the swami, despairing of being understood, gradually withdrew from them, the names which fill his diary prior to the New York visit appear less and less frequently after his return.

As for the public work which they had intended to spur, the opposite result ensued. When Paramananda started his Sunday lectures at the new hall, the attendance was almost half of what it had been at the Huntington-Chambers. Some of the weekly classes did not resume, and the new quarters specially rented for that purpose lay vacant five days a week. Not until May was the lost momentum partially regained. Two weeks later the lecture season ended.

In 1923, when the Vedanta Centre of Boston was a thriving reality, Paramananda recalled this early adversity:

When this work was first started, it was a question whether or not we should organize it as every society is organized, with by-laws and officers. Of course, organization has its advantages. It provides a background; but also spiritually it can weaken. I wanted to experiment, to build on a spiritual basis, laying just as little importance as possible on the mechanical side. It is no easy thing to begin a new work, especially in a strange country among strange people. In these circumstances many of my friends doubted the wisdom of trying to adopt new methods; but it was my firm conviction, and through Divine grace it has, I think, proved successful.

I have gone on quietly these years and I am perfectly willing to wait. What we are trying to do is to create an atmosphere with our life, our devotion and our spirit of service. If we had calculated how many came or stayed away, I think there would be few here now. That driving attitude for success would have made it impossible for me to endure the ordeal I went through right here in Boston. Today we have a big place and a large number of friends. It was not always so; but always I have had one Friend to guide me and always will I take the guidance of that Friend.

This incident was only one of a series of shocks which the naive young preacher had to face upon encountering the American public. He was offering them the pearl of great price; most of them wanted it only to add to their rhinestone collections.

He spoke to them of sacred spiritual values, of selflessness, purity, forbearance. "When I landed here, many years ago," he recalled toward the end of his life, "I used to speak of these things, just as I would speak of them in India. But soon I found that people were not interested. The Occidental audience, when someone from India comes, expects him to perform magic, or do some trick of jugglery. It was a shock to me."

Again, he reminisced:

In Boston, the first winter I was there, people often used to ask me to change the day or the hour of my classes. They would say, "Won't you change from Tuesday to Wednesday so we can all come?" and always I tried to do so, because my one desire was to benefit. Then, on a certain day, quite spontaneously, one of the ladies told me that the reason she could not come was because she had an engagement for a card party. It was a revelation to me. After that I found that almost invariably when I was asked to change it was because of something nonessential.

Even when people were genuinely interested in his teaching, Paramananda had to defend his philosophy against criticism that it was impractical, otherworldly, passive, or self-centered. Surprisingly enough, however, the greatest obstacle to Paramananda's acceptance in Boston was neither religious nor philosophical, but racial.

For all its pride in its abolitionist forebears, Boston was, and still is, a bastion of racial prejudice. Bostonians knew but one distinction, "white" and "colored," and Indians were definitely "colored." Swami Vivekananda, taken as a Negro, had been refused hotel rooms in Baltimore, and the *New York Herald* once referred to him as the "chocolate-tinted sage." Most of the early articles about Paramananda included descriptions of his complexion. It was one thing to learn Vedantic ideas from New England's own Ralph Waldo Emerson or even Mary Baker Eddy, but to apostle oneself to a "colored man," however finely wrought his features or Oxford his English, was worse than religious heresy; it was racial treason. To admit the wisdom of colored races was to deny the rationale behind the whole political and economic policy of imperialism to which Europe and America were plighted.

While Paramananda never directly spoke of the discrimination he faced, in a poignant fragment of dialogue he wrote years later, he has a child exclaiming: "Father, see how angrily that

man looks at our nice friend the holyman." The father replies:
"He does not understand him, because he is different and comes
from another race."

Paramananda resolved to meet all such opposition with faith,
surrender, and understanding, as he later stated in *Right Resolutions*:

> When my task fails to bring desired ends or leads me
> to defeat, I shall try to see the Divine Purpose which ever
> seeks to give me understanding even through pain and
> sorrow.
>
> When confronted with difficulty and perplexity, I shall
> try to be calm of spirit and strive to understand their
> meaning.
>
> When there are moments that provoke impatience, I
> shall guard myself with fortitude and perseverance.
>
> When unkind criticism is made, I shall try not to feel
> hurt or despondent, for have I not often been helped and
> spurred onward by adversity!
>
> If occasions arise to make me feel the lack of right and
> justice, I shall try to overcome these feelings with tranquility.
>
> I shall try to remind myself always that He, the All-
> wise Divine Dispenser, is ever just.

Upon his return from New York, Paramananda moved back
to Mrs. Bull's house in Cambridge. She had already left for
Norway, and wrote to him that she had extended her invitation
to him for two reasons: "most of all because your strength and
your interest are not equal; and secondly because you are willing
to venture — I have found — beyond your strength to bring out
results."

Devamata, who was still in India and was receiving letters
from Paramananda regularly, alludes to his overcoming repeated
trials:

> The bodily hardships formed only a small part of the diffi-
> culties encountered. Swami Ramakrishnananda followed
> the Swami's progress with the tenderest interest. Once

when the weekly mail brought word of the happy solution of a perplexing problem, he exclaimed with triumphant satisfaction: "Now the boy has won his spurs." And another day when he learned that a trying situation had been overcome, he said to me: "There is no doubt that Paramananda was born with realization. Otherwise he could not remain so steady under all circumstances."

One important new development which had begun to take place late in February and which gained strength after the swami's return from New York was his association with Miss Katherine Sherwood. After hearing Paramananda speak once, she immediately had invited him to hold a class in her home in Milton, a suburb of Boston. A matron of Boston society, related to Massachusetts' first family, the Saltonstalls, Katherine Sherwood was a formidable woman, large-hearted and broad-minded. Her inveterate interest in metaphysics had taken her from her family's Unitarian affiliation to Christian Science and then to an assortment of other philosophies. Twenty-four years older than Paramananda, she promptly assumed a protective motherly role toward the young swami, who reciprocated by calling her "Mai" (mother).

When the season was over in May, Katherine Sherwood invited Paramananda to spend a two-week vacation at her spacious Milton home. It was a time of relaxation and recuperation for him, for his health had suffered severely from the Boston winter, when often he had walked to his diverse classes in pouring rain or snowstorms, shivering from fevers or colds. Miss Sherwood and her other houseguests made him feel perfectly at home. In the morning they would play croquet or tennis, or receive guests, or pay calls on the swami's ever widening circle of friends. Often Paramananda cooked their dinner, an avocation he enjoyed, and they would eat in the open-air dining room beside the trickling fountain. In the evening they would read or meditate or listen to "gramaphone music." Sometimes Miss Sherwood gave dinner parties to introduce the swami to more people, hoping that personal contact would break down general prejudice. One gentleman who was an acknowledged leader of Boston society commented to Miss Sherwood at the close of one such dinner, "I do not know anything about your swami or his religious convictions, but there is no doubt that he is a thoroughbred."

The fortnight in Milton stretched into a month, and then two. Eliza Kissam visited from New York, as she had done three times already since her guru's departure, and spent a month with them. A taciturn woman in her mid-forties, descended from one of New York's old Dutch families, Miss Kissam was capable of deep dedication and hard work. The swami gave her the spiritual name "Satya Prana," meaning true-hearted.

Miss Sherwood's Milton home became Paramananda's headquarters. At the end of July he started travelling, to upstate New York and Vermont, and to lecture at the Greenacre Summer Conference in Maine. Several times he went to New York City, and he spent a week at a time at Ridgely Manor, visiting the Leggetts and Josephine MacLeod, Vivekananda's followers. But always he returned to Milton.

Katherine Sherwood's espousal of Paramananda as her teacher elicited ridicule from her Boston Brahmin family. Undaunted, she took him wherever she went, although her brother-in-law, Phillip Leverett Saltonstall, would not have the swami in his house when his friends were around. The general suspicion that the swami was a fraud and Vedanta a bogus cult, added to the stigma of fraternizing with a colored man, kept many doors closed to him. "This work will all be very slow," Miss Sherwood wrote in a letter, "but, oh how much it is needed. So much prejudice has to be overcome at every turn and that takes so much time—particularly because people never think they have any!"

"Religion means going steadily forward without heed to success or failure," Paramananda would assert. "We must have simple, child-like faith and a pure heart. Nothing else is necessary."

When autumn came, the swami began looking for a suitable

apartment in Boston. That spring he had seen a studio apartment on St. Botolph Street that he felt was the appointed place
to be a headquarters for the work and a living quarters for him.
When he went to rent it in September, he found that it had been
leased to a painter who liked the place so much it appeared
likely he would keep it indefinitely. The swami could find no
other apartment that felt right to him. He stayed in Milton, and
in October started giving a class there.

Meanwhile he had developed a chronic cough. He engaged
the Huntington-Chambers Hall for Sunday lectures again, but
the autumn chill afflicted him with a persistent hoarseness. After two attempts at public speaking, he had to abandon the
projected series.

Mrs. Bull, back in Cambridge once again, concluded that the
young swami's efforts to propagate Vedanta in Boston had failed.
She wrote to Nivedita in Calcutta recommending that the Math
authorities recall Paramananda to India. Nivedita, after conveying
the message to Swami Saradananda, replied:

> Now, if the travelling expenses can be found, they will be
> very glad to recall him. Meanwhile, your message will be
> treated, in any case, as confidential, and they will write to
> Paramananda that he is needed here. Swami Saradananda
> says that all the workers in the West find, after a year or
> two, that they have come to a sort of standstill. It is always
> one subject & one set of books, and unless they have
> some field of intellectual growth & labor, they are bound
> to become stereotyped.

Apparently Swami Brahmananda, who was in Puri at that
time, had more faith in Paramananda than the others, for the
final decision lay with him, and Paramananda was not recalled.
Friends, however, warned him against spending a second winter
in the harsh climate of New England. On December 3, he left
Boston and headed not for the mud-walled Indian Math, but for
the marbled halls of Washington, D.C.

6

Washington

WHILE PARAMANANDA WAS pitting his ideals against the harsh realities of Boston, his first disciple, Devamata, was enjoying unique opportunities in India. Sri Ramakrishna's direct disciples were greatly impressed by this cultured and competent American woman who had so committed herself to their Master and their cause. They accepted her into their lofty circle, as they had Sisters Nivedita and Christine before her. Mahendra Nath Gupta ("M"), the saintly recorder of *The Gospel of Sri Ramakrishna*, wrote, referring to Devamata, "I am exceedingly anxious to have a last look on this veritable incarnation of *Bhakti* at the Railway Station and bid her farewell." Many of the swamis shared his admiration.

Devamata spent most of her two years in India living across the road from the Madras Math, where she studied with and assisted Swami Ramakrishnananda. An astute stenographer, she had transcribed Paramananda's New York lectures for his second and third books, *The True Spirit of Religion is Universal* and *Vedanta in Practice*, which had appeared in 1908. She now rendered the same service for Swami Ramakrishnananda. Through her efforts and experience, his first book, *The Soul of Man*, was published. This was the beginning of the publication department at the Madras Math, which is now one of the large publishing houses of India.

Eager to learn all she could, Devamata steeped herself in Indian religion and culture, imbibing every detail, observing every nuance. When, eighteen years later, she published her reminiscences as *Days in an Indian Monastery*, the Indian press hailed the book as breathing "the very spirit of India," a unique achievement for a Western writer.

At one point Devamata paid a prolonged visit to Calcutta. There she was accorded the precious privilege of living closely with Sri Sarada Devi, Ramakrishna's consort and spiritual help-mate, adored by his devotees as "The Holy Mother." Devamata was allowed to take care of Holy Mother's room, make her bed, massage her rheumatic legs. Mother addressed her as "my sweet daughter" and showered blessings upon her. She entrusted Devamata with the implementation of her dream: a girls' school on the Ganges, where Eastern and Western pupils could study together.

In coming to India, Devamata had renounced the world and taken up the garb of the *brahmacharini*. She was known to every-one as "Sister Devamata." The general understanding was that she had come to give her life in service to India, as had her predecessors Nivedita and Christine, who at that time were teach-ing at Nivedita's Girls' School.

Her heart, however, was still tied to her young guru in America. When Paramananda had bid her farewell, he had said, "You are going to the land of great teachers. If you meet one whose disciple you want to be, do not feel bound by your rela-tionship with me." But Devamata's loyalty and devotion to Paramananda never wavered. While still en route to India, she wrote to him, "The greater the outer distance that separates us, the closer will our hearts cling together." As soon as she learned that he had left New York and was working alone in Boston, she longed to return and help him.

As for Paramananda, he was eager to see her accepted and appreciated in India, especially after the calumny she had had to endure in New York for his sake. Whenever he received letters praising her from his friends in India, he was overjoyed. "Oh! I long so much to see my Mother doing good work and appreciated by people. Do you know what a joy it brings to my heart when anyone speaks kindly of you. That is all I want, only to see you happy and blessed by the Lord. I want no other reward or return from you."

Still, he knew what an invaluable asset she could be to his new endeavor, and though he strove to be unselfish, he vocalized his need in terms she could not have, or would not have, ignored:

> How I wish you were here to help me. . . . You know how hard it is to build something new in the midst of strange people and one must go through certain discomforts and hardships. . . . You know, Dearest, what a comfort and help it is to have you near me, but I will leave your coming or staying entirely with you. If you are happier there, stay by all means. I never like to be selfish. I will try my best to do the work and if help does not come from anywhere, I will try to be contented, thinking it is Mother's will.

Devamata sailed from Bombay on September 17, 1909, for what most people thought was a brief visit home. Holy Mother saw further. She said to her, "Devamata, be careful. If you get even the hem of your garment caught in the American work, you will not get back." Hem—and heart—were already caught. She never returned.

On December 6, 1909, Swami Paramananda, Sister Devamata, and Mrs. Reukirt, a friend from New York, arrived in Washington, D.C. The swami had relinquished his notion of being a wandering Vedanta preacher. Immediately they began looking for a location to establish a new Vedanta Centre. After the usual frustrations of house-hunting, they fortuitously happened upon the perfect house to serve both as headquarters for the work and as living quarters for them.

The first floor was to be the meeting place for the public lectures and classes. The second was to accommodate "the workers," which included Satya Prana (Eliza Kissam) during her intermittent visits from New York and Katherine Sherwood once or twice. The third floor was to be the swami's bedroom and study, and the private shrine.

On December 20, amidst the commotion of workmen and renovations, they moved in, with five trunks and three cots as the sum total of their furniture. Getting the place ready and maintaining it were formidable tasks for the dedicated, but inexperienced, crew. Neither the two women of genteel birth nor the swami had ever managed an entire house before, especially one with such mechanical exigencies as a furnace. Sister Devamata gives a comic description of their plight:

> The furnace caused us continual disquietude. None of us had had experience with furnaces and we were constantly afraid it would go out. Swami would get up at five, go down and peer in to see if the fire was still burning; one of the workers, unaware of this early visit, would creep down at five-thirty; another would follow at six; and at seven the hired boy, who came night and morning to stoke it, would come and rescue it from too frequent shiftings of the damper.

Sister Devamata took the situation in hand. Eminently practical, efficient, and resourceful, she assumed the roles of housekeeper, laundress, and cook, as well as secretary, publicist, and administrator of the new Centre. With tireless dedication and zeal, she became the swami's one-person staff, and his invaluable partner in his undertaking.

They made an ideal team, for just as it was Paramananda's nature to treat his disciples as equals, it was Devamata's nature not to play second to anyone. An utterly devoted disciple, she nevertheless regarded herself as the swami's equal, not spiritually, but functionally. Paramananda deliberately fostered this attitude. When one student wrote to him, addressing him reverentially as "Beloved Master," he replied, "Do not address me thus. I like to feel I am your friend, a child of God." Even many years later, he appealed to his students: "I ask that you all pray for me, so that until the very end I may be able to work just this way, that I may not set myself up or have any desire to, because I would feel disconnected with you if I should try to sit on a higher level or pedestal. . . . Think of me always as your friend, so that I may serve and love you so much that you may feel there is nothing lacking in life."

To a large extent, Paramananda succeeded in staying off the pedestal. One early follower wrote to him: "You seemed more as a brother to me than a stern teacher to stand in awe of! And that is what I needed." Yet this stance, however conducive to Paramananda's humility, was hardly conducive to Devamata's.

On Christmas Day, 1909, Paramananda "installed the Lord" in the new house by setting up a shrine and invoking the Divine Presence with chanting, meditation, incense, and offerings of flowers and food. From that day on the household gathered before the shrine for worship in the morning, at noon, and in the evening.

These services were strictly private; the Vedanta offered to the public had little ritual or Hindu trappings. Still, the Sunday evening meetings, which began on January 2, 1910, were definitely services, rather than mere lectures as were given in New York. Paramananda began each session with a peace chant and ended with a benediction:

Thou, the Christ of the Christians, Jehovah of the Jews,
Allah of the Mohammedans, Ahura-Mazda of the Zoro-
astrians, Buddha of the Buddhists, Divine Mother and
Brahman of the Hindus, grant unto us light and understanding so that we may worship thee, Thou one Lord of
the Universe, with the true and universal spirit of religion.
Grant unto us Thy peace and blessing.

An article on Paramananda and his new center appeared in
the *Washington Sunday Star* two weeks after the Sunday services
and midweek classes had begun. The reporter apparently came
expecting to find a cabal of glazed-eyed initiates held in thrall by
an ornately adorned soothsayer. Instead he was surprised and
impressed by what he encountered:

> Coming out of the night into a long, brightly lighted
> room, absolutely devoid of all furnishings except the nec-
> essary chairs for the convenience of the little band of inter-
> ested listeners, the writer caught a glimpse of a boyishly
> slender figure clad in the delicate salmon-tinted robe of a
> Hindu monk, and as the words "peace, peace, peace,"
> reiterated in reverent monotone . . . fell upon the silence
> of the room, all preconceived notions of elaborate Orien-
> tal display and extravagant religious ceremonial were in-
> stantly dispelled by the solemn simplicity of the plea for
> the realization of the age-old ideal of mankind. . . .
>
> Bare floors, no furniture, no ornaments, no draperies,
> no music, no ostentation, no paraphernalia of any descrip-
> tion, nothing to suggest the atmosphere of the Orient save
> the faint odor of burning incense and the gentle courtesy
> of the sweet-faced, white-robed "sister" in her white veil,
> who presides at the door, certainly provide a most suitable
> and unusual setting for the quiet earnestness of the speaker.
> In excellent English, with absolute poise and unaffected
> manner, he makes a direct appeal for the true universal
> brotherhood of man, which is to live the life that the lowly
> Nazarene holds up as the straight and only path to immor-

tality, the goal of perfection and unity with God.

The simple teaching of the Swami throws a different light upon the tenets of the Hindu religion, a meaning entirely disassociated with the tinkling, glittering rituals of the land of Buddha as portrayed by the popular novelist, and a meaning which gives rise to the thought that many of the self-styled Christians, who desire to force their religious convictions upon the peoples of the east, might do well to pause long enough to realize the effrontery of such a course. All thoughts of the mystic, the occult, the promises of soothsayers, the prophecies of the seers, so generally associated with any of the teachers or 'holy men' of the east, melt away into nothingness before . . . the Swami Paramananda.

It was an impressive tribute, and one might think that it would arouse interest, or at least curiosity, among the people of Washington. But even on the evening after the article appeared, the attendance at the Sunday lecture was mediocre. The fact is, despite Devamata's ever-optimistic assessments ("the response was remarkable," "the attendance at the lectures and classes was unusually large for Washington"), Paramananda's diary reveals a consistent apathy in the Capital toward the Eastern teaching. Whereas Boston, even at its lowest ebb, had produced audiences of over a hundred, the group that came to 1808 Kalorama Road on Sunday evenings sometimes numbered only fifty, or forty, or even thirty. By the fifth week of the season the response had grown, so that the fifth lecture was very well attended, but the next Sunday was bitterly cold and windy, causing the audience to drop again. As Sister Devamata remarked, "The Washington public is very subservient to weather."

Nor could Paramananda attract crowds by his skill as an orator. His power as a speaker lay rather in the subtle calm he emanated. As the *Washington Star* described the swami's delivery: "The lack of gestures and repose of manner make him a restful speaker, and the constant kindling of the very expressive eyes keeps the listener interested."

Ironically, Paramananda could not have chosen a more difficult metropolis for propagating Vedanta than Washington, D.C.
Swami Abhedananda before him had tried and failed, as would
at least two swamis in later decades. When such unlikely out-
posts as Portland and Seattle had thriving Vedanta Societies,
Washington, D.C. still proved impervious to the movement. Perhaps the political capital of a nation is an incongruous place to
preach universalism, one of the cardinal tenets of Vedanta. As
The Washington Star quoted Paramananda:

> There has been a gradual awakening all over the world,
> and people are beginning to reach out after these univer-
> sal truths which, when generally accepted, will put an end
> to the intense strife between the different religions. The
> deep lines of demarcation drawn between the various sects
> will disappear, and each will allow that the other may be
> equally right and entitled to an equal share of respect. All
> warfare, bloodshed, and political contention for individual
> supremacy will cease when this doctrine becomes universal.

Such universalism was not only Paramananda's official message, but also his personal instinct. "I am very grateful," he once
declared, "for the spiritual training I received in India. I know I
could never be satisfied with an Ideal whose very foundation
principles were not love, tolerance, and absence of bigotry. . . .
If through some turn of circumstance I had been forced to sub-
scribe to dogmas or creeds, every bit of myself would have been
entirely outside of it."

Almost from the beginning, the question of closing the Washington Centre was debated. A terse comment by Sister Devamata,
the Centre's chief proponent, hints at the main obstacles: "As
the people are still strongly church-bound or absorbed in political and diplomatic life, any work of a serious or unorthodox
nature must necessarily progress slowly." The people of Boston

quibbled about religion, battled about religion, but cared about
religion. To the cosmopolitan population of Washington, on the
other hand, religion was as irrelevant as last year's fashions.

In the face of these persistent discouragements, Swami
Ramakrishnananda continually urged Paramananda not to be
disheartened:

> It is the will of Sri Sri Guru Maharaj [Ramakrishna]
> that the new center has been opened . . . because every-
> thing happens according to His will. He is the Doer, we are
> all instruments in His hand. This is the eternal truth. That
> one is a fool who thinks that he has achieved anything by
> his own strength and intellect, and takes credit. God Him-
> self will make you do his work; so, do not be anxious.
> Remember Sri Sri Swamiji's saying: "A hundred defeats
> must not frighten you."
>
> God manifests Himself in the heart of that one who
> has surrendered his self totally to God. You do not possess
> any ego, so He is manifest always in your heart. What an
> inexpressible bliss is experienced by the one who does not
> possess any ego! . . . That one is free and unconcerned be-
> cause he has known that he is an instrument in His hand,
> and so he is never unbalanced. Thus he relieves himself of
> pride, haughtiness, arrogance, jealousy, hatred, etc. . . .
> Never forget the great mantra, "Not I, not I; You, You." Never
> crave for your own name and fame. His will executes
> everything. Realize forever that not even a blade of grass
> moves but by His will, and thus remain free and contented.

Indeed, Paramananda had assimilated this ideal, and longed
to be only an instrument for the Divine action. As he wrote in a
letter from Washington:

> We are all His children and can be perfect channels for the
> manifestation of His glory, if we are only devoid of ego or
> lower self. This state of self-surrender or selflessness is
> indeed blessed and is the very height of Divine wisdom.

But let us not confound it with the idea of self-annihilation. On the contrary, this is the only way we may gain a hold on our true Self and understand its relation with the Divine. More we realize the Divine, humbler we grow and better fitted we are for His service. The tree which is full of fruit bows its head, as if in meekness and humility, while the fruitless, barren tree stands erect; similarly those whose life is full of love, charity and the fruits of nobleness are always the humblest.

To be sure, a nucleus of perhaps twenty or thirty people who were edified and inspired by the Vedanta teaching and the swami's presence gave the Centre wholehearted support and insisted on its continuance. But half of Paramananda's heart was still in Boston, and students there were clamoring for his return. His gradually improving health and the prospects of spring weather added to Boston's appeal.

An unexpected uproar clinched the fate of the Washington Vedanta Centre. They had deemed it efficient and thrifty to rent one house to serve all purposes, much the same as the New York Vedanta Society's home on West 80th Street. When Mrs. Reukirt and Satya Prana returned to New York in the middle of January, however, only Paramananda and Devamata were left living in the house. News of this incited criticism from influential Vedantists in New York and San Francisco.

The naive Paramananda saw nothing wrong in the arrangement, for he was young enough to be Devamata's son, and even as strict a moralist as Ramakrishnananda had praised Devamata's motherly affection and had bidden her to take care of the young monk. "I am very glad," Ramakrishnananda wrote to Devamata, "to hear that under your kind maternal care the health of Swami Paramananda has improved a good deal. Please remember me to Miss Kissam and Miss Sherwood. That is indeed heaven where three or four good people like you live together. How I should like to be in your company! . . . The ears should be made deaf to the remarks of men, but should be always kept open to hear the voice of the Lord."

The local followers, too, seem to have accepted the situation as quite natural and practical, for Paramananda's purity was beyond impugning. But rumors and calumny continued to be hurled from a distance. Josephine MacLeod and others who had supported Paramananda during the New York debacle suddenly were up in arms. Swami Trigunatita in San Francisco, whose friendship Paramananda had valued since their meeting in Madras, ignored his letters, and when the senior swami finally did respond to Sister Devamata, he pointedly avoided any mention of her teacher. These defections puzzled and hurt Paramananda, who was learning the painful lesson that human beings can be trusted only to be human. Stronger and wiser, he wrote to Ramakrishnananda, "In this world there is no friend except God."

As to whether he should act to quell the slander, or simply ignore it, the young swami was caught in a dilemna. While he did not believe in defending himself, not only his own reputation, but the reputation of the work was being threatened. In a letter he wrote:

> It is true that we have to go through many, many unpleasant experiences in the form of criticism and condemnation from the world, when we try to lead an ideal life of absolute devotion and renunciation; but it is true that the joy one feels in devotional life even in the midst of all external suffering is infinitely greater than any pleasure that the world can give us. So we must discriminate and stand by the right thing, no matter whatever may happen to us.

Swami Ramakrishnananda, who brooded over his protégé as devotedly as he had in Madras, at first advised him to ignore the prattle:

Do not pay heed to what people say against you. Let them say as they like. You do your duty and be contented. . . . Do not keep much connection with anyone; take shelter in Sri Sri Guru Maharaj and Sri Sri Swamiji, and carry on your work. There is no doubt that through their grace you will win. You are pure yourself. So, what matters to you what others say? Let them say as they like.

The matter eventually was put before Swami Brahmananda, the President of the Order, who directed Ramakrishnananda: "Write to Basanta that he does not stay with Devamata or any other woman in the same house. He can arrange to stay in some boarding house." Passing the directive on to Paramananda, Ramakrishnananda added: "Although he has particular trust in you, he has given this injunction to forestall people's criticism."

These letters were written in May. A month before that, indeed as soon as the cherry blossoms bloomed along the Potomac, Paramananda had returned to Boston, leaving Devamata in Washington.

"When man casts me down, God holds me up," had become his motto.

7

"To Infuse The Spirit"

THE FIRST ARTICLE about Swami Paramananda to appear in Boston newspapers began by quoting Booker T. Washington: "Down South it is not so hard to keep apace with religion, but here in Boston you have so many religions under so many changing names that it is hard to keep track of them. I must confess that I cannot." The article went on to announce: "It is but little more than a month since Booker T. Washington made 500 representative Boston men laugh by the above statement, but within that time a new cult has been born to Boston. Only last week 'Vedanta' made its debut. . . ."

Paramananda considered himself a man entrusted with a sacred mission, but did America, or Boston, already burgeoning with religious sects, really need Vedanta? The late 19th and early 20th centuries were a period of religious flux and experimentation. The Age of Reason had undermined the constituency of those churches based on dogma and the supernatural. It was the heyday of mind and matter; spirituality was as out of fashion as sailing schooners in the age of steamboats. Ethical and rational religions offered a plausible, if bland, alternative, but many people, especially intellectuals and free thinkers, could not see the necessity for religion at all. They denounced it as superstition, an opiate for the uneducated and weak-minded.

Then the "experimental religions" mushroomed: Christian Science, New Thought, Unity, Theosophy, spiritualism. They were in large part derived from Oriental teachings which had filtered into America through Emerson, the Transcendentalists, and current translations of Hindu scriptures, principally the Upanishads and the Bhagavad Gita. Indeed, the first thirty-three editions of Mary Baker Eddy's *Key to Science and Health According to the Scriptures* contained many direct references to and quotations from the Bhagavad Gita (which were mysteriously expurgated from all later editions, ostensibly to avoid the stigma of "Hindu influence"). But, despite their use of Eastern principles and methods, they were still very much religions of mind and matter. They taught that mind could control matter, and thus offered man power over his life and ills. Their goal seemed to be health, prosperity, and well-being, not God. Eschewing bondage to the physical plane, they penetrated the more subtle mental and astral realms, but they did not aspire to the pure spiritual realm, to mystical absorption in God. Indeed, in their efforts to improve their earthly lot, they used what they knew of the spiritual to enhance the material, while Vedanta teaches the use of the material to attain the spiritual.

Understandably, Vivekananda felt that the exalted principles of Vedanta had been misrepresented and exploited. He deplored the instant preparations and spiced-up-to-be-palatable concoctions which used India's sacred ambrosia as their base. Instead, Vivekananda and his successors offered the West pure spiritual food, with the Divine as its center and goal, yet rational, undogmatic, universal, and practical. They found that many were hungry for this pure mysticism which the traditional Western religions had either forgotten or expunged in their efforts to be "modern."

Mysticism, the direct experience of and union with God, is the ultraviolet ray of the religious spectrum, invisible to even the sharpest naked eye. Its revelations cannot be obtained through the senses or the rational mind, but only through the subtle, intuitive faculty of the soul. Those seers in all religions who have developed that subtle faculty through fervent love of God, prayer, meditation, and renunciation of the ego-bound self, testify to a God-permeated cosmos, which is the true reality behind all seeming appearances.

Vedanta preachers such as Paramananda taught the ultimate truth of that mystic reality and the methods to attain it. While the battle raged between the freethinkers who would cast off all religion and the dogmatists who would stifle man with one exclusive religion, between the worshipers of a remote-control God enthroned beyond the clouds and the petitioners of a Sears catalogue God dispensing household favors, Paramananda offered a nonsectarian religious approach consonant with St. Augustine's dictum: "God created us for Himself, and we will never rest until we rest in Him."

Vedanta did not claim uniqueness; rather the swamis asserted that the deep truths they taught could be found in all religions. But the fact was that these mystical principles and practices were downplayed or inaccessible in the Judeo-Christian establishment until, in the 1960s and '70s, the growing success of Eastern religious groups caused concerned ministers and rabbis to blow the dust off their own mystical traditions and offer their famished seekers something beyond ethics and organization. The current proliferation of courses in "Christian meditation" being offered in the churches and in Hasidism being given in the synagogue rooms which formerly housed only ways and means committees is a direct consequence of the trend quietly inaugurated by orange-turbaned swamis in the drawing rooms of Chicago, New York, and Boston so many years ago.

Paramananda never considered his aim to be the founding of another cult in an already proliferating potpourri. As he proclaimed:

I am not seeking to establish a new cult or creed. There are plenty of creeds already existent; another would be only one too many. Nor am I interested in a new dogma or in occult mysteries. I have only one fundamental interest uppermost in my heart and that is interest in humanity, its betterment, its unfoldment, its all-embracing unity. With these lofty and noble ideals we have established this work.

Once a gentleman asked Paramananda if he was a missionary. Paramananda replied that he did not believe in conversion.

"What is your work, then?" the man asked, surprised.

Paramananda answered: "My work is to infuse the Spirit which changes and transforms the lives of men."

———◆·◆———

While he was still in Washington, heedless of Sara Bull's assessment of his "failure," Paramananda wrote to Katherine Sherwood asking her to check on the St. Botolph Street apartment that he had tried to rent the previous autumn. It seemed to her like a futile errand, for the artist who lived there had planned to keep it permanently. She went anyway, and found that the tenant had just died and his wife was anxious to sublet it. It became the first home of the Boston Vedanta Centre.

The apartment, located at 16 St. Botolph Street, in Boston's artists' quarter, consisted of a large studio which could be used for the public meetings and two adjoining smaller rooms for the swami's bedroom and study. Downstairs on a floor just below street level were a large dining room, a kitchen, a laundry, a bathroom, and a storage room. The entrance to the apartment opened directly onto the street. In short, it was like a small house, without the bother of a furnace.

The swami was delighted with it, but he missed Sister Devamata's practical assistance. "I had such sick headache all yesterday afternoon & evening," he wrote to her, "& oh! how I missed your loving care, & said oh! if you were here you could remove so many little details from my hand & give me something to eat. All will come in time."

He decided to hire a housekeeper. The elderly woman who worked for the New York Vedanta Society was so devoted to the young swami that when she heard he had a place in Boston, she offered to move there and take care of it for him. Scarcely had she arrived when she fell ill, and the swami, in addition to the housekeeping, suddenly found himself playing full-time nurse. "We are trying our best to take care of her," he wrote to Devamata, "and she is very appreciative. Yesterday and today I have cooked some simple meals and I am learning how to wash dishes too. This is all for some good purpose. I like to nurse and the Lord has given me this little privilege so that I may learn to practice what I preach."

When the housekeeper recovered, she returned to New York, leaving the swami to himself. He resolved to undertake his own domestic chores, including cooking. His diet was simple and sparse, often supplemented by students who would bring homemade bread or dishes they had cooked. Once, a lady inadvertently sent some split pea soup which had turned sour. Paramananda dutifully ate it for several days, and after the Sunday service innocently asked her, "In America do they always put vinegar in pea soup?"

Meanwhile, Devamata, carrying on the work alone in Washington, felt dejected and discouraged. Having been rebuffed by her family and the New York Vedanta Society, now again she was the target for those prominent Vedantists whose disapproval she had aroused. A petite woman with a towering character, as strong in her opinions as in her dedication, wherever she went she made equally fervent admirers and enemies. Now she began to wonder whether she would be an asset or a hindrance to her gentle guru.

The naturally affectionate Paramananda let his love pour
out to her: "Now you see how it is turning. Those who tried to
put you out of the way have only brought you closer than ever. I
feel such longing for you at times, but I must wait patiently. Love
goes to you — oh! so freely." Again: "My heart is so full of love for
you that I hardly can write. You fill my life in so many ways that
you yourself even do not realize it."

Boston's Vedanta Centre gradually took shape. The swami
set up an impersonal altar in the studio and filled out the Sunday afternoon public services with readings from various Scriptures, music, and meditation. He conducted two evening classes
weekly, and a Saturday morning class on "The Bible in the Light
of Vedanta." On Monday afternoons he gave individual interviews to those who sought personal spiritual guidance. *Principles
and Purpose of Vedanta*, Paramananda's concise introduction to the
philosophy, was published that spring. Along with other books by
Paramananda and Vivekananda, it was distributed for sale, and
made available at the Centre's "reading room" each afternoon.

Slowly, undramatically, the work grew. Each week a few new
people appeared in the congregation, and the regular students
gradually deepened their commitment to the spiritual life and to
the Centre. This gradual growth, a few individuals at a time,
amply satisfied Paramananda's ideal. He used to quote Swami
Vivekananda's declaration: "Give me a genuine man; I do not
want masses of converts." Indeed, an early, handwritten set of
guidelines for the Boston Vedanta Centre states as its main object:
"to help each individual to unfold his or her spiritual or divine
nature by following the path of right thinking, right living, self-
control, concentration and meditation." Inspiring individual spiritual development was Paramananda's concept of his own mission,
a goal which eluded numerical assessments.

Although the format of the work revolved around public
lectures and classes, Paramananda felt strongly that true spiritual teaching was not given by words, but by example. In one of

his earliest sermons he declared:

> The only true help that you can render to mankind is when, by your very character, you teach others. Then you do good by your every word, your every movement. When, for instance, you remain steady under all conditions of good and evil, those around you learn the value of steadiness and begin to try to practice it themselves. Thus, by the example of your character, your whole life becomes a lesson to others. . . .
>
> Christ helped the world by His character. It is not that He turned this earth into a heaven. That is not possible. There was just as much evil in the world after He came as before, but by His example He is helping each individual soul to overcome its limitations and to strive toward perfection.

That May, Swami Abhedananda severed his connection with the New York Vedanta Society and, with a small group of disciples, took up residence at the Connecticut ashram, from where he would occasionally embark on lecture tours, his work henceforth independent of the Ramakrishna Mission. The New York Society wrote to Paramananda, inviting him to return and offering him complete charge of the Society. Faced with a choice between a large established center in New York and the incipient Boston enterprise, Paramananda chose the latter. He wrote to Devamata:

> I have made up my mind to work in Boston steadily and, if Lord is willing, to make this my headquarters. I do not feel in the least discouraged. Work like this grows very slowly. It is in its infancy and must be protected. His work He will do and no one can resist it.

The swami's Boston champions were not as patient. Katherine Sherwood, who considered Paramananda a rare spiritual manifestation, chafed at the blindness of people who did not see this light shining in their midst. "The meditation class," she wrote to Sister Devamata, "is much appreciated by those who come — also the Bible class, but the numbers are not as large as they should be, if the world were not asleep. I so often think of your expression in one of your letters — the unperceiving public — I could cry when I not only think of the public but the so-called Christian ministers — not one of them extending a hand to this blessed soul."

Paramananda rigorously shunned aggressive promotion, quoting Sri Ramakrishna's saying, "When the lotus blooms, the bees come of their own accord." He believed that the truths of Vedanta could be spread in a way commensurate with the exalted level of the teaching, that they need not resort to pragmatism and commercialism to teach idealism and spirituality. In contrast to later gurus, who would employ Madison Avenue techniques to attract mass followings, Paramananda deliberately avoided sensational publicity, printed the most modest circulars, and issued no tantalizing claims or promises, such as rapid enlightenment. On the contrary, he assured his students that the spiritual quest was a long, difficult struggle. Referring to learning to control one's mind, he said, "This is not the work of a day, but may take years; nay, lives." Hardly an inviting sales pitch. It was a paradoxical situation. Paramananda and his followers wanted the public to "wake up," but they declined to use alarm clocks, hoping instead that eventually the sun would rouse it.

Those who did find out about and attend the Vedanta Centre services heard no placatory platitudes or comfortable soporifics. Swami Paramananda, in the zeal of his youth, delivered a direct and uncompromising summons to renunciation and love of God:

> God is the source of all our strength and inspiration, but when we forget Him, through the charm of matter, we become spiritually blind. . . . You cannot have sincere love for God in your heart and at the same time fondness for

worldly enjoyments. It is impossible; it is inharmonious — as darkness and light. Thus the sages have declared boldly the thought of renunciation: Give up! Give up the world and love God, the Supreme Goal from Whom we have come into existence, in Whom we live and move and have our being. Do not forget Him, do not neglect to serve Him. Love Him and serve Him and let all else go.

At the end of May, 1910, the swami returned to Washington for a few days. The nucleus of students there was intent on keeping the Centre, and Paramananda was loath to abandon them. His relationship with his students was always a deep, personal bond. As an army Major in Washington had written to him: "We miss you very much, not on account of your teachings only, but principally on account of yourself. There are many people who teach and are respected or even revered by their disciples, but there are not many teachers who are beloved by those who learn. You inspire that kind of respect, dear Swami, the kind that makes of teachers, parents, and of disciples, children, and we — Mrs. Guzman and I — are two of the latter."

Accordingly, Paramananda devised a system whereby he would come to Washington in the early fall and spring and conduct six or eight weeks of meetings while Devamata carried the work in Boston. The rest of the time he would teach in Boston and Devamata would take charge of the Washington Centre. "If Lord is willing," he wrote Devamata at this time, "I think you are going to be a great help to whatever work He might want me to accomplish."

For Paramananda this was simply a logical and practical step. Devamata, with her natural talents, wide-ranging knowledge, Indian training, and leadership gift, was obviously qualified to teach Vedanta and manage the Washington Centre. The move appears revolutionary only when one realizes that no other swami of the Ramakrishna Order before or in the seventy years since ever allowed a woman to take the Vedanta platform on a regular basis. As in most other churches, the power was to be kept in the hands of a male hierarchy.

According to Vedanta philosophy, bodies and personalities are merely superimpositions upon the soul, which has neither form nor sex nor any limitation. Paramananda, who felt that his work was to deal with souls, not forms, took this principle in earnest. He accorded men and women the same opportunities, not because he was a militant feminist, but because it never occurred to him to do otherwise.

In this he followed his guru. The second person to whom Swami Vivekananda gave *sannyas* in America was a woman (Madame Marie-Louise). Indeed, Vivekananda had made equality for women a top priority of his mission, taking as his motto, "Women and the poor." "There is no chance for the welfare of the world," he had declared, "unless the condition of women is improved. It is not possible for a bird to fly on only one wing."

The breadth of vision of a great soul like Vivekananda inevitably becomes constricted by the generations which follow. In later years, Paramananda's practiced policy of sexual equality aroused increasing criticism from some of his younger brother monks. Nevertheless, he never debated the issue of equal rights for women. For him it was not an issue at all, but an axiom.

The regular round of services, classes, and outside speaking engagements at liberal churches and women's clubs was dotted by "banquets," which Paramananda loved to give. He did all the cooking and serving himself, Indian dishes such as pilau, chutney, sandesh. Often he improvised and named his creations, "Curry Unity in Variety," "Salad East and West." Miss Sherwood gives a glimpse of one banquet. She had brought her two servants, Bride and Katy, to assist. "When everyone had had all they could eat of two courses and fruit, Swami disappeared downstairs and served Bride and Katy and ate his own supper, telling them that he and they were helpers and would have their supper together."

The Boston work was proceeding so well that Paramananda decided to continue the Sunday services and Tuesday classes through the summer. When he left in August to give a two-week course of lectures at the Greenacre Conference on Comparative Religions in Maine, Sister Devamata took over the Boston meetings.

A *Boston Transcript* account of her advent describes her as a "foreign priestess . . . robed in spotless white." It continues: "There was a white light in the eyes of the comely woman and a brilliant sparkle to her words as she talked yesterday of what she hoped to do in Boston. 'I am not here to make any converts to Hinduism,' Sister Devamata said, 'nor to promote a creed, but to enlarge the atmosphere of belief.' " Curiously enough, she did not even mention Swami Paramananda in the interview.

During that summer Paramananda and Devamata were both guests of Katherine Sherwood in her Milton home, from where they commuted for classes and lectures. The swami's friends were concerned about his persistent ill health, for even in August he suffered from continuous "colds" (later diagnosed as hay fever). Perhaps as an attempt at therapy, Miss Sherwood sent him to Bermuda. While there he lectured to an audience of two hundred, the first time the teaching of Vedanta was heard on the island. Paramananda enjoyed four days of sightseeing, but with the brevity of the trip and the rough sea voyage home, it did not succeed in curing him. The night he returned to Milton he was consigned to bed again.

In September, the swami reopened the work in Washington, with Devamata continuing in Boston. The lectures went well, but the big house required too much care for one person. Paramananda decided to relocate closer to the center of the city, and found a suitable apartment. When he tried to rent it, however, he encountered the typical obstacle. The owner was an orthodox churchman, one of the pillars of the Church of the Epiphany, and he looked askance at a heathen faith holding meetings in his building.

Paramananda overcame the obstacle in a way that was also to become typical. He met the landlord personally and won him over by his gentle, disarming manner. The staunch Christian landlord not only rented the Hindu swami the apartment, but when another tenant objected to public meetings being held in the house, he threatened to cancel her lease. At the end of the year, when he heard that the swami was intending to give up the apartment, he wrote two full pages with his own hand urging the agent to do his utmost to keep the Vedanta Centre: "Give them whatever they want. I don't know anything about the Swami's religion, but it must be a good one to make him what he is. He is one of the nicest tenants I have ever had."

When Paramananda returned to Boston at the end of October, Sister Devamata resumed charge of the resituated Washington Centre. The surge of interest aroused by the swami's intermittent visits died down between them, so that Devamata often gave her informative expositions to meager audiences. "I remember one night when a storm was raging outside," she wrote, "and only three came to the Wednesday evening class. Two sat on the front row, and, exhausted perhaps by the battle with the elements, slept quietly, except for an occasional forward start to catch a sliding purse. The third one, still a faithful friend, sat on the very last row wide awake. I talked to her about the Upanishads for an hour, while she smiled and nodded assent to all I said."

The ever-zealous Devamata was not easily discouraged, however. Not only did she insist on keeping the Washington Centre open, but she was eager to forge ahead and open still another Centre in a different city. This plan would have effectively channeled her own dynamism, but would have overtaxed the swami in the process, for his health continued to be poor. Swami Ramakrishnananda indignantly rejected the proposal: "Devamata understands the Lord's work to mean only opening centres and delivering lectures. . . . The sincere worker is rare who sticks to one centre and carries the work quietly. Devamata may have devotion, but it is veiled by clouds in the shape of her desire for lots of work."

Despite their mutual affection and loyalty, Devamata and Paramananda differed vastly in temperament and methods, a reality which Paramananda did not have to contend with until after her return from India. Devamata had a penchant for organization, for rules and structures, for dignified but energetic promotion. Observing her in Madras, Ramakrishnananda had warned Paramananda of her "slight tendency to boss." Indeed, in the functioning of the Centres, Paramananda declined to over-rule her, preferring instead to balance her drive with his own mellow approach. Asked if Paramananda was afraid of Sister Devamata, someone who had known them both well replied, "No, he was not afraid of her. But he was afraid of hurting her."

Thus, while eschewing officers and bylaws, Paramananda intermittently yielded on the issue of formal membership. Some years there was a membership; some years there was not; but there were never such formalities as membership cards or fixed membership dues. Each one contributed whatever he or she could afford. Eventually, the swami's predilection prevailed, and membership in the Vedanta Centre became a self-declared spiritual affiliation only.

Paramananda was not only presenting a radical philosophy, he was presenting it in a radical way. His refusal to use organizational methods, standard publicity techniques, and the physical yoga instructions, so tantalizing to the public, bore out his advocacy of spirit over matter. For Paramananda, the materialism which dominated society and even religion meant more than hoarding money and worshipping possessions. It referred not just to values, but to perception. A materialistic society was bound to the gross, and was uncomprehending of the subtleties which compose true spirituality. To the accusation that he and his teachings were impractical, a charge which pursued him from the beginning to the end of his public life, the young Paramananda responded:

At present we have become so dependent on matter, and have so lost sight of the spirit that nothing seems practical but bread and butter, and such things as are perceivable and gratifying to the senses. If we weigh all our so-called intellectual arguments against the value of religion, we will see clearly that there is no other reason for our objections, except that we have formed a morbid habit of dependence entirely on matter — upon the external and transitory things of this world.

In his yearning to lead people to the mystic heights of truth and peace, Paramananda insisted on the supremacy of the subtle over the gross. He jumped levels, sang his song in pitches above the range of the human ear, called on people to develop new faculties rather than simply giving them new objects for old faculties. That is why he refused to feed their intellects with philosophical expositions, and their senses with a variety of external practices. People came to him expecting to be taught hatha yoga postures, breathing exercises, special diets; instead he shared with them his ethereal vision. As Nicodemus blankly wondered how a man could be born again, since he could no longer fit inside his mother's womb, most of the people who were attracted to Paramananda could not grasp the subtlety of his approach.

This lack of understanding was a source of repeated frustration for him:

> I am continually asked, "What do you do? What is your aim? Have you a method? Do you hope to obtain many converts?" and similar questions by persons who are well-meaning, but whose knowledge of things of the spirit is too weak to enable them to grasp the truth that not every idea for human good works in the open, or heralds its message through a trumpet, or depends on theory, dogma, or numerical strength for its ultimate fulfillment.

Typical of his emphasis on the subtle, Paramananda strove

to create not an organization but an atmosphere. He wanted to so charge the Vedanta Centre with peace and holiness that people could directly benefit just by entering the place. In November, 1910, Sister Christine, Swami Vivekananda's devoted disciple, and her friend Miss Haight visited the Boston Vedanta Centre. Afterwards Sister Christine wrote to Paramananda:

> We shall always remember our visit to Boston with the sweetest feelings. I came there very much disturbed in mind, but everything dropped from me as if by magic after the first day. You were so good and did so much for us. Everything — you, the house, the food and snatches of talk — had a sanctity about it. Even the theatre-going did not seem altogether frivolous. Miss Haight, in speaking of you on the train, said, "I shall always think of him as a pure young saint living his life in the midst of the world."

Such sensitive souls rarely passed through Paramananda's orbit during those early years in Boston. After more than four years in the United States, he was suffering from estrangement and loneliness, not for company (of which he had a steady stream), but for understanding. He felt ostracized by the other swamis in America. Among his own students were several earnest seekers, but no kindred spirits. Occasionally the idea of his visiting India arose, but Swami Ramakrishnananda, in April, 1910, had expressed his wish that his young protégé wait another year or two before making such a trip.

In spring, 1911, the base of good will which Paramananda had striven steadily to build up in Boston was dramatically shattered when the controversy over Mrs. Ole Bull's will came to trial. The innocent mockery with which Vedanta had been greeted gave way to a flood of hostility at the Eastern cult which had allegedly destroyed Mrs. Bull's sanity so that its proponents could snatch her fortune. Boston newspapers gave the case front page coverage every day for weeks, headlining sensational accounts of yoga practices and other "mystic rites." Witnesses on the stand gave elaborate descriptions of yoga postures and breathing exercises, while Mrs. Bull's maids and butlers testified about exotica ranging from pumpkin seed milk to a "pink radiance," all supposedly derived from the Vedanta teaching.

Although Paramananda's name, almost miraculously, was never mentioned, the case unleashed widespread distrust and denunciations of yoga, Vedanta, and swamis in general. A *Boston Herald* editorial entitled "Swamis and Others" charged that the typical swami was a "faker" as well as a *fakir*.

> So clever is he, however, in concealing these habits of his kind, and so successfully does he, when five thousand miles away from home, discover both the art of pleasing the American woman and the occult philosophy which she seems to crave, that he has often gained an authority as a spiritual leader entirely out of proportion to his own mental attainment or personal quality.

A letter to the editor signed "A Lover of Justice" (obviously Sister Devamata) refuted the editorial point by point, but others enthusiastically endorsed the attack, thanking the *Herald* for sounding a "much-needed note of warning" against "the cunning tact of the Swami."

Paramananda recoiled from the whole controversy. When one reporter ferreted him out and asked him if he had known Mrs. Bull, he admitted that she had come to some of his lectures, but he kept silent about the periods he had stayed in her home.

Nevertheless, he could not escape the effects of the scandal. Not only were his two years of effort in Boston suddenly devastated, but he was paralyzed from taking further steps under the hostile scrutiny of a rampaging press and an indignant, if ill-informed, public. The bitter climate hindered his work on many fronts. For example, each summer he had been invited to lecture for two to four weeks at the Greenacre Conference on Comparative Religions. This year the chairman invited him for only four days, explaining, "All this sad trouble about Mrs. Bull's will and the many unfortunate references to the things so dear to us both, have made some of the Greenacre friends feel we ought to modify our usual plans just a little for this year."

For Paramananda, this whole affair was simply another test, sent by the one Supreme Source, which he must pass by evenmindedness and submission to God. Describing his ideal of the transcendent character, he wrote:

> If he feels pain or if he feels pleasure, he recognizes that they come from the Supreme Source, and the consciousness that there is nothing apart from that one Source takes away all the weight of suffering. He knows that no real evil can come from that One who is his true Mother, his true Father, his true Friend and Protector, so he has no need to fear, and he remains always serene and cheerful. The touch of that philosopher's stone turns every pain and sorrow into blessing.

While the controversy raged, Paramananda was receiving disquieting reports about Swami Ramakrishnananda's health. The young swami longed to sit once more beside his beloved mentor and drink in his wisdom and love. Immobilized from any active work in Boston, on July 22, 1911, Paramananda sailed for India.

His ship took him to Naples, where he was to board the *Prinz Ludwig* for the journey to India. When he checked in at the steamer office, however, he was told that the *Prinz Ludwig* would not take any passengers from Naples on account of the cholera quarantine. He had already begun to reconsider the trip to India, perhaps feeling that it was self-indulgence to run back to the love and appreciation he knew awaited him there. As he was already in Italy, he decided to spend his trip touring Europe instead.

He took a train to Switzerland, where he revelled in the

natural beauty. "Now I am in this wonderful dreamland," he wrote to Boston. "No place that I have seen can compare with these lakes and mountains. I am enjoying every minute. . . . I am on my way to Interlaken to see that beautiful place and also to get a book with first lessons in French, German, Italian and English."

Shortly after his departure, the Boston Centre had received word that Swami Ramakrishnananda's illness had taken a dangerous turn for the worse. Devamata tried to relay the message to Paramananda, but her urgent cables and letters failed to reach him.

From Switzerland he travelled through Germany, France, and on to England. Everywhere he made friends and admirers. A prominent New York physician who had heard the swami lecture aboard ship followed him during the first stage of his journey and afterwards wrote: "It has been a great privilege to have met you, and for the first time I have seen Christ's teaching exemplified in a living character. I wish there were five thousand of your countrymen like yourself— pure, unselfish and universal in sympathy, to live among us Americans. We can't learn in the same way from books as from living characters."

Theodore Springmann, the German Vedanta student who had encouraged Paramananda to come to Frankfurt during the New York crisis, met him in Bremen. They spent two days together. Herr Springmann's letter to Sister Devamata described the swami as "one who in his childlike simplicity and purity is the real embodiment of what we dream and hope, of what many a speaker talks about and what many a soul struggles to attain. His perfect self-surrender, his combination of strength and modesty, gave us a greater lesson in those two days than we could ever get by anything else. Do you know what a treasure you have in Boston?"

In England, Paramananda stayed with Josephine MacLeod at Stratford on Avon, and delivered a lecture during the Shakespearean festival. The tense balance between England and India, the ruler and the ruled, made Paramananda's appearance a

potentially inflammable issue. The famous Shakespearean actor
Sir Frank Benson and a group of other prominent Englishmen
met with the swami daily. Afterwards, Miss MacLeod wrote to
Paramananda:

> In any case the East and the West met once — as equals.
> Mr. Cramb wrote to me of his indebtedness in meeting
> you: "So much simplicity of nature, so much nobility and
> utter clearness of sentiment, and withal so entire a de-
> tachment . . . as compels one to reconsider one's judge-
> ments upon the race or nation which can produce such
> a character. . . ."

In Stratford, Devamata's frantic messages finally caught up
with Paramananda. He cabled India immediately to inquire of
Swami Ramakrishnananda's condition. In response he received
the brief, ominous message: "Condition desperate."

From that moment Paramananda knew that he was racing
against time. He hurried to Genoa and boarded the first ship for
India. The boat seemed to plod through the Suez Canal, the Red
Sea, and the Indian Ocean while the young swami restlessly paced
the decks as if his longing could lend it speed. He landed at
Colombo on August 31, and the next evening crossed to the Indian
mainland at Tuticorin, only a few hours' rail journey from Madras.
As he stood in line waiting to pass through customs, his eyes
darted anxiously toward the waiting train. Three hundred and
fifty miles. Eight, perhaps ten, hours till the long-awaited reunion.

The customs officer asked to see his papers. Noticing that
they listed his vocation as a swami of the Ramakrishna Order,
the official remarked by way of conversation, "You know, a big
swami of your Order died last week."

Paramananda felt his heart stop beating. "What was his
name?" he asked.

The customs officer was concentrating on opening his luggage and poking his fingers around the layers of clothing.
Paramananda repeated the question, a little louder. "I said, did

you note the swami's name?"

The officer looked up with a start. "His name? Yes. Swami Ramakrishnananda."

He had lost the race.

———◆———

Paramananda crept into a corner of the railway car and sat there for hours, dazed, stricken, and heartsore. His mentor was only forty-eight years old. How could it be that he would never see his face again, without even a chance for final farewell? The young swami could not have known that just before Ramakrishnananda passed away on August 21 in Calcutta, his beloved protégé was poignantly in his mind. Biographies of Ramakrishnananda record how the dying monk asked to hear a song for which he wrote out the words, but no one knew the tune. The famous composer and dramatist Girish Chandra Ghosh set the lyrics to a new melody, and a well-known singer sang it over and over again as the swami listened with rapt attention. The biographers did not know that this was the hymn which Basanta had introduced to him, singing it for his teacher every morning at the Math on Ice House Road.

As Paramananda sat stunned and desolate in the railroad car, suddenly before his closed eyes rose the shining figure of Swami Ramakrishnananda, smiling radiantly. The vision brought with it a sense of relief which soothed the young swami's anguish. "I suffered much," he wrote, "but consolation came from the realization that he was free from all pain and physical suffering and was resting in the abode of peace. The vision of that smiling face brought me consolation."

During the last year, Ramakrishnananda had ended each of his biweekly letters to him with the assurance, "Know my heart's deep love and blessings." Indeed, Paramananda knew.

8

"The Heathen Invasion"

SWAMI VIVEKANANDA, in referring to the effect his passing would have on his disciples, said that saplings cannot grow in the shade of a big tree; only when the big tree is felled do the young ones shoot up. Paramananda grieved at the loss of his beloved Swami Ramakrishnananda, but the great teacher's demise somehow galvanized the young swami into a torrent of new enterprise and enthusiasm. Suddenly matured and self-confident, he was brimming with new ideas for the American work.

First, however, Paramananda had to cope with a problem in his motherland. It was easy, and perhaps natural, for some swamis in India to question the conduct of their brother monks living in affluent America, surrounded by women. Innuendos about them were constantly circulating (and to this day still are). Moreover, the New York schism and the Washington controversy had cast definite shadows on Paramananda's reputation. As one loyal South Indian friend wrote him upon his arrival in Madras: "I am afraid we all have our crosses to bear, and we have to live down prejudices. God knows how they spring up."

Paramananda had to prove his purity in the only way he could, by the silent witness of his being. After a bout of fever in

Madras, at Swami Brahmananda's request he went directly to Puri, where the head of the Order was staying with several of the older and younger monks. Paramananda rejoiced to be among them again. He quickly dropped back into his old manner of life, shaved his head, bared his feet, and donned again the ochre-colored loin cloth. Brahmananda was pleased by this spontaneous return to *sannyasin* habits. Once, when another swami suggested that Paramananda had been spoiled by his years in the West, Brahmananda reproached him, saying, "You only have to look at his face to know what he is."

Paramananda spent three weeks in Puri, two at the Belur Math, and a few days in Dacca with his brother, Bibhu Charan. Then he went south again, lecturing several times at Madras and Colombo. On November 12, he sailed for Italy. There he made a pilgrimage to Assisi and to St. Peter's Basilica. Both places deeply inspired him. Just before Christmas, 1911, he returned to Boston, charged with new zeal for his mission.

Already from India he had written Sister Devamata to concentrate her efforts on the Boston Centre and to suspend the Washington work, giving up the apartment there and storing the furniture. Reluctantly she obeyed, hoping to re-establish the Washington Centre soon. But Paramananda's new enterprises required her steady assistance in Boston. They opened a "Community Home," a second apartment on St. Botolph Street, a block away from the Centre, as a residence for Devamata and any other women who would offer their services either permanently or temporarily. Washington was relegated to a branch of the Boston Centre, with Sister Devamata going there to conduct one season of lectures and classes each year, until in 1917 she gave it up altogether.

Satya Prana (Eliza Kissam) finally renounced the world and moved into the new Community Home, donning the habit which Devamata, the former Episcopal nun, had designed for the incipient Order. By Paramananda's own description, Satya Prana was an "undemanding, faithful, unselfish" woman, who inspired the first line of his poem, "Ye who love and serve without thought of self." A rare reserved person among the swami's gregarious brood, though Satya Prana never stood out by personality or talents, she lived up to her name, which meant "true-hearted." She supported Paramananda through all the vicissitudes of his career, quietly filling in where she was needed. "She has at times taken care of me," Paramananda testified, "fed me and clothed me, often at sacrifice to herself." Many years later she would declare to the swami: "I have never changed my opinion about the holy orchid. When you first came to this country and I first saw you, I thought of you as an orchid. When you go to an orchid house, you walk through rooms of very beautiful orchids, and one or two more beautiful than the rest hang out as if they hung between heaven and earth. You cannot see what supports them there. That is the way I saw you, and I have never had reason to change."

It was a unique, lyrical tribute, for the taciturn Satya Prana usually broke her silence only with a few brusque words at a time. Once Paramananda, preferring that none of his workers be repressed, jestingly tried to draw her into speaking out. Her narrow lips pressed tightly together, two great tears welled up in her large, brown eyes. He never tried again.

His working force situated, Paramananda began to implement his ideas. He would build a house of worship, not Hindu nor Christian nor in any way denominational, but dedicated to the one Universal Spirit called by so many different names, where people of all religions could worship together in harmony. For this "Temple of the Universal Spirit," he purchased a large plot of land overlooking Boston's Fenway Park and began to sketch plans. The complex would include a spacious residence hall for a community of dedicated workers. Both buildings would open onto a common garden.

Moreover, because the written word could penetrate where

the spoken word could not, they would spread the message of Vedanta through publishing. They would issue a series of books compiled from the swami's lectures, which would be transcribed and edited by Sister Devamata. And they would launch a new magazine, to be called *Message of the East*. This would be published each month and would contain lectures by Vivekananda, Ramakrishnananda, and Paramananda, articles by Devamata, juxtapositions of quotations from Eastern and Western thinkers, prayers, poems, and reports of the Boston work and the Vedanta movement in America and India. Despite the warnings of well-wishers, Paramananda insisted that the magazine would not be defaced by paid advertisements or any commercial gambits. Maintaining that standard, the *Message of the East* was published continuously for fifty-one years.

The purpose of the *Message of the East* was to give Western readers exposure to genuine Indian philosophy, and thus counteract the rampant misunderstanding which had stigmatized all their efforts so far. Paramananda started the first issue (January, 1912) with the declaration:

> In the name of the Supreme Being of the Universe we send out this *Message of the East* with the hope and prayer that it may bring a clearer understanding between East and West and that its spirit may so touch our hearts as to awaken therein Divine harmony and peace. Uncharitableness, fanaticism and denunciation do not belong to the spiritual realm or, indeed, to true civilization; hence we should strive diligently to transcend them. God grant that . . . we shall always welcome the message of Truth with whole-heartedness, free from bias and prejudice, no matter whence that message comes. Truth is truth whether it comes from the East or the West. May we with the sword of wisdom therefore, cut down all the fictitious barriers that divide race from race, country from country, creed from creed, and find beneath them the underlying bond

of unity. Then we shall realize that we are members of one universal family, worshipping the same Supreme Being, and that, as the sages declared in the Rig Veda: "Truth is one, though men call it by various names."

The "uncharitableness, fanaticism and denunciation" which Paramananda referred to had only begun to mobilize. During 1912 and 1913, the Christian establishment, alarmed by the infiltration of Eastern religions into America, mounted a vigorous campaign against them, which effectively blocked Paramananda's most enthusiastic efforts.

According to G.G. Atkins, a contemporary historian of religions, "There was actually between 1890 and 1930, more radical and creative religious experimentation than, very likely, since the first three Christian centuries." Some of this experimentation, such as Christian Science, which spoke in terms of Christ and the Bible, and New Thought, which claimed to be the philosophical descendent of Ralph Waldo Emerson, was tolerated in varying degrees. But the Eastern spiritual movements which began to circulate in this country after 1900 were viewed as insidious competitors of Christianity. While Vivekananda could claim that Vedanta was a nonsectarian philosophy which taught the ideals common to all religions, Baba Bharati's Krishna cult, which he propagated in America from 1905 to 1909, was unadulterated Hinduism, complete with a Krishna Temple in Los Angeles. Murshid Hazrat Inayat Khan brought Sufism to the United States in 1910, followed two years later by Abdul Baha and the Baha'i movement. The Mazdaznan cult, a perhaps bogus derivative of Zoroastrianism, was founded in America in 1901 by Ottoman Zar-Adusht Hannish. By 1912, it claimed 14,000 followers in thirty cities of America and Europe.

That year, in the wake of the Sara Bull scandal, a rash of articles denouncing all Eastern sects (especially Vedanta and its swamis) appeared in American magazines. These articles inveighed against the "most revolting heathen idolatry" and "Eastern abominations" which were infecting Christian America. They contended: "Literally, yoga means the 'path' that leads to wisdom. Actually, it is proving the way that leads to domestic infelicity and insanity and death." As proof of that allegation, they listed several cases, including Mrs. Ole Bull, whom they maintained had been driven mad by the practice of Eastern rites. The author of the first of these articles, a Mrs. Mabel Potter Daggett, actually visited Swami Abhedananda's Vedanta ashram in Connecticut. At some length she describes the evening service there, with its serene setting, its tranquil meditation, and its lyrical quotations from the philosophy. Then she sums up the account with, "So poetically, so artistically, is paganism presented to persuade a Christian audience."

Hinduism in Europe and America, a book by E.A. Reed published in 1914, unabashedly charged that the swamis' motive in bringing Vedanta to the West was to make money and to cultivate the adoration and obeisance of white, Christian women.

Such tirades might be expected to find an enthusiastic echo in the Bible Belt, but even Boston, a reputed center of religious liberalism, was not free from these attacks. In May, 1913, Rustom Rustomjee, a Zoroastrian magazine editor from Bombay, was invited to address a meeting of Congregational ministers at Boston's Pilgrim Hall. He told the assembled clergymen, who were already uneasy about the influx of Eastern "sects":

> American women who become interested in the so-called Hindu religions that handsome young Swami fakirs bring to this country are in danger of the lunatic asylum. . . . There are three false religions—the Vedanta, Mazdaznaism, and the Yogi. . . . In New York a short time ago, I caused a place to be raided where one of these men was holding his "sacred rites." . . . There they drank wine from skulls in an orgy that shocked even the New York police. This religion is dangerous for American women in every way. They

become interested in it because it promises them eternal youth and beauty — without the aid of cosmetics. . . . I do not attack any one swami — they are all a bad lot.

The extent of the public confusion which made no distinction between one Eastern religion and another is revealed by the *Boston Herald*'s reporting of the above event. Although the article itself identifies this arch-critic of Hinduism as a Zoroastrian, the headline reads, "Hindu Exposes Swami Fakirs." Rustomjee was invited to repeat his denunciations several times in Boston, and created quite a stir, much to the ire of Katherine Sherwood, who could not resist paying him a personal visit to challenge his allegations.

It is thus no wonder that even Boston's liberal population should cast a suspicious eye upon Paramananda, that handsome young swami in their midst. Many people who might have been attracted to the philosophy would not risk the stigma of attending the services at the St. Botolph Street studio, and those who did come often hid their association from their friends. One student wrote to the swami begging him to pray for her, but not to send any letter in reply, lest her family should see it. Such stealth pained Paramananda, who years later recalled, "It is no easy thing to begin a new work, especially in a strange country. Out of many thousands you perhaps find one who has the courage and the conviction to stand up and acknowledge his belief. The majority are too afraid of public opinion."

As for his efforts to promote Vedanta, they were like planting flowers in a hailstorm. As the initial growth of the Centre levelled off, the plot of land on the Fenway remained vacant. The time was hardly ripe for the "Temple of the Universal Spirit." Rather than succumb to frustration, however, Paramananda regarded this adversity as an opportunity to practice persistence and faith. In a talk on "Secrets of the Meditative Life," which he gave in 1913, Paramananda declared:

Swami Vivekananda used to say, "Hundreds of times you may fail, but do not let that distress you. Get up again with fresh vigor." That kind of courage is necessary. This life is full of difficulties, and if we simply come to the conclusion that we are weak and miserable and can do nothing, that is the beginning of our downfall. The one who starts to doubt himself, who can save him? No one can make us believe in our own strength until we prove it for ourselves, and in order to prove it, we need wonderful devotion to our inner Ideal. What does such devotion mean? It means that day after day, night after night, morning after morning, evening after evening, we strive to make it our own through meditation. Sometimes we find satisfaction, sometimes we do not; yet we do not cease trying. We go on faithfully, without encouraging any doubt, without weakening our faith and fervor. Such one-pointedness in devotion is called *Ekagra*, and when we are well established in that, nothing can resist it.

Throughout this period of calumny, Paramananda refused to counterattack, clinging to his resolution never to entertain hostility toward anyone. "The strength of the Boston Centre has been harmony and tolerance," he reminded his workers. "To bring even a shadow of anything else would be to weaken it." Repeatedly, he quoted the words he had heard from Swami Vivekananda's own lips: "No opposition, no success." "No great success is ever accomplished without opposition," Paramananda told his followers. "We must hold fast to our Ideal in all circumstances, especially when there are occasions for failure and depression, misunderstanding and criticism. This is the way we prove our strength — our deep spiritual strength and our devotion to our Ideal."

Of course, many thinking people who were not swayed by hysterical polemics against swamis had serious reservations about what they understood to be the Vedanta philosophy. They recoiled from the Eastern ideals of renunciation, individual liberation, motiveless work, detachment, desirelessness, and the unreality of the phenomenal plane, believing that such values undermined the Protestant ideals of personal drive and service to mankind. As Horatio Dresser, a founder of New Thought and one of America's most liberal religious leaders, wrote:

> What effect does it [Vedanta] have upon conduct? It inspires peace, tranquility, passivity, contemplation of the Absolute; surely a noble result, and we cannot have too much of this spirit in our nervous Western world. But will this attitude solve the social problems which press so appealingly for solution? . . . If it be true that *aham brahmanasmi*, I am Brahman, then I am perfect, absolute, and why should I break my repose to succor suffering humanity, whose sufferings after all are unreal?

This threat of quietism offended America's activist spirit, which pours out to causes and movements the devotion which the East reserves for God. In those years just before World War I, Western man was intoxicated with the prospect that, with the aid of science and technology, he could soon conquer all the ills of the world. Indeed, America's liberal churches, from whom the swamis expected to get sympathy and support, found mystical Vedanta not so much blasphemous as irrelevant. It was, to use the worst of all possible slurs, "anti-progressive."

While ignoring the polemics, Paramananda addressed himself to these philosophical objections. Many of his lectures of the period are defensive, not in tone, but in choice of subject. Thus, the *Message of the East* summarized one discourse: "He corrected the prevailing false impression that Vedanta is a religion of quietism, by showing how the whole teaching of the Bhagavad Gita is based on the necessity for each man to fully accomplish his duty in the world before he can enter on the life of contemplation."

In another talk Paramananda delineated the four kinds of help which man can render his fellow beings:

We may give food, clothes or money to a needy man, but his need returns. Next we may offer secular education. . . . The third form of help is to save a man's life. This may seem the greatest, but death may seize him again at any moment. The fourth and highest help is to teach a man how to control and direct his thought properly, that he may gain understanding and wisdom, for this will save his soul. The first three forms of help are unquestionably very good; but the only permanent help is to give people the mastery over all their powers.

To underscore Vedanta's humanitarian commitment, almost every issue of the *Message* carried reports of the Ramakrishna Mission's charitable work in India.

Other lectures and articles were aimed at countering different accusations. In "The True Meaning of Yoga," the swami asserted, "This science is very old; there is nothing mysterious or horrible about it." Again, a *Message of the East* editorial explained, "The Indian doctrine of *Karma* is not fatalism as it is so often erroneously represented. On the contrary, it declares man to be the creator of his own destiny."

Primarily, Paramananda had to convince the Christian establishment that Vedanta did not seek to compete with any church, that it did not threaten their memberships, that Christians could be loyal affiliates of their own churches and still benefit from the teachings of Vedanta. As Sister Devamata put it, Vedanta sought to change the person himself rather than his religious affiliation. Referring to those who derived inspiration from the Vedanta services and then attended their own churches, Paramananda declared: "What do we say to such people? God bless you, because that is the way of the real spirit of religion." As he explained:

The purpose of this work is not to offer a substitute for existing faiths or to foster any spirit of rivalry towards them, but to lend a friendly helping hand to all who

earnestly seek after Truth. . . . Our object is not to ask
anyone to give up his or her own religion, but to aid those
who are striving along every path to realize the Presence
of God and to gain strength and inspiration to live bravely
in the face of many difficulties which confront them in this
battle of life. We do not call upon anyone to abandon his
faith, but to uphold tolerance, universal sympathy and
brotherhood, which have been often preached but not
always practiced. We are living in a time of growth, when
the religious ideal as well as all ideals must be expanded,
and Vedanta stands here to share with the West the wealth
of spiritual consciousness which India has accumulated
through the ages.

While much of his efforts were thus spent in refuting mis-
interpretations of Vedanta, Paramananda never entered into
direct debate against any accuser. "Our duty is to harmonize, to
sympathize, but never to antagonize," he wrote to Devamata.
"Sometimes it may take long to make people understand a great
ideal, but patience, perseverance and love conquer everything
in the end. . . . All are His children and everybody is dear to
Him." Paramananda was a man without enemies, even though
the target of mass enmity, because he simply refused to recognize any being as his foe.

In the following passage, written in 1914, he summarized the
inner stance he strove to maintain:

> To abide by one's Ideal necessitates undaunted courage,
> unfailing vigor, unwavering trust and selfless aspiration.
> In opposition we must be fearless, in failure we must be
> undepressed, in moments of darkness we must have faith,
> while love of our task must make us forget ourselves and
> all thought of gain or loss. These are the lofty virtues
> which adorn the life of every great messenger of Light. It is
> not that a message of Truth is always welcomed by everyone.
> It is not that noble efforts are at once crowned with success.

Nor is the path always smooth and clear. . . . In this battle
of life we must rise above self-seeking and learn to do our
part with no other motive than to accomplish with the greatest efficiency whatever we undertake. When we have something to give the world, we must be willing to give it for the
mere joy of giving, without stopping to see whether the world
recognizes our effort or not. Ours is to do what is laid
before us with bravery, perseverance and infinite patience.

As Devamata explained, Vedanta worked more as an influence than as an institution. In this the Centre's publishing campaign was its most effective endeavor. The *Message of the East*
was sent free to over one hundred of America's leading libraries,
at their request. By 1914, nine new books bearing Paramananda's
name had appeared, most of them on practical themes, such as
*Concentration and Meditation, Faith as a Constructive Force, Self-
Mastery,* and *The Creative Power of Silence.* All of these were
garnered from his lectures, as transcribed by Devamata. *The
Way of Peace and Blessedness* was put together by Devamata from
Paramananda's letters to her, with the addition of a few notes of
class talks. Helen Keller, upon reading a Braille copy of the book,
exclaimed, "Oh, this book is my creed!" During six weeks in
Italy in 1912, as a favor to his host and hostess, Paramananda
rendered a new translation of the Bhagavad Gita, the Bible of
Hinduism made famous in the West by Emerson and Thoreau.
One review called Paramananda's translation, "the Gita clarified."
Meanwhile, the Vedanta Centre was also publishing pamphlets
of lectures by Vivekananda, Ramakrishnananda, Paramananda,
and Devamata. Between 1912 and 1914, 10,000 books and pamphlets were issued.

While America was casting sidelong and usually harsh glances
at the swami, Europe was extending a beckoning hand. The
ardent young German devotee Theodore Springmann and others who had met Paramananda on his way to India appealed to

him to return and teach. Other voices were added to these. Madame Braggiotti, an American woman married to an Italian nobleman, heard the swami at the Boston Centre and invited him to Florence. Aline and TrauGott Pfaff, a Swiss couple trained in Christian Science, had been given a copy of the *Path of Devotion* while on a pilgrimage to India. Deeply inspired by the book, and assuming the author to be a classical figure of a bygone age, they wrote to the New York publisher of the second edition, asking for permission to translate it into French. Upon hearing that the Swami Paramananda was not only alive, but contemplating a trip to Europe, they wrote and persuaded him to stay at their chalet in Gryon-sur-Bex, Switzerland.

In 1912, Paramananda spent six months in Europe. In Germany he stayed with Theodore and Ruth Springmann and their children, conducting a daily meditation and study class in their home. As Herr Springmann described the impression Paramananda left:

> Great brain and extraordinary intellectual faculty, enormous energy which, if it were not checked, could break down everything that dares to oppose, and greater than all this, a never ceasing flow of love, that conquers the heart of all. I have never seen such an amount of love, which never changes if hatred and bitter feelings prevail all around. By his very presence, more so in silence than in speaking, he smoothed down all controversy amongst others, and brought all our little group so much closer together.

Even young Springmann's parents, who were so incensed at their son's hosting a "heathen priest" that they threatened to strip him of his patrimony, including the house in which he lived, were eventually pacified.

In Florence, "Monsieur and Madame" Braggiotti were anxious to start a branch Vedanta Centre. Paramananda stayed at their villa and gave a series of public talks there. He was so enchanted by the seven Braggiotti children that, in addition to his regular lectures and classes, he gave a weekly "Children's Service." Every evening the children would come to hug him goodnight, nestling against him as he held them in a loving bundle. "It looks as if we were going to have a Centre here," he wrote enthusiastically to Boston.

The month spent at the Pfaffs' chalet in Gryon, Switzerland was the most strenuous. "My time is quite full. In the morning there comes a group at ten and again in the afternoon at two or so. Then there is the regular class meeting at four-thirty and again in the evening a meditation class." He returned to Florence from Gryon, hoarse but happy because he felt he had reached a few souls. Madame Braggiotti, seeing how long it took his voice to recover, raged at those she called the "vampires" of Gryon. "He ought to have a body-guard," she stormed, "someone with a sword in hand to brandish it and say, 'Enough! You can go and wait till next day!' "

Among the regular attendants at these European meetings were some who did not understand English, but who came because they felt the blessing of just sitting in the swami's presence. As Theodore Springmann wrote to him, "O, I did not care as much for your words as for your being, your essence, your character, and I often sat there simply drinking the life water of your being and did not know what you said. It was as if I could finally satisfy a never-ceasing hunger."

Paramananda saw this as his true mission: not verbal expositions of philosophy, but direct transmission of spirit to spirit. "Lecturing is certainly the smallest part of the work," he wrote from Florence. "The main thing is to sow the seed. Those who are ready will feel the living quality just from the presence, without words."

It was a period of fluctuating possibilities for Paramananda's work. Herr Springmann was offering to help start a center in Berlin, while students in Geneva were anxious for their own center, not to speak of the Braggiottis' insistence on a Florence branch. In Boston, too, the work was at a crossroads. The hostile climate there had so thwarted the growth of Vedanta that Katherine Sherwood, and perhaps others, disgusted with the paralysis of the public work, suggested investing their energies instead in an ashrama, or retreat, where a small group of earnest aspirants could live and work with the swami. Devamata staunchly opposed this plan. She went ahead and procured a building permit and an architect for the Temple of the Universal Spirit. At that point, "an upheaval in labor conditions" brought the proposed construction to a standstill.

Faced with this plethora of alternatives, Paramananda, as usual, waited for "inner guidance." "I always feel sure that Divine Mother has some plan for Her work. God's power no mortal can resist. That is what I am conscious of all the time. The task may seem like cutting a road through solid rock, but everything is possible through His will and grace."

Paramananda returned to Boston in November, 1912. Just four months later, apparently at Devamata's urging, he abruptly sailed for Europe again. Perhaps she wanted to protect him from the Rustomjee furor, which was just breaking in Boston, or perhaps she was tantalized by the prospects of his greater success in Europe. Whatever the motive, his sudden, and seemingly forced, departure engendered resentment in Katherine Sherwood, who wrote to the swami that she missed him greatly. "Why is it that you cannot be at home here where you 'belong'? Just because someone else has other ideas—But I must not go into that."

Paramananda, travelling with the Springmanns in Italy and Switzerland, seemed equally unsettled about his absence. He admitted to being "quite homesick," and less than a month after his arrival in Europe, wrote, "Sometimes I have felt like returning to Boston at once and taking up the work there with concentrated energy. But the Lord will surely make His will known." A month later, he returned to Boston as suddenly as he had left, leaving his European friends surprised and disappointed.

Perhaps it was not so much Devamata's prompting as the friction between her and Katherine Sherwood which drove Paramananda from Boston. A congenital lover of peace, he cringed at having to work in a disruptive atmosphere. In 1913, these two powerful women were contending for hegemony of the Vedanta Centre and of the swami himself.

The rivalry between Sister Devamata and Miss Sherwood was probably inevitable. Devamata, the swami's first disciple, was like an adored only child who must adjust to the intrusion of new siblings. Miss Sherwood, too, while Devamata was in India and then Washington, had become used to her role as Paramananda's closest supporter, his indefatigable advisor and benefactor. Once Devamata took up permanent residence in Boston, the two women, so similar in background yet so opposite in temperament, were bound to clash. Katherine Sherwood, a born socialite, disliked the stringent personality of Sister Devamata, a born nun, while Sister Devamata doubtlessly disapproved of Miss Sherwood's liberality.

It was a losing contest for Miss Sherwood, for as her niece sardonically remarked, Sister Devamata "had the inside track." Whenever Paramananda was absent, Devamata had charge of the center, conducting all services and classes, and even giving private spiritual guidance to those who sought it. Her lectures were advertised in circulars and newspapers, just as the swami's were, and several of them were published as pamphlets. During the first half of 1912, after Paramananda's return from India, he and Devamata shared the platform. The swami conducted the Sunday afternoon service and Tuesday evening class; Devamata conducted the Sunday morning service and the Thursday afternoon and Saturday morning classes. Unmistakably, Sister Devamata was more than an assistant.

During that same period, Katherine Sherwood was trying to find her place in life and in the swami's work, feeling torn between the world and the life of consecration. At one point, she closed up her Milton house and moved into the Sisters' residence. She even put on the habit of the Order. Shortly afterwards, she took it off, for by nature she was more suited to ostrich-plumed hats than veils. Her intermittent yearning "to wear the dress and live the life that will draw me closer and closer to the Real" was not fulfilled. She felt herself increasingly superfluous to the swami's work as her duties were taken over by others. Eventually, just as she and Sister Satya Prana always sat in the back seat whenever the swami took them and Sister Devamata for a drive, so Miss Sherwood resigned herself to a back seat in his mission. She was always nearby, always ready to support and help between trips to Europe and other diversions, even conducting the public services in a pinch, but she stopped contesting the pre-eminence of Sister Devamata.

During Paramananda's two-month stay in Europe in 1913, a small group of his Swiss students formed a Vedanta Centre in Geneva. *The Path of Devotion* was translated and published in French, and the swami lectured in Paris. But even while the European work was blossoming, Paramananda felt that Boston was the place to concentrate his efforts. By the end of that year, the furor against Eastern sects had subsided, as all furors eventually do, and the Boston work was beginning to move forward.

Throughout this period, Paramananda's health was poor. After returning from Europe in 1913, he suffered a serious illness which drew grave concern from his friends there and in India. Even after he recovered, his fragile constitution never completely adjusted to the Boston climate. He suffered from the cold in winter and from choking hayfever the rest of the year. From India Swamis Brahmananda and Premananda were constantly importuning him not to work too hard, but just at that juncture the Centre was catapulted into a major advance which precluded all rest.

While the labor situation still held their construction plans for his "Temple of the Universal Spirit" in abeyance, Paramananda received a letter offering him a beautiful house on the most desirable corner of the Fenway. In addition, the owner agreed to take the land they held as part payment. "We had long coveted the property," Devamata remarks. "The house was already built and could be adapted perfectly to the Centre's requirements." It was not the dreamed-of Temple, but it could easily accommodate a chapel and the swami's living quarters on one end and a residence for the community and guests, with a separate entrance, on the other. As far as Paramananda was concerned, the Lord had made His will known. Sister Devamata, whose father apparently had not carried out his threat to disinherit her, or who had an independent trust, enthusiastically purchased the property in January, 1914. Shortly afterwards, the deed was transferred to the joint ownership of Swami Paramananda and Sister Devamata. In February, the remodeling began, including the conversion of the double living room into a chapel. The Dedication Service was set for May 21, 1914.

During this interval, almost as a precursor of things to come, two important speaking engagements opened up for the swami, both through his one unfailing technique: personal contact. Aboard a steamer returning from Europe, Paramananda had met a man whose brother was the president of the First Parish Club of Quincy, a city just south of Boston. This man spoke so enthusiastically of the swami to his brother that soon Paramananda received an invitation to address the Club, which was connected to Quincy's leading Unitarian Church. Similarly, the Women's Educational and Industrial Union, a bastion of conservative power in Boston, normally reserved its hall for staidly orthodox meetings. The president of the Union met the swami and was so impressed by him that, to everyone's surprise, she offered him the use of the hall for a series of lectures.

Although the swami had spoken frequently before such fringe organizations as the Theosophical Society and the Metaphysical

Club since his arrival in Boston, these new engagements were
the first breach in the wall of prejudice which surrounded the
city's establishment. After these, one opening led to another, so
that, although the wall never entirely came tumbling down,
Paramananda was able to pierce a door in it large enough to go
in and out.

It is significant that at the First Parish Club and later at other
churches, Paramananda's subject was India, not Vedanta. During
those early years, widespread calumny about India forced him to
serve not only as a religious teacher, but also as a cultural ambassador. He often addressed audiences for whom "swami" meant
a turbaned magician on the vaudeville circuit and India was a land
poised between heathen barbarism and Christian salvation.

It is difficult for us to realize the scandalous ignorance of the
Orient which prevailed in the West prior to the first World War.
Since the age of television, every twelve-year-old has become a
jaded traveller, as familiar with African bushmen and Japanese
geisha girls as with the local grocer. Before the age of television
and jet travel, however, knowledge of non-European peoples
came only indirectly, and from not altogether reliable or objective sources. The interested layman could read a book or attend
a lecture by white travellers who, not knowing the native
language, often derived distorted notions; by missionaries who
had a vested interest in focusing on the worst in non-Christian
cultures; and by scholars who were "experts" on a particular
country, although they had never been there and they derived
their knowledge more from ancient texts than current conditions.

Many of the resultant misimpressions about foreign countries were quaint; others were dangerous and destructive, for
they polarized humanity: Christian or heathen, white or colored,
civilized or barbaric. "The white man's burden" and "imperial
destiny" were watchwords of a cultural self-centeredness which
licensed the West to impose its religion and its civilization on the
rest of the world. Altruistic Western minds were indoctrinated

with books displaying illustrations of Hindu men burning their wives alive and Christian hymnals containing songs such as this one from "Songs for the Little Ones at Home":

> See the heathen mother stand
> Where the sacred current flows
> With her own maternal hand
> Mid the waves her babe she throws. . . .
>
> Send, oh send the Bible there,
> Let its precepts reach the heart;
> She may then her children spare —
> Act the tender mother's part.

As Vivekananda poignantly remarked, all the mud on the bottom of the Indian Ocean could not balance the filth that had been thrown at his motherland.

The most effective antidote for these noxious notions was to learn about other countries from their own people. The swamis who came to the United States were often the first "Hindoos" that their audiences had ever seen. Paramananda was amazed when people asked him whether Indian mothers really threw their babies to the crocodiles. As he told the Convention of Cosmopolitan Clubs in 1915:

> Superstition, prejudice and ignorance have held us apart long enough. Now the time has arrived when the two children of the same father, the East and the West, must join hands and look upon each other as members of the same family. . . . Unbiased and increased knowledge of Orient and Occident will dispel all mistrust and misapprehension from our minds and will help us realize the truth that "Above all nations is humanity" and the soul of the East and the West is one.

Paramananda's efforts as a pioneer of universalism were a major part of his mission. He worked not only as an apologist for

India, but also as one who deeply believed that "exclusiveness is always a great impoverisher . . . both in the individual and in the nation." He succinctly defined the twofold purpose of his work: "Although the vital aim of the work is to fulfill the spiritual need of those who seek it, it has also another definite purpose—to bring together East and West. . . . Our effort is to eliminate all feeling of harshness, discordance, doubt, and suspicion of one another; to break down all boundary lines." During the crucial period when a few groups of earnest Westerners were championing unity between East and West, Paramananda, by the testimony of his own being, convinced many Americans that the East was worth uniting with.

It is easy to look back upon an antiquated mode of thought, such as religious or cultural exclusivism, and to surmise that, like a man who has lived his threescore and ten, it simply exhausted its lifespan. Ingrained ideas, however, never die of old age; they are killed on the battlefield, and the hoarier their age, the more invincible they seem. Whenever history witnesses their vanquishing, we can be sure that certain pioneers' foresight and courage, not simply the calendar, mobilized the winning forces.

Surprisingly enough, nothing so overcame prejudice against the Vedanta Centre as its move from Boston's artists' quarter to its new home, the imposing and respectable house on the Fenway. On May 19, 1914, while the carpenters were still finishing the alterations, the swami and his community took up residence at #1 Queensberry Street. Sister Devamata describes the event:

> All the furnishings of the Shrine were packed into an old-fashioned horse-cab and we drove at solemn pace through silent pre-dawn streets to the new house. As we mounted the broad steps to the front door, the first rays of the rising sun shot out across the roofs and turrets of the dense city beyond, calling forth an answering gleam from the sacred vessels in our hands. We all stood for a moment in silent prayer; even the cabman bared his head. It was

the dawning of a new day for the Centre.

A solemn melodious Service followed; then the workers scattered to direct the coming and going of the moving vans. But the Swami remained almost continuously in the Shrine until evensong, spending the day in fasting, meditation, prayer and chanting. The little Sanctuary was vibrant with the power of his whole-hearted worship. . . .

A still more impressive Service came at the evening hour, when carpenters and painters were gone. At its close the Swami with the members of the household, carrying burning incense and lighted tapers, marched, a prayerful procession, through every room and hall and stairway, the Swami invoking the Divine blessing with such fervor that the whole house seemed filled with the spirit of devout consecration. From that moment it belonged to the Lord and became His dwellingplace.

That was Tuesday. They had sent out several hundred invitations for the Dedication Service, to take place on Thursday evening. For two days they scrambled, storing thousands of books from their stockroom, hanging curtains at forty windows, arranging furniture, and putting everything in order, as their high standard demanded. The Service itself was a heartening success. "The Chapel and entrance hall were packed from wall to wall," Devamata recalled, "there were people on the front stoop, down the steps and along the sidewalk." The guest speakers included the Professor of Sanskrit at Harvard, Professor Adams of Harvard, and Mrs. Adams, who frequently visited the Vedanta Centre as a "peace-break" amidst her busy days.

Six years before, in San Francisco, Swami Trigunatita and his Vedanta Society had constructed a spacious new headquarters which the sign at the entrance identified as the first "Hindu Temple" in America. Paramananda was insistent that his new chapel be dedicated not to Hinduism, but to all faiths. As he said in his dedication address:

Paramananda. Boston, c. 1910.

Sri Sarada Devi, the Holy Mother.

Bangalore, South India, 1908. Swami Brahmananda, center; Sister Devamata, right; Swami Ramakrishnananda, seated left; Swami Ambikananda, seated center front.

#1 Queensberry Street, Boston. Home of the Vedanta Centre, 1914-1925.

Entrance to #1 Queensberry Street, 1914. Left to right: Sister Satya Prana, Sister Devamata, Katherine Sherwood.

Chapel at #1 Queensberry Street.

Swami Paramananda. Los Angeles, c. 1916.

Sister Satya Prana

Sister Seva

Mary Lacy Staib (later Sister Shanta)

Sister Achala

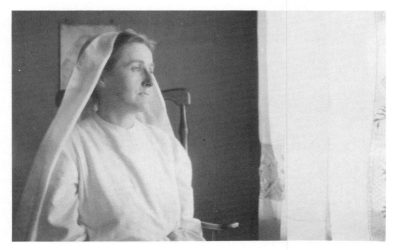

Sister Devamata, c. 1915.

Georgina Jones (later Sister Daya), aged seventeen.

Sister Daya. Boston, 1921.

In the name of the Supreme Being of the Universe, Whom
we invoke by different names, I welcome all friends and
guests to this home, dedicated to the all-loving Universal
Spirit. This altar stands here to represent a nonsectarian
conception of Deity and the ideal of love, of universal
sympathy and tolerance.

Whereas the San Francisco Hindu Temple, true to its name,
was an exotic affair of minarets, Moorish arches, and a towering
spired replica of the ancient Visvanath Temple of Benares, the
new Vedanta Centre had no trace of Oriental trappings. From
the outside, it was still the old Robert Treat Paine mansion, a
respected landmark on the Fenway. Even inside the chapel impersonal simplicity was the rule. The San Francisco Temple had
life-sized paintings of Sri Ramakrishna and Swami Vivekananda
on either side of its platform. The Boston Vedanta chapel had
no pictures at all; objects of personal devotion were reserved for
the private shrine room which adjoined the chapel. Carved on
the altar was the Sanskrit declaration: "Truth or God is one; men
call Him by various names." Above the altar was the chapel's
lone symbol: a great carved Sanskrit OM, or Logos, symbol of the
Absolute, against a thousand-petalled lotus representing realization. All in all, it was a setting in which even the most respectable Protestant could feel at home, and, quickly enough, many did.

Sister Devamata reports: "The tangible and convincing evidence of stability and permanence given by the imposing house
in the Fenway caused a rapid reversal of public opinion. The
Centre was no longer an alien; it became one of the accepted
religious organizations of Boston. Businessmen talked in their
offices openly and enthusiastically of their connection with it
and people came to it as they went to other churches. Prejudice
melted away."

Illustrative of the new-found recognition, many liberal Christian clergymen began to acknowledge Swami Paramananda as

their colleague, and some Unitarian ministers invited him to share their pulpits. Once they had opened up to accepting him as their peer, several realized that he was even more. A Lutheran minister from New York, declaring that he had derived great spiritual inspiration from Paramananda's writings, took up temporary residence near the Centre so that he could study with him. Another clergyman wrote to the swami:

> Frankly, you are the freest man I know in America. . . . Oh, yes, dear man, prophet from the Far East, you have the inborn technique and I laugh and bless you. But you're *sui-generis*. There's no one can invade your patents, only one in a generation of eels can wriggle through that chink in the walls about Eden. And you're the lucky eel and I watch and chortle. There's superb humor in the objection that I would not have a heathen like you appear at my church. If only they knew! Where do they dream they are? At the door of Heaven keeping out infidels? And the subtle Bengalee is occupying a front seat all the time. . . .

For Paramananda, winning over the Christian establishment was not a sudden victory, but a lifelong crusade. Devamata's metaphor, "Prejudice melted away," is apt. Like New England in spring where, long after the weather has warmed up, the remains of giant snowbanks continue to dot the landscape, even after the hostile climate in America had shifted, strongholds of orthodox resistance only gradually succumbed. Three years after the supposed melting away of prejudice, Sister Devamata, in introducing Swami Paramananda's latest booklet, "Universal Ideal of Religion," asserted: "It sets forth with force and clearness the broad inclusive attitude of Vedanta, and will surely do much to break down the sectarian prejudice and narrow-mindedness which many people mistake for religious fervor."

Indeed, the Catholic Church, which, around that time, came

to dominate Boston, never wavered in its stand that it was a mortal sin to enter even a Protestant house of worship, let alone a Hindu one. During the last three years of Paramananda's life, the city's Irish bureaucracy harassed him, insisting that the Vedanta Centre did not deserve tax exemption because it had no genuine religious standing. At the hearing on the matter, one city commissioner cross-examined Paramananda: "What do you worship? The sun? The moon? The stars?"

One day in June, a month after the dedication of the Queensberry Street house, Paramananda emerged from the shrine after the noon worship charged with the power and loftiness of the service. Stroking Devamata's head and laying his hands on her shoulders, he said to her:

"This is a wonderful place and you are very much blessed in being able to take care of it. Just lose yourself in that service. Everything will be all right. Nothing can touch you. Divine Mother will take care of you, and you know that there is one thing that will never change. What is that?"

"Your love," she replied.

"Yes," he affirmed, "that always flows over you. It is Her love, so it can never fail. Just to let Her love flow through my heart, that is my only mission in this world. If people want something more, I cannot help it. That is all I can do."

———◆———

On June 16, 1914, Paramananda left for Europe again. Although he felt most committed to the Boston work, his students in Geneva and Gryon were pulling on him. He agreed to stay in Europe for six weeks, but almost as soon as he arrived, he felt restless to return home. On August 1, World War I broke out.

Caught in a web of difficulties and adventures, Paramananda strove to extricate himself from the continent mobilizing for war. When he applied at the British embassy for a suddenly required passport, he was refused for lack of proper identification. He desperately searched his belongings for some acceptable evidence of his identity. All he could find was a copy of his latest book, *The Way of Peace and Blessedness*, in which his portrait appeared. Hopefully he handed it to the official, who perused it and remarked, "The Way of Peace and Blessedness. It does not *sound* seditious." The passport was issued.

Accompanied by his most devoted Swiss student, Mrs. Pearce, Paramananda made his way to Paris, where finally a fateful cancellation enabled him to procure the last remaining passage on a French steamer leaving for America. With barely a piece of silver to spare between them (his travellers checks were suddenly worthless) and no time to wire Boston, he boarded the ship amidst a panicky throng of refugees. A week later, late at night, he reached the house at #1 Queensberry Street.

> He ran up the front steps and through the hall, [Devamata recalled] looking at no one; but as he moved by us, we caught a murmur of the words, "Miracle— Divine Mother." He passed quickly through Library and Chapel to the threshold of the Shrine. There he laid himself prostrate and deep silence fell on everything. When he turned to greet us, there were tears of gratitude in his eyes and from the light on his face we could discern the unspoken prayer of his heart.

He never returned to Europe to teach. What happened to the proposed centers there? The Geneva group carried on on its own for several years, then disintegrated. The Florence branch was overruled by the Boston workers, who could not see the swami dividing his time and energy across an ocean. The Berlin center died with Theodore Springmann, who was killed in action fighting "The Great War."

9

The Tide Turns

WORLD WAR I shattered the self-confidence of Western civilization. The great god Science had turned into a death-dealing demon. Advanced technology, instead of succoring humanity, had maimed it. As lurid reports of the horror of The Great War reached America, a chastened people began to shake their heads at what they now called "the myth of progress." Peace was no longer an offering to be spurned.

For the cause of Vedanta, the tide had turned. Paramananda found himself being carried on a current that would grow in strength for the next fifteen years. America was finally willing to listen: to the East, to the claims of the spirit, to the quiet voice that assured them that meaning could be found — within.

The year 1914 marked a coming of age for Paramananda and his mission. The war reversed the climate of society; the new house on the Fenway confirmed the status of the Centre; and the swami, finally, turned thirty. The boyish idealist had become a mature man capable of dealing with American ways.

According to Carl Thomas Jackson, "The Boston Society rapidly developed into the most flourishing and most soundly based Vedanta organization of the early period. Much of this growth was owing to the leadership of Paramananda, in whom the Ramakrishna movement found a model monk to cope with the American environment."

The ingenuous young monk had had to learn to temper his spontaneity, grapple with negative realities, and meet American men and women on their own terms. "When I first came to this country," he once said with an amused smile, "I imagined that people expected me to talk philosophy, but I found out later that automobiles create a quicker point of contact. As soon as I learned to drive a motor car I had an unfailing topic of sympathetic conversation with everyone I met."

Eastern teachers in this country have always had to maneuver between the Scylla and Charybdis of becoming too Americanized on the one hand and remaining too rigidly Oriental on the other. Paramananda found his balance by dressing and acting like an American, while thinking and teaching like a Hindu mystic. He bought elegant (though used) cars which he washed, greased, and overhauled himself, wore fashionable suits (usually snatched up on sale), and played and talked tennis, cricket, and soccer as though he spent his days at the Harvard Athletic Club rather than at the Boston Vedanta chapel. But he would not compromise the philosophy to suit Western tastes. He taught the traditional Vedanta that Sri Ramakrishna and Swami Vivekananda* had. However gracefully Paramananda the man moved through the world, Paramananda the teacher did not disguise the aim of his philosophy: to transcend the world. His students quickly discovered that Paramananda, handsome, charming, debonair, was an enthralled lover of God.

Nor could popular demands cajole him into lowering the

*Wendell Thomas in his book, *Hinduism Invades America*, pejoratively classes Paramananda with Vivekananda as "conservative," because he refused to adjust Vedanta to Western values or methods of propagation: "Instead of sweeping history, science and western religion like Abhedananda to find illumination and expansion for his Hindu convictions, he [Paramananda] dwells forever on the cultivation of the 'inner,' or 'spiritual,' life by the methods taught in the *Gita*."

tenor of his teaching. For example, Paramananda's perennial youthfulness was a constant source of wonder. His face seemed immune to time. Once he related the following incident:

> Many times people have questioned me regarding what they call my secret for preserving youth. I remember one very pointed question asked me by a lady who saw me after an interval of a few years. She said, "You look at least ten or fifteen years younger." . . . Like a drowning person she caught hold of my hand. "Tell me your secret!" she exclaimed. "You can make a fortune if you will teach people how not to show the signs of age." I caused her great disappointment. . . . She thought I would give her a chant or mantram and say, "Hold your nose!" or, "Concentrate on your toe!" There are those who give such practices, but I was blessed with a glimpse of the Higher at the outset of my spiritual life, so I cannot confuse the spiritual with the material. I told her: "The only secret I can give is an open secret: Do not fill your mind with worries about yourself. Rather fill your mind with thoughts of constructive work, selfless service, and thus create a rhythm within yourself by trusting more and more in the Higher Power who always guides our destiny." This did not satisfy her.

To the increasing number of students who sought his guidance, Paramananda was friend as well as teacher. He took interest in their families and their avocations, visited them when they were ill or merely downcast, sent them notes whenever he went away. One student wrote to Sister Devamata in 1915: "I went to see Swami yesterday for spiritual help, & he took me to Child's for a cup of tea! Don't you love it? He saw how thoroughly worn out I was, & with that exquisite tact did not let me try to solve every transcendental problem at once then."

Where did Paramananda get money for travelling and for his personal expenses? Most of it was given to him by dedicated supporters such as Devamata, Satya Prana, and Katherine

Sherwood. In addition, he received honorariums from his outside speaking engagements and royalties from some editions of
his early books which, after he left the New York Vedanta Society,
were published by a commercial publisher. Money donated for
the Vedanta Centre was used exclusively for the Vedanta Centre,
but for the most part, close devotees preferred to give funds to
Paramananda personally, and from his pocket he met the expenses of the Centre. Those who would join the community
were free to keep their assets, or to donate or loan them to the
Centre as needed. Conversely, community members who had
no resources would be taken care of by the Centre. Consistent
with Paramananda's personal, rather than institutional, approach,
he himself bore the responsibility for the maintenance of the
Centre and its members, and his disciples trusted his intuition
and judgement in managing the funds.

———————————◆◆◆———————————

During the next few years, the Boston work grew steadily,
outside speaking engagements multiplied, and Paramananda
discovered a new field, the western United States. In the summer of 1915, barred from Europe by the War, the swami was
persuaded to travel to Yellowstone National Park and the San
Francisco Fair for a vacation. He wrote to a Minneapolis woman
who had stayed at the Centre that he would be passing through
that city. She promptly arranged two public lectures for him. So
went the holiday. He held informal meetings in Detroit and
Seattle and gave three public talks at San Francisco's Hindu
Temple and Pacific Vedanta Centre. On August 19, he arrived
in Los Angeles for what he thought would be a brief visit.

Swami Vivekananda and Swami Turiyananda had both
taught briefly in Los Angeles at the turn of the century, arousing
interest in Vedanta in that area which was to prove a hotbed for
sects and cults of every description. In 1903, shortly after arriving in San Francisco, Swami Trigunatita attempted to establish a

sister society in Los Angeles. In 1904, he sent to India for a swami to head this would-be center, and Belur dispatched Swami Sachchidananda. This young swami eventually had a traumatic falling-out with Swami Trigunatita. In 1910, after severing his connection with the Ramakrishna Mission, Sachchidananda wrote to Paramananda from the Vedanta Home in Los Angeles: "Consider me as being fully opposed and actively antagonistic to the Vedanta movement in America. With all my strength, I will devote myself to hinder and injure the Vedanta cause in America." After Sachchidananda's return to India, Trigunatita continued intermittently to work for a Vedanta Society in Los Angeles until a bomb set off in the Hindu Temple by a deranged ex-member ended his life in January, 1915.

Thus stranded, many Vedanta enthusiasts in the Los Angeles area extended an eager invitation to Paramananda while he was yet in San Francisco. He came, and found himself addressing audiences twice the size of those in Boston, and this although it was "off-season." He wrote to Boston:

> The lecture last night was a great success as far as the audience was concerned. I specially requested them not to take too large a hall. But the one they engaged proved altogether insufficient. They packed chairs from wall to wall without leaving any space between them. Many stood at the door and I do not know how many were turned away. It was a great surprise to all. . . . There must be some reason for my coming here. I hope Divine Mother will manifest some blessing through it all. I have felt very tired at times, but I am keeping on.

And a couple of weeks later:

> There is no doubt that the interest in the teaching is growing everywhere. They are very eager to keep me here permanently. People of San Francisco are also begging me to come back there. The Lord alone knows what He has in future for me to do. I know that I am more than anxious to

get back in my own little study and be in the atmosphere I
love most.

Prior to Swami Trigunatita's assassination, his San Francisco
assistant, Swami Prakashananda, and a group of dissident members had split off and formed their own organization, which they
called The Pacific Vedanta Center. After the death of their leader,
the San Francisco Vedanta Society appealed to Prakashananda
to return and conduct the services and lectures at the Hindu
Temple. He refused. There was talk of Swami Abhedananda,
who was in San Francisco at that time, taking over, but Trigunatita's
closest followers opposed this. When they met Swami Paramananda during his August visit, they were deeply impressed by
him and felt sure that he was the one to restore harmony to their
endeavor. They appealed to him to stay in San Francisco for a
few months as their new leader, but he wisely declined. Their
appeals followed him to Los Angeles and eventually to Boston,
until Swami Brahmananda at the Belur Math ordered Swami
Prakashananda to return to the original Society and merge the
two organizations.

Meanwhile, Sister Devamata wrote a letter to one of the San
Francisco leaders revealing Boston's opposition to Paramananda's
western involvements, a stance which would cause him considerable problems in the future:

> We can well understand that you must have had a
> strong desire to keep Swami Paramananda in San Francisco,
> but I fear that if you had succeeded, there would have
> been a terrible outcry in Boston, and a delegation would
> have started westward to bring him by force. People are
> too devoted to him here to let him be claimed elsewhere
> without a loud protest. . . .

After a few weeks in Los Angeles, Paramananda managed to
return to his beloved abode at #1 Queensberry Street. There he
could amply indulge the two hallmarks of his nature, sanctity

and playfulness. "If I should cease to be cheerful," he remarked one day, "my body would wither away, because it is so unnatural to me." He had retained his buoyant cheerfulness all through those first difficult years in America. When the woman who had been secretary of the New York Vedanta Society during Parama-nanda's ordeal there was sent a picture of him years later, she complained that it did not do him justice, for it was too severe. "I never remember him without a smile," she wrote.

During one visit to New York, he wrote to Devamata, "I arrived here safely without any difficulty and was greeted by my 'army' at the hotel." Devamata explained: "The 'army' consisted of one quite elderly lady who always bridled at any attack on the Swami. Sometimes she was his army, sometimes his navy, and they had frequent military drills with the stair railing as rampart of an imaginary fortress."

"Divine Mother wants us to be happy," Paramananda maintained. "When we allow unhappiness or depression to enter us, we act as though She were not sufficient for our joy. We are her children and we should be blissful."

In 1915, Paramananda took in an unlikely new resident at the Vedanta Centre. The janitor of the house had fallen ill and had to be hospitalized, leaving his motherless four-year-old daughter with no one to care for her. Paramananda and Devamata took the child, Helen Lortais, under their wings for two years. The swami played and romped with little Helen, calmed her with his imaginary "pills of quiet," and said her bedtime prayers with her with loving solicitude, while Devamata mothered and reared her. When Helen was later given to the custody of some distant relatives who curtailed her visits to Sister Devamata and eventually prohibited them altogether, Devamata suffered one of the most painful blows of her life.

Devamata as the surrogate mother effectively shatters the stereotype of Devamata as the austere nun. "I never had any children of my own," she wrote in the foreword to her book of children's poems, "but I have borrowed many and made them mine by right of love. The name I bear means 'Mother' and accords me the privilege of adopting all the children of the world — big and little, grown-up and new-born. To the little ones I now dedicate this book, giving to each one a hug and a kiss. . . ."

Like the Hindu goddesses pictured with many heads, Sister Devamata manifested an astonishing assortment of personae. To the public who frequented the Vedanta Centre, she was an affectionate, gracious, and witty hostess. Her files are full of letters from the swami's students in America and abroad, thanking her for her kindnesses, for her loving notes, and for her faithful remembrance of some long-distant devotee. To the monastic community which would be entrusted to her training, she was a stern, exacting prioress, relentless in her discipline, her unremitting sense of justice rarely superseded by mercy. To the swami, she was a loving disciple, for whom no task was too lowly, no challenge too great. He could jest with her and brood over her, grow anxious when she was ill and remonstrative whenever she lost sight of the higher ideals. Devamata had a scientific mind (she wrote her graduating thesis at Vassar on "The Rings around Saturn") and a fervently religious spirit. She wrote not only erudite articles for the *Message of the East*, but also children's rhymes, which she illustrated with her own drawings. She composed a volume of devotional poems, set many of them to music, and choreographed a dance to go with one of them. Just when we write her off as a bookish, cloister-bound nun, we read in one of her poems: "God is less in book or cloister/Than in the garden and th' open field." Indeed she claimed love of nature as second only to love of God among her sources of inspiration. Unfortunately, she alternated rather than integrated these various aspects of her personality.

In June, 1916, Swami Paramananda returned to Los Angeles

to lecture. He stayed in a hotel room from which he had to walk a mile to get anything to eat. Despite the general enthusiasm, specific offers of help were rare. He himself had to do all the clerical work, including stamping circulars and arranging every detail of the lecture halls, all amidst an unflagging stream of visitors. "People are really lively here," he wrote. "They are keeping me busy either over the phone or calling to see me. I shall soon have to make some rules and restrictions for my self-protection." In addition to the Los Angeles meetings, on Mondays he lectured in Pasadena, on Wednesdays in Long Beach, and on Fridays in Santa Barbara, all before freeways made travel fast and easy.

For the rest of his life, Paramananda would be caught in the irony of his own destiny. By temperament he disliked large crowds and furious activity, yet these were exactly what the success of his mission entailed. Neither a hermit nor a quietist, he liked people, but not throngs of them, activity, but not frantic hustle-bustle. Los Angeles, for all its easy success, was a perpetual invasion of his ethereal nature. When he had first arrived there, he had prayed to the Lord to make him less sensitive, so that he could withstand the frothy, restless atmosphere. Throughout his stay he alternated between gratitude for the burgeoning interest and sheer weariness at the hubbub. As a letter to Boston reveals:

> We had a curious experience last evening. We engaged Music Hall last Sunday and thought it would suffice for our audience, but the hall could not possibly accommodate the crowd. People began to be turned away so they opened Symphony Hall and we had to go back there. All this created confusion and delay. I felt very tired and was also a little disappointed that we could not hold our meeting in the smaller hall. These large audiences and excitements, instead of making me feel elated, seem to make me feel sad, and awaken a strong desire in my heart for a quiet and retired life.

Paramananda's ambivalence about his popularity in Los
Angeles stemmed from a deep distrust of worldly success, incul-
cated in him during his years in the Indian monastery. Amidst
hardship his inner life flourished, but could it withstand the
fame and fortune which were lavished upon successful preachers in America? As he had told a class at the Vedanta Centre:

> Sri Ramakrishna used to say that people who were carried
> away by too much outer activity, too great a desire for
> name, fame, success, it was very difficult for them to be-
> come spiritually engaged. . . . People who are over suc-
> cessful in life, who have great wealth, and much to do on
> the physical plane, are apt to be swept away by these
> things. They lose their equilibrium.

Moreover, Paramananda distrusted public adulation, which
he knew could evaporate into apathy or worse. Even in his brief
experience as a teacher he had suffered several abrupt, bitter
defections. For example, the Pfaffs, who had invited him to
Gryon and were so eager to translate *The Path of Devotion*, had
lavished accolades on him before and during his stay with them.
When he left, he sent them one of Swami Vivekananda's books.
Within a month they informed him that they could not accept certain of Vivekananda's philosophical assertions, and therefore they
were dropping Vedanta and returning to their original affiliation,
Christian Science, which was, after all, the only true philosophy.

In July, 1916, after several strenuous weeks of lectures,
Paramananda prepared to leave Los Angeles. He was tired of
the public work, skeptical that it was really reaching people's
souls and transforming their lives, which was his sole interest.
He longed for a few earnest disciples who would dedicate themselves entirely to his cause and for whom God-realization would
be more than a passing fancy in a plethora of pastimes. (So far
the community residence on the Fenway housed only Devamata,
Katherine Sherwood, Satya Prana, and a constantly changing

roll of guests.) His Los Angeles following, however, insisted not only that he stay, but that he establish a permanent center. Paramananda was torn between the alternatives, his "inner guidance" mute.

"My mind has been going through great perplexities about the Los Angeles work. To do or not to do is the most imminent question before me just now. The work here has come to a point where I must decide one way or the other. It may bring more workers to the general work...."

A few days later, he wrote to Boston again:

> My personal feeling all along has been to get away and take a rest; but there is some Power which holds me here. I naturally would like to come back and enjoy the privileges of an established home, but when I think of the earnestness of the people here and the start the work has received, I cannot consider seriously my personal pleasure. Ofttimes I am tired and feel a little lonely perhaps, but the joy of work makes up for it all.

"I am trying my best," he wrote the next day, "to break away from here and come back but—! I have been in such a whirl of activity that sometimes I have found it difficult to get something to eat. . . . My intention was to leave for San Francisco last Thursday. Then I thought I might get off to-night, but after much reflection I have decided to remain in Los Angeles and establish a Centre. Some Power has been holding me here. Every time I have tried to get away or write something definite about my plans some invisible Power has held my hand."

Even after they rented a house for the Centre's headquarters, Paramananda continued to vacillate. During 1917 and 1918, he spent as much time in Los Angeles as he did in Boston, impelled by the much larger California audiences. "It does not seem right to throw all this earnest interest away," he wrote, but he never felt completely at ease with the endeavor. "I do not see clearly what Mother wants to accomplish, but She must have some very good reasons for the work here." The Los Angeles Centre was always an exhausting enterprise. "I am tired," Paramananda wrote from there, "there's no doubt about that, and I weigh much less than last winter, but that is to be expected after all the struggle I have gone through lately."

Part of the cause of Paramananda's ambivalence must have been that Swami Abhedananda was also lecturing in Los Angeles at that time. After his separation from the New York Vedanta Society in 1910, he had taken up residence at his Connecticut ashram, from which he embarked upon occasional lecture tours. In 1915, just before Paramananda, Swami Abhedananda came to the Pacific coast. Although his main focus was San Francisco, where he eventually started a new Vedanta ashram, by late 1916 he had founded a Vedanta Society in Los Angeles.

It was a ticklish situation. In 1910, the authorities at the Belur Math had asked Swami Abhedananda to return to India. When he refused to do so, his name was dropped from the roll of Trustees. For the next eleven years, the remainder of his stay in America, he no longer represented the Ramakrishna Order. Thus, he could lecture independently in San Francisco, despite the existent Society there, and Paramananda could found a legitimate branch of the Ramakrishna Mission in Los Angeles without impinging on Abhedananda's prerogative. Still, it was awkward to see their lectures listed next to each other in the local newspapers, Swami Abhedananda's announcement invariably larger, with bolder print and sometimes a picture.

Indeed, their strained relationship from the New York debacle had been exacerbated after Paramananda's first visit to California the previous year. In January, Swami Abhedananda wrote to Paramananda from Los Angeles:

> I cannot believe my ears when my friends here and in
> Long Beach tell me that you played "dirty tricks" unbe-

coming to a Spiritual teacher, by telling *lies* against me and scandalizing my character behind my back. Is it possible that you would do such a mean thing as to spread gossips of spiteful and malicious women? If you are not broad enough to cooperate with me in the Vedanta movement, you should not go to my friends and students with your *lies* and *gossips*. And if you continue to do so my friends in different States as well as in Boston will take proper *legal* measures to stop you from defaming my character.

We do not know the basis of these allegations, or Paramananda's response to them, but they surely reveal a critical tension between the two swamis. It is little wonder that Paramananda felt uncomfortable in Los Angeles.

It was not long, however, before he saw the fulfillment of his premonition that a Los Angeles Centre might draw new workers for the cause. The first to offer herself was Mrs. May Gladwell. Born and reared as a Mormon, she began to seek other answers to the problem of existence. Somewhat psychic, she had a vision of a group of people dressed in foreign attire. At the center of the throng was a slight, bearded man, who beckoned to her. When she approached him, he said to her: "You belong to me." Then the scene vanished.

Finally Mrs. Gladwell hit upon a book by Swami Vivekananda, and was thrilled to find in it a philosophy she felt she could accept. She yearned to follow this teacher, and was plunged into disappointment when she discovered that he had passed out of the body years before.

Then, at the invitation of a friend, she went to hear Paramananda lecture in Los Angeles in 1916. When the swami stepped up to the lectern, she took one look at his youthful face and asked incredulously, "That *boy* is going to speak to us?" By the time the "boy" had finished speaking, she felt she had been vouchsafed a second chance to follow her ideal teacher. When she went to the Vedanta rooms for an interview with him, she spied a picture of the bearded man of her vision, Sri Ramakrishna.

A kind, warmhearted woman, adept in domestic skills, thoroughly giving of herself, May Gladwell's temper was nevertheless as fiery as her bright red hair. She was forty-two years old in 1917, when she followed Paramananda back to Boston. He named her "Seva," meaning "service," an ideal she was to embody for the rest of her life.

During Paramananda's cross-country trips, he sometimes stopped in New York to speak at St. Mark's-on-the-Bouwerie Episcopal Church, at the invitation of its liberal rector, Dr. William Norman Guthrie. Dr. Guthrie, who cherished his friendship with the swami, was delighted once to witness what he called "the hidden lightning-like supervirility in the gentle soul of Swami Paramananda."

Desirous of arranging a special tribute to the swami, Dr. Guthrie asked some local Hindus to engage Indian musicians to play native religious music as a prelude to the swami's next lecture. Of course, some Indians in America, then as now, were bitterly antireligious. In order to embarrass the swami, they arranged for the musicians to play and sing erotic songs. Paramananda, awaiting his cue in a private anteroom, was scandalized. Unaware, Dr. Guthrie came to fetch him. "What was my amazement when I beheld his countenance," the Rector recalled. "No Oriental God, created for the defense of a holy shrine, ever impressed anyone with such awe." Paramananda refused to take the podium and prepared to leave at once. Only Dr. Guthrie's assurance that the American audience was too ignorant to have understood the desecration, and his plea for the swami to summon his sense of humor, allayed Paramananda's flaming indignation. "He pulled himself together for a smile of pity, then of gracious humor, and all passed off to the utter discomfiture of the impious mischief-makers." Dr. Guthrie recorded what he knew to be a rare reaction, "lest perhaps the meek missionary of the Mother be misconceived."

These must have been difficult years for Sister Devamata. During Paramananda's prolonged absences, she was in charge of the Boston Centre, as well as the busy publications department. The greater his popularity, the greater the demand for his books. Although the swami was the nominal editor of the *Message of the East*, the work of transcribing and editing lectures for the monthly issues fell on Devamata, as did the bulk of the work load when he was away. Once the Los Angeles Centre was established, Paramananda could not leave its activities suspended for half the year. So, when he returned to Boston, he sent Devamata to take over the lectures and classes on the West Coast. This was undoubtedly a sacrifice for her. She had wanted so zealously to serve her teacher and now she found that serving him required almost constant separation from him.

Meanwhile, Sister Devamata was emerging as a teacher in her own right. Not only did she conduct all services during his absences, but also she was frequently invited for outside speaking engagements, and during her ever shorter visits to Washington, students flocked to her for private guidance. Indeed, some of the Boston students regarded Sister Devamata, rather than Swami Paramananda, as their "teacher." According to Cunard Nelson, one of the earliest Vedanta followers, who was a staunch admirer of Devamata, "When she lectured, students from local colleges sat on the edges of their seats, catching every word. She had much wisdom, had an answer for every question, and seemed to know everything."

As might be expected, Devamata attracted a following which differed from those who were drawn to Paramananda. Her commanding presence, intellectual precision, and sophisticated wit

appealed to people who did not respond to Paramananda's simplicity and ethereal spirituality. And, dangerously enough, she
knew it.

In 1917, the United States entered the European War. The
gory tales of mechanized death which Americans had been reading in their newspapers for three years they were now reading in
letters from their husbands and sons, or worse, in the dreaded
telegrams from the War Department. The horrors of trench
warfare, machine guns, poison gas, and armored tanks became
vivid experiences for 2,000,000 American soldiers in a war that
would leave over 10,000,000 men dead and twice that number
wounded or maimed. In only six months of fighting, 115,000
American troops were killed. The leaders of church and state
who had rallied their people to "make the world safe for democracy"
were discredited by a disillusioned and embittered populace,
making traditional deference for such institutions another casu-
alty of the war. American minds were pried open by the barrel
of the machine gun.

Amidst this national metamorphosis, Paramananda shifted
the emphasis of his message from universalism to "Spiritual
Awakening, the Crying Need of this Age." In offering people the
healing potential of the Spirit, he had to make a careful distinction between true spiritual living and the constricted realms of
dogma and hypocrisy which many thinking people equated with
religion. Paramananda told them that, while their grievances
were legitimate, the fault did not lie with religion but with its
application, or, rather, its lack of application:

> This is the great difficulty in the present day. Religion has
> become too superficial. A man belongs to a church or he
> subscribes to an organization; . . . whether he tries to live
> the life or not is of secondary importance to him. But, my
> friends, that is not the spirit of religion. The thing of pri-

mary importance should be to live the life. . . . At waking, the first picture in the mind should be of God, the first hour should be spent in communion with Him; thus man's consciousness would be so strengthened that he could go out into the world and remain firm in his spiritual life.

Paramananda believed that the antidote for all ills, whether they be personal problems or global conflicts, could be found by turning to the Divine within. It had worked for him, in the most trying circumstances, and he longed to pass on his secret: that there is a God, whom one could approach intimately and directly, without passing through the maze of dogma or the straits of exclusivism. As he told his audience at the Vedanta Centre:

> We must learn to open another eye, an eye that has not been developed in the majority of human beings—the eye of the Soul. And that eye can only be opened through the spiritual life. Religion does not call upon us to give up this life, but it asks us that in all our thoughts, words and actions we cultivate the sense of the nearness of God; for without Him we are lonely, without Him we are helpless, while with Him we have all things. It is this which the East gives to the world—a vivid sense of the presence of the Unseen. It holds out the hopeful promise that we can all prove for ourselves the reality of God and our oneness with Him.

While Paramananda taught no complex mental or physical exercises, the mystical approach he offered required a drastic shift of consciousness for his Western audiences, a complete reversal of orientation from outward to inward, from material assets to inner resources. Naturally enough, pragmatic Americans balked at any practice which smacked of passivity or, worse, unproductivity. Paramananda had repeatedly to prove to them that developing the inner self was the most practical step any person could take.

An amusing example of the difference between Eastern and Western approaches was related by the famous dancer, Ruth St. Denis, who invited Swami Paramananda to chant Sanskrit hymns for her dance school in California:

> The afternoon of his visit provided a disconcerting revelation of Western ignorance of the character and essence of the Orient.
>
> The girls, when they heard he was coming, were all aflutter. . . . He came very promptly, salaamed softly to us as he passed with that lovely, silent walk of the East Indian, and took his place on the pillow in an attitude of meditation. He closed his eyes and folded his hands. The girls were, of course, all eyes and ears, eagerly waiting to receive his slightest word. He began to breath rhythmically, and a peculiar aura of peace emanated from him. We waited and nothing happened. The girls looked at me, and earnestly looked back at the Swami; and as precious seconds turned into minutes I began to laugh inwardly, because I could read their minds. The active, pert member of the class was saying, "Well, why doesn't he begin" and furtively looked at her watch. . . . The Swami sat on and on, and just as their impatience was becoming more and more pronounced, an extraordinary tone came from his throat, the pronouncing of *Aum* (God) opened his prayer, and it was done with that extraordinary vibration which is like the striking of a great gong. . . . Of course the girls did not realize that he was teaching them their first lesson of the East — patience, reverence, and humility — but I do not think any of them ever forgot the effect of that afternoon.

That Vedanta offered a religious alternative different from that which had soured a whole generation of thinkers was attested to by John Spencer Clarke, a close friend of Emerson, Thoreau, and others of the Concord group. Brought up as an orthodox churchman, loyally subscribing to the imperative dogmas, including original sin and the literal accuracy of the Bible, Mr. Clarke's faith had been shattered by the scientific discoveries of the late nineteenth century, such as the geological proof of the true age of the earth and the theory of evolution. The Church has responded to this crisis, the triple onslaught of science, Biblical criticism, and comparative religions, by fearfully adhering to its dogmas more tenaciously than ever, labeling its estranged children as heretics. During the war, Mr. Clarke, by then a venerable octogenarian, decided to visit the leading churches of Boston to see what changes, if any, had been wrought.

"In the course of my peregrinations," he told a gathering at the Vedanta Centre, "I came upon your modest mission of the Vedanta; and I confess I was profoundly impressed by the vastness, the rationality, the inspiring character of the philosophic and religious thought here presented. The three great problems of philosophy: God, the Cosmic Universe, Man with his rational mind, were presented as a harmonious unity with infinite possibilities to the ever developing human soul." And to Sister Devamata personally, he confided that in the teaching of Vedanta alone had he found a God big enough for science.

As the Great War (Paramananda winced at the term, asserting that he saw nothing great about it) drew to a close, and ever afterwards, the swami spoke of the one portentous lesson to be learned from it: "That whenever one part of a body is struck, the other parts also feel and suffer; whenever one portion of humanity is afflicted—no matter who has caused the trouble or why—the rest of humanity is bound to suffer. . . . To my mind, it grows ever more and more vivid that we are fundamentally one." Had not the world seen that men and nations are inextricably linked, that one cannot better one's lot at the expense of another, that defeat for one means victory for none? For Paramananda war could produce only victims, not victors, for it outraged the sacred unity of mankind. It took twenty years for people to understand this point, and by that time the smug jubilation of Versailles had succumbed to the juggernaut of the Third Reich.

Two months after the armistice was signed, Paramananda was invited to speak at the First Unitarian Church of Ayer at a service being held especially for the returned soldiers. The minister was astonished to see how closely the congregation attended to the swami's every word, and how afterwards almost the entire crowd stayed to speak to the swami informally, holding him there until the time of the last train to Boston. "He lifted all to a new and higher plane of thought and feeling," the minister wrote. "That was the secret of the power of his discourse. 'The people heard him gladly.' My own great surprise was to find how many there are who in the depth of their hearts yearn for the larger vistas in religion and pure air of the region where such men as Swami Paramananda abide."

The West was ready for a new exploration, and Paramananda's years of ripening had made him a fit guide.

10

Queensberry Street

ONE FRIDAY EVENING in April, 1919, two Hindu students in Los Angeles invited Swami Paramananda to their apartment for dinner so that their friend Georgina Jones Walton could meet the swami. Georgina, a thirty-six-year-old Theosophist, had reached a doleful impasse in her life. As she described the fateful meeting:

> My spiritual need was very great and my heart was crying out, crying out for genuine guidance. . . . I looked forward to the meeting with an eagerness I myself could hardly understand. The few days of waiting seemed endless, but finally the appointed evening arrived. . . . I stood waiting in the small parlor — waiting and listening for the Swami's approach, while my hosts, along with another woman friend, were frying *luchees* [Indian puffed breads] in the tiny kitchen.
>
> At last I heard his footsteps, firm, light and rhythmic, on the steps outside. In another moment I had opened the door and he was in the room, his very presence like a light, conveying the strength and beauty and peace for which my whole being longed. There was just one moment of greeting, one moment to introduce myself and ask the question which somehow I felt I could not ask after the others came into the room. So, breathlessly and

217

without preamble, I said, "Swami, tell me, how does the supreme Vision come?" He looked at me with a certain tender compassion and replied, "It comes gradually, just like the sunrise."

Georgina Jones Walton, who would become Sister Daya, one of the foremost figures in Paramananda's life, was the youngest daughter of John Percival Jones, for thirty years United States Senator from Nevada. One of the barons of America's pioneer West, Jones had crossed the continent in a covered wagon during the Gold Rush of '49, had dabbled in early California politics, and had finally made his fortune in the Crown Point Mine of Nevada's Comstock Lode. He bought a ranch in southern California (now the site of Santa Monica, where his statue still stands) and built "Miramar," his mansion overlooking the sea. His second wife, Georgina Sullivan, was a highly cultured, liberal, cosmopolitan woman who, like many of the scions of America's best families, had been reared in France. She insisted on personally giving her children French lessons and training their tastes in literature, music, and art.

Georgina, who was born in 1882, was a happy, playful child until a protracted illness and subsequent operation almost took her life. During her long, painful convalescence, she was confined to a cot on Miramar's sweeping lawns, her playmates the birds and flowers of the garden, her playground the imagination.

She became, as she put it, the friend and protector of all helpless things. As she grew older, she spent her days tending elderly folks, wounded birds, stray cats. Three times after the turn of the century, her mother took her to Europe, trying out different mineral baths for Georgina's recurrent, agonizing kidney condition. One time in Rome, when the city was infested with rats, Georgina was sitting on a park bench. Suddenly a rat scurried from behind a hedge, and scampered directly toward her, under her skirt, and up her leg onto her lap. At that very moment, two professional rat hunters with guns dashed around the corner. "Have you seen any rats?" they demanded. Deftly placing her hand over the lump in her lap, she smiled sweetly and shook her head. The men ran along in the opposite direction. As soon as they were out of sight, Georgina lifted her hand, and the rat scampered down her leg and away.

Intellectual and literary, at the age of twenty Georgina moved to New York. There, while she worked at a Settlement House on the Lower East Side, she mingled with artists and musicians, such as Pablo Casals. She wrote poetry and later dramatized *The Light of Asia*, Sir Edwin Arnold's poem about the life of Buddha. Eventually her play was produced on the Broadway stage by Walter Hampden, the famous Shakespearean actor, but apparently Broadway was not ready for Buddha, for the play closed after only a few weeks.

Her naturally playful, humorous spirit continued to be routed by ill health. In 1904, she was hospitalized for a month. Probably during this bout, one kidney was removed. She took almost three years to recover. A decade later she was again suffering from an abscess, followed two years later by another operation. Her remaining kidney would never be healthy.

Although her parents were agnostics, Georgina was innately religious. Ardently drawn to metaphysics, in New York she joined the Theosophical Society. In 1911, she married Robert Walton, a lawyer and active Theosophist. They moved back to California in 1914, and later bought a house in Krotona, the national headquarters of Theosophy in the Hollywood Hills. Completely devoted, Georgina wrote articles and lectured on the philosophy, while Robert became one of the five Trustees of the Theosophical Society's American section.

Georgina's personal life suffered a mortal blow in 1912, when her longed-for pregnancy ended in miscarraige. Her jubilation at prospective motherhood, a role for which her whole being had been primed, plunged into heartbreak when the doctor informed her that her sutured body could never bear a child. Devastated, she wrote poems to her unborn baby:

> You left so soon—poor darling forced to go—
> You knew I loved you. You may even be,
> Unknown to me, within my lonely arms.
> My arms that ache for you and always will. . . .

Throughout it all, Georgina's disposition remained sweet, loving, gentle. To her husband, she was a Madonna; her friends considered her a saint, incapable of thinking or doing any wrong. Georgina herself, acutely aware of her own failings, protested that they did not know her. "There's evil in me. I am not all good," she cried in one poem, "But they would not believe."

Meanwhile, Robert Walton's delving into the occult aspects of Theosophy frightened and estranged Georgina. This conflict reached a fearful climax one day when Georgina, lying in bed recuperating from an illness, had a psychic vision of a terrifying creature. Their marriage unravelled when Robert joined the Navy during the Great War. Stationed in the South Pacific, he came home only one fortnight each year, always her good friend, but nothing more. By 1919, Georgina's state of mind was like a "parched desert" (as she herself described it). Then, like a spring shower, Swami Paramananda came into her life.

After that first meeting, Georgina attended the swami's lectures every night, and a few days later invited him to dine at her home with her and her friend, Elizabeth Jewitt (who later married the Prime Minister of Burma and became Lady Paw Tun). Just as Georgina felt an immediate kinship with the swami, so Paramananda seemed to experience an inner recognition of her as his disciple. That first evening at Georgina's house, Paramananda shared with them intimate memories of his experiences with his guru, Swami Vivekananda, and of his life with Swami Ramakrishnananda at the Madras Math. After he left, Elizabeth Jewitt remarked in wonderment that for them he had opened a door which he so obviously was accustomed to keeping shut.

Again, a few days later, Paramananda began giving Georgina instructions which he never imparted to casual students. She was sitting in front of a fireplace, holding her wet shoe to the flame in order to dry it.

"Fire is sacred," he said to her. "We do not dry our shoes in the household fire."

She was sitting on the floor, where she had been reading a book. Now she picked the book up from her lap and laid it down beside her foot. "Books are sacred," the swami admonished. "We do not place our feet upon them."

He explained that those who seek to cultivate a higher consciousness must at every turn take account of a living universe and their right relation to it. The elements were more than they appeared. They were the outer manifestation of an inner reality; and fire, of all the elements, was considered most holy, because it can purify everything without becoming itself impure.

"Why then," Georgina asked, "should one not dry one's shoes in it? One cannot pollute such an incorruptible expression of Deity."

"No," agreed Paramananda, "one cannot pollute it, but one can dull one's own sensibilities by a rude approach to great and sacred things. It is not that our actions can ever affect God but that we ourselves are affected by them. Without true reverence there can be no fineness of perception. The Divine Presence is so ethereal that man's whole nature must become ethereal in order to perceive it."

Looking at the swami, Georgina reflected that the man himself exemplified his teaching: "He was a living example of fineness and delicacy within and without. His very flesh seemed transparent, his atmosphere fragrant and his whole being perfectly balanced between the masculine and feminine principles."

Three weeks later, in early May, the swami returned to Boston. Georgina was faced with the excruciating choice of whether or not to follow him. From the train he wrote to her: "I am sending you these lines to assure you that my feelings & trust do not change so easily. *Eternal things never change.*" Although her marriage to Robert Walton was virtually over, Georgina felt bound by her commitment to Theosophy, despite her doubts and conflicts about its occult aspects. For weeks she struggled to weigh and compare the two philosophies, knowing deep within her that to join the swami's community meant a renunciation of more than Theosophy. It meant a renunciation of her life as Georgina Jones Walton. Irresistibly drawn to her new teacher, she wrote him a torrent of letters, laying bare her feelings and reservations. In her, Paramananda saw a reflection of his own simple, spontaneous nature. Addressing her as "Dear Child," he wrote, "I have truly missed you and I miss your childlike, enthusiastic and whole-hearted devotion. If it is Divine Mother's will, then I feel that you may become a great help in my work."

At the end of June, she boarded a train for Boston, calling her venture "a one-year trial period." By August, she informed her mother that she had decided to stay at the Vedanta Centre indefinitely:

> There are many reasons for this: The special training, spiritual and otherwise, I am getting here is rare and I feel I must avail myself of it to the utmost. I have chosen this life of spiritual aspiration, of religious service, and have chosen it with every particle of my being. I have struggled towards it and yearned for it for years. Now I have found the means and the way that so long I sought alone. I am entering into a new life, one in which I must, as Swami said today, make the most subtle spiritual conceptions living, burning realities in the heart—see God not as a principle to be conjectured about, but feel Him enter my heart as the great Guest. This, Mother, is a never ending task of great difficulty, but a task that rewards one with something worth every pain and every effort—worthy to be striven for with one's whole soul. . . .

I realize that you do not see this as I do—that you interpret it as selfish. If it were selfish, I could not stand for it as I do, I could not feel such depth of determination. It is not for my small self that I am seeking. . . . Many will not understand, will criticize and judge. I rely upon you to at least try to see it from my point of view. . . . Until I find Peace and permanence and Divine love within myself, I have nothing of real value for you or for my fellows. . . . I am not forgetting the world, only approaching it in my own way, and not permitting it to absorb my strength and scatter my forces for the present.

Being with Sister Devamata is a very special privilege, for she can teach me so much that will be invaluable in any future work I may have to do.

Her future work was laid out for her. She became Sister Daya, second only to Sister Devamata in Paramananda's work and closest in his heart.

———————◆◆———————

Meanwhile, Paramananda's public career was booming. In April, 1918, he had made a triumphant visit to Seattle, giving eleven public lectures and seven private classes in the span of fourteen days. The halls, even one which held three hundred and fifty people, were overflowing, and at one session a hundred people had to be turned away. They clamored for him to establish a Centre there, and invitations poured in from Tacoma, Spokane, and Portland. In 1919, he made his first visits to Louisville and Cincinnati, where the response was so overwhelming that branch Centres were established in both cities. "The work here has started very well, " he wrote from Louisville in March, "and I must confess that it has given me somewhat of a surprise. Yesterday I spoke twice and both afternoon and evening meetings were full. . . . When I ask people if it is wise to have two meetings a day, and if they would care to come so often to hear the same speaker, they tell me, 'You have no idea how hungry we are and how long we have been waiting for this.' First few days my body was very tired, but I am certain the Lord will give me the strength if He wants me to do His work."

The Lord must have given him the strength, for in 1920, Paramananda travelled 22,000 miles by train and motorcar, circling the continent twice. Los Angeles. Seattle. Tacoma. Louisville. Buffalo. Philadelphia. New York. Cincinnati four times. "I did not start out to travel twenty-two thousand miles," he explained simply. "Requests came from here and there and I responded to them." Sometimes he found himself addressing the most unlikely audiences, such as the Women's Suffrage Victory celebration in Los Angeles, or a crowd of nine hundred Masons in Buffalo. Many invitations had to be refused for sheer lack of time, for the man could not give more than two or three lectures in a single day.

"It is too much for any constitution, what I am doing day after day & week after week," he wrote from a rented flat in Los Angeles.

During one cross-country tour in 1920, he gave twenty lectures in nine days. "Only a few hours after leaving Boston," he wrote to his community, "I began to feel badly and at first tried to ignore it. I had violent nausea and the usual attack of hay fever in rather acute form. The train was an hour late [arriving in Cincinnati], but Mr. Johnson and Mr. Starick met me and took me to the hotel. Addressing the meeting that evening was the hardest thing I ever had to do. Without any voice and with every worst symptom you can imagine, I had to face this ordeal. The hall was full. . . . I do not see yet why they did not all walk out. . . . The days were very full and my body was far from well. I practically lived on malted milk as I could not retain any solid food at all. Many times I felt inclined to give up the trip, but something led me on. It is always very difficult for me to give up anything. . . . After four nights of discomfort, when I arrived in Seattle, Mrs. Weber met me and informed me that practically nothing was done, not even a place for my living was secured. . . . How happy I shall be to get back to my 'Bonnie Scotland.' "

"Bonnie Scotland" was the Boston Vedanta Centre, where the incipient community was steadily growing. Plagued by gnawing feelings of the superficiality of the public work, Paramananda longed to really kindle the Divine spark in even just a handful of souls. Public lecturing was a burden he shouldered partly because it was a requirement of his role, and partly because in every audience of five hundred he hoped to find one genuine aspirant who would recognize the pearl of great price and be ready to trade all the baubles of this world to procure it. The small community in Boston was Paramananda's dream, his laboratory where base metals could be transmuted into gold, his forge where sacred vessels could be shaped and offered to the Lord for His filling. He told his close disciples:

> Creating a community means transmitting something into the lives of people — a very different thing from delivering a few lectures, but that is the form this work has taken. I will never sacrifice my principle or inner vision to worldly wisdom. . . .
>
> What a wonderful thing it would be if all men and women, or even a very small group of men and women, could be so armed with Truth, with the feeling of love and beauty, that they would go forth into the world every day carrying their ideal as a living symbol; so that no matter what the world might do to them, even if it outraged them, they would always hold up their heads and glorify their ideal. Would it not minimize many of the cruel inharmonies in the world?

Freedom was to be the watchword of the endeavor. Paramananda envisioned a community held together not by external strictures, not by rules and disciplines, but by the inner promptings of each person's Higher Self. Jar lids and jammed umbrellas can be forced open; flowers cannot. What is material can be forced, but Paramananda wanted to deal with the essence within each of his disciples.

An ancient proverb declares: "In each person there dwells a King. Speak to the King, and the King will come forth." Paramananda was determined to address the King in each one, confident in the faith that, sooner or later, after all the imprisoning encrustations were penetrated, the King would come forth. Kings cannot be commanded. Speaking to the community, he said:

> I can make a lot of rules, but they are made for an inferior class of people. People who can have freedom and enjoy it and at the same time are self-governed, people who can maintain peace, give freedom to others, and have a proper understanding of freedom, they are the class of people we want to draw here and build up the work through that. . . .
>
> We have never had to make any rigid rules, and I am still hoping and praying we will not have to. It will be one of the greatest disappointments in my life if I have to make a lot of cut and dried rules.

Integral to such freedom was the principle, taught by Sri Ramakrishna, that for each individual person there is an individual path leading to Divine perfection. There can be no mass-produced roadmaps on the spiritual journey. Paramananda was intent on giving each soul the freedom to manifest its own uniqueness, work out its own destiny, face its own particular problems in its own particular way. He would not impose his brand of perfection on them.

Modern pedagogy confirms that a person develops through trial, failure, frustration, and trying again. The teacher who takes the pencil from his pupil's fumbling hand to write for him will end up with all correct answers, but a stunted student. Paramananda knew that freedom includes the freedom to make mistakes and to learn from them. On his pupils' winding path, he would be the loving guide, even the coolie to help carry their burdens, but he would not be the palanquin-bearer. He could not carry them up the mountain; they would have to walk on their own feet.

By 1921, the house at #1 Queensberry Street was well filled. In addition to Sisters Devamata, Satya Prana, Seva (May Gladwell), and Daya (pronounced Doy-a, meaning "compassion"), a thirty-year-old stenographer from Indiana had joined in 1918. Edna Massman was working for a prominent Boston attorney when she attended a service at the Vedanta Centre. The next day she phoned in her resignation and moved into the Centre. Efficient, practical, and determined, she was a prosaic woman, neither particularly mystical nor religious. Her devotion to the swami and his cause stretched her beyond her own limited dimensions. He named her Achala, meaning "unshakable," which must have referred more to potential than to fact for, as community living soon brought out, she was quick to cry — and not so quick to laugh.

Mrs. Glenn, Sister Devamata's eighty-year-old mother, also came to live at the Centre. (Paramananda encouraged his disciples to maintain good relations with their families. Through the years, the mothers of other sisters would take up residence at the Centre, whenever their need demanded.) When Mrs. Glenn fell and broke her hip, it gave ample opportunity for service to those who liked to serve, and to some who did not.

In 1917 Ramon Blanchart, a Spanish opera singer with the Metropolitan Opera Company, had joined the public work. Frequently he and his daughter, Salome, would sing for special occasions at the Centre. In 1920, Salome took up residence in the Sister's House, much to her father's satisfaction and everyone else's rue. She was unruly, disobedient, and lethargic, forever neglecting even the basic requirements, such as the care of her own room. When the swami admonished her, she defiantly answered him back. How to graciously remove Salome from the community became one of Paramananda's formidable problems. Knowing that spiritual communities tended to attract eccentrics, the swami emphasized "normalcy." "Let's not have any queer ones," he would say. Nevertheless, he had his share.

In 1919, Miss Camille Christians met the swami in Los Angeles, and zealously pledged herself to his work, following him back to Boston a year later. Camille was an overemotional nineteen-year-old with the ardent desire to become a saint and the unfortunate affectation of being one already. Paramananda would tell her again and again to speak and act naturally, for he disliked any pretension in the spiritual life, but Camille, soon named Amala ("pure"), never dropped her sanctimonious mannerisms. Whenever any of her seniors became upset, Amala would blithely approach with a Pollyanna smile and sweetly remind her of the virtue of evenmindedness. She was a trial for everyone.

Next to come was Galene Philadelpheus, a Greek social worker and teacher of the deaf. Intelligent, efficient, and universally competent, her career had accustomed her to supervising others, a habit not easily unlearned. She was talented and affable, and was considered a great asset to the community, except by those who found her vain and domineering. Galene was quickly given a position of authority, being chosen to speak from the platform when necessary. The public admired her gifts, and everyone expected her to become a sister, but after eight years, she returned to social work.

Mary Lacy Staib, who would become Sister Shanta ("peaceful"), was a devoted member of the Louisville group. She used to visit the Boston Centre for months at a time until, after her mother passed away in 1921, she moved in for good. Bred in the cultural aristocracy of the Old South, Mary Lacy was too homely to be the southern belle her mother had been. Instead, her interests tended to metaphysics. She was an avid reader and often attended New Thought lectures. Though one of the younger members of the community (she was thirty-one when she joined), Mary Lacy was mature, dependable, and practical, full of good sense and good humor. She went about her duties silently, selflessly. Paramananda used to laughingly call her his "Kentucky wonder." She never demanded attention or even recognition, but by the end of her life the community realized that their quiet sister had quietly developed into a saint.

Cincinnati contributed two additions: Mrs. Alice Affsprung (Vimala—"without stain"), a birdlike and dainty character who made frequent, extended visits to the Centre; and Hilda Johanigmann, a hefty German woman. While Alice flitted around, graciously receiving guests and acting as librarian, Hilda boomed and snapped, and kept everyone in stitches with her jokes and wisecracks. The swami delighted in the contrast between these two. Once he teasingly asked Hilda, "Why can't you be more like Alice?" "Why, I'd rather be dead than be like her," came the simple reply.

Two men also joined the Vedanta Centre community. Jack Miller was an ardent, young, Jewish man from Cincinnati who had been a New Thought student. His selflessness and devotion endeared him to everyone. The swami was particularly fond of him. A victim of tuberculosis, "Brother Jack" inspired the others with his cheerful endurance and tranquility. Lester Flint, who came from a suburb of Boston, had been a devoted student since Paramananda's first months in Boston. An enthusiastic young devotee, he brimmed with zeal and awe of the swami. One day during a period of housecleaning, when banana oil was being used liberally on the furniture, Lester opened the door to receive a visitor. The caller, stepping in, asked what that strange, sweet odor was. "Oh, that," replied the ingenuous Lester, "is the 'odor of sanctity,' emanating from the swami. You see, he is a very holy man."

St. John of the Cross, ardent ascetic that he was, claimed that the greatest spiritual discipline, greater than months on bread and water or nightly flagellations, was simply to live in a community. The household at #1 Queensberry Street would have amply borne him out. Paramananda, despite his love of harmony, knew that the inevitable friction among these disparate personalities he had collected would serve to rub off their sharp edges. After all, what could better teach tolerance, patience, and forbearance than to stand and dry dishes for a sister who washes them at snail-like pace and with aggravating thoroughness, or to have to daily rearrange one's bathroom accessories after the intrusion of three different sisters with other ideas?

"I like people who are outspoken," Paramananda once declared. Consequently his community abounded with them. One quiet Sunday evening after the public vesper service, a typical incident unfolded. Swami Paramananda, desiring a simple supper, asked Sister Devamata to have Amala (Camille) warm up a bowl of gruel for him. Fluttering at the privilege, the young novice set about her task. The ever-capable Galene happened by and made a constructive suggestion or two as to method. Then Sister Seva, the expert chef in the community, noted the scene and directed Amala just how to do it. Amala, of course, did not like to be "dictated to." When she finally presented the bowl of gruel to her teacher, it was quite late. Sensing the dissension that went into its preparation, the swami declined the dish. Amala burst into tears. Sister Devamata scolded Galene and Seva for interfering. Short-tempered Seva indignantly defended herself. And so it went, ad infinitum.

Paramananda founded his community on the principle that one can give most by being. He wanted to imbue his disciples with selflessness, magnanimity, joyousness, and infinite patience. So he provided the example of what to be, as well as the inspiration to strive to be it. Gathered before the fireplace in the evenings, he was not content simply to read them a play; he had to act out all the parts, even sing the songs when indicated. Similarly, he was not content to teach them the concept that this dual plane is *maya*, impermanent and illusory. He had to show them how to take life lightly, how to smile amidst hardships, how to remember the Eternal Reality even as the fleeting scenes of life whirl past. Life at the Vedanta Centre was a multilevelled circus, bombarding heart, mind, emotions, and spirit simultaneously. And Paramananda was the ringmaster, lion tamer, highwire walker, and clown in one. He guided them, chastised them, comforted them, cheered them, and rallied them to become twice as big as they thought they could be.

The community's life followed a simple pattern. Upon arising, each one was to meditate at her private altar in her own room. Then they gathered before the shrine for group worship, conducted by the swami or, in his absence, Sister Devamata. After breakfast they set about their duties: maintaining the large house, chapel, and surrounding garden; publishing and distributing the *Message of the East*, as well as the ever-expanding list of books which bore the swami's name; shopping and cooking for the community; and ministering to the shrine, which included dusting the altar, polishing the sacred vessels, arranging floral offerings, and preparing fruits and sweetmeats for the Lord. They met again for noon service, then dinner. In the afternoon, they might return to their tasks, or visit a sick member of the congregation, or take care of their personal washing and ironing, or practice the organ, or have a singing lesson, or take a drive with the swami in his Franklin Sedan. Vesper service came at sundown. After a light supper they would gather in the community hall and listen to the gramophone, or Paramananda would read to them or sing Bengali songs, losing himself in the strains of love and longing for God.

That was the warp on which their days were framed, but the

woof was entirely up to Paramananda's spontaneous spirit. In the middle of the day, with Sister Seva up to her elbows in canning eighty-four quarts of crabapple jelly and Sister Achala hurriedly typing final drafts for the next *Message* issue's deadline, the swami would announce a picnic at Revere Beach. In fifteen minutes they would all be piling into his seven-passenger Studebaker or the Franklin with Sister Daya at the wheel, and off they would go to swim or collect shells or run races in the sand.

Or Sister Devamata would be solemnly upbraiding the kitchen workers for their lack of tidiness when suddenly they would receive word that the entire community was summoned to the library. Murmuring among themselves as to what could be so important, they would enter the library and find themselves face-to face with their venerable teacher staring at them through huge goggles, outfitted in a jacket on backwards, stuffed with a pillow for a stomach, and coatsleeves for trousers, all rigged up with the aid of the serious Sister Satya Prana.

Or, again, two of the sisters might be arguing over the disposition of their duties when suddenly they would feel someone sweep past behind them. They would turn in time to see the swami costumed à la Petrucchio, with plumed hat and cape, cracking his whip, and pirouetting down the hall.

At Queensberry Street, Paramananda was free to be entirely himself. The self which emerged was alternately the playful child and the pleading mother-heart.

As the child, he was spontaneous, utterly unself-conscious. He would surprise his community with the most ludicrous costumes, delighting some and shocking others. One time he was Hamlet, in long cloak and turndown collar, wandering about the house with a melancholy and philosophic mien. Another time he appeared on the landing as a European prince, bedecked with jewels. Still again he would scurry about as a French chef, in tall hat and apron, waving a fan and exclaiming, "It's very warm in the kitchen! It's very warm in the kitchen!" Sometimes, entirely unfettered by sex distinctions, he would dress up as a Hindu lady, drawing his sari shyly over his head. He exploded all sanctimonious images of solemn saintliness, and his community, sometimes in spite of themselves, would roar with laughter.

"It is hard to stay gloomy long near him," wrote Georgina Walton four months after moving into the Centre. "He begs us all to be happy. He says that the Vision of Blessedness does not come to a depressed heart."

He would tell them: "Be cheerful, be serene, be bright! To be grouchy and go around with a grouchy face is pure selfishness. It simply makes those who love us most unhappy. I know that whenever I have shown sadness, it has given those near me much pain. I do not mean that we should be fickle or frivolous, but that we should carry a light within us that shines through."

He would entertain the community with nonsensical stories, reeling them off the top of his head. Invariably they would have a lofty moral, but the genre was definitely not allegory, but fairy tale.

He loved bargains. Coming home from a big sale with his booty under his arm, he would ceremoniously unwrap the package while all gathered around. Then the game of guessing its cost would begin. When the guesses soared far above what he had paid for it, he would beam with triumph like a small boy.

"More childlike we are," he would say, "more we have access to the Divine." And again:

> Let us learn the art of being like little children. We are so grown-up, we have such a sense of independence and self-importance, that we cling to our burdens. When we gain a trusting spirit and give them up in complete surrender and simplicity of heart, our burdens drop from us of themselves. . . .
>
> The thing is to be humble and loving, real little children. If we are grown-up, we can get nowhere. . . . Do not be too wise, too calculating. Do not feel that you understand the great, divine mysteries; just accept what comes with

grateful heart. That is the way I have done. Put aside all
cares and all unworthy feelings and think of yourselves as
in Divine Mother's arms, helpless — like little children.

By contemporary standards, the swami and his community
were unsophisticated. They would play at being the "Army of
Truth," with Paramananda as their Captain. In nightly drills they
would march behind their banner, emblazoned on one side with
their motto, "Humility, obedience, love, tolerance, peace," and
on the other side with *Jai Ma Anandamoyee!* (Victory to the
All-Blissful Mother). Paramananda took these drills in earnest.
One night he saw someone giggle, and he told them all, "You
should not laugh. You should treat this as part of your spiritual
exercises. In the monastery, when I used to practice these things,
I did them with prayer, and I used to feel a real spiritual glow.
Whatever you do, put your soul into it. That is the way spiritual
growth comes."

Paramananda made a careful distinction between being childlike and being childish. His behavior was neither immaturity nor
adult clowning, but a faithful adherence to Christ's teaching:
"Unless ye become like little children, ye shall not enter the
kingdom of heaven." In context, Paramananda fits somewhere
between St. Philip Neri, the learned sixteenth century churchman,
who, leading a distinguished group of cardinals up a flight of
stairs in the Vatican, would suddenly fall on all fours and begin
to crawl up the steps, and St. Therese of Lisieux, the "Little
Flower," who, with her "little way of spiritual childhood," has
become the most popular saint of this century. Indeed, Paramananda's teaching reveals an extraordinary similarity to Therese's,
as if, in this complex and sophisticated age, the simple way of
the child is being endorsed as the high road to heaven.

Yet, if he was the child, he was also the mother-heart of the
community. Each night before bedtime, they would all stand at
the bottom of the stairs, and Paramananda would pour out his

heart, his vision, his ideals. He had lofty aims for his spiritual children, and he longed to see them realized. Given the intrinsically autocratic nature of such a community, Paramananda's approach was remarkable. He could have commanded, domineered, exacted obedience, but he never did. Instead, he earnestly appealed to their higher nature. He pleaded with them. His guru, Swami Vivekananda, had asked him to beg food, not to satisfy his needs, but to prove his humility. Now the leader himself, Paramananda begged, not because he needed to, but because he was humble enough to do so. And those disciples who could not muster up gentleness, selflessness, forgiveness for any other reason, found themselves practicing these virtues out of love for him, because he begged them to:

> We must stand together, work together, pray together, do everything together. Remember always that if one of you hurts the other, even in the least, you are inflicting a wound on me. I do not expect you to be perfect. You may be impatient sometimes, but if one of you speaks a harsh word to another, it hurts me more than I can put into words. Even if one of you does not seem to be exalted spiritually, always remember that there is some reason for her to be here. . . .
>
> Do not have so much wrangling. Learn to endure; forget all pettiness. When a superior corrects you, or even an inferior, take it humbly, even though you are not in the wrong. Let no harsh note enter into your heart. Be peaceful, calm, serene. Please, don't have any wrangling. . . .
>
> I hope I will see real sisterly feeling between all of you. Gentleness, love, forgiveness, tolerance, endurance, surrender—these are the things which make the work strong. Real service and devotion to the guru is when you feel towards all that they are the guru. That means truly serving the Ideal. . . .
>
> Don't have a divided house. Be generous, loving,

forgiving. I don't like dissension. It pains me. When you feel others are not living up to the standard, don't criticize or condemn. . . . It takes a long time to get over short-comings, so be patient. I want to see nobility. Don't be petty. . . . How can anyone dare to be unkind?

The principle Paramananda used was simple: Love can empower one to accomplish what even inclination and determination cannot make possible. Vivekananda had pointed out that a young mother may be afraid even of dogs, but if a ferocious tiger suddenly appears in the path of her baby, she will dash to the very mouth of the tiger to protect her child. Thus, where will and courage fail, love succeeds. Paramananda believed in this miraculous power of love, and he let it work to lift his disciples to a level where their best intentions could never reach.

When, a year and a half after coming to Queensberry Street, Georgina Jones Walton was given the veil, becoming Sister Daya, bold headlines in the *Los Angeles Examiner* proclaimed: "L.A. SOCIETY WOMAN TAKES VEIL OF INDIAN CULT; SISTER DAYA MUST WORK AS SERVANT." Certainly no society woman was ever more eager to give herself to common domestic duties than the new Sister Daya. She bought a notebook and began to copy into it recipes for grapefruit marmalade and squash croquettes. Alas, life at "Miramar" had not prepared the Senator's daughter for a single practical skill. The first time the swami assigned her to cook, she burnt the rice to a crisp, and he relieved her of all further culinary duties. She turned her recipe book into a daily record of spiritual lessons, and found her post in the kitchen at the dishpan, where during the next thirty-five years she earned the title, "Champion Dishwasher."

Nor was it easy for Daya to conform to the meticulous standard of neatness upheld at the Vedanta Centre. By nature she was disorderly and disorganized, given more to poetic reveries than to cleaning her room or mending her cothes. Even as simple a chore as dusting posed challenges for her. Shortly after Daya's arrival at the Centre, Sister Devamata, at a loss for any other practical task to give her, assigned her to dust the library. Dustcloth in hand, the zealous novice began to dust the books with all the dedication she could muster. After a while, the title of one book caught her eye. Insatiable reader that she was, she momentarily set down the dustcloth and began reading. In a few minutes she was engrossed in the book. At that point, Sister Devamata walked in, took in the situation at a glance, and asked tersely, "Are you serving the Lord or serving yourself?"

To be sure, despite their similar interests and talents, nature could not have concocted two more disparate personalities than the tiptoeing Devamata and the skipping Daya. Even physically they were a caricature in contrasts, the senior sister's diminutive frame barely reaching five feet, and Daya towering over everyone at five feet ten. Those who knew Daya describe her in a single epithet: big. She was tall in stature, broad in mind, vast in heart. She could not easily be squeezed into the starched habit.

Sister Devamata, on the other hand, had in fact designed the habit, and, in her role of novice mistress, her most austere persona presided. After all, the new members of the community were no casual Vedanta students who needed merely some encouragement or camaraderie. They had joined the community because they aspired for the highest spiritual attainments, and Sister Devamata, scrupulously conscientious, meant to boost them toward it. Thus she imposed on them the austerity basic to her own spiritual life, which she regarded as a battle, requiring Spartan endurance and uncompromising renunciation. As one of her poems described it:

> Storm-beaten, whipped by frost and wind;
> Wounded and bleeding yet undefeated;
> Attacked on every side yet unafraid;
> Thus does the soul battle for its freedom.

Devamata herself had never flinched from discipline or trial. "Out of pain comes power," she once wrote. "The mightiest achievements are those that spring from a wounded life. Pain is a promise of God's bounty. He bestows his richest gifts there where suffering has made way for their coming."

Accordingly, she supervised her aspiring charges with a rigorous discipline, sparing neither herself nor them. "She was a disciplinarian," Daya recalled. "Though possessed of a tiny body, her will was adamant and was set on creating a perfect spiritual community."

> The Sister [wrote Daya years later, describing Devamata] was small and very active and seemed to be every place in the house at once. She taught the students that a heavy step, a high-pitched voice, were evidence of *rajas* or feverish restlessness, in other words, of ego. They must learn to speak quietly, move quietly, and quietly shut the door. They were to demand nothing, and with joyousness perform even the lowliest task. Furthermore always students must watch for ego in their every thought, word, and act, as the zealous cat watches for the mouse. To be late for a public Service was for the Senior Sister a major offense. More than once, slightly delayed, I tried to creep unheard down the long flight of stairs which led to the chapel, but always a board would squeak, and I would arrive at the chapel door only to face a devastating glance of disapproval.

The paradox of the Vedanta Centre community was that, although founded by the freedom-loving Paramananda, it was molded by the strict Sister Devamata. While he stood before them and beckoned, she stood behind them and pushed. Daya later chose two quotations from the New Testament to epitomize the training techniques of the swami and the senior sister. For Paramananda it was: "Come unto me all ye who labor and are heavy laden, and I will give you rest." For Devamata: "Whosoever will come after me, let him deny himself and take up his cross and follow me."

Ironically, Paramananda's insistence on freedom included giving Devamata the freedom to express her authoritarian nature. To be sure, he pleaded with her, as with the others, reminding her that, "Some aspirants must express their devotion through austerity; they are unbending and critical of others in the spiritual life. There is another type which employs only mildness, gentleness and humility in every task. Great souls belong to the second type." But he never interfered with her. Perhaps, too, he realized that Devamata's strictness balanced his own leniency. A structure must have walls as well as windows. Certainly the senior sister's firm hand took an independent and potentially self-indulgent group of women and forged them into a solid, disciplined sisterhood. Even the most recalcitrant ones were ultimately, if not immediately, grateful for her training.

In the throes of her struggle to adjust to community life, Daya knew that her adversary was not the senior sister but her own ego. Her pioneer father's taming of the Wild West was nothing compared to the taming of this errant lower nature which shrouded her higher Divine Self. Her pride, her vanities, her subtle desire to stand first in the swami's esteem—all had to be faced, admitted, and ultimately transcended. She laughed at those who called the religious life an "escape," a "hiding place." Living at the Vedanta Centre, one could escape from nothing. Every flaw, every attachment stood nakedly revealed, and there was no cranny in which to hide. Paramananda taught:

> It is ego that is the great bar to spiritual progress. If you want ego then you can't have God. If you seek God, then you must be crowned with humility.
>
> Ego is at the base of it all. Envies, hatreds, and all the things which torment us come from ego. It is like that story of the bird flying with the fish in his beak. He was pursued and tormented by the other birds till he dropped the fish.

Then he was left in peace. Ego is a fishy, smelly thing! It is
born out of ignorance.

Daya found that the ego is not easily dropped. The candid
record of her struggles revealed in her notebooks provides the
most penetrating picture of Paramananda as a teacher and of the
tribulations of a disciple. She strained every fiber of body and
mind to succeed in her spiritual endeavor, trying hard to become
orderly and practical, to perform her duties carefully and intel-
ligently. When the swami ignored her accomplishments and instead lavished attention and favors on the most wayward members of the community, Daya was plunged into disappointment
and indignation. The more she craved recognition, the more the
swami withheld it from her. Even the world, she protested, weighs
merits against demerits and hands out its rewards or denials
accordingly. Sometimes her inner rebellion would drive her to
the swami and she would pour out her complaints of injustice
and favoritism. Paramananda would listen in silence and then
remark, "I expect something better from you than this." Her
clouded mind failed to grasp the meaning of the assurance which
he often gave her: "Don't you realize that it is only those whom I
feel are close to my spirit—whose understanding I trust—whom
I dare to neglect?"

"When we dream of the coming of the Teacher," she wrote,
"we picture ourselves as being content just to give ourselves
completely with no thought of return. But when he is with us,
the subtle ego seeks to have its share of delight and instills the
poison of self into our very adoration. So sweet, so precious is
recognition from the Teacher that we long for it and work for it
with personal desire. . . . Others, perhaps, receive what we crave
and the sharp pang of disappointment or jealousy startles us. We
find that the initial impulse of selfless devotion is degenerating
into a mean struggle for favors, a comparing of benefits received.
We wound each other in a rivalry to serve, forgetting that the sub-

lime service of the Master is in being rather than in doing, in great-heartedness and love and humility rather than in any outer act."

One morning the swami reprimanded Daya for something she had seen another do with impunity day after day, right before the swami's eyes. A little later, she went to him and bitterly vented her grievance. "I realize," he replied "that the person you mention does offend in this way constantly. The reason I do not correct her is because the fault is so ingrained that it would do little good to mention it. It may take lifetimes for her to over-come it. In your case, however, that is not true. This particular fault is not native to you, therefore you can very easily get rid of it. These few words from me may be all that is needful to inspire you to do so."

Gradually it began to dawn on her that Paramananda was practicing a kind of spiritual socialism: From each according to his ability, to each according to his need. The question was not whether one deserved appreciation, but whether one needed it, to overcome self-doubt, to encourage a faltering faith in oneself. To those, on the other hand, who already had a strong self-image, a high opinion of themselves, such appreciation might serve only to fatten the ego, a lethal dose for a spiritual aspirant. The swami's exacting task was to intuit the need of each particu-lar soul and to administer it, undaunted by the weeping and whining of the disciples themselves.

One day Daya was standing, waiting for instructions, by the door of the swami's study. Paramananda and Devamata were talking together, not apparently in confidence, about a certain teacher from India. Daya listened with interest and eventually asked, "Who was he, Swami?" Paramananda gave her a quick glance and replied shortly, "Never be curious!" It was only a minor reprimand, a cursory lesson in manners, but it struck Daya at her most sensitive point, her pride in her own breeding and background. Was she not the Senator's daughter? Had she not learned etiquette and deportment in the cultural centers of

Europe? She fled to her room in tears and wept until her eyes were swollen.

Paramananda, for all his compassion and tenderness, never pandered to petty moods or the wails of a wounded ego. He sent for Daya and spoke to her gently, telling her to wash her face and pull herself together. At that inopportune moment, dinner was announced.

"I can't go down to the table!" Daya protested, painfully conscious of her red, swollen eyes. Had her pride not already been wounded enough for one day? She would go without dinner, she offered.

Paramananda smiled at the vainglory of those who hoped to attain humility without ever going through humiliation. "Oh, yes, you must come," he insisted.

She bristled, but she went. Years later she was to express her "gratitude beyond measure that with all his gentleness, the Swami never yielded to the importunities and demands of the lesser self."

It seemed to Daya that, despite the swami's unremitting efforts to bring her to a state of balance, she was forever either floating on the winds of exuberance or weeping her heart out in self-pity before her own little altar. Finally, one day after a particularly trenchant episode, she was jolted out of her self-centeredness:

> It was a look on his face—a look of deep hurt—a stricken, wounded look — which finally roused me from my self-absorption and proved a turning point in my new life. For me, it was all the more poignant because the Swami so seldom revealed the pain that these gloomy conditions must have caused him. Instead he would carry on with a brightness which it seemed must dissolve all clouds, however heavy. His household had come to take this attitude for granted. Therefore I felt as though I had struck down a blissful child, and I vowed then and there that, God willing, it should not happen again.

One is reminded of St. Teresa of Avila who, after twenty

years of vacillation in the spiritual life, was moved by an image of Christ sorely wounded. Her distress at his suffering catapulted Teresa out of her cycle of self-indulgence and self-recrimination, and set her firmly on the road to sainthood. In both cases, the pain of one whom they loved and idealized shattered their preoccupation with their own struggles and strivings, and thus accomplished what their most fervent resolutions had failed to do.

This was a cardinal principle for Paramananda: that the best way to transcend the self is not by grappling with the self, or working on the self, or conquering the self, but by forgetting the self, in love and service of a greater ideal.

Just as the "fishy, smelly ego" was the cause of all ills, so forgetting the self was the solution for all ills. One stormy evening, for example, Sister Seva, troubled with some grievance, voiced her complaint to the swami while he gazed meditatively out of the window, which was all jewelled by the rain. When she had finished, his only reply was, "See how beautiful the raindrops look as they run down the screen!" "Have you ever noticed," he would say, "that when the barrier of self is removed from someone who has been struggling, suffering, and is full of discontent, that he becomes a different person altogether? The whole picture changes."

He applied this principle in helping the Dobles, a couple who began attending the services at the Vedanta Centre about this time. Impressed by the philosophy, they drew ever closer, until they were spending almost every evening at the Centre, listening to music or to the swami's readings. Mr. Doble, however, was steeped in depression, caused by a severe financial crisis he was undergoing. While he attended to every sublime word about the real and the unreal, nothing could rouse him from his despondency and sense of despair.

Then one day Paramananda approached him and challenged him to a kite-flying contest. Mr. Doble, proper Bostonian businessman that he was, stammered and coughed while the swami explained to him that each of them would have to construct his own kite, and that it must be beautiful as well as flyable. Too much taken aback to refuse, Mr. Doble found himself supplied with paper, string, long slender pieces of wood, and artistic materials. The contest was on.

The swami sequestered himself in his study, and sitting cross-legged on the rug, with all the concentration for which yogis are famous, applied himself to constructing the most finely wrought kite imaginable. He whittled the sticks down almost to the breaking point, balanced the parts with exquisite precision, and tied the threadlike string with such delicacy that Sister Satya Prana, an expert in needlework, could only click her tongue in admiration.

Meanwhile, an incredulous Mrs. Doble reported to the sisters that her husband was avidly absorbed in making his own kite. During his leisure hours, instead of brooding over his ledgers, she would find him engrossed in measuring sticks, cutting out paper, and painting intricate designs.

On the appointed day, a cavalcade of cars drove to Revere Beach for the great event. The ostensible object was to bring down the other man's kite, but the rivalry was forgotten as the two men, clad in knickers and caps, ran along the shore maneuvering their creations amidst the billowy clouds. Spirits soared as high as the kites, and the tournament was extended day after day for a week or more, with each contestant growing more and more eager as new kites were devised and took to the skies. No one seems to remember who eventually won, but watching Mr. Doble frolic on the beach, laughing and calling to the others, Paramananda undoubtedly felt that they both had.

Once a year, in June, the swami gave his annual dinner, inviting his students from throughout the country. He loved to entertain and cooked the meal himself, directing the cutting of the vegetables and the decoration of the rooms with such calmness and poise that observers marvelled that seventy-five or more guests were really going to descend on the place in just a few hours. After the dinner and speeches, when the last guest had departed, the swami and household sat down to their own meal, for Paramananda was always too busy serving to ever touch his own plate. Then they attacked the task of cleaning up. "While we washed dishes and straightened up the rooms," Daya recalled one year, "Swami wandered from group to group begging to be allowed to help, but we wouldn't let him. He went to bed once and reappeared again, still not satisfied to be idle when we were working. . . ."

"Love, serve, and forget yourself." Paramananda repeated it like a *mantram*.

He told the community:

> Here is the true secret of happiness: Forget yourself and think of others. I don't know that I have ever expressed it this way before, but I feel it is the true way. In my life, my moments of greatest happiness have been when I have forgotten myself completely in serving others. When you feel dull and heavy and depressed, it is because you are thinking of yourself. . . .
>
> My greatest consolation and inspiration have been when I have found something to give, even when I have been in the depth of misery, whether physical or otherwise. When somebody comes in distress and I am instrumental in just doing something for them, that all goes away. I am electrified; that is the secret. I wish I could pound into everybody's mind, heart, and brain this idea. This would be a veritable heaven here.

During Daya's first few months in the community, her kidney condition flared up again. Some days she was so riddled with pain that it was all she could do to perform her allotted tasks and drag herself upstairs to her room. At night she could barely sleep, or even rest.

One morning she sat in Paramananda's study with him, feeling utterly weary and discouraged. The swami, sensing something wrong, asked, "My child, you look very bad this morning.
Are you feeling ill?"

"Yes, Swami," she replied. "I've had a very bad night and I'm
in pain."

Paramananda beckoned, and she went to him, kneeling beside his chair. Then he closed his eyes as if in prayer, and laid his
hand lightly on her shoulder. After a moment, he dismissed her,
and she rose to leave. The pain was gone. She went to perform
her regular duties, bracing herself for its renewed onslaught, but
it never returned.

Although Paramananda never claimed to heal, Daya maintained that her agonizing, lifelong malady had been cured by
him, or rather, by the Divine grace invoked by his love and
prayers. Other sisters testified to similar experiences. Years later,
Sister Achala, who suffered from a chronic lung condition, was
diagnosed as having tuberculosis. When she informed Paramananda, he grew very grave and told her to ask the doctors to take
another X ray. The second X ray came out perfectly clear.

As for Paramananda, he claimed to be only the instrument
through which the Divine power, albeit imperfectly, operated.
As a teacher and a leader he claimed no infallibility. One night,
as they were all gathered in the hallway before bedtime, he said
to them:

> I do not ask you to follow me. If you do so, you do so of
> your own free will. In the path I may stumble, I am not
> certain always of my own way. But if I find high and
> beautiful things, I am glad to share them with you all. I
> want you, each one, to feel perfectly free to leave me if you
> find something greater and better. . . . If I should ever
> fail—I might fail, I am human, I have weaknesses—I beg
> of you to hold to the great main ideals we follow. They are
> true.

He gave them all freedom, but he held them with his love. As their own self-confidence and fortitude fluctuated, his faith in them, in their Divine potential, never wavered. "O! You are all going to be wonderful," he would tell them. "I am very optimistic. I shall never let go of you till you are."

He loved even the most disagreeable of them with a tenderness conceivable only in the light of the divinity he discerned within them, which he alone discerned within them. "You are all dear to me," he told them. "You are a great comfort to me. I want you to know there is nothing I would not do for any of you. I love you all, with every fiber of my being." As he expressed it in one of his poems:

> Ye are like my limbs.
> My love for each and every one of ye
> Is like unto breathing, perpetual and natural.
> If ye are hurt, I am hurt;
> If ye be sad, my heart is sad;
> When ye rejoice, my soul delights;
> When ye are well, I flourish;
> When ye are united, I am strong.
> In your joy, I am joyous.
> In your grief, I grieve.
> Come ye then all in harmony.
> Be one in love
> One in hope
> And one in cheer;
> One in trial
> And one in work,
> And lend me your share
> For the fulfillment of my task.
> Amen, amen, amen.

Paramananda used many methods in teaching and training his disciples, but it was by his love that he transformed them.

11

Sister Devamata

ON FEBRUARY 13, 1921, Swami Paramananda was scheduled to lecture before a large New Thought meeting in Covington, Kentucky. The regular hall being unavailable because of renovations, the New Thought congregation applied for the use of St. John's Episcopal Church. Rev. Francis Bliss, St. John's young minister, readily consented. He had heard Paramananda lecture in Cincinnati, and was deeply impressed with him as a genuine man of God.

The night before the lecture the church vestrymen sent a representative to Rev. Bliss's home to inform him that Swami Paramananda would not be allowed to speak at St. John's. "I was astounded," Rev. Bliss declared: "I had heard the swami deliver a lecture at the Gibson Hotel, and found him to be a remarkably spiritually minded man. He seemed to me to be Christian-like in the broadest and best sense of that term."

The vestrymen were adamant. Rev. Bliss resigned in indignation. The next day, unaware of the cancellation of the lecture, hundreds of people gathered in front of St. John's Church. The doors were locked. Local newspapers blazoned the clash in front-page headlines, with photographs of Rev. Bliss and Swami Paramananda.

It was just the kind of notoriety that Paramananda abhorred. The season before, he had written to Daya, "I am feeling more and more strong revulsion towards the public life." Between 1915 and 1921 he had travelled more than 150,000 miles by train and motor. On February 11, 1921, he had embarked on a tour of the branch centers in Cincinnati, Louisville, and Los Angeles, planning to stop also in St. Louis, Kansas City, and Washington state. A week later he wrote from Louisville:

> I do not know why, but lately I have been feeling very lifeless, and very little enthusiasm is left in me for the public work. Everything was successful in Cincinnati, but I could not get up any enthusiasm in me. My body is very weary and mind, too, so I am going back to Boston.
> I have a strong feeling that I am not essential in anybody's life, and if anyone finds that they cannot live without my help, they will find their way to me.

He was particularly troubled, as he had always been, about the Los Angeles work. The most devoted of the California students had followed him back to Boston, leaving behind a large group whose interest waxed and waned with disconcerting fickleness. During the swami's absence, certain students were designated to take turns reading transcripts of his Boston lectures at their weekly services and classes. Late in 1920, he wrote to them: "Not a word from any of you, but I hope that all of you have not lost your enthusiasm and interest at once. It is better to take turns, as you do about the reading."

Early in February, he sent Sister Daya to take charge of the Los Angeles work. Two weeks later his long vacillation ended. He wired Daya to close the center, sell the furnishings, and return to Boston. "I am in no mood for competition with anyone," he wrote. "I like to leave the whole field to those who are keen for it." Ironically, only five months later, Swami Abhedananda left the United States for good.

Shortly after his return to Boston, Paramananda was hospitalized for minor surgery, the removal of a cyst. His friends urged him to have the operation, and, in his childlike way, Paramananda went along with them. Major complications ensued. For ten days he suffered high fever and excruciating pain. When the doctors performed a second operation without ether, Paramananda exclaimed that he was near the end of his endurance. A week later, thin and weak, he was released from the hospital, but it was a month before he could get out of bed, and two months before he could resume his public duties.

When a devoted Cincinnati student expressed his distress that the swami should have had to undergo such needless agony, Paramananda wrote to him: "If we shrink from a little pain or suffering, how will we be able to understand the suffering of other hearts? I am grateful to the Divine Mother for every experience that She puts me through. . . . Now I can sympathize more truly with those who are in pain."

His convalescence, combined with his chosen retrenchment from lecture touring, gave the swami six uninterrupted months at his beloved Centre. In January, he had told the Boston members, "There is one thing I must impress upon your minds, that all these travelings and all these other connections of different Centres do not in any way lessen my interest here. On the contrary, it increases it. I feel more interested, more strongly in love with this work."

Paramananda considered the Vedanta Centre a shrine, a place consecrated to the Lord where the living Presence of the Divine actually dwelt. He tried to imbue his disciples with a "sense of sanctity," a sensitivity to that immanent Presence in everything that surrounded them. He pleaded with them:

> Feel the living Presence in this house. It is alive with power. I never go into the shrine without feeling that living Presence. It is not merely superstition. It is a sacred, holy place.

We are living in the heart of the shrine. We should care
for our rooms as though they were a shrine. If your rooms
were untidy and I should come in, how would you feel?
One far greater than I may come night or day. So we must
be ready. . . . In the monastery, everything was done for
the Divine Guest.

Paramananda himself lived in perpetual readiness for the
Divine Guest, even to the extent of carefully combing his hair
before going to bed at night. There were to be no unwashed,
matted-haired ascetics in that house. Every person and every
thing was to be kept immaculate and well cared for, for the sake
of that One to whom all belonged.

One day the swami discovered that a chaise longue in a
small study had been forced back against the wall so roughly
and so frequently that it had caused a long gash in the wallpaper
and plaster. This distressed him, for he actually felt that even
inanimate objects were permeated with the omnipresent Divine
consciousness, and must be treated with sensitivity. "People
should show care and delicacy," he told the community that
night. "They treat the Centre as if it were a thing of block and
stone instead of something living. As long as they feel this way,
they will make no progress." And he added that when things
were injured in the Centre, it was just as if someone had struck
at him.

Again and again he charged them to develop fineness of
feeling. "One must *feel* in the world of religion," he would say.
"Spirituality is a matter of feeling." It was not enough for them to
mouth the Vedantic assertion that God permeates all existence.
They must live and act as if God were right there, in the tools
they used, in the food they prepared and ate, in every object
which served them. Then there would be no mechanical observance of ritual; every act would be the natural expression of that
finely tuned consciousness. As Daya recorded, "He wanted us to
become so aware of the Divine Presence, even in the dust be-

neath our feet, that our consciousness gradually would become suffused with it and our very footfalls would grow gentle."

While the swami encouraged sanctity, he discouraged sanctimoniousness, to which spiritual communities could easily fall prey. His approach was not meant to be moralistic, just spiritually practical. Thus, the ethereal atmosphere which he wished to cultivate at the Centre naturally precluded boisterousness, vulgarity, and worldly habits such as cigarette smoking. But when he noticed that Galene had developed a "holier-than-thou" attitude toward people who smoked, he immediately acted to break it up. He announced that he wanted to try smoking, and he asked Galene to please go to the store for him and buy him a pack of cigarettes. Scandalized, she nevertheless obeyed. As she watched her revered and holy teacher puffing on his first Camel, her prejudice quickly went up in smoke.

Paramananda was equally deft in squelching other spiritual vanities on which an aspirant's ego can subtly feed. When members of the community came to him to relate some experience which they felt indicated spiritual advancement, such as seeing a light or hearing "Om" during meditation, the swami showed not the slightest sign of being impressed. Once, during Sister Daya's early days at the Centre, she lingered in meditation alone after shrine service. Suddenly the supper bell rang. Jumping to her feet, she hurried toward the door, but, confused by the interruption, she stumbled over the corner of an outside altar and fell full length upon the floor. The sound instantly brought the swami, full of deep concern. As he helped her up, she explained that she had fallen because she had been too absorbed in deep meditation for a quick adjustment to this physical plane. At that, the swami replied curtly that meditation should give one greater mastery over one's mind and body, not less.

Paramananda was not about to have a community of dazed visionaries and glassy-eyed ecstatics. He wanted alertness and intelligence from his disciples. Once, when one of the sisters made an excuse for some negligence on the grounds that she had renounced the world, he smilingly replied, "No one asked you to renounce your brains."

In a field reputed for its complex mysteries and intricate practices, Paramananda championed simplicity. His inspiration, Sri Ramakrishna, had stripped three millennia of Hindu scriptures and rituals down to their bare essentials, love of God and renunciation of self. Faithful to that example, Paramananda proposed to present the exalted teachings of Vedanta in a clear, practical way, so simple that people could live by them, but not so easy that they could exploit them for self-aggrandizement. He offered nothing to titillate the ego through feats of physical or intellectual gymnastics. As he told the congregation at the Vedanta Centre:

> Of course, there are people who love to use foreign terms, and also there are those who love to hear them, especially when they do not understand their meaning; but this is not going to satisfy me in the least. I want to give you something that will be of value; therefore, I am going to present the Yoga teaching in a simple, direct way, leaving aside all elements that might seem occult or mystifying. . . . After all, the profoundest Truth comes in utmost simplicity. The greatest men speak a language that a child can understand, while the poorer type of mentality uses words, words, words—expressions which have no sense and only add to our lack of understanding.

Paramananda preferred to impart what he had to offer without "words, words, words." Sometimes he would call Daya to his study and, after dictating a short article, would ask her to stay on while he worked. She would sit quietly watching him at his task, or would busy herself with some writing of her own. Not a sound would pass between them, but when the time came for her to leave, Paramananda would look up with a smile and say, "What a happy visit we have had!" And Daya would feel that she had received something tangible and deep, for which words could have been only the surface foam.

When Daya first arrived at the Centre, fresh from Theosophy with its esoteric intricacies and occult mysteries, she went to Paramananda and asked, "What method do you want me to follow in meditation?" She expected him to instruct her in an elaborate system of yoga, visualizing *yantras*, repeating *mantras*, and delving into secret rites known only to the adept. Instead Paramananda answered: "Just lay yourself at the feet of the Divine Mother." She was taken aback and disappointed at this simple instruction, but twenty-seven years later she testified, "That little sentence spoken so long ago has drawn my mind, my heart, my whole being deeper and deeper into a one-pointed effort which has induced meditation and which must ultimately destroy . . . the very tap-root of ego-consciousness."

He taught his students that they need not practice severe austerities or elaborate rituals to obtain the highest blessings. Whatever they sought with sincerity and genuine yearning, they would be given. Once Sister Daya asked him, "What can one do when one doesn't have true humility, and yet desires it with all one's heart?"

Paramananda replied, "If you desire it with all your heart, you will get it. There is no doubt about that."

"But," Daya continued, "when one struggles and struggles and finally realizes one is in a prison which one seems incapable of escaping from?"

"When one feels utterly powerless like that," Paramananda assured her, "then if one can admit one's helplessness and call on the Mother in surrender, true humility will come."

To those seeking keys to the transcendental, Paramananda offered his magic formula: humility and surrender. "Direct, simple, child-like method is the best. All great characters have exhibited simplicity and directness. This is a Divine gift. It is much easier to go by the direct path. Calculation, mental analysis and all such things entangle us and our mind becomes confused. When we have a true sense of consecration, we are always simple, child-like and full of selfless devotion."

The community continued to grow. When the Los Angeles Centre was closed, another California student came to live at the Boston Centre. Margarite Morgan (named Mangala, "auspicious") was an attractive, humorous, easygoing, and somewhat coquettish young woman. She never became a sister, but spent the rest of her life living alternately in the community and with her mother and brother in Monterey.

The attendance at the public services was also increasing; between 130 and 160 people were coming each Sunday morning. By 1921, the Vedanta Centre had outgrown the twenty-room house on the Fenway. Wishing to expand into the country, Paramananda looked at several farms in central Massachusetts, but he was advised that maintaining a farm in that rugged climate was more work than it was worth. Instead, they decided to make extensive additions to the Queensberry Street house. They built a fourth story and a new wing at the rear of the building, thus adding six bedrooms, two bathrooms, a laundry, and two storerooms. They also increased the seating capacity of the chapel, and enlarged the dining room and cellar. From the sun parlor on the new fourth floor, the community could enjoy the entire panorama of the Fenway, as well as sunrises and sunsets. There, too, distinguished guests such as the Nobel prize-winning poet Rabindranath Tagore and Dr. J.C. Bose, the pioneer researcher of sensitivity in plants, would be entertained, Tagore returning to India to report to Paramananda's sister, "He is sitting there in America, emanating splendor all around."

The new construction was a strain on the entire household,

especially Sister Devamata, who supervised the work. "It entailed a thousand and one complications, caused chiefly by a dishonest contractor," Daya recorded. "The strain upon all was terrific, for the work lasted from July to the middle of the next February, and during that time there was never one night that the three long flights of stairs, front and back, did not have to be swept clean of debris in the form of lime-dust and shavings and blocks of wood and great lumps of plaster, and the whole house more or less gone over. Sister Devamata was everywhere from garret to cellar, climbing ladders, directing workmen, and generally wearing herself out."

One day Sister Devamata summoned Cunard Nelson, a member of the congregation and a manager of the Boston Edison Company, for advice on light fixtures for the new sun parlor. Although the room was almost completed, the stairway leading up to it had not yet been constructed. Never daunted, the prim senior sister climbed out a third-floor window and scaled a ladder to the new room. Flabbergasted, Mr. Nelson could do nothing but scramble after her.

It was a trying year for Sister Devamata. Her mother, during a brief visit to her other daughter, suddenly had suffered a stroke and died. During the swami's illness and convalescence, Devamata had to take all the public services and classes, as she did also during his extensive lecture tours. Sometimes while he was in Boston, she went to lecture at the Louisville and Cincinnati branches. Relentlessly she drove herself and everyone else. Even on Sundays, between giving two public services, she would sit in the living room busily darning socks. Once a weekend guest, Mrs. Nelson, reproved her for failing to rest on the Lord's Day. "Every day is the Lord's Day," she replied, without missing a stitch.

Devamata was a woman tyrannized by "shoulds," for herself and others. Even her children's rhymes abound in moralisms, such as:

A little tune plays inside of me
　　All night and all the day;
And this is what it seems to say:
　　"Be quiet" and "Be good" —
　　　I wish I could.

If she goaded the rest of the community with her expectations of perfection, she was no less demanding on herself:

Scourge, O Lord, my wayward heart
　　with uplifted rod;
Call my wandering thought apart
　　from unchastened ways.

Purge, O Lord, each word and deed
　　by Thy cleansing touch;
Then plant Thy fructifying seed
　　in my furrowed soul.

The foible of the strong is that they use their own strength as the parameter to judge all others; this lack of empathy for human weakness becomes their fatal weakness. Expecting perfection from others, Devamata became annoyed by their every lapse. In the resultant tension, as she later realized, she grew "harsh and critical and out of rhythm." Paramananda wrote to her: "All your earnest service will surely enrich your life with true understanding. Remember that complete surrender alone makes us clear channels for the Divine."

Unfortunately, it was her attachment to Paramananda that she was least able to surrender. After years of individual attention, she could not adjust to sharing him with an entire community. Desperately clinging to the old mode of fond and exclusive closeness, she sought to monopolize him. During the day, she spent hours sequestered with him in his study, working on the *Message of the East*, discussing matters which she brought to his attention, taking letters (although Achala was perfectly competent to act as his secretary). At night, after instructions in hatha yoga exercises and their "drill" with the banner, the community would gather at the foot of the stairs for some inspirational words and an impromptu prayer, which they all repeated after the swami, line by line. Then Paramananda would disappear up the stairs to his room. Invariably, Devamata would come to his door for an individual "Good-night".

Regarding herself as his peer in administering the community, she expected to be consulted on all decisions. Sometimes she openly challenged his judgements, or even tried to overrule him. If Paramananda, who loved driving his "machine," wanted to motor to one of his distant speaking engagements, Devamata would veto the proposal, calling it "impractical" for him to arrive at his destination tired. When the swami and Lester Flint planned a two-day motor excursion to Dr. William Norman Guthrie's summer home in the Catskills, Paramananda gleefully wished to buy a tent and camp out during their night on the road. Devamata and several others argued that they should check into an inn, have a hot bath, . . . Behind her back, the community nicknamed her, "But, Swami."

One evening Paramananda took the community to the theater. He drove up to the marquee and dropped them all off, asking Amala to please wait for him at the entrance with two tickets while he parked the car. Sister Devamata raised her eyebrows. "Why, Amala is only a child!" she reproved him. "It's perfectly absurd to have her stand there all by herself. You don't know how long you'll be."

At this Amala fired back: "There is no age, and I'm not a baby. I hope to ever stay this way and be only as Divine Mother wishes me."

Devamata pursed her lips, glared at Paramananda, and then turned and stalked into the theater. The swami asked Galene to wait with Amala. All that evening and throughout the next day, a shadow hung over him.

Devamata had become so used to being obeyed that she could not stand to have her will opposed, even by Paramananda. She realized that she had come to a dangerous state: She was competing with her own teacher.

Years before, Paramananda had written to her, "Mother has made you so one with me that it is impossible not to feel any-thing that comes in your life, whether good or bad." Now he felt her struggle, and it scourged him.

That year he spent Sri Ramakrishna's birthday alone in his study, immersed in reading the Master's utterances as recorded in the *Gospel of Sri Ramakrishna*. When he emerged the next day, he was indrawn but radiant. He said to his community: "I feel so well today; I feel light and free as I used to feel. I have not been able to feel that way for a long time. It is because I have been away from creatures—have been with the immortals. I have a new definition for mortal mind. Mortal mind is the mind that gets in touch with mortals and becomes entangled. I must be free and unattached. When I am attached, I cannot help anyone."

———◆———

A decade had passed since Paramananda's 1911 visit to India, and recurrently he felt pulled to return there. His bond with his motherland was strong. According to Swami Akhandananda (one of the direct disciples of Sri Ramakrishna), Paramananda showed more interest in the Ramakrishna Order's Indian proj-ects than any of the other swamis living in America. Using money he earned from his lecture tours, profits from the sale of his books, and personal contributions from some of his followers, he sent a steady stream of aid to the Boys' School in Madras, the charitable dispensaries in Dacca and Allahabad, the orphanage in Murshidabad, the Home of Service in Benares, and the hospi-tal in Hardwar, as well as to the Belur Math itself. At one point the Madras monastery was almost wholly supported by the sale of Paramananda's books, sent free from America. Keenly aware

of the high standard of living that residence in America provided him, Paramananda had only to hear of an elder swami's
need or illness for him to underwrite that swami's medical or
living expenses. Whenever disaster hit India, Paramananda, with
help from Devamata, organized a famine or flood relief fund.

Other causes in India also reached out to him. Paramananda's
oldest sister had been left widowed with four daughters. The
eldest daughter, his childhood playmate Charushila, enrolled in
college to learn teaching for a livelihood, but her meager scholarship could scarcely support the family. Hearing of it, Paramananda
sent regular drafts to them, for which the aging woman gratefully wrote, "This money is a great help in my old age, disease,
and grief."

Bibhu Charan, Paramananda's older brother, was an attorney with poor health and many children. Recurrent sieges of
illness kept him out of work for months at a time. When he did
work, he counselled Dacca's impoverished Muslim population,
from whom he had not the heart to extract payment. All principles and no pocketbook, Bibhu Charan reluctantly sought help
from his brother. As early as 1913, he appealed to Paramananda's
generous nature:

> The condition of my health is such that I may not live
> long. Although you are a *sannyasin*, you are the one I
> request to take care of and support these children. I have
> no one, no friend, no relative on this earth except you. My
> life appears to be a great, great failure. At this age it is
> hard to carry the burden of the family, and I am unable to
> do proper duties towards them. This very thought pains
> me. You are the 'saviour of the clan.' Do remember me
> and the children.

Paramananda responded by sending draft after draft. During Bibhu Charan's extended bouts of illness, the family, including widowed sisters and orphaned nieces and nephews to whom

Bibhu Charan had opened his home, virtually lived on Para-mananda's aid. In 1922, Bibhu Charan wrote to the swami: "Without your help, this family could not and cannot go on."

Although, in becoming a monk, Paramananda had renounced his family, his family had not renounced him. The whole Guha Thakurta clan looked to him for spiritual counsel and emotional support, as well as financial aid. His third sister, overwhelmed with grief at the death of her young daughter, wrote: "Brother, you have approached God. Show me the path. I am broken mentally and physically. Show me the path to salvation." Bibhu Charan, Charushila, her mother, and other cousins, sisters, nieces, and nephews complained constantly that he did not write to them frequently enough. "Do you know how mush strength, how much hope your letters carry to me?" wrote Charushila, summing up the sentiment of them all.

Despite his straitened circumstances, Bibhu Charan, a pro-gressive and an idealist, was intent that all sixteen of his children, girls as well as boys, should become educated. When Mahatma Gandhi launched his non-cooperation movement in 1921, he called on Indians to boycott British schools, which included all the universities in India at the time. Accordingly, Bibhu Charan's eldest son, Prabhu, refused to continue his college education, and joined the nationalist movement. Fearing that the boy would end up in a British jail, Bibhu Charan begged his brother to take Prabhu out of India and educate him in Boston. Paramananda complied, and in 1923, Prabhu Guha Thakurta enrolled at Harvard, taking up residence at the Vedanta Centre.

Paramananda's connection with his family provides another striking parallel to St. Therese of Lisieux, who said: "I love my little family very much. I don't understand the saints who don't love their family." Moreover, his unmonklike financial support of his family had its precedents, even in the Ramakrishna Order. Swami Saradananda had accepted money from Mrs. Bull not only for the upkeep of his parents and siblings, but to finance his brother's education in Japan. Nevertheless, Paramananda was leaving himself wide open to censure. In the Order in India, a new generation of monks was emerging, disciples not of Vivekananda, but of Swami Brahmananda. Some of these men were jealous of Paramananda, of whom they had to hear such extravagant praise from the elder swamis. Paramananda, after all, had practiced no rigorous austerities, had not even graduated from the university (as most of them had), and was living a life of comfort and adulation in the United States. They were galled by his unorthodox behavior, such as living with a community of women and allowing women to teach Vedanta from public platforms, thus putting them on par with the swamis themselves.

Despite Vivekananda's dream of a women's Math, succeeding generations gave no priority to making room for women within the Order or contiguous to it. Indeed, women in Bengal at that time were still in *purdah*, hidden away in the inner apartments of their homes, prohibited from going out in public or being seen by any male adult outside their immediate families. The swamis in India could not understand why Paramananda was devoting so much of his efforts to the spiritual development of females. Unwilling to acknowledge women's claim to the loftiest spiritual direction, some of Paramananda's antagonists imputed baser motives to him. Naturally, Paramananda's patronage of his family gave these critics more ammunition to hurl against him. Nevertheless, he never curtailed that support, even during his own years of financial struggle.

The age of psychology was dawning in America, and Clubs of Practical Psychology were mushrooming throughout the country. Considered more personally relevant than science and less superstitious than religion, psychology offered people a methodic way to understand and improve themselves, a claim similar to Vedanta's.

In September, 1921, Paramananda was invited to address the Convention of Applied Psychology in Cleveland. Three thousand people heard him speak, and the response was overwhelming. Invitations deluged him from throughout the East and Midwest. In November he embarked on a tour which took him from Rochester and Syracuse through Ohio and Indiana to St. Louis. In twelve days he delivered twenty-two lectures in seven cities, sometimes lecturing three times a day. During the tour, 1,800 of his books and pamphlets were sold.

Early in 1922, the swami developed a strategy which enabled him both to tour and to carry on the Boston work. After conducting the Sunday services in Boston, he would leave for New York State or Ohio, returning in time for next Sunday's services.

The audiences he addressed at the Psychology Clubs were larger than those organized under New Thought or other religious auspices, usually numbering between 500 and 1,200. Once, in Cleveland, he was scheduled to lecture in the auditorium of the Hotel Winton, but the crowd which gathered a half hour before the meeting was so huge that the organizers began searching for larger accommodations. When they could find nothing spacious enough, someone suggested opening the cafeteria. It was quickly filled, and in order to be seen and heard, he had to deliver his talk standing on the lunch counter.

It was not Paramananda's style. Although he was gratified to see many helped by his message, he recoiled from the carnival atmosphere of mass movements. Throughout his life this conflict would tear him. Swami Yogananda, who had come to America in 1920, was lecturing to thousands every night; his public healing meetings and prayer affirmations were a sensational success throughout the country. Before Yogananda would enter any city, a staff of volunteers would go before him and prepare the way by advertising in newspapers and on billboards, arranging as many meetings as possible in clubs and liberal churches.

The tactics and pace of such barnstorming ministry did not

attract Paramananda. "I strongly disapprove of this rushing from hotel to lecture hall and from there to the station in mad rush," he wrote to Boston. "At St. Louis I almost missed the train, but they held it for a few minutes. . . . In Cincinnati we rushed to the hotel in Dr. Boike's Buick, driving part of the time forty and forty-five miles an hour, but of course this is a secret. Poor man has enough trouble without getting into trouble with the traffic officer."

What attracted the admittedly unmystical psychology audiences to Swami Paramananda? For one thing, Paramananda always presented Vedanta not as an abstract philosophy, but as a practical method to deal with the challenges of life. He discounted any religious approach that did not teach people how to live from day to day, how to overcome their anxieties, how to get along better with their families, how to withstand tragedies and trials. Referring to religion, he said: "It is not found in theory, rather is it in our practical life that we find it. This has been the dominant thought in every word that I have spoken from the public platform, in intimate talks, and in all my written books."

Still, what he said did not impress his audiences as much as what he emanated. As he himself declared, "I believe absolutely that the greatest amount of good we can do in this world lies not in what we say or in the opinions we advance, but in what we are, the atmosphere we carry with us." More than teach his listeners how to find peace, in the course of an hour's lecture the swami actually seemed to impart peace. A woman who had heard him speak at the Convention of Applied Psychology wrote to her mother-in-law: "While he said little of psychology, there was so much of peace and blessedness that he radiated that we were indeed carried away from these troublesome material things, and for the first time in two years I felt at peace. Oh, how I wish I could hear him often. . . . I never in my whole life met anyone that so rested one, just to talk to him."

Profulla Ghoshal, a young Hindu studying Western drama in New York City, described Paramananda's appearance before

1,200 people at a Fellowship of Faiths meeting there: "When he came in and sat on the platform, the very sight of his serene and youthful face calmed my over-strained nerves." Nor was Paramananda satisfied simply to disseminate such peace from the podium. As Profulla recorded: "Perhaps he had detected my suffering, for he said that he would like to have me with him all day. I actually spent the whole day with him. Just before boarding the train, Swamiji said: 'What else can I do for you, Profulla?' and I could only reply, 'You have done enough, Swamiji.' "

In March, 1922, Paramananda was lecturing in Memphis. He addressed an audience of one thousand on "The Conquest of Fear," and was scheduled to deliver more lectures in Memphis and eight other cities. On the 22nd he received a wire from the Vedanta Centre which made him abruptly cancel all his remaining engagements and take the next train back to Boston. Sister Devamata had suffered a collapse.

At first doctors diagnosed it as a nervous breakdown, caused by the strain, partially self-imposed, of the last year and a half. For weeks she lay in bed, showing no signs of improvement. Further tests revealed a more dread diagnosis: encephalitis (sleeping sickness), inflammation of the brain tissue, a fatal disease for which no cure was then known.

On the evening of May 10, Sister Devamata's illness took a turn for the worse. The doctors declared that death was imminent and notified the Board of Health. The household murmured that the soul had already left the body, and that only the vital organs and a senseless speech continued to function, sustained by the might of her teacher.

Devamata called the swami to her bedside. He came, prepared to give her all the strength and light she might need at this final hour. She did not want strength and light; she wanted life. She told him that she felt herself slipping out from the body, and she implored him to save her. She pleaded that she knew she had brought this illness on herself by her ambition. Even though her yearning to live sprung not from any fear of death, but from her desire to remain with the swami, she promised him that if she lived, she would never again trouble him by her attachment to him. She insisted that he could save her by his intercession, whatever the doctors had said.

Paramananda looked at this stricken figure on the bed, his first disciple. How many times he had declared to her, "Ordinary love fluctuates and changes; my love will never change!" Gazing at her now, he knew that it never had. He knew her better now than in those early days in New York, but he did not love her less. Fifteen years before, she had offered her life to him; could he refuse it now to her? Although willing to let her go, he did not want her to go in this state of darkness and resistance. He would do what he could. He took her hand and told her not to worry. "Had not Lazarus been raised from the dead?" he muttered as he turned and left the room.

Paramananda summoned the community to the dining room. They gathered solemnly, expecting to hear that Sister Devamata was gone. Instead, he announced that they were going to hold a vigil in an effort to save her life. He explained that for the next three days, around the clock, different members of the community would take turns keeping a prayerful vigil before the shrine, while the altar flame would be kept burning steadily.

That night, at 10:30, they began with a special service. Then Sister Seva took her place for the first watch. Paramananda remained in the shrine, lying prostrate before the altar, his whole being a supplication. Finally he heard a voice, which he took to be the Messenger of Death, say: "Very well, but you will pay for this."

He began to feel ill. He left the shrine, went upstairs to his room, and stretched out on a rug on the floor. Suddenly a violent sickness seized him, as if some malicious force were trying to knock him out. It felt like a boxing match was going on inside him. He had never known anything like it. Overcome by an uncontrollable nausea, he bounded across the room, but could not even reach the bathroom in time. He vomited on the rug. Then the illness left him as quickly as it had come.

Lying in her room below, Devamata knew nothing of the vigil, but in the middle of the night she suddenly felt a heavy burden drop from her. She who for days had been too weak even to move rose from her bed and walked across the large room to her chair. The registered nurse who came on duty at dawn would not have been surprised to find her patient dead, but she was shocked to find her sitting in her chair across the room.

During the course of the morning, the attending physicians came to examine Devamata. They were stunned at the change in her condition. One said to the other that they could take no credit for the miraculous, indeed impossible, recovery. The nurses shook their heads in wonder, murmuring that they had never seen anything like it.

The vigil continued for the full three days and nights; then for nine more days special vigil lights burned in the shrine as the swami and the household came and went at will. At the end of the last day, Paramananda gave each member of the community one of the vigil lights which had burned in the shrine. "Devotees should be able to do these things," he told them. "Not that any person does it, but we can make ourselves pure channels. . . . We cannot do it through our own will. He who thinks he can accomplish this through petty, personal will is mistaken. It is only by utter and absolute surrender."

Gradually over the next few months, Sister Devamata regained her strength. Each day Paramananda would visit her and read to her from some sacred book. Daya recorded:

> He has given Sister practically every breath she breaths, spiritually he has supported her dead weight. . . . He has lightened every difficulty, has carried on the public work, done the entire editing of the *Message*, been the light and

life of the house, and has carried his burdens in such playful spirit that people who do not know would think he was doing nothing.

Devamata never entirely recovered. One side was left partially paralyzed, so that she walked with difficulty, her speech was garbled, and her face slightly contorted. She lived for another twenty years, but she never again spoke from the public platform. The dynamic figure who had been "every place in the house at once" became a semi-invalid, moving about stiffly and haltingly. Henceforth, she straddled a dual role: the first and the last among the sisters. Nominally, she was still the senior sister. She consulted on their affairs and even supervised a couple of major projects. But she was impotent to discipline others. The least productive of them now, her chief contribution became the writing of her books: a biography of Paramananda, another of Sri Ramakrishna, a monumental compilation of Paramananda's utterances in the form of a daily devotional (*The Book of Daily Thoughts and Prayer*), *Days in an Indian Monastery*, and others, plus numerous articles and a copious worldwide correspondence. As an aspirant who had prayed for humility, she now had an excellent chance.

Her life returned, Devamata was not able to keep her deathbed promise to the swami. More attached than ever, she followed him wherever he went, like a dwarfed shadow, even hovering at the door of the bathroom while he was inside. As the voice had warned, Paramananda paid for interfering with destiny.

———◆———

One Thursday evening just after the fateful vigil, Paramananda was standing at his study window, watching a steady stream of people arrive for the weekly class. It had come true, he thought. What many had called his pipedream had come true. Without planning or organization, without advertising or extravagant promises, people were being drawn in ever-increasing numbers. Less than ten years ago the small studio on St. Botolph Street had been ample; now even the newly expanded chapel could not hold them. "O Thou unasked, unceasing Giver," he thought, and then the lines cascaded into his mind:

O Thou unasked, unceasing Giver
Thou has given me Thy endless blessing,
Thou hast drawn me close to Thy heart.
Thy bounty runs through my life to overflowing.
Yea, tender Lord, by Thy magic charm Thou hast
    driven away all my past wretchedness.
Can we with all our might, offer Thee aught worthy
    in Thy blessed sight?
Can we ever make our heart so free of earthly stain
    that Thy light of love may shine and glow unceasingly?
Thou art ever merciful to the lowly;
We bring Thee our humble hearts.
No merit have we save our faith in Thine
    infinite compassion.
Do Thou make of us Thy tools that at all hours,
    in work and play,
We may revolve in Thy safe-keeping.

Quickly he jotted down the words, just as he had heard them inside his head, and then hurried to the class.

The next morning he beckoned Daya into his study and handed her the paper, saying, "These lines have come to me in this special form."

She read them slowly, then, staring at Paramananda, exclaimed, "Why, this is poetry! Beautiful poetry!"

After that three more "poems" came in rapid succession, all in the same way. Paramananda had played at writing rhymes and jingles before, but these verses were profoundly different. He did not compose them; they surged up in his mind and he had only to grab the nearest scrap of paper and take them down,

his hand rushing to keep up with the flow of syllables, later
changing perhaps a word or two. He considered himself not a
poet, but the Lord's instrument:

> A glance from Thy smiling eyes hath poured
> Upon me a shower of countless blossoms.
> Now I gather these scattered flowers
> Day and night with ecstatic joy,
> For they bear the blessing of Thy divine fragrance.

The muse had taken possession of him. Sometimes as many
as six poems came in a single day. One evening he was so swept
up by the force of inspiration that he came upstairs trembling all
over. By the first of August he had eighty poems, enough for a
book.

Soul's Secret Door came off the presses in October. The critics
lauded it as high-calibre mystical poetry, one reviewer even comparing it to the psalms of David. Even the Mammon-oriented
New York Post commented, "The book sheds an almost tonic
sense of peace and repose." The *Literary Digest* selected several
of the poems for its December issue, and later others were included in the *Book of Modern Poetry*, a distinguished anthology
of the best poems being written in America.

Although the swami did not calculate it that way, his poetry
found inroads into sectors which would never have glanced at
his books on Vedanta. The *Methodist Review* printed two of them,
and the *Literary Digest*, which only ten years before had published the inflammatory "Strange Gods of American Women,"
commented, "Writing in free verse, a devout Hindu gives us a
book of poems, 'Soul's Secret Door,' and it is interesting to note
how essentially Christian is his Oriental faith." Paramananda's
poetry books, which numbered four volumes by 1929, spread
the sentiment of universality among even the most bigoted literati.

Poetry readings became the favorite evening activity at the
Vedanta Centre. The community and closer members of the

congregation would gather in the sun parlor, and the swami would recite his poems in a sonorous voice, never failing to be moved by them himself. Coming during a time of great strain, he cherished them like a gift sent to lift him above all his troubles. "I forget difficulties and problems when I begin to write poems," he said. "When the inspiration comes, it wipes out all shadows."

Nor was the inspiration limited to poetry. In November, a five-act play, *The Veil of Twilight*, came to him. For seven hours scenes, characters, and action spanning ballrooms in Cambridge and gardens in the Himalayas poured through him, as Paramananda paced the floor of his study, dictating the lines to Sister Achala, who struggled furiously to keep up with him.

The muse was kind to come, for the year had been fraught with more than one sorrow. A few days before Good Friday, Paramananda had experienced severe mental suffering. The household attributed it to Sister Devamata's desperate condition, but two days later the swami received word from India that Swami Brahmananda had passed out of the body on that day. "I have heard of sacred grief," Daya wrote, "but I never witnessed it till I saw that Divine child of ours with the tears flowing down his cheeks as he spoke to us of his beloved friend and teacher." Vivekananda, Ramakrishnananda, Brahmananda—one by one the giants in his life had fled, leaving him among the pygmies. That night at dinner, Paramananda told the community that he felt his work was entering a new phase.

12

Ananda Ashrama

PARAMANANDA was an inveterate dreamer, always astir with visions of the wonders that might be:

> I am dreaming, dreaming all day and night; Dreaming of
> life in ceaseless harmony. . . .

The farm idea of 1921 gave way the following year to his recurrent dream of a temple: "The Temple of the Universal Spirit." Not content with the converted sitting room of a city house, he dreamed of building an artistic, freestanding structure. In an unprecedented (and never to be repeated) appeal for funds, Paramananda alluded to the temple's cost during the Easter service of 1922. Various members of the congregation and community submitted designs and ideas for the structure, and a miniature model was installed in the entrance hall of the Centre.

By the middle of the next winter, however, Paramananda's dream for the Centre's much-needed expansion had taken another turn. Perhaps it was six months of steam heat and icy roads which made visions of California dance in his head. "When we get into the turmoil of the cities, the man-created chaos of life," he declared, "how little of Nature, how little of that which is true and unspoiled, is left for us. This means we have to create a new setting." The unlimited possibilities of wide open spaces and year-round outdoor living incited what was to be the greatest dream of his life: Ananda Ashrama.

The sages of ancient India had lived with their disciples in ashramas, or forest retreats, where they sought and taught the highest Truth, bequeathing their realizations to the world in the form of the Upanishads. America had seen three attempts at ashramas: Swami Abhedananda's two in Connecticut and California, and the Shanti Ashrama founded by Swami Turiyananda. By 1923, all three were defunct.*

Paramananda's idealized haven was to encompass more spheres than its predecessors, which had been simple, meditative retreats. He envisioned a place, set in the serene beauty of nature, where all facets of human expression would be encouraged: art, music, drama, agriculture, animal husbandry, and a variety of crafts, all issuing from the substratum of spiritual consciousness produced by continual prayer, meditation, and selfless service. It would be the home of his monastic community, women and (he hoped) men, and of families who shared their aspirations. Guests could come for short or long periods, partake of the peace and exalted atmosphere of the place, and carry them back into the world. It would be a lighthouse on land, a shrine dedicated to all world religions, a refuge for world-weary souls, an abode of truth, beauty, and high ideals.

> Where souls of men delight in others' happiness,
> Where hearts of men sing to awaken other hearts
>   from slumber!

In short, it was to be a heaven on the earth of California.

"In zero weather, you cannot imagine outdoor life," Paramananda told his Boston followers. "We shall create out there a place where a community of workers can live and express their talents along different lines—music, art, industry. It will not be limited to religion, although that will be the soul of it. Silent

*Shanti Ashrama was revived in the 1930s under Swami Ashokananda.

living, people who dare live and wait patiently, whether the world gives any recognition to them or not: this home is going to be created for that purpose. It is not a sudden change. For some time I have felt the need of a different line of action. Life is to be put on a simpler basis. It does not mean giving up anything; it means only expansion. We are going into something bigger."

Paramananda's concept of a utopian community (he never used the term, but his vision was nothing less than Utopia) focused on three ideals: self-expression, service, and *sadhana* (spiritual practices). The swami wanted his followers to be paragons of selflessness, but he knew that self-sacrifice without self-expression could lead to a diminishing of the person rather than his or her blossoming. Self-expression without service, on the other hand, could lead to egocentricity. In the end, the goal was neither to reduce the self nor to enhance the self, but to transcend the self and live in that higher sphere of love and all-encompassing vision. Paramananda, whatever the methods he employed, aimed to produce neither artists nor humanitarians, but saints.

"Let us hope for big things," he exhorted his community, "not only what is good for us, but what is good for the whole. Impossible hopes, let us dare to hope for those. What if the world calls us dreamers! Let us dream those dreams which will lift us from the dilemma of selfishness and self-seeking. Let us soar high with the wings of hope and dream into the transcendental."

On January 24, 1923, with almost three feet of snow on the ground outside, Paramananda first broached to his community the idea of moving the bulk of the work to California. Less than three weeks later Sister Daya boarded a Los Angeles-bound train to search for suitable property for the new ashrama. The place would have to be accessible to nearby cities, but removed from congested urban atmosphere; unspoiled in its natural beauty, but developed enough to be feasible; and the price would have to be within their modest reach.

"Arriving in California," Sister Daya wrote, "I did not find my task a simple one." The Golden State was experiencing one of its periodic booms, and the price of property had soared to dizzy heights. Two weeks of assiduous searching produced not a single possibility within their price range. A defeated Daya wired the discouraging news to Paramananda. On March 4, the swami arrived in Los Angeles to see for himself.

Paramananda revealed his approach to finding the desired land in a letter written to the Boston household the day after his arrival in California: "We will wait and see what the Divine Mother has in store for us." Indeed, years before he had written, "When the right time comes, we shall have a nice Ashrama. A place is waiting for us somewhere." One of Paramananda's cardinal teachings was that when one is in rhythm with the Divine, everything moves in perfect step. Coming up against repeated obstacles often indicates that one is "out of rhythm." One has to listen to the Divine beat and move with it. Thus, after a fruitless week of land-hunting, exhausted, bedraggled, and disappointed, Paramananda began to wonder whether he was pursuing the Divine Mother's will or his own.

One afternoon, Paramananda seemed particularly troubled. Finally he confessed to Daya, who was driving him through Laurel Canyon in a borrowed Ford, that he felt someone pulling on him. He asked her to take him back to his hotel in order to see if there was any message for him.

There was. Sister Devamata had forwarded a cable from Paramananda's brother in India. Bibhu Charan was about to give his second eldest daughter, Gayatri, in marriage, and was asking for Paramananda's blessing on the union.

The year before, Gayatri had written to the swami asking to join his community. "I understand that you have American women in your community helping in your work," wrote the idealistic fifteen-year-old, who was determined to dedicate her life to something other than marriage and children. "Would you like to have an Indian woman, too?" The sisters and the swami were delighted with the request. Yes, he did want his community to be drawn from both East and West, but he never answered the girl's letter. Perhaps he felt that she was too young, that the time was too soon.

Now, just a year later, suddenly the time was too late. "The cable from India was a real shock to him," Daya wrote to Boston, "and I confess it made me feel terribly. He was very quiet, but I could see how it affected him."

Given that there were many other women in India available to join his community, Paramananda's intense reaction is understandable only in the light of the future role that this particular Indian woman was destined to play. In an uncharacteristic act of intervention, Paramananda cabled to Bibhu Charan: "STOP THE MARRIAGE."

The cable arrived the night before the wedding, with the house full of the groom's relatives, the arrangements all completed, and the prenuptial festivities in full swing. Horror-stricken, Bibhu Charan called Gayatri to him and asked her what he should do, for he had plighted his word and to cancel the wedding at that point would mean disgrace and dishonor. She read the telegram, looked up at her father's tormented face, and handing the wire back to him, replied, "What else can you do? Do what you are doing." The wedding took place.

Perhaps Paramananda intuited the futility of his cable, or perhaps the fruitless search for an ashrama had defeated him, for when Daya parted from him that night, "He seemed so terribly discouraged and down." The next morning Daya, feeling helpless and weighted by the swami's depression, drove to his hotel for another arduous day of land hunting. A buoyant Paramananda came striding sprily down the hotel stairs. Joining Daya in the Ford, he told her, "A poem came to me last night. Would you like to hear it?" Then he read:

Anything or nothing—I am content if it be Thy Will.
When Thou dost dwell in my heart, I feel no lack of
  things of this world.
Only one thing I ask of Thee:
That Thou dost abide with me always and evermore.

As they drove into the foothills, Paramananda was singing.

A couple of days later, after more leads and dead ends, they stopped for tea at the home of Seymour Thomas, an artist friend of Daya who lived in the valley of La Crescenta. In the course of their conversation, Thomas mentioned that he believed that the Fusenot property of about 140 acres, a little farther up the valley, was for sale, although it was not generally known to be on the market.

When they had exhausted all other possibilities, Paramananda and Daya drove up toward the Sierra Madre mountains. Sixteen miles from Los Angeles, they turned off the main highway onto a steep, narrow road skirted on either side by untouched fields of scarlet larkspur, wild lilac, and purple lupine. At the top of the hill, a mass of lavish green set against the sagebrush mountains beyond, they drove through the gates of the Fusenot estate. The automobile climbed from terrace to terrace, past lines of tall, shimmering Lombardy poplars, fruit orchards, vineyards, acacia and eucalypus trees, Himalayan deodars, Japanese plums, and an exotic array of other choice shrubs and trees planted by the artistic French owner. The road ended at a small house, white stucco with red tile roof.

Paramananda and Daya got out of the car and walked to the edge of the terrace, 2200 feet high, 500 feet above the valley of La Crescenta. For ten minutes the swami stood there, looking out at the valley, the Verdugo Mountains beyond, and, in the distance, the dim blueness of the Pacific. Then he turned to Daya and said, "This is the place I have been seeking." Later he told her that he had had a dream of the stucco and tile house, exactly as they saw it.

Inquiring of the caretaker the price of the property, they were amazed to hear that it had somehow eluded the boom that had catapulted all other real estate beyond their reach. The price was reasonable, the terms of payment satisfactory. Paramananda probably had arranged to borrow the downpayment from Sister Devamata, who was now half heir to her mother's legacy.

They got back into the car and drove directly to the Anderson Real Estate office in Montrose, with which the property was listed. Foregoing the usual bargaining and negotiations which accompany such large transactions, Paramananda simply walked in and announced to Mrs. Anderson, "I am ready to purchase the Fusenot place. Please have the papers made out at once." When Mr. Anderson returned to the office, he found his wife leaning breathless against the wall. "You won't believe it," she said, "but in the course of the last ten minutes, I have sold the Fusenot property."

A week later Paramananda installed Sister Daya in the old La Crescenta Hotel and returned to Boston. Two weeks after that, Sister Devamata, Sister Seva, and Mangala, dubbing themselves "the ashrama pioneers," set off for their California adventure.

Paramananda followed them, and on April 29 the first public service was held on the new grounds. The surrounding beauty of nature seemed to fulfill their most euphoric expectations. As Daya described the occasion:

> The platform upon which the Swami stood was of grass. Locust trees in full blossom, masses of yellow broom, white syringa, wild sage, and the lupine made the air fragrant around him. . . . As beautiful and profound as the Swami's words have seemed to his listeners in Boston and in other places, even more simple and beautiful did they there on the natural altar of Ananda Ashrama. Little lizards ran up the limbs of the tree above the Swami's head and shyly made their way over the grass at his feet, birds hopped

trustingly near and hummingbirds flashed through the air. . . . His Sanskrit prayers had a new majesty, heard out of doors with the undertone of nature, and his peace chant mingled with the peace of the hills and seemed to flow forth over the world below.

At the end of May, Paramananda again left for Boston, obliged to pacify both the congregation and the remaining community members there, who were feeling neglected and somewhat jealous at the swami's intoxication with his new child. He raved constantly about the enchantments of the ashrama and of his many plans for it, causing Galene to exclaim: "I hope that at least once you will come to Boston and be wholly here."

Undaunted, Paramananda continued to unroll ashrama maps and blueprints and to share with them his dreams and ideals for the new retreat:

> My motive in having the ashrama is not for personal pleasure or benefit, or a retreat for a chosen few. It is for the good of the whole, the world. Some of you have selfish ideas of only a few, but whatever I am instrumental in doing I want for the good and benefit of everyone. I wish to create something beautiful and inspiring, from where on the mountain top thoughts of good and love may spread all over the world.
>
> We must depend on the Higher Power. I am not doing anything; it is a Higher Power that does all things. And we must be full of love. What is it to have lofty theory without living? We should live, love, and be love. . . .

In hoping to benefit the world through the ashrama, Paramananda did not mean to draw enormous crowds to his public lectures there. On the contrary, he hoped eventually to abandon such formal preaching entirely: "The real teaching cannot be given to order. I wish I were not bound to set classes. I wish I could give freely—just speak and those who have openness, they would get something from it, but not be bound by form. This is the original idea of an ashrama, and it will come."

Paramananda's dream of spreading a world-healing power from the mountain top was based on a subtle concept common to Hindu, Buddhist, and Christian contemplatives. That is, that God-consecrated thoughts and actions even behind steep monastery walls in the middle of a desert exert a force that will ultimately redeem the world. Paramananda felt that if the consecrated workers of the ashrama could direct their minds and lives to the highest ideals of love, peace, and noninjury, they would create an influence that would radiate far and wide, "not only to just a few people who come to it," Paramananda exalted. "It will have world-power behind it."

The Boston members had no need to be envious, for the "ashrama pioneers" were hardly having a romantic time of it. Used to the comforts of Queensberry Street, which lately had included frequent theatergoing and ping-pong matches, they found themselves isolated on a mountain with no modern conveniences. The house, however charming and artistic, had no electricity or telephone. The icebox, which stood in the living room for lack of space in the tiny kitchen, had to be stocked with ice brought by Sister Daya from the nearest town. During their first weeks there, the high fog from the ocean still deposited its damp chill, while the open fireplaces of the house yawned blank and empty, for Sister Devamata was there to instruct them that, according to Indian tradition, in a holy dwelling the first fire must be lighted by the hand of the teacher. Shivering at night, the sisters had to resign the last vestiges of privacy permitted them by community life, for the small house did not have enough rooms to accommodate the four of them individually. Seva and Mangala had to share a bedroom and Daya slept on an army cot in the living room.

During the day, they scrambled to get things done, overwhelmed by the enormity of the task before them. The indefatigable Seva irrigated orchards and trees into the late hours of the night, for in that arid region the lush verdure of the estate depended on regular irrigation. She also dug holes to bury the garbage, plowed a field with a little hand plow, and planted a melon patch and a vegetable garden. Her efforts produced long rows of shining corn and luscious-looking watermelons, which she later picked with pride, only to discover that the possums had scooped out the center of each melon with their little hands, leaving nothing inside.

Mangala and Daya had never wielded either hoe or hammer. They knew enough about flowers only to pick them, but, confident of the fertility of their home state, they stuck flower seeds into the hard, sun-baked soil near the house, and watered them daily on the run with a little water poured from a milk bottle. "Imagine our surprise and aggravation," Daya later related, "when not a single sprout appeared above the surface to repay our toil."

As for Sister Devamata, her health made her alternate between periods of independence and helpfulness and periods when she herself became one more care for the others to tend.

Even the peace which the mountains had promised them seemed to be teasingly withheld. Mr. Fusenot's caretaker, who stayed on for a while after the change of ownership, was disgruntled over the loss of his job. In a one-man campaign to scare off the newcomers, he expatiated on the miseries of poison oak, in which, he said, the place abounded, and waxed eloquent in describing the fierce winds which periodically swept the hills, ravaging the property and shaking the little house. His ten-year-old son, Delbert, would race his bicycle around the main house in a perpetual marathon, grating on the sisters' nerves, already frazzled by a host of minor inconveniences and major responsibilities. Sometimes the mother's voice could be heard yelling, "Delbert, give me that ear," causing even the usually tolerant Daya to later exclaim: "As the ear was attached to the boy, I for one wished she would get it and never let go."

From the beginning, major projects had to be tackled. More workers, so direly needed, could come only when there were more accommodations. Aside from the stucco house, the estate had only a two-room structure made of native stone and the caretaker's rather ramshackle cottage. In June they contracted for the building of a row of primitive cabins. In anticipation of the arrival of Mr. and Mrs. Doble and her sister Miss Eaton, "the faithful trio" as Paramananda called them, who were eager to join the new community, the caretaker's cottage was lifted and moved from the gate to a site near the main house.

When Paramananda arrived with "the faithful trio" in mid-July, his dream suddenly plummeted and hit the hard earth of reality. He was staggered by the realization of the undertakings required to make the ashrama fit for a large community. The main house would have to be enlarged to accommodate the rest of the sisters waiting at Queensberry Street. Another devoted Boston family, Mrs. Fischer, her two young sons, and her daughter and son-in-law, Ruth and Cunard Nelson, were also anxious to move to the ashrama. Another set of cabins would have to be built for them in Ward Canyon. The public services could not be held outdoors during the upcoming rainy season; they needed to construct an auditorium to make do until the "Temple of the Universal Spirit" could finally be raised.

Other technical problems beset the fledgling community. The property's water supply from its own mountain spring—one of the attractions which had originally delighted the swami—was being seriously depleted. In order to tap an adequate supply for the growing community, they would have to tunnel hundreds of feet into the mountain to the water's source, and then expand two dams in Ward Canyon to store the flow. Moreover, all this construction would require new roads to make more of the property accessible.

In the face of these huge enterprises, the available manpower was pitifully small: the swami, Mr. Doble, and Jack Miller, the ardent young Jewish devotee whose body was already ravaged by tuberculosis. "When I first returned," Paramananda wrote to the Boston household, "and found everything rather in a chaotic condition, and dire need of workers, my heart was very heavy and sad, and outlook at the time seemed very dark." The following Tuesday, as if in answer to his yearning prayer, three men suddenly showed up: Lester Flint, the here-again, gone-again brother, arrived from Panama without any notice; Harold Camerford, a sailor in the merchant marine, asked to join the community; and one of Paramananda's Los Angeles students came for a visit. The swami, in order to encourage them, was outside working at 5:30 each morning. Making light of his resultant fatigue, he would come in at the end of a strenuous day remarking, "My legs are complaining; they say, 'Monsieur Paramananda, won't you please give us a break?'"

Nevertheless, it was internal friction, more than external exigencies, which burst the bubble of the swami's dream. He had asked nothing of his disciples except that they live according to his ideals, those lofty principles of peace and love which were his very life's breath. Referring to the guru's role of shouldering the accumulated karma of his disciples, Paramananda wrote:

> It is a very hard task for one to carry a burden and still harder for him who removes it. How can we repay his debt? Only by living a true and pure life according to his teachings. *There is no other way. There is no other way.* Material help, service, is nothing. . . . Know perfectly well that you can never satisfy nor serve me unless you live the pure and true kind of life.

Therefore, Paramananda was deeply shaken when he returned to find his abode of peace rife with discord. As Daya described their state in a letter to Mary Lacy:

For a long time we have had our moods, we have had
our selfish demands, we have often been unloving one to
the other, critical, harsh. . . . It was when he came home
to us here at the Ashrama and found cruel mental conditions,
sickening disharmony and wrong spirit that his inner Self
was actually wounded. "When one has had a great dream
and seen it fail, then one is crushed"—These were Swami's
words. His great dream for the Ashrama, his joy in it, fell
to earth with broken wings those first tragic two weeks.

One afternoon, two weeks after his return to the ashrama,
Paramananda was erecting a trellis near the parking place. When
he finished, he slowly plodded back to the house, his cheeks
flushed with fever and his eyes unnaturally bright. He fell onto
his bed and lay there feverish and delirious for several hours. In
his delirium, instead of rambling incoherently, he poured forth a
steady stream of spontaneous poetry.

At first they thought it was influenza, but after days of burning fever and congested lungs, the doctor diagnosed it as bron-
chial pneumonia. When the lungs still refused to clear and other
symptoms developed, the doctor confided to them that it might
be tuberculosis.

According to the Vedantic concept of karma, every action,
good or bad, produces a like effect which must eventually be
borne by the doer of that action. An illumined soul, however,
can take upon himself the negative karma of his disciples and
suffer its effect in their place. It operates like the Christian doctrine of Christ taking upon himself the sins of the world.

The sisters were convinced that the swami's illness was a
direct result of their friction. "Whose was the fault?" Daya wrote.
"The fault lay in all our hearts, small and personal. If one injured,
the other reacted, and so the atmosphere was like a poison into
which our Swami came with his glowing dream. The illness may
have seemed to have an outer cause. This was the real cause."
Her letter continued:

Again and again during that time Swami said: "Someone must be willing to lay down his life for a cause if it is to live." And of course it was his life he was offering. How close he came to laying it down, I do not yet dare to think. . . . His illness, his danger, has healed and redeemed. In those hours of uncertainty, we could only lie at Divine Mother's feet and offer our all renewed intensity of devotion, with hearts aching with suspense and contrition. It has been a purifying fire that has swept the Ashrama and nearly consumed our blessed one. . . . His dream will come true. We will be big enough to forget ourselves in God's service.

His lungs cleared. The danger lifted and Paramananda, weak and prostrate, began to recover. "The work here will go on now," he told them. But the doctor warned that he must take it easy for the next few months, otherwise he would drag along for a long time, never becoming completely restored, and opening himself to other troubles. "Influenza weakens the heart for a time," Daya wrote ominously.

The swami's dream proved as buoyant as the man himself. By the end of August activities and spirits around the ashrama were flourishing, and Paramananda was jubilant:

I realize more and more that this new work must be built up on a basis that is of love, earnest zeal, and selfless aspiration, and I am happy to see these elements so marvelously manifesting in the lives of our small pioneering group. That alone is such a soul satisfaction to me that my suffering is of very small consequence. . . . When I first undertook this new venture, I had many high ideals and dreams, but some of the happenings have already gone beyond my expectations.

The new set of cabins in Ward Canyon was underway and a road was being constructed through the orchard to the site. Lester painted the Dobles' cottage inside and out. Brother Jack, his health somewhat revived, was able to irrigate the poplar trees and do other light chores. Mr. Doble tended the grapevines, planted lawns, put in a rose garden, and threw himself into a dozen other projects. The young fruit trees on the ashrama were yielding abundantly: peaches, apricots, pears, and walnuts.

Amala arrived and was put in charge of cooking and provisions; she would sit on the screened porch preparing vegetables and singing the swami's poem, "It is dawn, It is dawn!" Sister Seva, in addition to her constant gardening, assumed the care of sixteen newly-delivered hives of bees, an apiary that would soon be producing a ton of honey yearly. Mangala flitted here and there, busy washing, housekeeping, and sewing curtains for the cabins. Daya taxied up and down the hill for supplies, mail, and visitors who took the streetcar as far as the highway below. During the swami's illness and absences, she conducted the public services, quickly changing her successive Sunday roles from dishwasher to chauffeur to minister.

Guests coming to the mountain retreat were impressed and delighted by what they saw. Marion Forster Gilmore wrote: "My experience revealed to me something of the blessed meaning of a Peace Retreat. Spontaneous co-operation and joyfully consecrated activity are actual forces, not mere theories, in the daily life of the household. It is at once a wholesome, mutually helpful community and a family, bound by spiritual ties."

The community was rapidly expanding. The Fischers and the Nelsons arrived from Boston and occupied two double cabins in Ward Canyon. Small, bare frame structures with a common outhouse, they were a far cry from the Boston home that they had given up, as Mr. Nelson's physical labors were a far cry from his engineering desk job with the Boston Edison Company.

Ruth Norton, one of Paramananda's Los Angeles students from the early years, and her fifteen-year-old son, Earl, joined the group. As a little boy tagging along with his mother to the Vedanta meetings, Earl had told Paramananda, in a burst of juvenile magnanimity, "Swami, if I ever get rich, I'll buy you a goat!" Moving to the ashrama, he brought with him like a sacred dowry his own livestock: nine goats, a donkey, hens, a cow and a calf. Corrals, pens, and later a barn were constructed for them. When Earl returned to high school in the fall, Brother Jack would sit in the main house living room with him each night, helping him with his algebra homework. The boy was jubilant when he came out at the head of his class, for he felt that he was working for the glory of Ananda Ashrama.

A person's noble dreams may or may not come true, but the person himself becomes nobler for having dreamed them. Paramananda felt that he was no more a visionary than those who dreamed of gaining wealth or worldly pleasures, only the caliber of the dream differed, and mattered. Just as a man shapes his dreams, his dreams shape the man. As Paramananda cried in one of his poems:

In this world of dream, my soul,
    dream a truer dream,
Whose mighty pulse will lift thee
    to a high pinnacle
And make thy body vibrant with new life.
Dream, my soul, of that happy realm
Where joy abides alone in unbroken oneness,
And life reigns in eternal surety.
Dream, my soul, where love dwells in harmony
And beauty in its virgin loveliness.
Dream of divine ecstasy
Whose eternal melody is sung by all created things.
Stop not dreaming this great dream
Till its image speak to thy soul
    with a living tongue.

Despite intermittent idyllic periods, reality never quite caught up with Paramananda's dream. As one visitor put it after being shown the ashrama: "It was most beautiful, but more beautiful to me was the swami's vision of it."

————————◆◆————————

In mid-September, sooner than the doctor had wished, Paramananda felt pulled to return to Boston. The disposition of the work there was a critical problem. Some members of the community felt that he should give up the Boston Centre entirely and concentrate his energies in one place, that sustaining the work in Boston amidst his frequent absences was not worth the effort he would have to put into it, that repeated crossings of the continent would put a lethal strain on him. Indeed, ever since Sister Devamata's retirement from speaking, the interest and attendance of the Boston public rose and fell strictly according to the swami's presence at the Centre. For example, on April 15, the attendance at the Sunday service prior to Paramananda's departure for California was 181. The very next Sunday only 82 showed up to hear Miss Sherwood's service. The congregation further diminished with each passing week, until the swami's return made it soar again. The move to California was a crippling blow to the Boston Centre just when it had reached its zenith. Without Paramananda's continuous presence, its prospects were bleak. Besides, two centers meant splitting up the community, and Paramananda himself declared, "I could never be happy with a divided household."

Boston had, however, a devoted nucleus of students whom Paramananda could not bear to abandon. As he told them that autumn: "In the beginning, but for the earnest spirit of a few people, I might not have established a work here at all. It was those few people who held me." Now, again it was the few who held him. He decided to keep two or three workers in Boston, sell the Queensberry Street house, and continue the Vedanta Centre in smaller quarters. Having moved into the Centre the day after Sister Devamata left, a reluctant Katherine Sherwood

Left to right: Sister Devamata, Salome, Swami Paramananda, Georgina Jones Walton (later Sister Daya), Edna Massman (later Sister Achala). 1919.

Left to right: Paramananda, Sister Seva, Edna Massman (later Sister Achala), Galene Philadelpheus, Sister Satya Prana. Queensberry Street house, 1920.

Paramananda constructing a kite.

Paramananda flying a kite. Revere Beach, 1922.

Kite flying contest, Revere Beach, Massachusetts, 1922.
Left to right: unknown, Mr. Doble, Grace Eaton (Doble's sister-in-law),
Paramananda, Camille Christians (later Amala).

Paramananda hiking at Ananda Ashrama, 1923.

Panoramic view of Ananda Ashrama grounds, after construction of Temple.

P & O. S. N. Co.
S.S. Rajputana
Jan. 29th 1926

Dear ones,

I place my hand of love on each one of you & I pray that God may make your hearts glad. I am always full of gratitude that He has given me so many true hearts to love & serve & to be loved & protected through their pure consecration. May you all live each day to glorify Him. Through your selfless devotion I am so very bound to you that distance cannot diminish it, nor can separation prevail against it. I am bound to you through love (the gentle word) but strongest of all fetters. This moment my heart is overflowing with such tenderness that there are really no words — no words but that which / needs no words at all.

Ever & ever yours
Paramananda

Facsimile of Paramananda's handwriting, letter to ashrama community, en route to India, January, 1926.

Standing, left to right: Mr. Doble, Grace Eaton, Mrs. Doble, Sister Seva, Paramananda, Sister Devamata, Sister Daya, Dr. Belle Barnard, Hilda Johanigmann. Kneeling: Dr. Robinson, Amala, Mary Lacy. Ananda Ashrama, December, 1923.

Standing, left to right: Sister Seva, Mr. Doble, Prabhu Guha Thakurta, Mrs. Doble, Paramananda, Ralph Fisher, Mrs. Fisher, Sister Devamata, Ruth Nelson, Earl Norton, Cunard Nelson. Seated: Mangala, Grace Eaton, Amala, Dr. Robinson. Ananda Ashrama, 1924.

Dedication of Ashrama Cloister, November, 1924. Standing, left to right: Sister Achala, Katherine Sherwood, Mrs. Doble, Sister Devamata, Mr. Doble, Paramananda, Sister Daya, Sister Seva, Hilda Johanigmann, Grace Eaton. Seated: Mangala, Amala, Mary Lacy, Dr. Belle Barnard.

Ananda Ashrama Cloister, rear view, 1925.

Gayatri Devi. 1927.

Gayatri Devi. Ananda Ashrama. c. 1926.

Gayatri Devi and Sister Daya. Ananda Ashrama, 1926.

agreed to conduct the services in the swami's absence. Galene eventually replaced her, while Sister Satya Prana was left in charge of the shrine.

Two trying years passed before they found a customer for the huge house. Finally, after long negotiations and a tenuous financial arrangement, the Home of Truth, another unorthodox religious society, took over the building. On June 2, 1925, the Vedanta Centre moved to its new home at 176 Marlboro Street, leaving its members and the swami to lament forever the beautiful Queensberry Street house they had left behind.

To keep both the Ashrama and the Centre buoyed up by his presence, Paramananda bounced like a tennis ball from coast to coast, often crossing the continent at two or three-week intervals. Most of his time he gave to the ashrama, never spending more than a month at a stretch in Boston.

He always broke the long railroad journey with speaking engagements in Cincinnati, and often in Louisville, Chicago, St. Louis, or Dayton. Since the departure of Swami Abhedananda in 1921, Paramananda was the only Vedanta swami touring America. The two other Vedanta societies in New York and San Francisco were headed by swamis who were distinctly withdrawn in their public approach. Dedicated to their own centers, they made no attempt to spread the message of Vedanta elsewhere.

To be sure, the membership of the New York Society had declined from 200 in 1906 to 50 in 1926. Many Vedanta sympathizers in New York were disappointed with the leadership of Swami Bodhananda, Swami Abhedananda's replacement, whom they considered a faithful but uninspired representative. They repeatedly urged Paramananda to found a second branch there. Dr. Guthrie, rector of St. Mark's-on-the-Bouwerie Episcopal Church, had even offered Paramananda the use of a building adjoining St. Mark's for such a Centre, and was crestfallen when he directed his expansion to California instead. Paramananda's keen consciousness of his role as the sole national representative of his Order goaded him to do more travelling than his health would permit, so he never entirely recovered his strength after the 1923 bout of pneumonia.

When Paramananda returned to California in December of that year, he brought with him all the rest of the household who could be spared: Sister Achala, Mary Lacy, Hilda, and Dr. Belle Barnard, a physician who had taken up residence at the Vedanta Centre six months before. Part of Paramananda's dream was to have ashrama doctors and ashrama nurses, but Dr. Bernard, too diffident and phlegmatic to ever start her own practice, was not much help at the ashrama either. With the transfer of the book department and the *Message of the East* to California, the move was complete.

During 1924 and 1925, the development of the ashrama proceeded at full swing. The workers cleared brush, cut trails throughout the property, built stone walls, and planted flowers broadcast. Sister Devamata planned a chapel garden beside the main house; with the labor of several friends, it soon grew into a riotous tangle of color climbing its way over carefully designed stone walls and steps, along stone-edged and tree-bordered paths to the rose garden beyond. A hired crew dug a six-hundred-foot tunnel into the mountain to tap the source of the spring, laid thousands of feet of pipe, and enlarged the two dams in Ward Canyon, thus creating two crystal pools in which the sisters planted Indian lotuses.

Sixteen years before, as a young swami in New York, Paramananda had written to Devamata: "Mother, you know that Paramananda's one thought is to be unselfish. I may fail many times, but still I try to get up with fresh vigour." Now he experienced the fulfillment of that struggle. Sitting before the fireplace in the ashrama living room one January evening in 1924, he told his community:

If I had been seeking my own comfort, it would have been easy for me to settle down and enjoy a certain amount of ease. But now my whole life is to give to others. The only reason I have become engaged in such a big undertaking is that many may receive blessing from it.

In May, 1924, the crucial expansion of the main house was begun. Elmer Grey, a distinguished architect in the new congregation, offered his services and designed a twelve-room addition to the original stucco and tile cottage to serve as a living quarters for the sisters and women workers. Conceived under Sister Devamata's counsel, the building, not surprisingly, turned out like a medieval Spanish cloister, complete with four wings, an enclosed courtyard, flagstone arcades with a pergola, arched porticos, grilled windows, and beamed roofs, all constructed of unhewn stone gathered from the ashrama itself and joined with rough, surface pointing.

On November 2, the "Ashrama Cloister," as it was inevitably named, was dedicated. Five hundred people, many of them curiosity-seekers, motored up the hill and gathered in the new courtyard to hear Paramananda proclaim his ideal for the new work.

He began with the Buddhist prayer which had become his personal ideology: "Let all beings that breathe — without enemies, without obstacles, overcoming sorrow and attaining cheerfulness — move forward freely, each in his own path."

Then he continued:

In spiritual life we require courage. Sometimes we have to stand alone. If the measure of success lay in public recognition, the very first year of this work would have been the last one. The measure of success is not in what others give us, but in what we ourselves receive from the joy of giving. Our concern is how much we are able to give, not what we may get from people; that is the leading spirit of our work. We have gathered here, a band of conse-

crated workers, not because we want something for ourselves, but because we believe in the power of this ideal. . . .

Dedication of a place can only be accomplished with a
sense of spiritual presence. We can build castles and
churches and magnificent palaces, but sometimes they are
cold and lifeless. No place is of any great interest or benefit to people unless it becomes living and vibrant; and we
make a place living by our own life, by our love and our
interest in humanity. . . .

I hope and pray that those who come within the radius of this work may be imbued with this spirit, and that
they may carry that message out into the world, because
the world needs it.

About the same time, he wrote the poem which became the
theme for the ashrama and was later inscribed in nine-inch letters on the Temple arcade:

Hold aloft this light and stand firm to thy post,
Till all wandering souls have reached their goal
    in safety.
Service brings strength and renewed life
Love cures all weariness,
And Faith, the shining jewel of life,
    performs all miracles.

Paramananda soon found that it was not easy for human
beings to "stand firm to their post." Aside from the staunch
nucleus of sisters, the personnel at the ashrama was constantly
shifting. Lester and Harold both left less than two months after
their arrival, Lester returning to Panama and Harold going back
to sea. The Fischers and the Nelsons, after six weeks of roughing
it, moved to a house in nearby Glendale. Mangala was away for
months at a time visiting her ailing mother in Monterey. In July,
1924, Mrs. Norton and Earl returned to the town they had come
from, leaving their livestock behind to supply the ashrama with

milk, cheese, butter, and eggs.

The saddest loss was Jack Miller. The first man to give himself wholeheartedly to the swami's work, Brother Jack, after a temporary rallying, again succumbed to tuberculosis. In March, 1924, he was moved to a private sanatorium in neighboring Tujunga, where the swami and sisters visited him regularly, always marvelling at his patient, undemanding, quietly joyful spirit. "Just when he felt he was most useless," Daya wrote, "he was doing the greatest possible service to us all, for he was showing us by his living example the true spirit of discipleship, unwavering faith, undaunted courage, marvelous patience and sweetness in the midst of pain and discouragement." His one sorrow was that he bitterly missed the daily worship services at the ashrama. Hearing of it, Sister Daya came every day and conducted a little service by his bed with the accustomed prayers, songs, and meditation. On July 24, 1924, he died.

"I sometimes feel the grief of others more than a mother feels for her only child," Paramananda told the community two days later. "That boy is closer to me than when he was in the flesh. He had given his best without demanding anything.

"It is one of the blessings of this work that we can feel the grief of the world. There is a great joy in it—the sweetness of pain. If you have a heart which is loving and vibrant, you will understand."

Despite his human sorrow, the swami's general feeling was that Jack was released from a broken body to a higher plane commensurate with his soul's lofty state.

Paramananda considered the ashrama a sanctuary for every animal, bird, and insect which happened to cross its boundaries, not to speak of human beings. Yet death seemed to stalk the ashrama that July. Less than two weeks before, a seven-year-old child drowned in the upper dam. Vernon DeHoog, his brother Norman, and their friend Harlem, who lived a short distance from the ashrama, had walked up the hill to watch the workmen on the tunnel. Coming back, they decided to take a dip in the upper pool. The cold mountain water cramped their muscles and Vernon and Norman sank into deep holes in the otherwise shallow pool. Harlem's shouts brought workmen, sisters, and swami. The workmen pulled the boys out and revived Norman. Sister Daya ran for a doctor and the fire department, who came speeding up the hill with a pulmotor. They tried every possible means to resuscitate little Vernon, but, even as the sisters gathered hurriedly in prayer and the swami stood over him in ardent supplication, the boy died. "I do not know how I seem on the outside," Paramananda told the sisters later, "but I think no one would suspect how I feel inside—all bleeding and weeping."

The swami felt that, as always, subtle realities were behind the gross manifestations, that the community's own failings had opened the way for such a tragedy to happen on the sacred precincts of the ashrama:

> We must learn from this that all of us must live in such harmony and rhythm that there will be no possibility for such happening as this. Freedom from all inharmony will create a natural protection all about the ashrama. . . . Things do not happen by accident. They always happen through some very good reason, and we should be just like sentinels, protecting the sacredness of this place. If you can all be so absolutely full of prayer and sacred feelings at all hours of the day and night, no evil could ever trespass the threshold of the ashrama's life.

Paramananda was discovering that the ashrama's wide spaces and wild naturalness, which had originally drawn him, also had their drawbacks. The Santa Ana wind proved as destructive as the former caretaker had warned; it periodically swept the property, breaking limbs, uprooting trees, snapping the cement pillars of the rose arbor, and decimating the grapevines. Skunks and coyotes broke into the chicken coops and killed the chickens. Frequent brush fires on the surrounding hills perpetually menaced the ashrama grounds. On Christmas Day, 1925, the first fire on the property broke out and destroyed an acre of brush. The next day a blaze consumed one of the cabins.

The forces of nature and human nature—both seemed unmanageable in the vastness of the ashrama. "I sometimes feel that I have undertaken too much, too great a responsibility," Paramananda told the community during that tragic summer of 1924. "My body will not stand it. My buoyant nature is decreasing and I feel the burden. . . . My grip and strength shake a great deal these days.

"You must all help. Do not yield to your emotions and human feelings. Impatience or when any of you holds unkind or resentful feelings against another means that you have not the proper feeling for me. I do not always speak of these things, but it is not because I am not conscious of them. Use your will power to overcome these moods. Make a vow to yourself that you will rise above them. . . . Have I spent all these years gathering material that is worthless? You all have great worth. You would not be here otherwise."

In the Boston house togetherness was easy, inescapably so. When the chimes sounded for service, everyone gathered from the different rooms where they were working, and no one was ever more than a shout away. Life spread out over 140 acres, on the other hand, conduced to disunity. While clearing brush in the hills, the sisters and the brothers found it easy to skip midday service, or to have no idea when it was being held. Meals were similarly elusive. Ever reluctant to impose outer regimens, Paramananda repeatedly appealed to his community to establish their own unified program: "I plead and pray that you all join efforts and establish certain regularity in all the routine of the ashrama life. This will please me more than anything else."

The greatest problem during those first years was lack of manpower. Paramananda had wanted every project on the ashrama to be done as a labor of love, just as devout volunteers had raised the Gothic cathedrals of Europe. He was disappointed to have to hire men to build the cloister, develop the water supply, and do the heavy chores around the place. "What is the matter with American men?" he wrote in May, 1925. "There must be some who have nobility of purpose and true manhood. I pray that He may send us a few for this great work."

Two weeks later they started to come. Walter Kissam, Sister Satya Prana's middle-aged nephew, believed in community, but not in God. True to his claim not to exclude any sincere soul, Paramananda accepted Mr. Kissam as a member of the community. "The Godly Atheist," as they called him, never attended a service, but he was a loyal member, a skilled worker, and an amiable personality. An electrical engineer, he proved invaluable when they finally brought electricity to the ashrama in 1926. Later he hooked up an intercom system which connected all the far-flung buildings. He was also an adept cabinet maker, and constructed the community's custom furnishings, such as long dining tables and a loom for weaving.

William Verbeck, with his brother and sister-in-law, attended the Sunday services for a few months and then asked to join the community. A melancholy, artistic young man, whose repeated threats to commit suicide were taken less seriously with each passing year, Willie did woodwork and odd jobs around the ashrama. A Mr. Patterson also moved into the ashrama during this period.

With the aid of these and other willing men in the congregation, who often came up to help on Saturdays, Paramananda's dreams could more readily be implemented. For example, during one of his first hikes on the property, Paramananda had discovered a secluded ravine, shaded by great oak trees and sycamores, enclosed on all sides by sage-covered hills. He envisioned it as a perfect open-air temple. Almost two years later he decided that the ashrama's second anniversary service should be celebrated in this natural sanctuary.

With two men to help him, starting only ten days before the celebration, he marked out a trail, determined the necessary filling and leveling of the canyon bed, cleared the brush, and pruned the trees, climbing them to cut off a protruding branch or tear down a rat's nest. The day before the anniversary a dozen volunteers joined them. They cleared a wide trail to the site, cut steps in the hard soil of the bank, leveled the canyon floor, and then spread a carpet of small, dry live-oak leaves. Walter Kissam made a rustic gate for the entrance; Amala carved a sign, "Open-Air Temple"; one man built redwood benches; Mr. Doble constructed a platform; the swami gathered the young sycamores that had been cut down and made of them a backdrop for the altar. The next morning the sisters wove garlands of wild flowers and hung them on this rustic reredos. A jubilant Paramananda directed all the activity, feeling vindicated to see that it really could work, that with true spirit of service and co-operation, it all really could work. . . .

Paramananda's gentle nature did not mean that he was a lenient supervisor. On the contrary, a perfectionist with infinite ideas can be a demanding leader for whom to work. One evening after Paramananda had arrived at the ashrama from Boston, Mr. Kissam quipped: "Swami has been here only a few hours, and he has already laid down work for me for six months." Sister Devamata proudly pointed to the swami's "extraordinary record of large books put through the press in two weeks, a number of the monthly magazine prepared and published in five days, successful entertainments organized in a few hours or important enterprises set on foot overnight." One can imagine that not all his workers shared her admiration.

Nor would he allow slipshod performances. He watched his workers with a vigilant eye, correcting them on minutiae that they themselves would not have noticed. Once Cunard Nelson was helping to clean up after a public luncheon. As he removed an oil cloth from one of the tables, he heard the swami over his shoulder tell him, "Mr. Nelson, be careful. Don't roll that oil cloth too much. It will crack." With another worker who took care of the grounds, Paramananda made a game of grading him for his work, an A for this, a B for that. One day a small tree needed pruning. Having no proper shears with him, Mr. Belcher used a small, dull axe that was handy, and mangled the tree. When Paramananda saw it, he commented, "I'm afraid I'll have to give you a minus Z for that job."

One of the most industrious volunteer helpers was George Weigand, the thirty-four-year-old foreman of the Pasadena Ice Company. George was more interested in socialism than religion, but something had drawn him up to the ashrama for a Sunday service. Once he heard the swami speak, he kept on coming. Softhearted and tender on the inside, disguised by a gruff exterior which children and animals immediately saw through, he attracted them like a cross between the Pied Piper and Will Rogers. Sometimes he would shyly leave his own home-baked pies and cakes in the ashrama kitchen, then quickly disappear. Once Hilda spotted him slipping out the kitchen door and called after him, "Oh, Mr. Weigand! Please thank your wife for the pies." He turned and glowered at her: "I ain't got no wife."

Indeed, he was free, free to spend his vacation at the ashrama in September, 1924. Hailing from a Kansas farm, George was a skilled dairyman, mason, mechanic, and builder. His presence that September was particularly timely. Paramananda had designed a two-story, fifteen-room guesthouse to accommodate the many visitors who came to the ashrama from all over the country. News of the unique retreat in the Sierra Madre foothills had spread through the swami's tours, the *Message of the East*, and the network of Vedanta followers stretching from San Francisco to New York. Some who made the pilgrimage roughed it in the ashrama cabins, others stayed in nearby hotels. Two days after George Weigand arrived for his vacation, he, the swami, and Mr.

Kissam started clearing brush from the site chosen for the new Community House on a knoll three hundred yards below the Cloister.

On Thursday morning, September 24, George returned to his job at the Pasadena Ice Company. All he could think about was the ashrama. On Friday afternoon he drove up to La Crescenta and announced to the swami that he had obtained a two-month leave of absence in order to supervise the construction of the guesthouse. Forty-two years later Brother George was still supervising at the ashrama.

While the Community House was under construction, another facet of Paramananda's dream was realized. He launched the arts and crafts department with incense making, teaching the sisters how to mold incense in the Indian fashion using sandalwood oil mixed with herbs they gathered from the ashrama hills. Seva and Achala packaged the incense in paper boxes which they made and hand-lettered, "Ashrama Incense."

Shortly after moving to the ashrama, Sister Devamata had bought drawing pads for Amala and Jack. Amala evinced real artistic talent, which the swami was quick to encourage. With the opening of the art department, Amala tooled leather bookmarks and bookcovers and illuminated Paramananda's poems on parchment and bookmarks, being taught by a new member of the community, Concorde Brodeur.

In her late twenties, Concorde was an attractive, charming, French-Canadian divorcée, with gay humor and unlimited talents. She sang, played guitar and mandolin, sewed expertly, wove ultrafine cloth, did calligraphy, painted, and was an experienced nurse, cook, and housekeeper. Those in the community who had a tendency to be jealous found ample opportunity with Concorde.

The other addition to the group in 1925 was Alice Affsprung (Vimala), who, after her many extended visits to the Boston Centre from Cincinnati, finally left her husband a note on the kitchen table and moved to the ashrama. With her degree in music and accomplished skill as an organist, she extended the ashrama's artistic prospects to another area.

Not all of Paramananda's dreams materialized. He spoke of a fully equipped publication house with printing press and bindery, but their little press, moved from Boston, printed only cards and pamphlets, while the *Message* and the swami's books continued to be produced outside. Blueprints were drawn up and approved for the intended large auditorium and library, and Paramananda proudly exhibited parchment drawings of it in Cincinnati and Boston. The building was never constructed.

The probable impediment was lack of funds. The water development, including thousands of feet of pipe, had cost $10,000. Construction of the Cloister and Community House, plus mortgage payments for the property and salaries for hired men, had exhausted most of Sister Devamata's legacy. Two extra years of paying mortgages and heating bills for the sprawling Queensberry Street house, followed by meager, sporadic payments from the Home of Truth, left Paramananda with little capital to purchase the new house on Marlboro Street. Besides, his many charities in India depended on his regular drafts.

In mid-1925, the dreamer Paramananda suddenly woke up to his critical financial plight. From Boston he wrote to the ashrama:

> I do not think I have ever been through such a situation as I am facing now in all my experiences in this country for last nineteen years. Ashrama has been a very great financial drain for last two years. We have spent money ruthlessly and extravagantly, but the situation must be saved. It will require all my personal attention, courage, and full cooperation from every one of you. I feel that I have been 'napping' a little too long and no person in my position has any right to be 'napping.' Of course this constant going back and forth has kept me very much unsettled. No work can succeed with only visionary ideas. It requires practical wisdom and selfless devotion. This rare combination in a

character makes one invincible. It is not enough to make
up a budget of what we are going to expend, but [also]
how wisely we may obtain it. We must increase our resource-
fulness and to this end I hope to work next few months.

The weight of responsibility hung heavily on what had been
a light-stepping and buoyant nature. "If I could only give up
being a leader," he often told them, "what a relief it would be to
me." The usually joyful Paramananda periodically had experienced bouts of waning enthusiasm and withdrawal from people
and activities. These states had always dissipated in a few weeks,
but during 1925 he seemed to be increasingly swathed in a
cloud of depression which his inherent mirth only occasionally
pierced.

In January he wrote from St. Louis, "Here I am again in this
dirty city, gloomy even with the sunshine. . . . My heart is very
far from all this public work and its artificiality and it is quite
possible that I may suspend it for a time if it is His will."

Apparently it was not His will, for the demand for Paramananda
as a lecturer only increased. From New York, where an enthusiastic
audience drew him for weekly lectures and classes, he wrote:
"Life is a funny thing. Whenever I try to cut down all my activities and retire to the background, I am pushed more to the
foreground than ever." He complained of feeling weary, uninspired,
lacking in his usual vigor, eroded by physical and mental strain.

True to his own teaching, he did not allow himself to be
utterly submerged in this malaise. Again and again he roused
himself to his accustomed state of lightness and humor. From the
train speeding through Kansas, he wrote a typically playful letter
about the hailstorm he had just seen, estimating the hailstones
to be a "couple of pound apiece." Then he went on tongue-in-
cheek: "I wonder if I ought to send such jumble to such a holy
and saintly household. I sincerely hope that the saints will see
through my motive and not be bed-ridden with shock. Why! this

letter was meant for the 'hail' and hearty only and I thought I had a great deal to say on the subject."

But he could not shake the shadow of suffering which seemed to be pursuing him. A fortnight later he wrote from Boston:

> Two days ago I felt like a "man of sorrows" overwhelmed with the suffering of the world. Galene has brought to my notice especially these last days so many cases of helplessness and suffering. There is a woman from Chicago poor and destitute and she thinks "that Swami can do anything for her if he would only lift his hand in blessing." My heart was very sad over her, but Galene told me last night that she has got a position now, the best one so far. I hope she can keep it. Other day I felt so keenly, that I was almost reluctant to eat while there was so much suffering in the world. I know that such impulse is foolish and yet I would not be without it.

He continued to cherish his dream for the ashrama: "What a tremendous vista of creative usefulness it opens before those who are not overcome by fever of selfishness. . . . 'Hold aloft this light and stand firm till all wandering souls have reached their goal.' This is not preaching or teaching, but a burning flame, a constant passion of my soul."

Still, a strange detachment had crept over him. He told his disciples one day:

> I am just at the breaking point, losing my temper, and it is not natural for me. Your earthly feelings cannot hold me — tears, love, etc. — anymore than those things held me before. You do not know me. I am gentle and full of love and compassion, but there is another side you do not know. . . . I was too bound, too attached to a place, to an institution, to people, and my soul must be freed from it. . . .
>
> Let this house represent the highest Ideal, or don't let it exist at all. I don't want any success here unless it is through Divine will. If it is His work, none can thwart it.

You will have a lot of difficulties, a lot of financial struggle, but if it is His work, let it be. If not, the sooner it goes, the better. I will be freed.

In autumn he received a notice that the first convention of the Ramakrishna Math and Mission would be held in Calcutta during Easter week, 1926. It was fourteen years since he had seen his motherland. He suddenly announced that he was going to India, and he could not say when he would return.

The community was stunned and distraught. Achala, Hilda, Amala, and others feared that he would never come back. He had to reassure them: "This does not mean I am withdrawing to the extent that I am abandoning you all. . . . This is the time for every one of you to prove your real worth, that is all." He wrote a letter to them in October and signed it, "I am ever yours, bound for life and maybe longer and forever, Paramananda."

It was as if the wounds of the last three years had gouged a channel to his inmost self and the essence of the man stood nakedly revealed. In his farewell to the ashrama, given in the newly dedicated Community House on the Sunday after Christmas, 1925, he delivered an address which he called, "My Message to You." In it he summed up everything he had tried to impart during his nineteen years in America. There was barely a dry eye among the 225 people in the room.

As I turn over page after page of my book of life, filled for the last nineteen years with the most intense activity, I find but one thought in all that I have done, but one thing that comes before me with vivid, glowing reality, and that is: the heart of humanity. If I could put my finger on any one thing as being fundamental, as being the essence of what I have tried to convey to you through all these years of preaching, I think that would be the gist of it. . . .

How do we know that God exists? How do we know that He is all-loving and beneficent? We know it because we see these attributes exhibited in men's lives, in charac-

ters which have been blended with that eternal Principle.
That to me is the sum and substance of religion.

Peculiar phases of religious development, mysteries
and complicated matters, these do not interest me in the
least, but there is a way of reaching the heart of humanity,
and we must find it. First, however, we must reach our
own depths. . . . We may preach to others and try to convert them, but do you suppose we can ever really convince anyone until we have awakened in our own soul
such ardour for the spiritual Principle that we can convey
it without a word?

If I have given any message with special insistence, it is
that people may know their own worth. . . . Whenever
we have occasion to touch a life, some struggling and des-
pondent soul, and can awaken and quicken in that soul a
ray of hope, we have done our part. Whether that soul is
true to us, or turns to something else, should not be our
concern. The great Lao Tze once said something very wise.
He said: "When you have done good work and another
has benefited by it, why do you look for the third thing as
the fools do?" That is one of the greatest lessons I have
learned through life, and today as I am about to depart I
want to share it with you.

People often have said to me, "Why do you not do
more public work?" The dewdrop that falls upon the
flower bud, so gentle, so unostentatious, is symbolic of
spiritual work. It does not make any noise, but it opens
and brings forth a blossom. Is it not sufficing for the dewdrop to know that it had a part to play in the blossoming
of a flower? It may sound abstract to you yet it contains the
secret of life. . . .

I am powerless to express all that I should like to express;
but this I must say to you, and it is the greatest tribute I
can pay you: I have lived with you here in a country which
ordinarily I might consider as alien; yet I have never had
that consciousness, that word is not in my vocabulary. I

have moved freely both here and in Europe, and it has been my special privilege to feel in return a kinship, a friendship which is more than friendship, which is a soul relationship. That this instinct may be awakened in mankind is my greatest hope and prayer. To that end this place has been established. That to me is life, philosophy, and religion. . . .

We have, each one of us, our part to play in human destiny, and if we are fulfilling our part, that much of the world will be made better because of our existence, because of our love. If instead of holding the sordid idea that the world is all wrong and that we cannot and should not trust our fellows because they are full of evil, if instead of that we began to believe men to be better than they seem, and to trust them because fundamentally they are children of God, would it not transform life for us and for them?

Let us all rise with prayer in our soul, with love in our whole being, that through our intensity of feeling, we may feel the Presence of that great Reality and we may learn to convey it to others. Oh, let us give our heart and soul and body and mind to that One from Whom we have received the blessing of life. Let us withhold nothing, so that we may be sanctified, that we may be purified and inspired to do His will.

On January 9, 1926, leaving a trail of poignant farewells behind him in California, Cincinnati, Boston, and New York, Swami Paramananda, accompanied by Mrs. Cara French, an old Vedanta student from San Francisco, sailed for India. From the ship he wrote to his beloved ashrama: "May you all live each day to glorify Him. Through your selfless devotion I am so bound to you that distance cannot diminish it nor can this separation prevail against it. I am bound to you through love, that gentle word, but strongest of all fetters."

13

"Love Will Conquer"

PARAMANANDA returned to an India different from the one which had nurtured him. Most of the great souls, the shining lights which had kindled his spiritual consciousness, were missing. Not only Swami Brahmananda, but the Holy Mother, Swami Premananda, Swami Turiyananda, Girish Ghosh, and most of the other direct disciples of Sri Ramakrishna were gone. It was symbolic that the first convention of the Ramakrishna Math and Mission was being held; what had been a fellowship of spiritual geniuses had turned into an organization.

The eager boy who had sat at the feet of the great masters was now himself one of the senior swamis of the Ramakrishna Order. Paramananda, at forty-two, had twenty-five years' tenure in the Order and the status of a celebrity. For years members and friends of the Mission had been reading reports of his exploits in the *Message of the East* and in the Order's Indian magazines. Two flourishing centers, a large and dedicated American following, and an international reputation as a lecturer and author had brought him great prestige in India. When Swami Paramananda, accompanied by Mrs. French, docked at Bombay on February 12, 1926, the shy young monks who waited on the pier to greet him held their offerings of garlands in sweating hands.

They both expected and feared that Paramananda had been spoiled by the West and his own fame. The enigmatic figure who appeared before them, dressed in a Western clerical suit, a turban, and an Indian shawl, did nothing to assuage their suspicions. Only later, in the ashram on the outskirts of the city, did he prove himself one of them. As Swami Yatiswarananda, the head of the monastery, wrote to Ananda Ashrama:

> Some of the members here at first thought that the Swami might feel some discomfort in our simple and small monastery, so very different from yours at La Crescenta. But to the surprise of these and the delight of all, he began to move about like one of the inmates from the very first moment of his arrival. He became in dress and other things the old Hindu monk again.

Wherever Paramananda went, during his week in Bombay, his months in Calcutta, and his visit to Delhi, the swamis and devotees scrutinized his every move and gesture, anxious to see if the years of adulation had corrupted the inner man. Mrs. French wrote: "There are many watching everything he does or says: his manner; his dress; how many suitcases he had and what they contain . . . They have been appraising him with closest scrutiny."

In each place he visited, he was showered with public addresses of welcome, garlands, and fruit offerings, and besieged with invitations to speak. For a public reception held in Calcutta in honor of "His Holiness Srimat Swami Paramananda," odes to him were printed in three languages. The reception committee itself consisted of more than sixty high-ranking citizens, magistrates, professors, and gentry.

He intrigued them. His youthful appearance, a topic of speculation among his American audiences, seemed to belie his twenty-five years in the Order. His manner of public speaking was casual, even intimate, compared with the orators they were used to hearing. He would mingle with the people as if he were one of them, and not the famous personage he was.

Reclining beside one of the chapels on the Belur Math grounds one day, Paramananda overheard two swamis conversing around the corner of the building.

"Have you seen Paramananda yet?" asked one of the swamis.

"No, I am afraid to," replied the other.

"Don't be," remarked the first. "He is just the same."

Swami Virajananda, the foremost disciple of Swami Vivekananda and a future President of the Math, wrote to Sister Devamata about Paramananda:

> I cannot tell you how delighted I was to meet him at the Math after nearly twenty-two years, and I found him as sweet and loving as before, as childlike and unassuming as was always his nature when he was unknown to fame and honour. Just as years have lightly touched him, so have name, fame and affluence.

All the swamis who had known Basanta, Ramakrishnananda's gentle protégé, found him unchanged by his years in the luxurious West. Some of the younger swamis, however, watched him being driven around Calcutta in the shiny Rolls Royce made available to him by the Countess of Sandwich, the niece of his old friend Josephine MacLeod, and wondered.

One of them, Swami Vijayananda, remarked critically to Mrs. French: "You know, when they come back from the West, we watch them: Bodhananda, Abhedananda, Prakashananda, Paramananda. We count the luggage. Abhedananda — so many pieces! Paramananda — oh, he is *all* gone!"

Paramananda had returned to India with the avowed intention of restoring his shattered health, but from the very beginning the trip proved counterproductive. On the first leg of the sea voyage he had become so sick that, arriving in London, he was unable to make the connection for the India-bound steamer. Only after ten days in bed and the extraction of a wisdom tooth was he able to continue the journey.

Shortly after his arrival in India, the stifling summer heat descended. Recurrently Paramananda fell ill; for days at a time he lived on nothing but fruit juice. Meanwhile, the demands on his time and energy were incessant. "Everyone hanging around him, and he gets no rest," declared the attendant assigned to him when Paramananda succumbed to a serious siege.

During a week's visit to Delhi, where one day he had engagements consecutively for eight hours, Paramananda himself wrote: "I have been kept constantly busy here ever since my arrival, and now the invitations are pouring in from different parts. . . . There is really nothing radically wrong about me except a very over-tired body and it is impossible to get any rest here in India. They are quite ready to kill me with kindness."

Mrs. French described how one Monday afternoon in March an urgent request was delivered to Paramananda to address the Vivekananda Society in Calcutta that evening. Feeling feverish, he declined, but, several other speakers having cancelled on them, the messenger begged Paramananda to reconsider. Finally he acquiesced. When Mrs. French joined them at the ferry landing, she noticed that Paramananda looked pale and nauseated. During the boat ride across the river, he chatted cheerfully with his escorts, but while they waited for a taxi on the other side, she saw him furtively step aside and vomit. Apologizing, he rejoined the group, and they continued to the meeting.

One of Paramananda's principal ideas in coming to India was to find one or two qualified assistants for his work. Both the New York and San Francisco centers had assistant swamis, and for years the superiors at Belur had been urging him to accept a helper for his strenuous undertakings.

Before Paramananda's departure from New York, an influential Indian friend, the head of a couple of large Hindu cultural associations, had encouraged him not to restrict his search to the Ramakrishna Order. The gentleman was disappointed in too many of the swamis who had come to the United States, for while they were intelligent and well-versed in the philosophy, they lacked the charisma and enthusiasm to spread Vedanta as Paramananda was doing. Paramananda, on his part, had in mind his own special requirements: idealism, simplicity, flexibility, and a willingness to fit into his established community. He would take whoever met his standard, in the Order or outside it, man or woman. "I do not care which sex—whether man or woman!" he declared, and added: "This is woman's age."

Wherever Paramananda went, at every meeting, conclave, and reception, he scoured the group for the person who he felt would be compatible with his work and his methods. Weeks passed and he found not a single candidate who met his requirements, except his niece Savitri, a brilliant and gifted young woman full of idealistic zeal, who was already married and therefore unable to follow him.

When he returned to Calcutta from Delhi, he was met at the station by two monks from the Math and his brother Bibhu Charan. Bibhu Charan had with him two of his daughters, Maitreyee and Gayatri, whose marriage Paramananda had tried to stop three years before. Now nineteen years old, Gayatri made an uncanny impression on Paramananda's mind. A few days later he disclosed to Bibhu Charan: "Gayatri's eyes haunt me."

Despite the censure of his scrutinizers, Paramananda spent much time in Bibhu Charan's rented Calcutta house, where the meals were cooked specifically for his indisposition. During these visits he could not help but notice Gayatri's aptness. She knew Sanskrit (the language of India's scriptures) and could speak, read, and write English. An inveterate idealist, she had gone around in homespun saris, five inches too short for her lanky frame, in support of Gandhi's boycott against British cloth. Material possessions and married life seemed to hold little interest for her, though she dutifully did what was expected of her. Her husband had fallen gravely ill with meningitis just before Paramananda's arrival in India, so she spent most of her time nursing him.

Paramananda felt a deeply rooted bond with Gayatri, akin to what he had intuited upon meeting Daya and others of his disciples. "She might have been my daughter, had I not become a monk," he confided to Mrs. French. One day Gayatri and Maitreyee were serving lunch to the swami and Bibhu Charan. After the meal, when Bibhu Charan and Maitreyee briefly stepped out of the room, Paramananda looked directly at Gayatri and said, "You know, you belong to me." The girl was struck speechless.

In March Paramananda made a week's visit to Dacca. When he returned to Belur, Mrs. French told him of rumors that the Math authorities had assigned a new assistant swami to San Francisco and were about to select one for him also. "It is being settled for you," she remarked. Paramananda replied dryly, "I may have something to say about it."

The Convention of the Ramakrishna Math and Mission began on April 1. Paramananda was accorded the privilege of reading the President's address on behalf of the frail and aged Swami Shivananda, Brahmananda's successor. On the fifth day of the Convention, Paramananda addressed a public meeting of a thousand people on the ideals of Sri Ramakrishna and Vivekananda. "Ye, the young of the country," he implored, "recognize the Swami [Vivekananda] in his full color and follow him with fervor, enthusiasm, and selfless devotion. This is the morning of your life, and, in the words of Sri Ramakrishna, butter churned in the early morning is always best. Do not trouble your head with intricate theological discourses and perorations; the vital truths are as clear as daylight. Feel an impetus from within. . . . From intense feeling will come all the strength you require."

He concluded by quoting Swami Vivekananda's appeal: "The world is burning in misery. Can ye sleep, ye heroes? What the world wants today is twenty men and women who can stand in the street yonder and say that they possess nothing but God. Who will go?"

Indeed, "Who will go?" had become the gnawing problem for Paramananda. Young swamis of the Order poured into Belur for the Convention, and there were one or two whom he "was watching," but in general he was disappointed with their lack of simplicity, idealism, and spiritual ardor. He sensed in these young men, most of them university graduates, a worldly-wise sophistication, a tepid conventionality, a preoccupation with forms and structures which seemed to obscure the essence of what Sri Ramakrishna and Swami Vivekananda had come to teach.

Indeed, three years later a group of these young swamis launched a mutiny against the venerable authorities at Belur, shaking the Order to its very foundations and eventually seceding from it. When one loyal swami wrote to Paramananda, plaintively asking why such felony and treachery should be factionalizing their sacred brotherhood, Paramananda revealed to him what he had observed in silence while in India:

> I am opening my heart to you, brother, because you have asked me sincerely why such things are taking place. . . . Where are the noble, holy and consecrated ideals which must inspire every Sadhu? Can ambition and power, cleverness and intrigue, make up for our soul impoverishment? Can back-biting, slander, gossip, idleness, help but undermine the very foundation even of the strongest structure?

Gayatri's husband died during Paramananda's stay in India. Seeing her in tears, Paramananda asked her, "Are you going to cry, just like any ordinary girl?" Gayatri quickly dried her eyes. Indeed, in this delicate, intense young woman, charged with inner fire, Paramananda saw depths of promise for the ideals he cherished. The ardent fifteen-year-old who had tried to rebel against the societal mill which churned every female into a wife and mother had been subdued, nearly stifled. But beneath the diffident exterior, Paramananda sensed a spirit capable of the ultimate dedication. Every quality he craved to elicit from his

struggling community—gentleness, joyousness, serenity, love—
he discerned embryonic within her. Even her exacting nature
and strong will needed only purpose and direction to become a
powerful force in the Lord's service. When he looked at Gayatri
he did not see his niece nor a young Hindu widow; he saw a
vision of her soul unfolded. Here at last was his ultimate dream,
not a panorama of hills and canyons, but a vista of human
possibility, an infinite potential poised to blossom.

Upon her husband's death, Gayatri's status in Indian society
became the pitiful position of a childless widow: prohibited from
ever remarrying, confined for life to drab garb and diet, and
thrust upon the charity and domination of her husband's family,
to whom she technically belonged. Bibhu Charan was beside
himself at the prospect of his daughter's bleak future. "You are
doing penance for your parents' sin," he cried, remembering
how he had pushed her into the marriage.

The solution was obvious to all of them; the girl's unan-
swered letter and the swami's unheeded telegram were finally
finding their fulfillment. She was free to follow him if she dared.
Her final obstacle was her scruples over leaving her mourning
in-laws, who claimed her as their own. Her husband's father
harshly accused her of faithlessness should she even consider
abandoning them. After five weeks of vacillation, no less harrowing
for Paramananda than for the young widow, Gayatri made her
decision. On May 2, 1926, Swami Paramananda, Gayatri Devi,
Mrs. French, Swami Dayananda, who was bound for San Francisco,
and Swami Akhilananda, who had been assigned as Paramananda's assistant, sailed for America via the Pacific.

Paramananda immediately began Gayatri's training, which
he called his "special work." To develop her English aptitude and
her appreciation of Christianity, he had her read aloud to him
from his book, *Christ and Oriental Ideals*. He described to her all
the members of the community, their strengths and their weak-
nesses, asking her to pray for each one. He thus inaugurated her

life of prayer and forestalled her critical tendency by making their foibles an object for her prayer rather than her derision.

According to Indian custom, she wore the plain white sari with narrow black border and partook of the strict vegetarian diet prescribed for a widow. Paramananda wanted her to feel that she was beginning a new life, without holding on to the trailing end of an old one. He encouraged her to eat fish and chicken, as he himself did, and one day, surveying her coarse white sari, remarked, "No one else would dare to travel with me in rags."

Gayatri was equally critical of the way Paramananda dressed. She had never seen a swami wearing Western clothes, fashionable knickers, and dapper suits. Nor did she understand or like his casual manner, his unorthodox habits. She remembered the day, shortly before their departure, when he had come to take her to the government offices for her visa. She had emerged from her house to find the swami seated in a Rolls Royce, singing to himself, "Ta, ta, my bonnie Maggie dar-r-rlin'," rolling his r's like a native of County Cork. Here on the boat, too, he sang a medley of curious songs in the latest Harry Lauder brogue. Gayatri expected swamis to chant Vedic hymns, not American pop tunes. While all her life she had dutifully respected and deferred to elders, Paramananda encouraged her now to express herself freely. She did. She fired her criticisms at him. Paramananda never restrained nor rebuked her.

He spoke to her in English; she stubbornly answered in Bengali. Only when they sailed into the chill air of the Malay States would she don the warm clothing, shoes, and stockings which he had purchased for her despite her protests that she would never wear them.

As outspoken as she was with the swami, among strangers she was shy, even timid. A nineteen-year-old girl for the first time out of her sheltered environment, she clung to Paramananda, becoming nervous whenever she was away from his presence.

Paramananda sensed this, and kept her with him as much as possible. Meanwhile, it seemed to Mrs. French and to Swami Akhilananda, a mild-mannered, good-natured monk of seven years, that Paramananda was squandering his time and attention on a pretty Indian girl, an inexplicable weakness.

One day in early June, they were descending the stairs to the dining hall from the upper deck. Paramananda slipped and fell, lacerating both shins even through his heavy socks. Fully believing that outer happenings were the manifestations of inner states, Gayatri felt certain that her critical, cutting attitude was the cause of the swami's injury. She took one look at the streaks of blood on Paramananda's delicate skin and her haughty heart melted within her.

Some seeds lie dormant on the forest floor for years, designed to sprout only when touched by fire. Her contrition at Paramananda's minor wounds was the fire which made the dormant seed within Gayatri's soul sprout. From that day, her spiritual consciousness grew and flourished. She resolved to try to understand and cooperate with her new teacher. As she observed him more closely, she noticed that the tongue which sang such frivolous tunes never uttered a harsh nor angry word, and that under the dapper suit beat a deeply dedicated heart. Soon she surrendered to him completely. When, fifty years later, Gayatri Devi published her autobiographical sketch, dedicated to "the one whose faith, love, and guidance made the dream of one small life come true," she could appropriately preface it with the quotation from Ruth: "Whither thou goest, I will go; where thou lodgest, I will lodge. Thy people shall be my people, and thy God, my God."

Aboard ship young Gayatri was not Paramananda's only critic. Even in India Mrs. French had begun to question Paramananda's ways. As she would be sitting on the verandah of the Belur Math guesthouse with Josephine MacLeod, Paramananda, bubbling over with childlike enthusiasm, would come to show them an album of Ananda Ashrama photographs, or would read to them his own poems. Was this not conceited? Why did he spend so much time at his brother's house? And on the train back in America, why did he wash his hands and don a glove before opening the door to the dining car on the way to dinner, whereas every other swami she had known disdained such pica-yune matters?

Mrs. French had come to India under awkward circumstances. A disciple of Swami Trigunatita, she was a devoted student of Swami Abhedananda during his years in San Francisco. It was Swami Abhedananda who wrote encouraging her to come to India to visit his Darjeeling ashrama. Having made one ten-day retreat at Ananda Ashrama, Mrs. French asked Paramananda's advice about going to India, and in response received an invita-tion to accompany him. When she reached Calcutta, she found that both Swami Abhedananda's Math and the Belur Math had arranged to accommodate her. She chose to stay at Belur, but was perplexed and uncomfortable whenever the mention of Swami Abhedananda's name evoked a stony silence. The shadow of this conflict hung over her Indian stay.

Much to her satisfaction, Paramananda had indicated that he had a place for her in his work, but when the time came to return to America, she was disappointed at having to leave with-out seeing the rest of India. She had not even managed to get to Darjeeling. Disgruntled at having to tackle visa offices on behalf of Gayatri, she was offended when Paramananda reprimanded her for telling another swami that the decision for her to return to Ananda Ashrama was his, not hers. Aboard ship, Mrs. French was ill part of the time from poor accommodations, which she blamed on Paramananda, and was vexed by Gayatri's persistent monopolizing of the swami, whose "tenaciously eager plans" for his niece bored her. Nor could she understand why Swami Ak-hilananda and Swami Dayananda were travelling second class when the rest of them were travelling first class, nor why Paramananda gave so little time to the two younger swamis. She developed a warm friendship with Swami Akhilananda, who she felt had taken these slights with admirable equanimity.

In trying to understand spiritual figures who claim to be guided by an almost prophetic intuition, it is tempting to use the future to explain the past. Gayatri would indeed become Paramananda's lifelong helper and eventual successor, while the quiet Swami Akhilananda would threaten the very solidarity of his work, but were these the cause or the result of Paramananda's differential treatment? Whatever the case, by the time they docked in San Francisco harbor on June 18, 1926, the alliances—and enmities—of the future were already forged.

Paramananda returned to an ashrama riddled with discord and factionalized by cliques. The new Community House, which he had so lovingly designed and dedicated, had turned into a nest of sedition, fomenting criticism against the ashrama, against the sisterhood and brotherhood, and against the swami himself. The Community House was occupied by Mrs. Jewell, Mrs. Oliver, Alice Affsprung, Melissa and Edwin Phillips, an elderly couple who had come from Vermont to join the community, and Mr. and Mrs. Allan, long-time Vedanta students from San Francisco who had begun paying week-long visits to the ashrama shortly after its founding, and who had moved into the guesthouse in April, 1926. Mrs. Allan was the chief instigator of the discontent which, as Paramananda put it, was like a drop of poison added to a bowl of fresh, pure milk. Her insidious criticisms poisoned other minds which were "fresh, full of faith and consecration." The sisters and brothers in turn were indignant and resentful against their critics. While some passively turned their backs, others lashed out in counterattacks, not realizing that the swami himself would be the victim.

On Saturday morning, one week after his return, Paramananda called together the ashrama members. "I must confess," he told them, "I have felt the broken harmony since I returned. It has not been a very lovely home-coming for me for that reason.

"If you become instrumental in building up something, everything pertaining to it becomes part of your own life, almost a part of your flesh, and if anything happens to any of its parts, you feel it intensely. And that is exactly the way I feel, and I am speaking right out of my heart. If there is any shadow of unhappiness, lack of peace, it is not a question of what causes it, but I feel it just as intensely as you feel it if someone cuts your flesh, causing a wound, and I suffer intensely whenever any such thing happens.

"This work, as you know, is my very life to me, because I have put the very best efforts of my life into it, and my whole zeal is to always maintain its standard. So that if there is anything at anytime, any unhappiness, any shadow, I feel it intensely.

"I have called you because I have great love for every one of you, whether you can understand its measure or not. I believe love will conquer your ills. If there is anything, any ill, real love will conquer it, heal it, restore you. And this whole work is based on that. It is not an experiment with me. For over nineteen years I have been blessed and privileged to carry on a work, and there has never been any dissension. . . .

"Criticism is a good thing if it is constructive. Otherwise, it is hideous; otherwise it means a wagging, idle tongue. I fight with the armour of love. Tolerance is a beautiful thing, but it does not mean compromise. Untruth and truth do not blend together. . . . We cannot be namby-pamby when situations arise. We have to face them."

Paramananda was forever quoting Jesus' injunction: "Resist not evil, but overcome same by good." Now he was determined that the ill will undermining the ashrama could be overcome, not by counter harshness nor by passivity, but by a more zealous adherence to his cherished panacea, love. He charged his monastic workers to meet every critical onslaught with a vigorous reprisal of unstinting love.

Unfortunately, this factionalism was Swami Akhilananda's introduction to the ashrama. He was housed in a two-room suite in the Community House. Mrs. French was also given a room there and the assignment to look after his quarters, laundry, etc.

Ten days after returning, Paramananda left for Boston, taking Gayatri with him. Akhilananda found himself like a spare part introduced into an already adequately functioning machine. Upon Paramananda's departure, Sister Devamata, as she had done for many years, took over the daily worship in the shrine, and for the first week Sister Daya resumed her conducting of the public services and classes. This infuriated Mrs. French, who felt that both positions should be relinquished to Swami Akhilananda. She bristled to see him, as she put it, "treated just as any ordinary student, with no special consideration." When she undertook to make the new swami a robe for lecturing, she was supplied with cheap material and a nightshirt pattern used for Swami Paramananda by which to cut it. The sisters, in their turn, were displeased by Swami Akhilananda's attitude toward their leader and themselves. Commenting on the new-comer in her diary, Amala wrote: "He did not talk with respect to our beloved Paramananda. Swami Akhilananda seemed to think that we do not know anything."

In the Community House, on the other hand, as Mrs. French recorded, "Swami Akhilananda was placed at the head of our table and the honor due was paid to him." Several residents asked him to conduct an early morning worship in the shrine of the Community House before the established service in the Cloister, and Swami Akhilananda obliged. The Community House faction had found their leader.

Soon Swami Akhilananda was given charge of the Sunday service and one of the weekly classes. Academic and scholarly, his presentation of Vedanta differed considerably from Paramananda's. For the class he chose as his text the Bhagavad Gita,

using the translation by Swami Swarupananda rather than Paramananda's version, which was used daily by the community.
Such actions must not have endeared him to Paramananda's
loyal followers. The ashrama founder was absent barely a month,
but before he returned his quiet assistant took a stealthy, duplici-
tous step. He sent a letter, whose critical contents we can only surmise, to the head of the Order at Belur, making it appear as if Mrs.
French were the source. As Mrs. French recounted in her memoirs:

> One morning just as I was finishing the usual daily
> tasks in his rooms, Swami Akhilananda lowered the shades,
> then asked me to remain for a while and meditate with
> him. I complied; but my mind was very disturbed. Added
> too was the fear that prying eyes might report this—along
> with everything else—to the major-domo of the Ananda
> Ashrama.
>   Swami Akhilananda urged me to write to Swami Shi-
> vananda [the President of the Order]. How *can* I? What
> can I say to him? I asked in perplexity. So he bade me get
> my stationery: and word for word followed dictation. Then
> instead of placing it, addressed to Swami Shivananda, in
> the general mail, I walked down to the village and posted
> it myself.

Paramananda returned to Ananda Ashrama on July 29. Although he had originally intended to send Akhilananda to Boston
immediately, he now decided to keep the younger swami with
him for a few more months.

During Paramananda's six-month absence in India, the attendance at the public services and classes had plunged. After
his return it did not rise again. Sunday after Sunday during the
hot summer of 1926, the swami addressed meager congregations
of eighty or ninety. Always insistent that the work must be built
up from within, through the spiritual centeredness of the community, Paramananda launched the "ashrama summer school."
At 7:30 each morning, even before the regular service in the

shrine, the community would gather under the acacia tree beside the Cloister. Sitting cross-legged on the grass, they would listen to Paramananda expound the ideals from the *Book of Daily Thoughts and Prayers*, which Sister Devamata had compiled from his own utterances and published as a surprise for him during his trip to India. At noon they would again assemble, by the stone bench in the cool shade of the chapel garden, to hear the swami read and comment on the Dhammapada of Lord Buddha or the Upanishads. The last class, at four o'clock, used as a text the Bhagavad Gita, and flowed naturally into the evening worship performed in the shrine.

Despite this idyllic routine, this noble effort to permeate the atmosphere with lofty thoughts and teachings, Paramananda himself felt restless and overburdened. The maintenance of the ashrama, not only spiritually, but physically and financially, was a massive load which weighed on him even more than before his journey to India. "The estate we have here," he wrote to Swami Shivananda, "is really in many ways a princely estate, requiring a great deal of wealth to maintain it, and is really meant for a multimillionaire. Its present financial responsibilities probably exceed all our American Centres put together, and it does not seem to me a logical way to develop a spiritual work."

One Saturday evening that summer, Paramananda announced to the community that he was thinking of selling the ashrama and moving the whole work to India. He even dictated to Sister Achala the names of those who would be likely to go. A few of the sisters were thrilled at the prospect, others were alarmed, incredulous that he could actually consider giving up the place into which they had already poured so much effort and expense. A paradoxical detachment had taken hold of him. He loved the ashrama, its hills and canyons, the open-air temple, the quaint cloister, the imposing guesthouse, yet the sisters realized with horror that he was indeed capable of turning his back and, in the blink of an eye, walking away from it all.

In the months that followed, driven by an inner urge which never quite snapped into focus, Paramananda's dream shifted with the staccato abruptness of a slide show. The idea of moving to India was replaced by visions of a villa on the French Riviera, serving as a center for Vedanta in Europe. A fortnight later it was the Italian Riviera. Two months after that, Malaysia. He called in real estate agents to discuss the sale of the ashrama property, then thought of keeping just Quail Canyon and building a temple and a new house for workers there. Later, convinced that the present site was too far away from the public, he envisioned moving to a small estate in Pasadena, and even had one picked out. When the Boston Home of Truth continued to default on their payments for the Queensberry Street house, the swami toyed with the idea of repossessing it and returning the community to its original home. Again and again, he spoke of dropping everything and returning alone to India, then would reproach himself for faint-heartedness.

The future of the Boston work, where he went at intervals, spending three to six weeks at a time, was equally uncertain. The new home on Marlboro Street was proving unsatisfactory, too expensive and too much work for the skeleton crew which consisted of Sister Satya Prana, Galene, Dr. Belle, and Miss Lillian Engstrand, the thirty-six-year-old head nurse of Boston's Floating Hospital for Children, who had been attending the Centre's services for several years before she moved in in 1926. The work there had severely diminished, due to Paramananda's long and frequent absences and to lack of ardor among the workers. Galene, never reconciled to that interloper, the Ananda Ashrama, was seething with discontent; Sister Satya Prana, ever faithful and dependable, exuded no potent power of attraction; Dr. Belle was still her bland, phlegmatic self; and Lillian, a keen intellectual graduated from Johns Hopkins, alternated between tender devotion and agonizing skepticism.

In October, Sister Daya accompanied Paramananda, Gayatri,

and Miss Sherwood to Boston. She had to be in proximity to New York in order to confer about her play, *The Light of Asia*, which was about to be produced on the Broadway stage. Two weeks after their arrival, she wrote to Mary Lacy:

> The congregations here as in California are not picking up as they should do and I think it troubles Swami and depresses him. . . . Of course, Swami has withdrawn himself, he really is no longer here, and I am sure that is the reason why this time he feels a lack of vitality in the work. Boston is like a very sick child; she has had too many shocks, I suppose. Yet the feeling for Swami and the work is still here, very strong.
>
> About Swamiji—the same strange, restless mood is with him, perhaps even more intensely. It isn't a mood—something far deeper, the resistless urge of that Power which controls his life, and nothing can stand against it. On the train he said, "The same urge that brought me to America in the first place is now taking me back." He is not so depressed as he was at the Ashrama during the hay fever period but he is just as much withdrawn from this work. I cannot begin to tell you, however, how many times he speaks of the Ashrama and of the workers individually. For instance, he will say, "Just about now they are having service at the Ashrama," or "They must be having dinner now." . . . Sometimes I feel that I cannot bear to see him so tied down, especially when his heart, like a bird, is longing for freedom and the free spaces.
>
> I think we must make up our mind that Swami is going this time for a period of readjustment. He said the other day that he might be gone one year, he might be gone two years, but he had to get away and get his adjustment.

Lines from one of his poems confirm his feeling:

How oft I feel distressed and desolate.
Stranded and helpless I look for my course. . . .

Wilt Thou not show me mercy,
    Thou Friend of the lowly,
And halt Thy march a little moment?
Have pity on this poor pilgrim
And let him once worship Thy holy feet.

As he wrote, "only the trailing light" of the Lord's garment drew him on.

Occasionally, even during this period, Paramananda would pierce the clouds surrounding him with a ray of playfulness. Thus, he would close a serious letter to the ashrama: "As ever & ever & perhaps forever (if it is not too dull), Yours with love, Paramananda."

One day, Paramananda happened to pass the old St. Botolph Street studio, the first home of the Centre, and found it unoccupied. He came home brimming with glee at the possibility of moving back there and continuing the Boston work on a smaller, more manageable scale. Wrote Daya, "Swami is happy as a lark at the mere thought of this tremendous burden slipping off and says that now he begins to have renewed interest in the Boston work."

For some reason, the move was never made. The Centre remained on Marlboro Street for another difficult year. In late November, Paramananda called for Swami Akhilananda to come to Boston in order to conduct the services during his absences.

Throughout this turbulent time, Paramananda's greatest consolation was Gayatri. By her ingenuous, loving nature, she had endeared herself to the whole community. "There was about her a spontaneity, a freshness, a naturalness," testified Daya, who observed with admiration how the swami redirected "a certain self-will and tendency to rebellion on her part" into "high and constructive channels."

Although all her life Gayatri had been nicknamed "Burru" (old woman), because of a precocious depth and wisdom, at the ashrama she became transformed into "Baby" for everyone. She treated each of the sisters like a mother, calling Daya "Mâm" (meaning Mother), Achala, "Twin Mâm" (because she received the veil on the same day as Daya), and Mary Lacy, "Choto-Ma" (Little Mother). She lavished affection on all of them, sometimes flinging herself into Daya's arms with such zeal that she almost bruised her. From across the continent she wrote to Daya, with whom she felt a sacred bond:

> If all the thoughts and feelings that rise in your Baby's heart concerning yourself could be put on the paper, they will make a book, not a letter. Not a day goes by when I do not feel you in the depths of my heart and myself right in your bosom. . . . Things I cannot share with others, I send you in silence. Do you ever see your baby kneel by you? She does in her mind. Many other things she does but they are too sacred to be talked about. People must think I am crazy, but I know I am not.

Paramananda was delighted with her purity, her childlike candor, her depth of feeling. In Bengali he addressed her as "Baby-Jewel" and "My heart's treasure." Deftly, he pointed her strong will inward, so that she imposed her rigorous demands on no one but herself. During that first year, he gave her private lessons in the Upanishads, and took her with him each time he crossed the continent. In gloomy Boston she brought a brightness and in the ever-agitated ashrama she exuded serenity.

"All of them love you so much and show you such affection," he wrote to her, "and this arouses wondrous joy in my heart. . . . You silly girl, you do not understand how pleased I am with you, nor do you know the extent of my faith in you." Then he added portentously, "Through you great, great feelings will manifest. Many people will receive joy and peace. It is not necessary for you to know all this. . . ."

And another time: "That your tenderness and sensitivity really touch my whole innermost being—how can I make it known in a letter? Indeed, my intuitions regarding you when I first saw you are today proving true to a large extent. Sometimes I myself doubted a little about my feelings. This you know. Now you are showing those deeper sides of your soul. . . . Here I have much work to do. But you are not someone related to my external life."

Amidst the problematic atmosphere of his outer life, Gayatri was an oasis of otherworldliness. To be sure, she was the only dream of his life which did not lose its luster when the twilight of reverie gave way to the harsh glare of reality. On the contrary, as time passed, she grew more ethereal, more intuitive, more one with his spirit. Among those close to him, she was the only one who never disappointed him, never wounded him. "You are a goddess," he said to her more than once, much to her embarrassment. Relentless in her drive for perfection, in the outer world and in her inner life, Gayatri burned with aspiration to be what he saw in her. By the end of her life, everyone agreed that she had vindicated his vision.

Paramananda's problems, with Ananda Ashrama, the Boston Vedanta Centre, and the finances needed to maintain them both, continued to harass him. One of the Boston members introduced him to Mr. Moonan and Mr. Keele, two enterprising young stockbrokers who showed fervent interest in the swami and the Centre. It was the 1920s, when all of America was dallying with the stock market. Paramananda, ever adventurous, was quite willing to experiment with what Moonan and Keele assured him would be a simple way to solve his financial dilemma. Not only did Paramananda give them a substantial part of his own money to invest, but he shared his glowing prospects with those of the sisters who had assets.

Moonan and Keele turned out to be swindlers. Paramananda declined to register any complaint against them, but the rest of their clients prosecuted. The two men ended up in jail, and the swami and the sisters never saw their money again.

Meanwhile, despite Paramananda's pleas and injunctions, the ashrama continued to be racked by pockets of criticism, the clique in the Community House instilling its hostility into some of the public and engendering in turn harshness and countercriticism from the dedicated workers. Paramananda refused to take the easy solution of expelling the dissidents; he would not rule by fiat, but by love. Always believing that inner states, not outer threats, determined one's lot, he focused his attention on the conduct of his followers rather than on the misconduct of his adversaries. One night in February, 1927, as the household was gathered in the living room before bedtime, Paramananda formulated for them what had become the ruling passion of his life:

> Unmistakable language of love—I hope and pray, pray with all my soul, that we may be able to hear the voice of love ourselves, and that it may speak through us. Then I am quite certain that the confusion, whatever confusions that have been in the past, will be eliminated. It is something worth trying.
>
> We are not here for any ordinary purpose. We are here because we believe in a very great cause, and do not let us do it in any half way. We do not want to only speak of love, but we want to really sound it through our life and through our action. I believe that the whole atmosphere will change. . . . If we can speak with the voice of love, or if the voice of love can speak through us, I am certain nobody can go away from here with injured spirit. It does not matter what other people do, or think, or contrive against us, love will conquer. . . .
>
> Every one, every one of you, no matter what others say or think—people from outside may sometimes say things which may offend you, hurt your spirit—but may you always speak with the voice of love, or may that voice of love speak through you. It requires tremendous amount of tolerance. . . . I cannot see that our life can bring any

sense of completeness because we have a beautiful place, enjoyable community. We are here to render service. . . . Merely having a happy life, which you all have, I have had, living in a peaceful community, is very wonderful, it is blessed, but I think another turn comes in the work when we must learn to forget ourselves. Let us form the habit of not criticizing anyone. Let this be like those idealistic communities who really felt for humanity. Whenever anyone comes, if crippled morally or spiritually or physically, may we have enough love and sympathy to give healing balm. . . .

We must live, feel, give, help, sustain when people are in need. Even when another person blunders, we must be patient and tolerant. Let no one go away from here wounded, even if they should wound us.

Wounded or not, they did go away. Both the Allans and Mrs. French returned to San Francisco. The community regained its lost harmony—for the time being.

In 1927, Paramananda suddenly leapt out of the quagmire that had entrapped him. He emerged rallying to bigger and bolder vistas than ever before. Instead of focusing on a select few, he was now sweeping all humanity with his gaze. "The gigantic responsibilities which we have been obliged to carry in connection with this work," he wrote in February, 1927, "seem very little in comparison with its spiritual blessings and the hopes that it holds for the future welfare of a larger humanity. This I know, that the Great Power that led our steps to this place can make all things possible, and if it is His will to make this place of universal spiritual significance, nothing can hinder it."

After years of wincing at public lecturing, suddenly he was reaching out to a larger audience through a half dozen different channels, the most innovative of which was radio. In February, a friend and neighbor, Frederick Robinson, invited the swami to take part in the opening of his new radio station KGFH, broad-

casting out of La Crescenta. The response to Paramananda's
short message was so favorable that a regular Wednesday night
program was scheduled, with the "Ananda Ashrama Choir" (Concorde, Daya, and Amala) providing musical preludes. When an
invalid in a distant town wrote, expressing deep appreciation for
the broadcasts, Paramananda became enthused about the far-
reaching potential of the new media. "Lately I have been convinced," he wrote to Swami Shivananda, "that this is a new way
of rendering service, not only to a new public, but to those who
are blind and crippled and unable to come in direct contact. No
one can measure the extent of its influence." In May, KHJ, the
large broadcasting station of the *Los Angeles Times*, invited Paramananda to give a series of Tuesday night talks.

The most significant event of 1927 was the long-awaited
consecration of the ground for the Temple of the Universal Spirit.
After all Paramananda's far-flung dreams, the temple was to be
erected not on the French Riviera, in Malaysia, or in Quail Canyon,
but on the ridge overlooking the Cloister. Nor would it be the
elaborate edifice he had originally designed, approached by a
stone bridge amidst pools and fountains. Still, after fifteen years
it was finally to become reality. Brother George with his tractor
leveled the hill, and the grounds were consecrated on Easter
Sunday.

That summer Paramananda established a Vedanta library
and reading room in Los Angeles and another in Pasadena. Both
were open to the public all day every day, staffed respectively by
Amala and Miss Blandy, a local follower. On Wednesday nights
Paramananda gave a class at the Los Angeles rooms and on
Thursday nights at Pasadena, in addition to the regular Tuesday
classes at the ashrama.

He also began giving public lectures in Los Angeles, first
under the auspices of other groups, and then independently, for
the first time since he closed the old Los Angeles Vedanta Centre in 1922. The crowds which gathered in Symphony Hall to

hear him were enthusiastic, increasing to 550 by the third week of the series.

At the zenith of the giddy materialism of the twenties, American society was showing signs of what one Methodist minister called, "the reawakening of mysticism." Writing in the *Methodist Review*, the Rev. John Moore claimed: "Everywhere there is the witness of spiritual pauperization in both Romanism and Protestantism. Neither of them seems to have enough truth and spirituality to satisfy the religious demand. Everybody experiences the feeling that there has been a profound materialization and secularization of life. Yet there are signs of subtle change; . . . signs that make for the reawakening of mysticism."

Paramananda's work was being spurred into a dynamic new phase. The attendance at the ashrama services shot up. Sri Ramakrishna's Birthday was celebrated in Indian style, with the feeding of two hundred people in the open, Paramananda cooking the meal himself. Many guests came to stay at the Community House, among them the conductor Leopold Stokowski and his wife. Other artists, such as Ruth St. Denis, began to frequent the hilltop retreat.

Paramananda was loath to interrupt the heartening momentum of the California work for a trip East, especially since he had accepted Stokowski's invitation to travel to India with him in October, but suddenly in late August he received an urgent call to come to Boston. A crisis was disrupting the Vedanta Centre.

The catalyst was Swami Akhilananda's traditionalism, in contrast to Paramananda's spontaneous spirituality. Boston's women workers, accustomed, like the ashrama sisters, to Paramananda's egalitarian treatment, refused to accept any male leader who presumed to put himself above them, whatever title he might bear. In assigning Swami Akhilananda as assistant swami to an already long-established community, the Belur Math could not have understood that it was less like appointing a new vice-president to a corporation than transplanting a new vital organ into a body. When a body rejects such a transplant, it throws the whole organism into cataclysm.

Certainly, Swami Akhilananda's orientation and methods differed radically from Paramananda's. The scholarly and conventional young monk was critical of the senior swami's freewheeling ways. They were both, after all, members of the Ramakrishna Order, an organization with specific rules, regulations, and written guidelines, to which Paramananda paid little heed. The Belur Math Rules, for example, specified a set term for a postulant before becoming a novice, and another set term before being initiated into *sannyas*, or full monastic vows. Some of Paramananda's workers, however, had been in the community for years without any ceremony of initiation at all, while Sister Daya had received the veil after only a year and a half.

In ritualistic matters, too, Paramananda took broad liberties, while Akhilananda endorsed literal adherence to the Scriptures. Despite Paramananda's attentive ministrations to the shrine, which he considered the heart of the Centre and of the ashrama, he bypassed most of the elaborate rituals enjoined by Hindu tradition. "Know that the real thing necessary," he wrote, "is to have true devotion in your heart. When you have that, it does not matter whether you say any *mantram* or not, it is always accepted. . . . If we can only offer our heart's love and devotion, then alone we worship Him; otherwise no amount of offering can ever please Him."

Akhilananda openly expressed his criticism of the elder swami, thus eliciting from Paramananda a rare explanation in a letter to the Boston household:

> You see, the whole evolution of this work . . . through my humble instrumentality has been not so much through rules and regulations made by others, ideas and ideals offered by books, but rather through spontaneous and direct feelings of the soul. I do not think it will be possible for me to suddenly change these for ideas and ideals which

might appeal for the time being to some people, but I must keep on the way I have been doing and where I believe the Lord can use me to best advantage. I never interfere with others' freedom consciously (and, I hope, unconsciously) and my spirit must have freedom for self-expression, and this to my mind never clashes with the great and fundamental ideals of life and spirituality.

Not all the Boston Vedantists objected to the younger swami. Some, like Lillian Engstrand, the nurse, were attracted to Akhilananda's more intellectual approach. Mr. and Mrs. Worcester, who had never cared for Paramananda as a teacher, became very enthusiastic over Akhilananda. Anna Worcester, as a matter of fact, believed that Swami Akhilananda should have the leadership of the Boston Vedanta Centre, and she encouraged him to claim it. They maintained that Paramananda should relinquish the Eastern work and satisfy himself with California.

Paramananda was not so easily severed from a work into which he had poured almost two decades of his life. He still felt what he had expressed a few years before, when the Boston members held a reception in his honor to express their love and gratitude:

This work is not less dear to me today than it was fifteen years ago. If anything, it is dearer. You know how it is when you build up something; you give your whole heart and devotion to it. You are very reluctant to part with it. It is a human feeing which we all have. That human feeling I have more than perhaps you realize. From the point of view of human love and affection, I cherish it, and over and above that I have something more—the feeling that comes in connection with spiritual realities.

Although the Boston work was flagging, Paramananda was determined to rally it, and wrote to Swami Shivananda: "Boston for the last fifteen or sixteen years has been one of our strongest

and most influential Centres in the United States, and it sad-
dens me to see it dwindle to such a small nucleus. However, I am
going to do my utmost, and if it is His will, the former dignity
and strength may be restored."

Indeed, early in 1927, the Boston Centre had started showing signs of new life. A prominent young Boston artist, Kenneth
Clark Pillsbury, who had been attending the services regularly,
asked permission to paint Paramananda's portrait. When the
finished portrait was shown at the Boston Art Club's winter
exhibition, it aroused a flood of interest. The *Boston Transcript*
and *Boston Herald* both reproduced the portrait, and the secretary of the Art Club said that he had never heard so many
comments made about a picture before. The attendance at the
Centre's services swelled.

But the Akhilananda faction continued to beleaguer the Vedanta Centre, even after Lillian, still beset by conflicts and doubts,
moved to Ananda Ashrama in July. Surreptitious plotting as
well as overt maneuvers finally goaded the irate Boston members to send an urgent call to Paramananda in late August. He
rushed east, leaving Gayatri behind to take classes (much to her
surprise and horror). He arrived to find the Centre bristling like
an armed camp, both sides intransigent.

According to a letter from Akhilananda to Swami Shivananda, a few female workers at the Boston Centre were rude to
him. He expected Paramananda to offer his support, but Paramananda remained aloof. Paramananda, of course, never took
sides in altercations between community members, and what in
India might be considered impudence, he had permitted as free
expression. Nevertheless, when Paramananda finally did show
the junior swami sympathy and affection, Akhilananda declared
that it was too late.

On September 21, an embittered Swami Akhilananda left
Boston for New York. Paramananda wired the ashrama to send
Gayatri to take over the public services in Boston. And he asked

them all to hold vigil for a few days "to clear the atmosphere."

The following week the Centre moved to a still smaller house at 875 Beacon Street, and, in its eighteenth year, Paramananda finally allowed the Vedanta Centre to become incorporated, so that their mortgages could stand in the organization's name, rather than his own.

The volcano had erupted, but its lava continued to seethe and burn for over a year. Paramananda deplored the whole Akhilananda episode, not only the conspiracy and intrigue against him, but the behavior of his own followers. Indeed, he was stung more by the vitriolic defense of his supporters than by the vicious attack of his adversaries. For Paramananda, defeat could never be inflicted by external enemies, but only by internal failures. He had recently written the poem which epitomized his credo, "Thee I love in all." Now he felt that his community had betrayed the very essence of the work. He who had so often told them, "I have given myself to you completely; you can either make me or break me," again plummeted into the slough from which he had so laboriously extricated himself only nine months earlier.

The crisis had prevented Paramananda from accompanying the Stokowskis to India in October, but he resolved to go alone before the end of the year. Once again at the ashrama in November, he wrote to the Boston household:

> I feel very broken, body, mind and morale. My heart often bleeds thinking over the past. Know that I have no blame in my heart for anyone, because that would be nothing but cowardice to blame anyone. I suppose it was natural for all of you to take the attitude you took, but it does not alter my own inmost feeling, so I have made up my mind to get away from everything, and Lord only knows what this will result in. . . .
>
> I hope you will understand my spirit. I cannot help but feel that the whole affair could have been averted if we had let our inner and spiritual feelings guide our course.

Too much human will and boisterousness lead to disaster, and I hope and pray every moment that at least I can abandon pursuance of human will. One of the strongest thoughts that come to my mind is that wherever I am, whatever may be my work, it should never become so small, narrow and exclusive that it should exclude anyone. If it becomes that, it also excludes me. . . .

Whatever happens, I want everything to be done with a deeper spiritual consecration and insight. Too much scheming and planning and discussing rob us of our clear vision, and we can never expect to be a right channel. Wherever I am — India, Europe, or in this country, whatever may be the situation, I am convinced that spiritual revival, renewed consecration, is the only way to solve our perplexities. "Thee I love in all, and all I love for Thee." Beginning and end, and all that is between, my spirit pulsates with this fundamental thought. Try to understand it and you will not misunderstand me. Love and more love, and yet more love, will overcome what is not loving and lovable.

The affair was far from over. In November, Swami Akhilananda moved in with the Worcesters and began delivering lectures in Cambridge.

He had the support not only of the Worcesters, but of most of his young brother monks in America. The roster of Ramakrishna Order swamis in this country had shifted dramatically during 1927. The old guard had effectively passed with the departure of the assistant swami from New York and the death of Paramananda's beloved associate, Swami Prakashananda of San Francisco. These were replaced by two of the new generation, who were Swami Brahmananda's disciples, as were the new assistant in San Francisco and the founder of the Portland center, Swami Prabhavananda. Swami Prabhavananda, who was now founding another center in St. Louis, called Akhilananda his "twin brother." The only remnant of Vivekananda's disciples left in America was Swami Paramananda and Swami Bodhananda in New York (who never had had any rapport with Paramananda).

This group of younger swamis endorsed Akhilananda's bid either to take over the Boston Centre or to start a second one in neighboring Cambridge. After facing years of antagonism from conservative Christians, Paramananda was heartsick at this opposition from within his own Order. It was the culmination of an arduous period and his mind was turbulent as he sat with the ashrama community one night in November and poured out his heart to them:

> Today I have come to the point where I cannot stand any cross current. I shall have to make a complete change. I cannot get away from it all soon enough. . . . Today I stand on the threshold where I can make complete renunciation again. My pull is my love for you all. Even if the whole world should say, "He is no good," it does not make any difference. You know what Swamiji [Vivekananda] did in his last days? He withdrew himself. . . . I have a little bit of the same spirit.
>
> After all, it is not my work. People don't understand this. I cannot even convey this to people who are most immediately connected with me. One thing I must have: people who understand. I do not want to go about with a sledge hammer. It is not my mission in life. Those who do not understand, there are plenty of opportunities in the world for them. I am not the only swami by any means. As far as that is concerned, I am very insignificant. That is one thing I can tell you. There is no fever of ambition in me for rising to a great glory. Some of you may think, "He has lost his mind." It may seem that way to the world in general.
>
> If anybody out of over-zealous nature does something to misrepresent their ideal, it wounds me to the core. I am not just a fool that I want to see myself always flattered. Sometimes it is sickening when people give me flattery.

Pretty strong forces are at work here. I may have made a lot of mess. Every man has to go through these things. Sometimes it seems inevitable. No matter which way you want to go, it is sort of a turn of destiny. Also it is a test. If you come out of it, you are better for it.

It is a very strange thing. If you rise up in the world, you are like a target. If your work is a failure, you escape; but if you become somebody, you become a target for hatred, envy, jealousy, condemnation. I am almost standing as a target. Everybody is throwing things at me. Swamiji suffered. He told us sometimes he felt like committing suicide many times. I am telling you these things because I have been so puzzled about myself lately.

A few days later, as he prepared to depart for India, Paramananda again unveiled his heart to his community:

The other day I was brooding over it: Have I not blundered? Have I not imposed myself and my suffering on others, people who are close to me? And a voice gave me assurance, "It is the only way. There is no exception. Everybody has done the same thing; you are no exception to that. Anybody who is trying to do any good — that is man's destiny." . . .

It is an interesting thing. My life has been more or less easy. Whatever I have tried to do, I always had the resources and help. I do not mean only material resources. Always Divine Mother has given me a push and it has gone, and if today I am put through this ordeal, the reason is not that I am lacking that support, but there has been a whole lot of cross current. People have destroyed many of the fine forces. When I went to India, you know, I said I place you all as sentinels on the watch tower. I poured out my heart and soul. You let the wrong element come in.

I pray so hard that there will be no snapping with each other, no harsh word. And loyalty — fight tooth and nail anyone who comes with disloyal spirit. Somebody comes

A Bridge of Dreams

and strikes at the very root. "Oh well, I will tolerate him."
That is not the way of tolerance. Somebody came to Sri
Ramakrishna and talked against Swamiji, and he actually
took a club and drove that man out of his room. He did
that much for his disciple. If you cannot do that for your
guru, you are no good. . . . That is what has weakened
this work. But it is not going to die. Neither is the Boston
work, know this. I have been very tender and gentle and
everything, but now another spirit is rising in me. If I have
to fight, I know how. Silence is my weapon. Freeze outside;
there is no entry here in my house. I give royal welcome to
everybody, even a beggar, but not those who come with
fault-finding spirit. I will not tolerate it.

I do feel very strongly, for the preservation of this
work, that there should not be any division on any ground.
I have suffered terribly under it, and I think perhaps my
broken health and broken spirit is greatly due to that. . . .
Finding fault is not going to lead us anywhere. Disputing,
discussing, are not going to solve problems. I say again
and again, let us go close to our Ideal—meditation, prayer,
communion with the Supreme, and then all these clouds
will vanish.

On December 12, 1927, Paramananda, accompanied by Katherine Sherwood, sailed for India via the Pacific, even as the
construction of the Temple of the Universal Spirit was beginning.
He left Sister Daya to take the services in Boston and Gayatri
Devi to conduct the services and classes at the ashrama, in Pasadena, and in Los Angeles.

Two weeks later, from the mid-Pacific, Paramananda wrote
to the Vedanta Centre in that light vein which always seemed to
run through even his darkest times:

You have all been in my thoughts constantly, specially
during this season. What is Xmas without Boston chill and
snow? And as for New Year, it should not be begun except
at the great Hub. There is plenty of wind and abundant

chill too at North Pacific Ocean, but it lacks that cutting something which Boston wind alone has. Oh! how I miss it. Dear old Hub, I wonder if she still loves me or she is getting modernized and fickle. These changes will come and we have to get used to them. Alas! Alas! for our deep attachments. . . . This letter is meant for New Year's greetings, but so far I have overlooked all the solemn ceremonies. There is only one ceremony logically possible for me to perform now, and that is baptism. There is plenty of water for it.

The voyage through the Far East turned into a triumphant tour. At Manila an official delegation met Swami Paramananda at the steamer and entertained him during his stay. At Singapore, five hundred people gathered on the wharf to receive him. The garlands, bouquets, sprinklings of rose water, ceremonials, and addresses of welcome (printed on satin and read before public receptions of thousands) accosted him at every stop during his two-week tour of Malaysia. He delivered lectures before huge crowds, unveiled a sacred image at a Hindu Temple, rode in solemn processions in his honor, and was feasted and feted at every turn.

This unexpected appreciation in such a far-flung corner of the world rekindled Paramananda's dampened enthusiasm. His mind burst aflame with the idea of "world unity." He began to envision a string of centers, in Hawaii, Malaysia, India, Europe, and America, necklacing the globe like luminous gems, proving to all the oneness of the human spirit.

"This may not sound like a vacation," he wrote from Singapore, "but it is impossible to refuse these enthusiastic people. Mai [Katherine Sherwood] is doing her best to keep my spirit down. This morning we had quite an argument over my new plan of extending the work over here. She is strong for the Ashrama, and of course she is right in a way, but my spirit cannot be bound. . . . I am a dreamer and I suddenly cannot cease to be one on anybody's account. Many of my dreams have come true, and why not this one? Mai feels that I am always inclined to undertake too much and she is right. But to me nothing seems too much."

During his five days in Rangoon, also, there were public lectures, receptions, countless ovations, and showings of moving pictures of Ananda Ashrama, which he had brought with him. On his last day there he lectured to an audience of Indian women holding and nursing their crying babies, as interpreters translated the address into Bengali and Tamil. At the conclusion, echoing Vivekananda's motto, "Women and the people," Paramananda asserted the right of women to become equal companions to their husbands and to hold a more equitable position in the family. "If this is not done," he concluded, "there is no hope for India." The women exclaimed that no one had ever spoken to them like that before. "I have hardly caught my breath since," wrote Miss Sherwood. "We are told that Rangoon was never so roused before by anybody."

Paramananda's stay in India lasted scarcely a month. Its most important outcome was the decision to bring back with him Charushila Devi, his niece and childhood playmate, who for years had been working as a schoolteacher to support her mother and sisters. At forty-two, Charushila was a petite ball of fire, spirited, quick-witted, and hard-working. This time, Paramananda did not even bother to look among the young swamis of the Math for an assistant.

He did, however, confer with Swami Shivananda about the Boston situation. The President of the Order averred that it was improper for Akhilananda either to displace Paramananda or to start another Centre only a few miles away from the Boston Vedanta Centre. He pledged his full support to Paramananda. In a letter to Devamata after Paramananda's departure from India, Swami Shivananda wrote:

There is no doubt about his greatness—loving, solicitous and sympathetic, too, to the extreme. All these qualities of his head and heart were palpable to me during his recent visits. We were all very glad and happy to see and feel how Sri Guru Maharaj [Ramakrishna] helped him to develop during all these years. It was simply wonderful. Surely he will have our full support. We had discussed the matter over here and have assured him of our support. We cannot do anything which will hamper him in his work.

Even so, the opposing forces were only beginning to mobilize themselves. In March, 1928, while Paramananda and Charushila were still en route from India, Mrs. Worcester wrote him a letter from Cambridge: "Just a few lines — unfortunately we definitely understand that you are trying to have Swami Akhilananda removed from here. We can only say don't tear down this work. The consequences will be very serious, perhaps you do not realize it now. It will be far-reaching."

In May, 1928, a month after Paramananda's return to America and two weeks after his coming to Boston, Swami Akhilananda sent for Swami Gnaneswarananda. The two of them requested a conference with Paramananda, and closeted themselves with him in his study for three hours. The younger swamis demanded that Paramananda amalgamate Akhilananda's fledgling Cambridge work with the Boston Centre. When he declined, they insisted that he immediately telephone Swami Madhavananda in San Francisco, and submit the dispute to his arbitration. Paramananda refused.

He later declared, "My attitude towards Swami Akhilananda —I have no ill feeling. On the contrary, I feel great pity for him. But I would not let him do the same trick again, to come and rupture my work." He stood firm in his refusal, despite pressure from the other swamis and Mrs. Worcester, whom one swami later described as "a holy terror."

Rumors began to be circulated that the authorities at Belur had instructed Paramananda to turn the Boston Centre over to Akhilananda, and that Paramananda had flouted the Order by refusing to obey. This story is clearly refuted by Swami Shivananda's own letters. Although the President of the Order preferred that Akhilananda return to the Boston Vedanta Centre as assistant to Paramananda, for he was always gravely concerned about Paramananda's health, barring that possibility, he gave explicit alternatives which never once included Paramananda's giving up the Boston Centre.

As tales of Paramananda's obduracy spread through the American Vedanta societies and ultimately reached Belur, he, as usual, offered neither defense nor explanation of his position. Two of the loyal Boston members, Agnes and Jennie Reymond, did write to Swami Shivananda, explaining why they refused to reconcile with Akhilananda. When Paramananda read a copy of their letter, he replied to them: "Your letter to Swami Shivanandaji, the President of the Ramakrishna Mission, was all right and will undoubtedly serve a purpose. I have not written or given any explanation of the situation. You know I am always reluctant to do such a thing."

In June, Swami Akhilananda informed Swami Shivananda that he had received enough funds to open a new center from an anonymous donor who stipulated that it must be in an Eastern city. Swami Shivananda wired back: "CABLE CONSIDERED FULLY PROCEED WITHOUT HESITATION TO ST LOUIS ANY OTHER CENTRE INADVISABLE."

Unwilling to go to St. Louis, Akhilananda replied to Shivananda that it would mean forfeiting the anonymous donation. He met again with Paramananda, who gave him leave to start a center in any Eastern city outside Massachusetts. Swami Akhilananda promptly founded a Vedanta Society in Providence, Rhode Island, forty miles south of Boston.

After that, relations between Paramananda and Akhilananda were friendly, even warm. Akhilananda would invite the senior swami to lecture at his Society and would cook dinner for him and his companions, graciously serving the meal himself. Paramananda, in turn, often invited Akhilananda to lecture at the Boston Centre.

But Mrs. Worcester's ominous prophecy proved true; the consequences of Paramananda's opposition to the coalition of young swamis was far-reaching. He became an outcast among them. The most successful of them all, Paramananda was repeatedly under fire from their criticism, which condemned his liberal ways and the opportunities he gave to women. Pointing at the suave image projected by Paramananda's physical beauty which, as Katherine Sherwood remarked, glorified every garment he wore, and at his charisma, which elicited such personal devotion from his followers, they called him "the Hollywood star swami." As soon as Paramananda passed away, only twelve years later, his centers, with their female leadership, were disowned by the Order, and Swami Akhilananda was able, at long last, to establish his own center in the heart of Boston.

14

The Swami's Calamity

THE TEMPLE OF THE UNIVERSAL SPIRIT was raised during Swami Paramananda's 1928 trip to India. On January 3, at 6:45 A.M., all twenty-four members of the ashrama community gathered in the Cloister shrine for the regular morning worship conducted by Sister Devamata. Then Gayatri Devi, conducting the daily class for the household, told them: "Let us all think of Swami today and think of his message to each one of us, try to be close to That which he represents to us, and eliminate ourselves absolutely, our little whims and likes and dislikes and desires, put them all to one side and make ourselves just channels, free, clear, and open, and then the Divine Power will really work through us."

With that everyone marched up to the Temple Hill singing, "This is the Temple of the Lord," "Holy Sanctuary," and "Take My Life." Gayatri chanted in Sanskrit. Then vigil in the shrine began, each one taking a turn sitting in prayer and meditation. The next day when Brother George and the other men were ready to excavate the foundation, the community reassembled on the hill and each member in solemn succession took the shovel and pick and dug up his or her sacred scoopful. A telegram was received from the Boston Centre: "MAY TEMPLE BE REARED IN GLORY MAY EVERY STONE RADIATE SPIRIT OF SWAMI."

Paramananda himself, aboard ship somewhere in the North Pacific Ocean, wrote:

> If you are instrumental in building a Temple whose pillars shall be no other than the sacred manifestations and revelations of ages, 'THE TEMPLE OF THE UNIVERSAL SPIRIT' once dedicated must be served perpetually by unfailing and unfaltering devotion. . . . My dream is that some sacred heart must be in prayer every hour of the day and night without cessation. It will require many — perhaps — but when heart is fired with devotion, one become many. If He has chosen me to do this task of blessedness, I cannot escape. If He chooses you, you cannot fail.

The Temple of the Universal Spirit was the culmination of Paramananda's lifelong dream. Dedicated to the one God of all religions, it would stand as concrete testimony to the oneness of the human spirit, towering above all superficial distinctions of nationality, race, and sect. On its nine tall, leaded windows would be stained glass depictions of a Christian cathedral, a Jewish synagogue, a Hindu temple, a Moslem mosque, a Buddhist stupa, a Greek temple, a Chinese Pagoda, an Egyptian temple, and a Shinto shrine, illustrating the principle that, as the same light passes through all these windows, so the one Truth shines in and through all religions. Its walls would be lined with arched niches in which would be inscribed passages from the different Scriptures of the world. At the far end, next to the steps leading up to the inner shrine, on one side would be a statue of the Buddha, on the other a statue of the Madonna. And in the inner shrine itself, curtained off except during the times of services, surrounding an altar to the Absolute, would be installed the prophet of universality, Sri Ramakrishna, and Swami Vivekananda, and the Holy Mother, on the breadth of whose love and teaching the whole edifice would stand. Paramananda described the temple as a "monument which may stand here on the mountain top as a beacon light for aspiring humanity."

When the swami returned on April 20, he found the unfinished temple complex, which included a library, a publications storage room, and living quarters for himself, all connected by wide arcades, well under way. Much of the work had been done by the dedicated brotherhood, which included a few new young men, under the direction of an expert builder and supervised by Sister Devamata, who followed Paramananda's original plan with one, perhaps symbolic, omission. There were several narrow side doors, but no wide main entrance. Paramananda called forth men and machinery and had them knock out a huge portion of the end wall, which was also symbolic of the man whose destiny it was to turn walls into doors.

The Temple of the Universal Spirit was to be dedicated on July 22, 1928. Reading the announcement of the grand event in the *Message of the East*, people came from throughout the Midwest and the East coast, only to find that the building, depending mostly on the labors of the dedicated community, was far from complete. A disappointed Paramananda decided to hold what he called "a preliminary dedication service" in the unfinished temple.

After that, workers scrambled to finish, working long days and sometimes whole nights. Mr. Kissam installed decorative electric fixtures, Willie Verbeck painted floral borders on the walls, Gilbert Dawes finished the woodwork, Concorde wove the curtains to partition off the inner shrine, Jessie Trueworthy, a new member and miniaturist, painted the inscriptions from the various Scriptures in the niches, Lillian wrote words and music for a new hymn to be sung at the dedication service, and Amala lettered the quotation over the shrine: "Where I am there is peace," which Paramananda loved, jestingly, and justifiably, to paraphrase, "Where *I* am there is no peace!"

On October 21, India's Festival of the Divine Mother, the final dedication service was held. Six hundred people climbed the hill for the two services. Paramananda was on fire with the

ideal he had vocalized throughout southern Asia: the Commonwealth of Humanity.

> Today it is not the sect, not the dogma, not the creed that
> is winning the souls of men. I have realized this more and
> more as I have gone about in my travels. Everywhere peo-
> ple are reaching out for something bigger, more inclusive.
> In spite of themselves, they want to merge, to come together,
> without any limitation, in the great dream of brotherhood,
> the great dream of unity, the great dream of the realization
> of One Deity. Last year when I stood there in the Malay
> States before an assembly, not just of one or two national-
> ities, but of Americans, English, Europeans, Chinese, Ja-
> panese, Siamese, and Burmese, this dream of the Common-
> wealth of Humanity — the Temple of the Universal Spirit —
> which had been burning in my soul, took definite form.
>
> In every turn of life we must seek to realize that we are
> children of Divinity and as such, as a part of great humanity,
> all are our brothers and sisters. First, last, and forever we
> are one, because we have one origin; but it takes strength,
> courage and inspiration on the part of man to realize this.
> It is not enough to form a league or a society of universal
> brotherhood. We must become charged with the spirit,
> the immensity of it.
>
> This little house of worship stands here to remind us
> of . . . the great concept which we have enshrined here. It
> is a great concept. We all recognize how much it is needed
> in the world today for the healing of the nations. Even
> though we may not be interested in it from the religious
> point of view, just for the preservation of the human race
> we need this unity. . . .
>
> We are all looking for saving grace. What is going to
> protect us? What is going to save our civilization? Every-
> one is asking this. Guns will not do it; nor inventions, nor
> science, nor poison gas. What then will bring us peace?
> "Where I am there is peace." Not in wealth, not in worldly
> possessions, not in kingdoms, not even by selling our own

soul shall we find it; but—"Where I am there is peace." Only
when man senses the Divine Presence can he know peace.

Such are the thoughts which we want to radiate from
this place. . . . Our objective is that we may be inspired to
live the ideal life, the life that brings man face to face with
his Maker. And may our hearts be so freed from the blemish of petty feelings, hatred, anger, misunderstanding, lack
of balance, that we may be secured by the Spirit of God,
and help to extend that security to our fellow men.

To be sure, the "blemish of petty feelings, hatred, anger,
misunderstanding, lack of balance" had been spattering the community's inner temple ever since the swami's return in the spring.
Sister Devamata, always made tense by major responsibilities
which she nevertheless insisted on undertaking, was in a cantan-
kerous mood. There was jealousy toward Charushila, growing
irritation with Amala (whom even Paramananda called "arti-
ficial"), and the inevitable frictions of community life, exacerbated by the pressure and fatigue of the temple construction.
Paramananda, as always, was susceptible to every disharmony
within the community. Once, at the breakfast table, after a bitter
exchange between Achala and Amala, Paramananda, pushing
his plate away from him, remarked to Gayatri: "If they only
knew, when they speak to each other like that it puts a knife
through my heart." From Boston in May, Daya wrote to Mary
Lacy: "My heart aches over what you tell me of conditions at the
Ashrama. . . . Will there never be an end to Swami's crucifixion
in that direction?"

Ironically, even as the temple dedicated to tolerance, understanding, and world brotherhood was being built, *Mother India*,
Katherine Mayo's scathing indictment of Indian society and Indian
women, was published. After a scant four-month stay in India,
augmented by twenty months of scouring newspapers and commission reports, Miss Mayo had produced what Mahatma Gandhi

called, "a drain-inspector's report." Indignant Hindus in America rebutted with a wave of books and pamphlets, such as *A Son of Mother India Answers, Sister India*, and the acerbic *Uncle Sham*, which, using the same method of distilling newspaper and commission reports, depicted American society as rampant with crime on the streets, political scandal, and marital infidelity, abuses which India could smugly disavow.

India was in the limelight, and the inveterate American sense of fair play rebounded to give Paramananda's work openings and opportunities where it had previously met only indifference. Gayatri Devi was suddenly invited to lecture on "Ideals of Indian Womenhood" before a half-dozen establishment organizations, including the prestigious Los Angeles City Club. Sister Devamata's memoir, *Days in an Indian Monastery*, which fortuitously came out that same year, was reviewed in journals which otherwise would have ignored it.

Paramananda himself, however, refused to plunge into the fray. When a Hindu association approached him for a statement refuting *Mother India*, he curtly replied, "I have two Indian women living right here in my community. They are my answer to *Mother India*."

He was busy and overburdened, shuttling between Boston and California, lecturing in Columbus, Cincinnati, Louisville, Chicago, and Grand Rapids, giving Tuesday night classes in Pasadena, Wednesday night classes in Los Angeles, a series of Sunday night lectures in Symphony Hall, all in addition to the regular Sunday morning and Sunday afternoon services at the ashrama. An article on *The New Religions of America*, published the previous year, had called Paramananda, "the best known present-day swami." It was an appellation he had earned. He was still giving radio talks over several stations and speaking before a variety of organizations whenever he was invited. Then, too, during most of 1928, there was the supervision of the temple construction and the working out of the Akhilananda situation, which was not settled until late that year.

"My soul cries out for inspiration," he wrote on the train to California. "What will I do with all the mental cogitations of this wide world? A little inspiration and peace, let all else go."

On the eve of Sri Ramakrishna's birthday, he opened his heart to the ashrama members:

> We are living too much in the outer life. Work, organization, all these things are assuming too much proportion, it seems to me. If we can just be really holy, consecrated, devoted, dedicated, united, forgetting all our personal differences, becoming part of real God-life, something that is worthy of Sri Ramakrishna, then it would be really worthwhile. I feel it tremendously, that the best preparation we can have for the work is giving ourselves to God. We must do it.

He was trapped by the one temptation he seemingly could not resist, "The hand of the world professing love and tender friendship led me on through many glittering roads, ever promising freedom, peace, and joy. And with sweet voice filled my ears with hopes for ever greater service."

Responsibilities and worries crowded in on him. Gayatri's and Charushila's visas were gnawing problems. America's immigration laws had been passed only a few years before, purposely to limit the influx of Asians, eastern Europeans, and other "undesirable groups." Upon arriving at San Francisco harbor, both women had been detained for hours by immigration clearance, and then granted only short-term visitor's visas. Gayatri's expired in June, 1928, and on the 9th of that month she was notified that she would have to leave the country within nine days. Paramananda was intent on keeping her here. After frantically trying every available means, he sent Sister Daya on an eleventh-hour mission to Washington, where through her late father, the senator, she had a connection with the Under-Secretary of Labor. After much bated breath, at the very last moment a six-month extension was granted. In December, the whole nerve-racking process had to be repeated.

During the Akhilananda episode, Paramananda had resolved that the Boston work would again become a thriving center. Arriving there in November, 1928, with Charushila Devi, he threw himself into reviving it. The community there now included some of his strongest workers, Daya, Mary Lacy, Charushila, in addition to Galene, Dr. Belle, and Amala, whom he called East after Christmas, much to the relief of the ashrama members.

The house at 875 Beacon Street, purchased at Galene's prompting, had proved too small and crowded during this year of occupancy. In December Paramananda bought a new home for the Centre at 32 Fenway, overlooking the same park of their Queensberry Street days. All were overjoyed that, after the two unsuccessful ventures on Marlboro Street and Beacon Street, the Centre would finally be settled in proper quarters. The swami announced that the ground floor of the new house would be turned into a Boston "Temple of the Universal Spirit." He brought Stanley Dawes and Willie Verbeck to Boston to assist with the transformation.

Finally, too, the swami with the reputation of never asking for money conceded to share the financial burden which for two decades he had been shouldering practically alone. First in California, then in Boston, an "Association of Friends" was formed. Whereas neither the Vedanta Centre nor the Ananda Ashrama had formal memberships or dues, the "Friends' Association" had both. As the *Message of the East* explained: "The swami and his immediate household have carried the burden so cheerfully and efficiently for the past . . . years that the public has imagined that it was an endowed work. Now the members of the larger household have asked to have their share in bearing it." On Thursday evenings the association would gather for an informal talk by Paramananda and a "Hindu dinner" cooked either by the swami or by Charushila in Boston or Gayatri in California.

The associations helped until the Depression made funds too tight even for "friends."

The new momentum of the Vedanta Centre was so encouraging that Paramananda decided to give it added impetus by spending Christmas there for the first time in years. By the end of January, the *Message* could report: "Never before has there been manifested a more enthusiastic spirit than during the last few weeks, nor greater response from friends old and new." When the new Temple of the Universal Spirit was dedicated on February 24, 1929, 250 people crowded into the Fenway house for the morning service and again for the afternoon service, and another 125 came for the evening ceremony. Spirits ran high; the swami was radiant.

They were barely settled in the new quarters when a rapid succession of illustrious guests from India came to pay their respects: C.F. Andrews, Gandhi's and Tagore's English apostle; Sarojini Naidu, famous poetess and former President of the Indian National Congress; and Dr. James Cousins, eminent educator and cultural ambassador. Paramananda had also become friends with Krishnamurti, who wrote to the swami with almost boyish enthusiasm: "I just want to say how glad I am that we have met each other. I hope we shall meet each other very often and become real friends, if we aren't now! . . . We must see a lot of each other, next year, that's if I may."

In order to sustain the public's enthusiasm, Paramananda had to come to Boston more frequently and not stay away for more than four weeks at a time. Thus, in 1929, he made the train journey across the continent ten times, often at two or three week intervals. "It is a bit strenuous," he admitted, "but worth doing."

The ashrama members were disgruntled at this sudden shift in concentration; they especially felt bereft at Christmas. Gayatri, in California, wrote to Daya about "the silent opposition to Swami's present movements." She continued: "As far as I am concerned, I can tell Swami never does anything that is not born of higher vision. . . . I do not really know what is good and what is better, so I like to have absolute trust in Swami. I said this to Sister [Devamata], and she shut me up saying, 'When you carry the burden with him, you know what it is.' "

By mid-1929, it was obvious that Paramananda's frequent absences from California were not due solely to Boston's need. The continual skirmishes in the ashrama community were beginning to take their toll on its peace-loving leader. "Swami seems strange," Gayatri wrote to Daya in May, "most of the time very indrawn and thoughtful. He talks of the weariness of the public life, of the desire to retire, and so on. . . . I do not care what he does or where he goes as long as he feels lighthearted and free. Your song-bird hardly sings at all, even the smile often one has to ask for. I pray intensely that Mother will lift his heavy burdens. There is always disturbance, annoyance, confusion, contradiction, selfish demand going on day after day . . . and is it a wonder that he wants to go away from us all at times? What infinite patience, what unbounded compassion we see, yet how little we learn!"

Even during such discouraging periods, his love for his errant community never wavered. "My own all, more than flesh and blood," he called them, and appealed to them: "Let the very air we breathe be permeated, the whole atmosphere! This place which he has given us, let every particle of this place be blessed and radiate the joy of God."

Despite such oft-repeated pleas, the ashrama members continued to tussle with each other and with the swami. For instance, Stanley once dented the ashrama truck. George scolded him for his carelessness, so Stanley threatened to leave. George whistled, pretending he could not care less.

Or again, while they were sitting around the Cloister living room in the evening, the swami attempted to speak to them. Mr. Eldridge remained engrossed in a conversation with Mangala; Lillian, straining to hear what the swami was saying, snapped her fingers at the pair and silenced them with a chilling "shush." A look of pain passed over Paramananda's face, ending with a smile. "Be rhythmic," he told her. "Be gentle, even in your casual relationships with one another."

Another time, the swami was telling the community about a man who had offered them the use of a hall. Various people interrupted with objections, minute questions, adamant opinions. When the din subsided, Paramananda said in a discouraged voice, "You all say, 'Swami, follow your inspiration, do what you feel is best,' but you break in with your trivialities and self-will, and the inspiration is lost. I don't even remember what I was going to say."

Were they a particularly unsuited group of aspirants, insensitive to higher ideals or even common courtesy, immune to the nobler impulses which inspire even those who have not renounced the world? Hardly. All of them in their letters and diaries revealed a burning zeal to realize God, a sublime understanding of spiritual truths, and depths of aspiration to fulfill the swami's vision of their souls.

Lillian, the gruff and compulsively efficient nurse, ever tormented by her doubting intellect, wrote in her diary:

> The only abiding, really important thing is that that gentle, tender Divine Love manifest thru this our instrument. Nothing else is of any lasting import. In the end Love is all that matters, not whether we have done a certain thing in a certain time, etc. We try to do a certain thing very well; we have a high ideal as to how it should be done; somebody interferes with our doing it, or obstructs thru lack of cooperation, low ideal of perfection, etc. Then all that matters really is that that gentle, tender Love keeps on flowing thru us and secondarily we do what we are doing as well and as promptly as we can under the trying circumstances. This is the course I must adopt. I must be gentle, tender, loving as Swami—as Jesus—this body and mind consecrated to the exclusive use of Divine Love.

Sister Achala, the swami's petulant secretary, who repeatedly smothered his dreams with her practicality, wrote to Daya shortly before the anniversary of their receiving the veil together:

> Now that the 19th of October is so near at hand, I want to send you more tangible proof of my thoughts and unchanging love for you. No matter how silent, or how far distant we may be separated, I know the memory of that sacred day will draw us closer than any outer sign. It is such a big and long journey we have undertaken, and if I thought always of my failures and mistakes I could be so discouraged, but one unfailing thing always brings the courage and strength to go on and on in spite of all the failures, and that is the fact that we have eternally our Blessed Swamiji's guiding hand to direct us and lift us up every time we fall. How richly and rarely blessed we are among human beings!

All of them, the stern Devamata, the grouchy George, the self-absorbed Amala, betray in their letters depths of love and tenderness that would have made the swami's heart swell with satisfaction. Why, then, the tragic hiatus between their aspirations and their attainments?

In order to understand the cross which Paramananda had to bear because of his own disciples, one must recognize the inherent strains of monastic community living. First of all: celibacy, which means not only to sublimate natural human instincts, but also to be deprived of the consolation and security of a spouse, someone with whom to share one's burdens and joys. Although surrounded by people, monastics are individuals alone. The unrelieved intensity of their situation drives them either Godward or crazy, or simply ripples through the community as tension.

Then there is the onerous condition of being with the same people for every waking hour. The same sister whose chattering annoyed you all day long while scrubbing walls, in the evening is sitting beside you clanking her knitting needles while you are trying to read. The same brother who left your tools outside where the rain could rust them goes off to bed leaving his dirty dishes in the sink for you to wash. At the end of a hard day, you do not go home, kick your shoes off, and put your feet up on the table. For the residents of the ashrama there was no escape, not on evenings or weekends or holidays. Relaxation meant you all went to the beach together, like it or not.

Add to that the unremitting stress of constant striving, for their primary occupation, aside from maintaining a 140-acre ashrama, was to utterly transform their human natures into divine ones. While one is paring vegetables or milking the goats or extracting the ashrama's yearly tons of honey, one also has to be striving consciously to remember God, to practice humility, to not let a critical word cross one's lips or mind. So, if at the end of a day, one can look back upon an arduous task completed, a momentary snapping at a fumbling helper is enough to over-shadow all sense of accomplishment. It was rather like holding down two full-time jobs simultaneously. And full-time meant not forty hours, but ninety.

Why did Paramananda not make it easier for them and thus for himself? It was a question which some of his workers ruefully asked. He was committed not to their ease, but to their spiritual growth. Every spiritual teacher knows that evolution takes place faster in a pressure cooker.

As Paramananda himself put it: "Sometimes people I love most dearly, I put them through hardship. At the same time, I know it is going to bring them out in a beautiful way. For instance, I feel about Gayatri, she is going through a tremendous ordeal just now. I know it is going to be the making of her. It is bringing out all the fine things I saw in her. I had the faith in her. I practically dragged her out of India. Now she is finding out I made no mistake."

Saint Francis, that gentle, loving master, once commanded his shyest disciple to strip himself bare, and naked walk into Assisi, enter the grandest church there, mount the pulpit, and preach a sermon. Mortified, the disciple obeyed. Stripped naked, he entered the city amidst the jeers and taunts of playing children, entered the church to the shock of the finely arrayed burghers, and climbed up to the pulpit. Just as he was about to begin speaking, Francis, also stripped naked, ran in, ascended the pulpit, and, hugging his triumphant disciple, preached to the astonished congregation on the glory of self-surrender. One notes that Francis did not revoke the disciple's trial, but rather shared it with him.

During 1929, and intermittently for the rest of his life, Paramananda buckled under such sharing. Why did he persist in what surely seemed like a Sisyphian task? His hands were glued to the boulder by his faith in his disciples, and he could not conceive of ascending the mountain without that sacred burden. "True devotion has wonderful power," he had cried decades before. "Through it a devotee can bring out divinity even from a stone." Now he believed, with an appearance-defying optimism reserved for saints and madmen, that at the top of the mountain the boulder he pushed would indeed manifest divinity. He would never let go of it until it did.

"I place my faith in you anew every day," he wrote to them during this period. "Why do you doubt yourself? Why do you make yourself insignificant by small thoughts? Onward! In the march of life ever steady & onward!" And again: "I feel such love for you, for every one of you. I have such faith in you & your ability to do everything. You are all noble souls, unselfish and true. Sometimes you forget your divine nature and allow yourself to sink in despair. Let me be instrumental in reminding you of your true heritage."

This was Paramananda's concept of his own role: to have such faith in their infinite essence that it would become a reality even for the most petty of them. As he expressed it in a lecture:

> At present we think ourselves weak and we have become
> so, but let us cease to think it and all weakness will drop
> off. Do not remind anyone of his weakness. Make even a

criminal feel the best that is in him. If you wish to help anyone, do not regard his weak side, but call out all that he has of good; only so will you help him to realize his better nature.

One moonlit night the community gathered in the Cloister courtyard for meditation. Afterwards, Paramananda spoke to them from his depths, intoning his words slowly, softly, like a prayer:

> Just know that you are part of that pure spirit. Meditate on it, think on it, carry it in your consciousness, pure and fine, untouched by any earthly sin or sorrow. Just carry this thought in your heart tonight so truly, so potently, that you may realize in a conscious way how much the welfare of a sacred shrine like this depends on you and what a tremendous contribution you can make with your prayers, with your heart's love. Forget all pettiness and smallness. They don't belong to you. . . .
>
> When you feel discouraged, just remember that through His grace nothing is impossible. Through His grace the lame can cross the mountain and the dumb speak. . . . It is all so easy if you can only have faith. If you could only see with the eye of understanding, everything would seem so easy. . . .

In July, 1929, Gayatri Devi accompanied Paramananda to Boston. One morning there he asked her, "Why can't I stay at the Ashrama, the heavenly spot?" She wrote this to the California community, adding:

> Who knows why he does not? You know the life is so different here, all morning has gone by quietly and smoothly, each one is absorbed in his or her own duties. Swamiji is resting peacefully, there is not a noise, disturbance is out of the question. If ever the California work becomes the same, Swamiji will not be so anxious to get away.

In another letter she commented wistfully, "His spirit is free in Boston."

His spirit was not free in California, where the demands of the sprawling community beset him at every hour. Once he was sitting in his study when a poem began to come to him. He reached for a pencil to take it down when suddenly he heard a knock at the door. Sister Devamata had an appointment with him. He knew that if he interrupted the flow of inspiration, the poem would be lost. Again the knock. He quickly got up, climbed through the window, and escaped into the chapel garden, even as the knocks on the door grew louder and more insistent.

"I have sometimes felt," Paramananda confessed, "the ashrama is my calamity."

Despite his growing fatigue and repeated disillusionments, he was never at a loss for new dreams. In June of that year, at the bargain price of $2,000, he purchased twenty wooded acres in Cohasset, a seaside town twenty-three miles south of Boston, to serve as an ashrama for the Boston Centre. The "baby ashrama," or "ashramette" as they liked to call it, quickly became the delight of the swami, the household, and the congregation alike.

Every Saturday they would pile into as many automobiles as the swami could conjure up and descend on the pristine little ashrama. Paramananda would hold a service under the pine trees, then Charushila would serve dinner to everyone on the porch of a portable house set seventy-five feet up in the air on one of the property's huge glacial boulders. Afterwards, they would gather on "the high rock" for a sunset meditation, the tranquil spell of which would captivate even reporters who came to cover the new retreat. As an article in the *Boston Herald* put it: "Deep in the heart of the Cohasset woods, Swami Paramananda has established his Ananda Ashrama, which in English means 'Peace Retreat.' The name is well bestowed; here peace is indeed to be found."

Lola Haynes, wife of William S. Haynes, the inventor and

world's foremost producer of the silver flute, had begun attending the Vedanta Centre the year before. She quickly became
one of their most intimate members, as well as the swami's East
Coast secretary. An astute businesswoman, office manager of her
husband's company, at the same time she had keen spiritual sensitivity. Lola regarded the new ashrama as a fantasyland of natural
and mystical beauty: "Great white cottony clouds changed to rose
pink as we sat on the rocks in the stillness. Little birds sang softly
as though making a gentle accompaniment for Swami's rich voice.
Peace and joy wrapped us as with a soft garment. Cleansed,
healed and refreshed, we drove homeward, singing. . . ."

The little ashrama was the site for many such sacred hours,
and proved a balm to the swami as much as to the others who
sought its peace. At the preliminary dedication service, he defined the purpose of the ashrama by pointing to trees up on the
hillside. They had obviously weathered many gales and storms,
and were bent and gnarled. Then he pointed to the tree under
which he was standing, a straight pine seventy-five feet high,
sheltered from the winds by surrounding trees. He explained
that it was beneficial for everyone to leave the storms of life
occasionally and to retreat to a sheltered spot, so that his life, in
spite of the winds of circumstance which beat upon it, might
nevertheless grow straight like a tree. The Cohasset woods reminded Paramananda of the forest retreats of ancient India,
from where the Upanishads had issued. He explained to a reporter that out of such retreats had come the great thoughts, the
spiritual impulses, and creative energies which were the life-
blood of India. Undoubtedly the swami hoped to renew his own
spiritual impulses and creative energies in that setting.

But for Paramananda even recreation was strenuous. Accompanied by a small group or large, he made the hour's drive to
Cohasset almost every other day that summer, often not returning to Boston until close to midnight. At the ashrama, in addition to the idyllic services, there was dense underbrush to be

cleared, poison ivy and cat briar to be pulled, thorny vines to be cut away, as well as plans to be made for future construction, for the one portable house on the rock was hardly sufficient for the community and congregation members who wanted to stay there. Besides, it was only a summer cottage, and the swami dreamed of making the beloved ashrama usable throughout the year. "Swami delights so in dreaming the buildings one way and another," wrote Lola, "that it seems a shame to put up anything tangible which he cannot move about at will."

His body could not possibly keep up with his dreams, but how it tried! He would give an eight o'clock class on Wednesday night in Pasadena, then dash to catch the 10:15 train east. Arriving in Boston early Sunday morning, he would bathe, change his clothes, and be on the platform in time to conduct the 11:00 service, and the 3:30 service (added for the benefit of the many out-of-towners who were beginning to frequent the Centre), and the 8 P.M. service. Twice that summer he had to run down to Washington, D.C. to plead for another visa extension for Gayatri. *My Creed*, his fourth (and last) book of poems, had to be prepared for publication. Then the stock market crashed in October. "My body wants rest," he told the household more than once.

On Sunday, November 10, 1929, Swami Paramananda addressed a full congregation in the Boston Temple on "Let Your Light Shine." Forcefully he told them that there are two ways of approach to God, one by the intellectual faculty, trying to discern the heights and depths of the Divine, the other by laying oneself completely in God's hands, saying, "Do with me what Thou wilt." He had made his choice the latter path, he said. After the sermon, offertory, and announcements, Paramananda, standing, was about to close with the final benediction, as was the custom. Suddenly he sat down in his chair. "Let us enter into the spirit of holy silence," he said to the puzzled congregation, adding: "Go forth in peace." Mystified, everyone just sat there. Then, with the words "Mother, Mother," on his lips, Paramananda's head fell back and he slumped into the chair unconscious.

In a flash, Mary Lacy and Charushila were beside him. Two men from the congregation lifted his limp body and carried it upstairs to his bedroom, while the stunned congregation sat there in silence until Charushila calmly dismissed them.

When Paramananda again opened his eyes, he found a bevy of anxious faces peering down at him. Trying to summon up a reassuring smile, he said, "Didn't I stage that perfectly?" No one responded.

The episode sent a shock wave as far as the Belur Math. A concerned Swami Shivananda wrote to Devamata: "Twice when he was here, seeing his frail constitution and hearing the amount of work he does and how exhausted and tired he feels, I repeatedly asked him not to strain too much. . . . If he lives, many people will get solace by coming in contact with him personally, and hearing him many will be able to solve the greatest problems of life."

The doctor diagnosed it as complete exhaustion, and prescribed prolonged bed rest. The swami's heart was all right, he reassured them.

Paramananda dutifully obeyed while Charushila conducted the public services, as she had been doing during his absences for the past year, especially since Daya went west in June. After ten days he was feeling so renewed that when Jennie Fraser, a close devotee, brought her new Hupmobile for the swami to christen, he decided to take it for spin. He drove for an hour, past Jamaica Pond, through Franklin Park, and out to the sea by City Point. When he returned home, he was feeling spry enough to speak of going back to California soon.

That night, however, he slept restlessly, and the next morning was coughing and looking drawn. He blamed it on the weather, for the season's first snow was falling, but later he confided with amazement to Charushila that that little outing must have been too much for him. "It is a revelation to me how

exhausted I have become," he told her. "The day before yesterday I thought that I was just fooling, resting all the time in bed.
Today I've realized how the least little bit tires me." The next day
Jennie took him to the bank. By the time he finished his business
there, he was trembling from the exertion.

Nevertheless, a week later, he was on the platform to give
the Thanksgiving service. He was intent on returning to California, where, even before his collapse on the platform (and
before the stock market crash), they had bought a house in Los
Angeles to spare him from staying at the ashrama. The four-day
cross-continental train journey was, of course, out of the question,
but the swami was exploring other alternatives. A boat through
the Panama Canal was the most restful possibility, but too expensive and time-consuming. He decided to take a boat to New
Orleans, from where the train route would take only two days.

Amala was to be his travelling companion. His attempt to
settle her in the Boston community had failed miserably, for,
after less than a year, Mary Lacy and others were threatening to
leave if Amala remained. While professing childlike simplicity,
the twenty-nine-year-old Amala had a genius for intuiting people's
most sensitive spots, then harpooning them with fiendish precision and infuriating frequency. When the victims reacted, Amala
would get hurt and depressed, and would complain that they
were "touchy" or harsh. She burst into tears with little or no
provocation, and was as hard to take in her affectionate effu-
sions as in her ceaseless needling.

At one point, Amala was so abrasive that Mary Lacy, Charushila, Jennie, and Lola launched a concerted effort to counteract their own negative reactions with prayer for her. Each day, at
precisely noon, they would stop whatever they were doing, and
individually would direct their energies and prayers in a healing
effort. Within a week Lola claimed that "already we see a great
change in her. She seems more relaxed, more reasonable, and
less irritable."

It did not last. Two months later Lola was writing to her confidant, Sister Daya, that "Amala is worse than ever." A Dr. Mattinson, who was coming to the Centre's services, heard Amala's complaints about feeling sick and overtired. He offered her twelve free osteopathic treatments and put her on a special diet. As Lola described the developments:

> For three days she had only orange juice, but on the fourth began to cook for herself, buying the most expensive fruits and foods in the market, including a jar of real cream daily for personal consumption—do you sense Mary Lacy's horror? . . . She talks diet and treatment and Dr. Mattinson until . . . each of us stands for all he is capable of in the way of listening to her dissertations then fairly runs from her presence. It is a lucky thing for her we all have a little self-control, else we might add wild screams as an accompaniment to our hurrying footsteps. One night last week we were driving up from the Ashrama. She, Mrs. McCoy and I were sitting in the back of Swami's car. From the time we left the Ashrama until we reached 32 Fenway, that girl never once stopped talking and every word she said concerned the three subjects already mentioned. I wished she would faint or go to sleep, but no such merciful thing happened.

Paramananda's faith in disciples such as Daya and Gayatri was hardly noteworthy, for he was acknowledging what almost everyone saw in them. His faith in Amala, on the other hand, must have seemed like praising the Emperor's new clothes. "I always feel your purity and power of devotion," he wrote to her, "which none but selfless heart is capable of producing. I have invested my trust in you, which is most sacred. Nothing can shake that trust because that is part of the Divine principle. . . . I understand your inner spirit, which is always loving and beautiful. Do not be discouraged, my child. I have great faith in you, and how I delight in you when nobility takes possession of all your thoughts and actions. How it lights up your whole being and makes you rhythmic and true."

Nor did he voice such faith simply because he thought it would be therapeutic for her to hear it. After Amala's return to California, Paramananda wrote to Daya there: "Watch over Amala as you have always done. There is a future there, I feel confident, and I know that patience and lovingness will help her to unfold some of her sterling qualities which she has within."

He defended her against the criticisms of most of the community, pointing out her good qualities, repeatedly praising every little service she had rendered. "Let those who find fault with her," he exclaimed, "be as earnest and sincere. Then they can talk." He was not oblivious to her foibles; indeed, he was usually the brunt of them. But he could not think of rejecting one who had taken shelter in him.

One afternoon in Cohasset he spoke to the group of the great need there is in the world for harmony and peace and lovingness toward one another. He told how Swami Brahmananda was once reproached by a disciple for his tolerance toward a fellow disciple who had caused the swami infinite anxiety and trouble. Brahmananda answered, "But I cannot do without any one of you. All are necessary to me." Paramananda went on to say that if he was willing to accept trials and wounds inflicted upon him by those who knew no better, then the rest of them should be willing to support him in that.

A year and a half later, when Amala was taken ill, Gayatri wrote to her of the effect the news had on Paramananda: "Amala, you perhaps will never know what it did to your Swamiji. All day long, you were his first thought, and it almost brought tears to my eyes to feel the blessedness of his love, now so full of anguish at your distressed condition. No mother with a single child could have loved her baby more tenderly, more yearningly than his heart brooded over you."

At that time Amala was in the throes of emotional turmoil,

and had gone to live with her family temporarily. Paramananda himself wrote to her:

> The loving faith I placed in you twelve years ago is no less today; in fact, it is stronger and greater through the ordeal of time. Things of the flesh change, but that which is based on spirit is of everlasting endurance. Remember this, and be of good cheer. If I told you all the thoughts which rise up from the innermost depth of my being when I consider your spiritual radiance, your love, your devotion, and your unselfish service, I am afraid it would move you to tears.

Swami Paramananda and Amala reached California on January 13, 1930. The very next day he dedicated the house at 745 West Adams Street as the Los Angeles Vedanta Centre. The weekly class which had been held in the Music Arts Building was transferred to the new house, and henceforth the regular Sunday 8 P.M. service was to be held there instead of at the ashrama. Most important, Paramananda himself took up residence there, at a safe distance from the strain and harangue of the ashrama.

Instead of being given her old room in the Cloister, Amala was assigned a room in the Community House. She felt chilled by her cold reception, smarting from remarks made to her by Hilda and Achala. Paramananda solved the problem. He had her move into the West Adams Street house.

Nor was she the only other occupant of the supposed retreat house. Daya, Gayatri, Concorde, and Achala were more or less permanent residents, and a half dozen others came and went for meals, two-night visits, etc. Paramananda drove to the ashrama almost every day; from February on, he slept at the ashrama Friday and Saturday nights. One wonders if, with so many people at West Adams Street, the ashrama was not now the quieter of the two spots.

Indeed, his love for the ashrama, his reverence for it, had not abated. One afternoon, walking through its hills, absorbing its beauty, feeling the sanctity of the place, he exclaimed, "I feel the blessing of God upon the ashrama!" Later he added: "I said it because I could not help repeating what I felt so much."

The public work boomed, as it usually did when Paramananda returned. For Sri Ramakrishna's birthday celebration, fully three hundred people attended the service and the dinner afterward, cooked by Gayatri Devi. For the Easter sunrise service, which by then had become traditional, people began to arrive in the pre-dawn darkness and take their seats in the specially arranged "Sunrise Terrace," until all three hundred chairs were filled. Then breakfast was served, then the 11:00 service, then luncheon in the Community House, then the 3:00 service. The Thursday night "fireside chats" and Hindu dinners, which had been discontinued during the swami's absence, were revived at the West Adams Street house, where setting up and cooking for forty to sixty people weekly could not have added much to the restful atmosphere.

During this period a curious development took place. Swami Prabhavananda, one of the younger monks of the Ramakrishna Mission, left the Vedanta Society he had founded in Portland, Oregon, and established a new Vedanta Society in Hollywood. Two years before, while the debate was still raging about Swami Akhilananda's Cambridge center, Swami Prabhavananda had come to Los Angeles and given a series of three lectures at Symphony Hall. Paramananda had received him courteously and had even missed his own Pasadena class in order to introduce Prabhavananda's first lecture. The following Sunday he had invited the guest swami to speak at both services at the ashrama. Now, shortly after the opening of the Los Angeles Vedanta Cen-

tre on West Adams Street, Swami Prabhavananda was holding
Sunday morning services and midweek classes in neighboring
Hollywood. Coming as it did on the heels of the Akhilananda
episode, it is little wonder that some of Paramananda's followers
took it as a territorial invasion.

Paramananda himself did not bother to react. He invited
Prabhavananda to the ashrama and asked him to speak at one of
the Thursday night dinners. But the relationship between them
would always be touchy until, at the end of Paramananda's life,
all attempts at fraternal harmony would be explosively abandoned.
Eventually, after Paramananda's death and until his own passing
in 1976, Prabhavananda would become the most dynamic and
successful Vedanta swami in mid-century America, a powerful
speaker and a charismatic leader. He would attract a large
following, including such notables as Christopher Isherwood,
Gerald Heard, and Aldous Huxley; would found a large community of nuns and monks; would expand his Hollywood Center to
include a convent in Santa Barbara and a monastery in Trabuco
Canyon, under the new name, "The Vedanta Society of Southern California"; and would disseminate the spiritual classics of
India to a wide, general readership through his clear, lyrical
translations, done in collaboration with Isherwood and Frederick Manchester. But during his early years in southern California,
the energetic Prabhavananda labored arduously in the shadow
of the senior, well-established Paramananda. As one of Prabhavananda's first disciples, Sister Amiya, described that early
period in Hollywood: "The growth was slow and painful. Seekers after truth were few and far between. On many occasions
Swami would stand and lecture for the full hour before a mere
handful of people scattered among the empty seats."

In retrospect, in reading an intimate portrait of Prabhavananda
such as Isherwood's *My Guru and His Disciple*, one is struck by
the similarities between Paramananda and Prabhavananda: their

loving natures, their childlike simplicity, their devotional approach, their zeal to propagate Vedanta. But while they lived, their differences predominated. Prabhavananda, who always worked closely under the direction of Belur Math, disapproved of Paramananda's independent, innovative ways, and considered them the immodest expression of an inflated ego. He once complained to a senior swami in India that Paramananda had introduced him to his devotees as a fellow countryman. Apparently he would have preferred to be introduced as a fellow monastic member of the Ramakrishna Mission, an identity which he valued more than did the non-organizationally inclined Paramananda. Paramananda's followers, on the other hand, considered the chain-smoking Prabhavananda not to be in the same class as their holy teacher; to them he was jealous and competitive. The hostile feelings between them erupted periodically during the 1930s, and, indeed, for decades afterwards. Only after Prabhavananda's passing in 1976 would his Vedanta Society's extensive bookshop, which sold books by hundreds of spiritual authors, consent to stock the books of Swami Paramananda.

———————— ◆ ————————

Just when the prejudice born of ignorance of the East was being assuaged, Paramananda found himself accosted by a backlash born of contact with the East and its representatives, false or otherwise. During the Roaring Twenties, interest in yoga and Hindu metaphysics had surged. This demand was both cultivated and met by a rash of teachers who claimed to impart the ancient secrets to "health, youth, success, and happiness," as one Swami Bhagwan Bissessar advertised. Emphasizing the physical benefits of hatha yoga and charging tidy fees for their instructions, either in person or by correspondence courses, these teachers incited a wave of suspicion against all Eastern teachers.

Some of these popular teachers, such as Sri Deva Ram Sukul

and "Super Akasha Yogi Wassan," were genuine Hindus. Others, such as "Oom the Omnipotent" and Prem Lal Adoris, were Americans who had studied in India. Still others were charlatans who got rich by posing as Hindu adepts.

In a report to the Belur Math, Sister Daya wrote:

> You will understand from all this that Swami's work has been of a slow, permanent growth and has taken deep root because of its pure and holy character. There are plenty in this country who are lighting hay fires by means of excessive, sensational advertising, some from India who call themselves saints and yogis, and degrade with their vulgar methods the sublime teachings of India. No not degrade, they cannot do that, but they grossly misrepresent it in the eyes of the western peoples. Crowds flock to them, seeking mysteries, and turn against them as quickly, and of course, the inevitable reaction and antagonisms aroused react against all Swamis, for the people at large, especially in the Occident, do not discriminate. However, they cannot really harm any true work; but they make the way a little harder and I know that Swami is saddened by these things.

Even genuine Hindu spiritual teachers like Swami Yogananda projected an image of Hindu spirituality different from the one which Paramananda for two decades had sought to establish in America. Using Madison Avenue techniques such as promotional letters and prominent newspaper and billboard advertisements, Yogananda offered, for $25, a three-part correspondence course on spiritual techniques. Paramananda's followers were shocked to see pictures of Swami Yogananda smiling down on them in the Boston trolley. Paramananda responded sometimes by becoming even more low-key; when he saw Swami Yogananda's large advertisements in the Los Angeles newspapers, he withdrew his notices entirely.

As for those who embellished the spiritual teaching through

the promise and display of psychic powers, Paramananda responded by delivering lectures on the difference between "Occultism" and "Spirituality." He denounced psychism as a dangerous sidetrack on the spiritual path, which could "fatten up the ego" and distort one's sense of values. He especially disavowed those who collected money for supposed healings; he maintained that the Divine power to heal was cut off as soon as mercenary motives were introduced. He never condemned any figure, but to his community he disclosed his disdain for "anyone who goes after sensationalism." "This is not a cheap philosophy," he declared. "God is never a popular subject, and those who have tried to preach Him have never been widely accepted."

Despite all disavowals, Paramananda could not escape the effect of the backlash against other Hindu teachers. Once he was scheduled to speak in Louisville immediately after Swami Yogananda had appeared in that city. The Christian clergy's protest against Yogananda's advertisement appearing on the Church Page made the newspapers reluctant even to announce Swami Paramananda. His lectures had to be listed as "Reverend Paramananda." "I cannot tell you," he wrote to the Vedanta Centre, "how sorry and distressed I feel when I come upon these episodes."

By 1930, he was again plagued by the old doubts about the meaningfulness of the public work. Often during his lectures of that year, his voice betrayed the irritation of one who is asked to repeat the same message for the fifteenth time to a deaf audience. He knew where the pulse of the public was, and how shallowly it beat. He was tired of their insistence on pat answers, easy enlightenment, ten-step methods to superconsciousness, as if God-realization could be bottled and sold. With his repeated admonitions to love one's enemies and renounce selfishness, he was accused of preaching "old-fashioned religion," when the demands of the day were for yogic techniques and esoteric secrets.

"I tell you this very frankly," he declared during one service. "I have no price for these teachings. They are India's great heritage. The only reason I would ever give them is when I see a clean, pure, unselfish, true life. Many people think they can go to the market and buy Cosmic Consciousness by paying so much for it. But it can come only from within. What does not come that way is no good to you or anyone. I state this definitely because I want you to know it. I do not make any compromise."

He was not impressed with the large numbers that filled the temple Sunday after Sunday that season. So, Vedanta was in vogue today. Tomorrow a new sensation or fad would arise, and the crowd would follow. The crowd always followed. "Anyone who thinks constantly, 'Are they going to criticize or applaud me?' becomes the slave of public opinion," he declared. He would not tailor his teachings to suit this year's fashions. Public success no longer mattered to him.

One Sunday morning service in May, standing under the acacia tree at the ashrama, he unveiled his heart to the congregation:

> Practical, practical, practical religion! That is my plea. And yet some of you say, "Why does he not give us practical teaching like the psychologists?" My friends, I am not on the market for sale, and I never shall be. What are you seeking? Are you seeking God, Truth, or do you want someone to think for you, and give you your salvation, your liberty, and your illumination? . . .
>
> Someday you may find that I shall change this public activity; often I feel the uselessness of it, the futility. The only thing that counts is living the life, creating a power that no one can resist. I speak very frankly to you. I did not know that I was going to speak this way—I have no written sermons—but perhaps it is because these are thoughts that you and I both need.
>
> It does not make any difference what you call yourself; be something that satisfies your own soul. Do not always look around to see whether your friend or your neighbor or the public approves; gain the sanction of your inmost

being. The recognition that you desire from others, seek it from within. . . .

Did that mean that, less than two years after the dedication of the Temple of the Universal Spirit, Paramananda was losing his interest in the "larger humanity?" On the contrary, his urge to alleviate human suffering was more zealous than ever before, but he was becoming increasingly convinced that real help could not be given by words, but by the vital influence of one's own ideal life.

> If you find somebody who you feel has gone astray, and who is not living according to your ideal, do not go to him with long lectures; overwhelm him by your own conduct and love. . . .
> We cannot convey a great deal by preaching, no matter how full of beautiful sentiment our words may be. We need to live the sermon, radiate the sermon, that in our dealings with humanity, even in a casual way, people may come to realize that our faith is living. . . .
> The thing is, to hold to the one, single, definite, spiritual fact that we radiate light only as we possess it.

The point was too subtle to be grasped by most people. Even those not seeking health or longevity came to the services, or tried living in the community, hoping to learn the specifics of Indian philosophy. They were disappointed to find that a person could attend Paramananda's lectures for years and still not know what the Mimamsa school represented, or the dates the Vedas were consigned to writing, or how Sankara's teaching differed from Ramanuja's.

One young man named Henri de La Riviere lived in the community briefly and then left, complaining that he wanted definite study and more set training, which neither the swami nor his assistants provided. It was a common complaint against the ashrama's unprogrammed lifestyle and lack of real study classes. Late one night, just before retiring, Paramananda talked to the household about how India's ancient sages, or rishis, had handed down their wisdom to worthy disciples informally, by word of mouth.

> You say, "Why did they not write books?" Because the real import cannot be imparted by mechanical means. Some day people will understand what I mean when I talk of these things, that you cannot learn by mechanical means. We have too much mechanical education today, and our inner life is devoid of grace, of beauty. . . . It is only the example that teaches.
>
> The rigid thing never appeals to me. I am not suited for that—do this now, do that. It is all mapped out, no inspiration, no freedom. I have always been a great believer in freedom. That is the reason I never bind people through promises and vows. If your own feeling, your own sense of sanctity, your own inner devotion, do not make you do things that are right, why, the vows do not do any good. They only create another bondage.

Paramananda's "escape" to West Adams Street had, of course, proved a fiasco. Living with the combination of Concorde and Amala was like building a peace retreat under the Coney Island roller coaster. Whereas the others at least made an attempt at tolerance and peace, Concorde deliberately baited and taunted Amala.

A high-strung personality to begin with, Concorde was showing sides of her nature which, during her first "honeymoon" years in the community, had rarely surfaced. The sisters accused her of being flirtatious, worldly, and, worse, insincere. They maintained that the flood of affection and service she had given Gayatri since the girl's very landing was nothing more than a ploy to win Paramananda's regard. If so, it worked. Paramananda wrote to Gayatri of Concorde: "She has endeared herself greatly to me by her care of you."

But that was in 1927. Paramananda eventually tested each of his disciples by withdrawing his attention and appreciation for a time, to see if their devotion and service were solely dependent on ego reinforcement. With Concorde, evidently, they were. Deprived of the personal relationship with the swami which she craved, Concorde began to turn against him. Early in 1930, complaining of sinus trouble and nervous strain, she moved to the isolated top floor room of the West Adams Street house to get away from the group.

On May 26, Paramananda called in two real estate agents to put the West Adams Street house on the market. The next day he left California, not to return for six months. He might be pardoned the indulgence, for he was feeling pains in his chest.

From Boston in June, he wired Sister Daya to put most of the ashrama property on sale. He was asking $150,000 for the upper terrace including fifty or sixty acres, $120,000 for the lower terrace with the Community House and Oak Canyon. The Cloister and the Temple of the Universal Spirit they would keep. "NO REASONABLE OFFER WILL BE TURNED DOWN," he added.

No reasonable offer was given. The country was deep into the Depression, and Paramananda found himself stuck with the ashrama, the Los Angeles house, and the 875 Beacon Street house in Boston, with mortgages on all three.

Nor, with the stock market so low, could he depend upon aid from the sisters, as he previously had. Quite the reverse, he felt personally responsible to take care of those who had given their lives to the work. For example, Sister Daya, whose legacy from her father had been almost wiped out by the crash, long before had lent Mr. Doble $2,000. By July, 1930, he still owed her $900 which he could not pay back, nor could Sister Daya bring herself to ask him, although she needed the money. Paramananda came to her rescue by giving her the $900 and asking Mr. Doble to transfer the note to him. "I can always help you out, remember that," Paramananda wrote to Daya.

On June 23, Gayatri received irrevocable notice that she would have to leave the country within five weeks. Despite all Paramananda's efforts, no further extension could be granted. He was informed, however, that if from outside the country Gayatri applied for a permanent resident's visa, in a few months she would be readmitted under the new status. Paramananda decided to send her to Europe.

The big question then was, who would accompany her? The swami himself would have loved to go, for he had not been to Europe for years, but manifold responsibilities bound him. In addition to all else, construction was about to begin at the Cohasset ashrama. After elegant dreams of buildings on different rocks connected by quaint bridges, Paramananda decided on the most modest and inexpensive possibility. A garage which had come with the property would be converted into a cottage, complete with fireplace for winter gatherings. Brother George, Jessie True-worthy, and Concorde came east to execute the transformation.

When Concorde heard of Gayatri's trip to Europe, she begged to be allowed to go with her. Concorde, however, was penniless; Paramananda would have to pay for both passages as well as several months' expenses in Europe. If Sister Satya Prana went, on the other hand, she would not only pay her own way, but would assume Gayatri's expenses also. In those Depression times, dollars made decisions. Sister Satya Prana and Gayatri sailed in July, leaving behind a bitter Concorde. This was a severe test for her, as Daya explained: "Swami Vivekananda used to say that it was one thing to serve a far away God whom you do not see and whose Will you can persuade yourself is in harmony with your own secret wishes, and quite another thing to serve a living Master who can speak to you face to face and whose discipline may often go contrary to your own desires."

During that summer of 1930, Paramananda remained aloof from the California ashrama. He sent his love and his prayers, but he stayed clear of its snapping jaws. When he received news from Daya of further contention there, he responded to her:

> Please do not feel unhappy or worried about anything. The Great Mother has Her way and though apparently things may be unsettled and there may even be suffering — it is only for a moment.
>
> Why I am not rushing to the Arena, even when I hear these things, I cannot tell, except that my spirit is very still and my deeper nature makes me realize that the Power that works through me must have its own course.
>
> A large, heterogeneous community — I do not think it is the way to build up a great work. The aspect of show and bigness appeal to me less and less. I know how you would love the little house we are building at Baby Ashrama, so free from ostentation and unnecessary frills. Who knows? Perhaps this little insignificant cottage will give us the start for a better and more ideal Ashrama to be. You know I am always full of enthusiasm, optimism if you want to call it that. These are my natural traits. Without them, my life fades greatly. Fear, suspicion, and unloving spirit are not the setting in which my spirit flourishes. Freedom I must be willing to give those who come within my radius and freedom I must have to work for the cause of freedom.
>
> I can always open my heart to you because I know you understand these things, and I want you to know that I do speak to you often even when thousands of miles away. You see, some of you have grown deep and profound, not that you have performed great, formal spiritual practices, but your nobility of purpose, your dedication, your selfless devotion to an ideal have brought you up and nothing can stop the process of this upbuilding. Just a few I want like that, well chosen, harmonious and true to the core.

He was still suffering pains in his chest. Everyone at the Vedanta Centre had his or her remedy — diets, "electric treatments," salt baths—and Paramananda submitted himself to them one by one. But when Concorde engaged a woman faith healer to come in and lay hands on him, the others rose up in protest. The woman had been introduced by Concorde's family in Boston, who had never approved of Concorde's involvement with Vedanta. Why should they suddenly be so anxious to help? The Centre residents did not trust this healer and were not about to subject Paramananda to her.

Concorde was irate. She would not be shunted aside so easily. By the patient's bed they argued it out, and so fiercely that Paramananda later exclaimed, "The battle of Rama and Ravana took place right in my room!" He did not know that he had only begun to sample Concorde's fury.

15

Concorde And Discord

THE GREAT DEPRESSION was more than an economic collapse. It was a national state of despondency, a mass depression in the psychological sense of the word. An entire society which had put its faith in financial institutions, banks, and corporations now found itself betrayed and bereft. With the crash of the stock market, tycoons and laborers alike saw their cherished hopes for security and prosperity obliterated.

Yet disillusionment with the ruined economy did not turn men's minds to the eternal verities. On the contrary, the material concerns which had been their dreams and enterprises now became their obsession. As the breadlines grew longer, men's vision grew shorter.

People had lost more than their bank accounts; they had lost their faith in themselves, their drive, their sense of possibility. They took the failure of the market as their own failure. They were a nation which had failed, a nation defeated, with no victor to blame, an embarrassment to themselves. A feeling of impotence had gripped the nation.

For the next few years, Paramananda's message was a rallying cry. He told people not to waste their energy cursing their fate, but to discover the blessing inherent in every trial. Summon-

ing his audiences to be strong, again and again he would quote
Carlyle: "The block of granite which was an obstacle in the path
of the weak becomes a stepping stone in the path of the strong."

> This depression — the handicaps, the encumbrances which
> are weighing upon us — perhaps it is the very thing which
> will bring out vital issues from our life and fire our heart
> with new consciousness. . . . I often look upon the strug-
> gles I have gone through as my greatest blessings, and I
> think every truly thoughtful person can say the same thing.
> The hours of trial are the hours which make us strong. . . .
> Thus hard conditions may be for you like a little bit of flint
> striking upon you to ignite the fire of real life.
>
> Today on all sides we hear people complaining about
> the misery of existence and there is held before us so
> constantly the picture of a world going to pieces that al-
> most we believe it is so. Is it not time for some men and
> women to become imbued with another concept, to cre-
> ate a different picture which will show us that we are
> placed here by a Divine hand and are fulfilling a Divine
> purpose? Such an attitude would change the whole mean-
> ing of life for us. . . .

Two decades before the swami had admonished, "Do not
give your children the weakening thought that they must depend on material things for their happiness; but tell them from
their childhood that they are Spirit and not the physical body;
that they are the Immortal Self, which is above all external
conditions. Only thus will you make them strong." Now, while
the nation was grasping desperately for remedies to its plight,
Paramananda dared to declare that the need of the times was
not a return to wealth and dependence on wealth, but a realization of one's own inner, divine resources.

> The world today needs, more than gold, the under-
> standing hearts who will by their staunchness of spirit heal

the wounds of humanity. . . .

Our real emancipation comes through the mind. . . . I want men who will show by their lives that they have something other than just a material background. I want individuals who, when men are puzzled as to what is to be done and how they are to do it, will awaken them to the invincible power within. To you, my friend, who feel that your life is discarded because you can no longer earn a few dollars in a machine shop, to you I say, "You are going to be a producer not just of machines, but of thought, ideas, and idealism." . . .

The real heritage of man is within himself. Let him discover it. He who does so becomes a beacon light for his community.

While the swami gave due credit to public works programs and the plethora of social service efforts which had sprung up, he tried to make people aware of a need deeper than hunger and a solution more lasting than food.

"We are doing our part," you say. "Men are hungry and we have given them food. Men are cold and we have given them clothes." That is right. To help others is the first step. But the hunger returns—do you not see?—and the clothes wear out and again there is lack, and there seems to be no end to the struggle. The thing is, there is a fundamental need which we have not met—the need of spiritual knowledge. . . .

Often I have spoken about the significance of feeling a Divine Presence in our life, a Presence that does not leave us, that we carry with us, a Presence so constant, permeating, and pervading that as long as we are aware of it, nothing can molest us or thwart our purpose. That is the dawning of our spiritual consciousness.

Central to Paramananda's philosophy was the importance of the individual. "The destiny of man can be revolutionized through the individual," he used to proclaim, and would give the illustration of a city in darkness illuminated by a single man who kept his vigil lamp burning. Likewise, he maintained, the despair of whole families could be dispelled by a single person with clear vision and undaunted spirit.

> If we carry the joy of God in our soul, others will feel it, for joy of God is also infectious. That is why great souls, even without a word or any organized method, succeed in minimizing the miseries around them. There are human beings so radiant and vital that wherever they go they counteract all darkness and deadness — they bring a new feeling, they create a fresh atmosphere. Even one who is overwhelmed with grief, or in pain, feels new life on meeting them.

He spoke from his own experience. Wherever he went during this last decade of his life, his audiences testified to a new influx of hope and inspiration in their lives. One woman, for example, who heard him at the Louisville Truth Center, had been crushed by an agonizing marriage to an alcoholic, a miscarriage, her own poor health, and having to take care of her ailing mother. The bankruptcy of her husband's business at the onset of the Depression drove her to the verge of suicide when a friend brought her to hear the swami. He gave her no special instructions nor private time, but after that she picked up her life, moved her mother and herself into an apartment, started her own business, and from somewhere found the energy and the courage to make it work. Forty-five years later, self-confident and well-situated, she wrote her story to the Vedanta Centre when ordering one of Paramananda's books to replace her worn-out copy.

How did Paramananda's own centers fare during the Depression? Sister Achala counted the carrot slices allocated to each person's plate and Sister Devamata fretted over the failure of the West Adams Street tenants to pay their rent, while the swami juggled finances and jumped at bargains in the basement of the stock market. The cows, goats, and hens proved themselves the true benefactors of the ashrama, providing enough milk, eggs, cottage cheese, and butter to feed the community and have some left for barter. Sister Seva's beehives were then producing three tons of honey yearly, most of which was sold for profit. The Arts and Crafts Department, created as a means of expression, became a valuable source of income. Gayatri wove scarves, shawls, and bureau covers on the loom Mr. Kissam had made her; Amala and Lillian illuminated bookmarks and the swami's poems for framing; Jessie painted miniature portraits which were then in vogue; while others hand-tooled leather bookcovers and continued to gather herbs from the ashrama hills for making incense.

Their financial situation was always strained, and always demanded Paramananda's attention and ingenuity. He wrote pleading letters to the bank explaining that they could afford to pay the interest, but not the principal, on the mortgage of 875 Beacon Street, which was still unsold and whose tenants were more truant than those occupying 745 West Adams Street. Once the bank sent him a letter stating that the $30,000 mortgage on 32 Fenway was due the following month. "And they sweetly ask me to pay the entire amount," wrote the swami. "It has caused us many laughters." Nevertheless, when the laughing died down, he had to scramble to appease them.

More and more, albeit reluctantly, he was forced to turn to the public for support. Mrs. Hagerty, a new devotee in Los Angeles, was permitted to launch a fund-raising campaign. The *Message of the East*, in reporting a 1931 dinner at the Vedanta Centre, recorded: "The Swami made it very plain that it was an utter physical impossibility for him to carry all the responsibilities and details of both the Boston Centre and the Ashrama in California, unless people who valued the existence of the Boston work came forward with their material help." Many did, and somehow they scraped by, although Paramananda always regretted this dependence on the vagaries of public support. He would quote the Hindu Scriptures: "He who is dependent upon others brings misery upon himself."

Instead he spoke of simplifying, of reducing their needs to the bare minimum, even if it meant sacrificing his own princely standard. "The public would come to hear me just the same, even if I spoke from a hovel," he exclaimed, "and it would be much more in keeping with the teaching." But his own nature recoiled from such ascetic frugality. When Daya offered to come across the country in an Austin, rather than make him pay the $100 train fare, he absolutely forbade it: "Before any of you do such a drastic thing, I shall be the one to set the example, and I do not think any of you will allow me to go through privation; and as your place is behind me, you cannot do these things until I have set the example."

At the seventh anniversary celebration of the Ananda Ash-rama in 1930, Paramananda told those assembled:

> What is the significance of this work? Often I have rebelled at the idea of its scope. At the very outset, the dawn of my early life, did I not renounce the world and its complications? Why then should I be involved with these things now? Certainly it has not been for my own benefit. On the contrary, it is the one thing that has ever brought to me any weight, any burden, any element of misunder-standing. Why then have I assumed it? The answer lies in those who come here and find solace, a true interpretation of life, and healing. Who are we? We are nothing but trustees, that is all.

That trusteeship wore heavily on him. As he wrote to Mary Lacy late in 1930: "I am so sorry that our life is so terribly involved, but I can only hope and pray that the future may lend us greater wisdom and bless us with simpler life. I feel harassed beyond words, but there is nothing to do but wait patiently and do

*Paramananda leaving on the Santa Fe,
October 14, 1925.*

*Pasadena railroad station, October 25, 1926. Left to right:
unknown, Amala, Vimala, Sister Devamata, Sister Seva,
Paramananda, unknown, Sister Daya, Gayatri Devi,
Mangala.*

Hiking at Ananda Ashrama, 1925. From left: Sister Achala, Mangala, Amala, Hilda, Mary Lacy. Front: Sister Devamata, Paramananda.

Left to right: Paul Wiegand (George's brother), Mr. Carlson (Lama), Willie Verbeck, Brother George, Bryon and Catherine Dunn.

Planting in orchard, Ananda Ashrama, 1924. Left to right: Earl Norton, Ruth Norton, Mangala, Mary Lacy, unknown, Concorde, Paramananda.

Paramananda with his brother Bibhu Charan's family. Dacca, 1928. Left to right, rear row: Ranu*, Atreyee, Kanai*, Sita (Chokanu)*, Sati. Second row: Bibhu Charan, Savitri, Paramananda, Maitreyee, Bibhu Charan's wife, Charuprava. Front row: Khana, Ballai, Arundhuti, Roma Nag. (*Later came to America.)

Temple of the Universal Spirit, Ananda Ashrama, 1929.

Interior of Temple.

Cohasset ashrama, "House on the Rock," August, 1929.

On the "High Rock," Cohasset ashrama, c. 1929.
Paramananda, center rear; Gayatri Devi to his left.

Swami Paramananda. c. 1929.

Left to right: Concorde, Gayatri Devi, Paramananda,
Sister Daya. Ojai, California, 1927.

Left to right: Mary Lacy, Sister Daya, Paramananda.
Cloister patio, June, 1926.

whatever we can to get out of it." He spent the rest of his life trying to disentangle himself from his financial encumbrances, but for Paramananda external simplicity was an even more elusive goal than God. He never attained it.

In November, 1930, Paramananda, accompanied by Sister Satya Prana (who had just returned from Europe with Gayatri), George, Jessie, and Concorde, returned to California after his six-month absence. He was suddenly ready to cope with the challenges of the ashrama, for he was lifted beyond their reach by an exalted consciousness which could only have been the product of mystical experience. He never disclosed these sacred inner events, which were the oxygen that sustained his whole being, but was he not speaking of himself when he declared during that period: "There are times when a human being becomes mad with the ecstasy of divine recognition. There are times when he hears a voice like the thunder, convincing, strong, yet full of music, proclaiming: 'This whole world is full of God!' Suppose all books and teachings were taken away, and that one sentence remained shining, glowing, before us. Would it not be enough?"

For Paramananda, during the next two excruciating years, it was enough. Fortified by that realization, he became increasingly convinced that all bleak conditions were merely passing phantoms which could not affect the Divine Reality behind and within. The result was a growing transcendence. "Life is all a fun," he wrote Gayatri early in 1931, "and I hope as long as I live I shall not lose that sense and take it too seriously." The waves of circumstance that had formerly submerged him he was now surfing upon.

And waves there were aplenty. Concorde and Amala turned the West Adams Street house into a battleground, driving the swami back to the ashrama to live. Sister Daya had to be hospitalized. Sister Achala's chronic lung problem flared up, keeping her on her back as much as on her feet during the next few months. In January an influenza epidemic swept the community, leaving half the household in bed and the other half scrambling to take care of them amidst their now doubled duties. Paramananda, concerned especially over Daya, wrote Gayatri: "Oh, how I suffer when any of you are not well and suffer physically or mentally! If it is my lack, I am afraid it will always be there."

Still, he was now the spectator of the drama rather than its weeping protagonist. A sense of the fleeting unreality of it all was overtaking him, and increasingly during the early 1930s his mood became lighthearted and playful. He headed one letter written while travelling: "Scenes From My Latest Moving Picture." When trouble renting the Beacon Street house cost them further loss, thus agitating and distressing Sister Devamata, Katherine Sherwood remarked, "Yes, not everybody can play with life as Swami does." He gratefully acknowledged the support and devotion that the community poured out to him, writing from the train shortly after leaving the ashrama: "With so much love surrounding me, I cannot help but be well and feel like a lion (but not fierce)."

His attitude toward the ubiquitous public work reflected this growing release. He had always claimed that the success of his work depended on the inner unfoldment of its members rather than their number, and refused to compromise his standard to attract huge crowds. Nevertheless, large attendance at a public celebration always excited him, while low numbers disappointed and discouraged him. Now, however, he was shifting his attention from the size of the audience to its spiritual quality. Rather than proudly citing numbers, he would effuse over "the best class of people we have ever had."

"You see," he wrote to Gayatri, "I am becoming more and

more bent on the quality of things, and if we can maintain the highest quality with all the sincerity of spirit, it will win. I am rather interested in seeing this change come upon me, because as you know I have been used to a great deal of public activity, adulation and ovation, and this change comes upon me sometimes with a great and benign sweetness."

In February, 1931, exciting news came from India. Three months before, unable to renew Charushila Devi's visa, Paramananda had had to send her back to India, planning to bring her again when the time was right. Upon arriving in Calcutta, Charushila went to pay her respects to Swami Shivananda, the President of the Ramakrishna Math and Mission. The venerable swami asked her why, with her qualifications as a teacher and her recent training under Swami Paramananda, she did not endeavor to do something for India's women?

Charushila became fired with the idea. After two years of working amidst independent and educated American women, the dire plight of her Indian sisters must have seemed especially pathetic to her. She returned to Dacca, the capital of East Bengal, and, in the name of Swami Paramananda, founded an Indian branch of the Ananda Ashrama dedicated to the upliftment and education of destitute women.

Starting with thirty unmarried girls, widows, and abandoned wives, she rented a house, enlisted a handful of teachers who, like herself, would work without salary, and launched a school, vocational training, and cottage industries. Emphasizing eventual self-sufficiency, the high school taught nursing, hygiene, and domestic science along with its academic curriculum, and seven other departments gave practical training in weaving, dying, tailoring, etc., while spiritual teaching formed the backdrop of it all. A breathless Charushila wrote to Paramananda, reminding him of his dream of a string of ashramas throughout the world: "Let your golden dream come true!"

Paramananda was thrilled. His longing to help India preyed on him even in these straitened times. Only a few months before, he had written Daya of a new investment he had made with funds that were given to him personally: "I also feel happy that at last I can do a little which will help India today, materially. How happy I was yesterday when I was able to send a few checks there out of my present venture. I was really in ecstasy and no one can say that this is money they have given me for something else."

About this time, an insidious problem began to overshadow the community. Amala was complaining that she was being "mentally attacked" by Concorde, who had always been fascinated by occultism and magic. Agitated and sometimes hysterical, Amala claimed that the Devil himself was working through Concorde to unsettle her and destroy her faith in the work to which she had dedicated a third of her young life. But the community had grown impervious to Amala's habitual complaints and imaginings. No one paid any attention until February 15, 1931, when Amala suffered a nervous collapse and left to live temporarily with her sister. Three weeks later she was diagnosed as a severe diabetic. Then followed months of treatment, insulin, two short hospitalizations for insulin shock, and repeated mental setbacks as her mind revolved on the harm Concorde had done her. Paramananda, regretful that he had not heeded her warnings, buoyed her up with phone calls, visits, invitations to go to the beach with the community, and encouraging letters, trying to resuscitate her moribund faith:

> The present condition is nothing but a passing, cloudy sky. It will not last. Call forth with your fervent spirit, all your soul qualities—beauty, simplicity, purity, faith, and holiness. These are the things which abide. . . . The other things belong to a perishable world, and if we dwell on the things which are perishable, our mind takes the tincture

and through it the body suffers; then everything connected with our life is thrown into chaos. Trials and tests come to all, especially to those who have chosen the spiritual path, but when through Divine Grace we conquer them, how great is our solace, how wonderful our victory!

Paramananda himself was struggling with a body which would not heal, no matter how much California sun he gave it. His weight, never above 136 pounds, dropped. At five feet ten inches tall, he was almost as light physically as many people sensed him to be spiritually. As one new student described him: "He looks strong but he gives the effect of great lightness of body—a peculiar effect—of resiliency of body, as if the physical man might move away easily, disdaining all laws of gravitation. Just rise and go away with the ease of his own lightness. I have never seen any man before whose body impressed me like that, as being a strong body, and yet, curiously, hardly more than an envelope for his spirit."

In May, he wrote from the ashrama: "I have not felt well for many, many weeks now, and it has been difficult for me to account for it except that I have thought at times there is some outside influence which tries to destroy my body and its usefulness, but I know there is no power greater than God, and my childlike dependence and unconscious attitude which have always pre-served and protected me will do the same now."

By that time the community had come to believe Amala's reports of Concorde, for they were witnessing what Daya charitably called, "a deep warp in her character." The handsome woman who used to play the mandolin and sing sweet renditions of the swami's poems had turned into a vindictive shrew, flying into mad rages, firing outlandish accusations at the sisters, disrupting the entire household. "She was like an utter stranger," Daya later recalled. "Someday I can say more fully what I felt and saw—an insincerity that suddenly revealed itself to me and made me feel ill. It came like a flash of revelation, the sham of so much that I thought was true." Other sisters whispered that Concorde, her drive to control frustrated, had opened herself to the power of evil, that even her physical features had become contorted.

In Boston that June, Paramananda was feeling indrawn. He wrote the ashrama:

> Certain it is that great clouds have hung over us for a long time, but now, through Divine Grace, I feel the Light is finding its way through them and I know that it will dispel all the doubt and depression and the material problems which have been so overwhelming that I have remained quiet and silent, doing only the things immediately before me. . . .
>
> Please do not have anxious thoughts about me or anyone. The only cure for difficulties is wholehearted prayer and faith in the Divine.

The light did come, but only after the clouds had burst their storm over the ashrama. Ida McCarthy, an affable young woman who, with her eight-year-old son Jackie, had come to live at the Guest House the year before, fell under Concorde's sway. When Paramananda returned to California in July, the crisis broke. As he recounted the story in a letter to Gayatri:

> Almost from the very first moment my feet touched the Ashrama ground, I sensed a spirit of conspiracy which tried to mar my homecoming. It was very obvious that Concorde was out of tune and she was deliberately trying to do as much damage as possible, although outwardly she professed great devotion to me.
>
> To make a long story short, Concorde announced that she was leaving the Ashrama. . . . Also she had conspired with Ida, and Ida was also leaving with Jackie. You can imagine how I felt over this whole situation. In the midst of all their preparation, Ida came back one afternoon and

one talk with me straightened her mind, and she told me it was as if she were under some strange influence. . . .

One point you must clearly understand: that Concorde was not put out, unless it was from some Higher Power. Everyone was most kind, even making serious mistakes in giving her sole freedom in connection with the Guest House during my absence, and she certainly did enough mischief there to wreck a kingdom.

To Mary Lacy he wrote:

The things she has said can only be invented by an insane mind. Poor soul, I pity her from the depth of my being and pray that the Lord may give her a different turn of mind so that she may not wreck herself completely.

It is strange that her going has practically left no gap here at the Ashrama, and the atmosphere is so completely changed that it is really like a different place. . . . I think through her delving into psychism and occultism, she brought a very alien atmosphere and her constant nervous outbursts were certainly poisonous for this community. . . . You have no idea how she has desecrated everything in her mad, uncontrolled, vicious outbursts. But I know there is a Power which will always protect this work and I feel deeply sorry for anyone who tries to hurt it.

Try to hurt it she did, and with all the power she could conjure. Frustrated in her effort to take Ida away from the ashrama, Concorde left with only one ally, Khagen, a young Indian man who for a while had lived with them at 745 West Adams Street. With Khagen's help, Concorde launched a campaign aimed at destroying Paramananda and the work he had built. Immersed in occultism, she tried to direct a psychic bombardment against the ashrama and its members. At the same time, she spread the calumny that Paramananda had practiced black magic on her.

Paramananda responded to Concorde's attacks with a stalwart inner dissociation, believing that she could hurt them only if they gave her inner access through their own negative reactions. "What is the use of dwelling on these things?" he wrote Gayatri. "I have not allowed my mind to be disturbed by them, although it was not easy. I realize more and more that it is the power of the Spirit which can set right what is out of rhythm." Accordingly, the morning after Concorde's departure, he rose before five o'clock and encircled the ashrama singing and chanting the Lord's name. After that, everything took a dramatic upswing: the atmosphere of the ashrama, the spirit of the community, the public work, and even Paramananda's health. "Spirit always conquers," became his new motto. Concorde was pitting her power against his, without ever fathoming his power's source.

Paramananda continued to pray for Concorde, but he took stern measures to safeguard his community from her malevolent schemes. He bid them to cut off all avenues of Concorde's influence by not speaking about her or thinking about her. Those members of the congregation whom she managed to win over, he politely asked to stay away from the ashrama at present. His prayer for his disciples was to "feel a lightheartedness and a joyousness that transcends all earthly pangs and disappointments." His own lightheartedness was unmarred by Concorde's machinations. He had a wonderful summer.

With his new-found health, Paramananda plunged into activity. He undertook to cook dinner offerings for the shrine every Tuesday, Thursday, and Saturday, days considered especially sacred for the worship of the Divine Mother. "These things in the eyes of rationalism may not have much value," he declared, "but I see their effect almost like fragrance that comes after the blossoming of a flower. Several times I have noticed an entirely different atmosphere. . . . These things have made me happy because they always stimulate my interest in the Ideal which is first and foremost in my life."

The close friends of the ashrama (Polly and John Verbeck, Mr. and Mrs. Hagerty, Mrs. Evelyn MacMinn, the Dunns, Mr. and Mrs. Starick, who had moved from Cincinnati, etc.) were invited for the Saturday night dinners, so that the swami usually served between twenty-five and thirty-five people. Every weekend different guests came to stay at the Community House. The newly instituted Thursday night "moonlight services" in the Temple patio drew unexpectedly large crowds, which, Paramananda was quick to point out, were as sincere as they were large. Mrs. Hagerty, to replace the weekly city class which had been moved from West Adams Street back to the ashrama, offered her Hollywood home for Friday night classes. It became the new "branch center" in town. In addition, the swami continued to lecture outside at clubs and churches and occasionally over the radio.

Daily excursions to the Santa Monica beach (an hour's ride from the ashrama) were somehow also wedged into the schedule. As he described it with irony in a letter to Boston:

> My vacation this summer has been as strenuous as ever you have found me. Going to the beach is observed most religiously every day with the exception of Sunday, and even that we have sometimes over-ruled by going at night. In short, when these beach parties are arranged, seating provided for a great regiment, luncheon discussed and executed, going through the same performance coming back—all this leaves very little time for other duties. . . . So I have taken vacation only in letter writing.

Daya added her own description of that arduous summer:

> Always when Swami comes we are busy, as you know. Yet this visit seems to me to have surpassed everything in strenuosity. . . . It seems to me that I go steadily from 5:30 A.M. to 10 P.M. Swami has cooked three days a week in

addition to many other things, and you know what that means. But he is well. I have not seen him so well for a long time. It has been a very trying summer as you may imagine, but the beach has saved the day. Swami actually sunburned. . . . New people are coming with their complications to add to the general collection, but through it all Swamiji smiles.

The public work was thriving, stimulated by a proliferation of special celebrations observed (or should we say invented) by the swami. In addition to the customary celebration of Easter, Christmas, Thanksgiving, New Year's Eve, Durga Puja, Dipali, and the birthdays of Sri Ramakrishna, Swami Vivekananda, and the Buddha, as well as the anniversaries of the founding of the Vedanta Centre, the Ananda Ashrama, and the Cohasset ashrama, Paramananda was now commemorating the anniversaries of the founding of the *Message of the East*, of his first coming to America, of his first coming to Boston, and of practically any other event which he could dredge out of his memory. How the swami did love to give a party!

The publications department was also flourishing. Although they did practically no advertising of Paramananda's more than thirty books and pamphlets, within the first half of 1931 alone book orders were received from practically every state in the Union, as well as Australia, Italy, Hawaii, Germany, Africa, South America, Alaska, and Canada.

Yet, even in the healthiest body, individual cells are constantly dying. So, while the work as a whole was thriving almost as if in defiance of Concorde's threats, the individual workers were undergoing their own cataclysms. During the period 1931 to 1933, almost every member of the community at some point underwent a physical or emotional crisis. Some of them, such as Amala's, were attributed to Concorde's doings. When reports came from Boston that Gayatri looked "thin and colorless," having gone down to eighty-eight pounds, some people testified that Concorde was performing black magic on her, that she had actually bought a doll and was practicing voodoo.

Sister Daya, who, according to Paramananda, had done most for Concorde, was the special target of her ire. In September, Daya wrote to Gayatri, "This summer has been a terrible struggle for me in which sometimes I have felt beaten down to the dust." Her sensitive nature seemed to bear the imprint of every tear shed anywhere in the world. The tense global situation, especially India's struggle for political freedom, tore at her. "Sometimes," she wrote, referring to India's plight, "my heart is in hot rebellion against this cruel world." That year her longing for her "baby" Gayatri was particularly acute. From La Crescenta she wrote to Gayatri in Boston, "I have a great yearning to be with you, not only for the human personal relationship, but for the inner comradeship of love and prayer. It seems as if this platform work would forever keep us apart. I would like to be with you for a while in Boston *very much*. And yet really I do not want—I am learning not to want—anything other than what is."

Lillian was suffering from severe depression and nervous anxieties. On the outside she was a talented, competent, and somewhat aggressive woman. Inside she trembled with fears and panicked whenever she had to carry responsibility. A prolific reader, she was well-versed in all the answers philosophy could give, but her mind harassed her with endless doubtings and questionings. Her life was a perpetual tug-of-war between Paramananda's faith and her own despair. Her case, poignantly documented by her own diary, gives an intimate picture of Paramananda's methods:

Mon., Aug. 17
Deep depression. I tell him that I feel no love in my heart. . . . If there were a way out of existence, I'd have taken it long ago; but I must have tried it in some other

life, & therefore I have this strong sense that there is no escape from existence. "So recently you seemed to have so much insight. Why do you have this feeling now? You know when these attacks are coming. Why do you not prepare yourself, make yourself strong? I, too, sometimes have such feelings, but it is only love for others that gets me out of them."

"Yes, there you have it. You are never without love, but I am without it. I have none in my heart."

"You love me. That is enough to start with."

Sunday, Aug. 30

After evening family service, I ask to see Swami and break down in an orgy of despair telling him all this difficulty of getting away from *Maya* and of the "blessed extinction" that can't be gained, . . . and question whether God *is* anything but Existence. "Why do you tear everything to pieces, yourself, and me, and God? . . . You know nothing and I know nothing, but there is One who knows. Yes, God *is* Love. This whole universe is full of love. . . . Become as a little child. You know that I am childlike in heart. Have you faith that I can help you? . . . There, I will quiet you." Places hand on my back.

Mon., Aug. 31

Go to beach & gradually with no effort on my part, cloud lifts. When sun in sky comes out after being behind cloud, Swami looks at me & smiles, & says, "Now will you have faith?"

Wed., Sept. 16

After doing my own work & getting Hilda's cooking done, I speak impatiently to Swami who is going out to dinner with Ida and Miss Sherwood; because I feel that he is rather unfair & unreasonable about asking us again & again to do Ida's work so that she can go & come as she pleases. When he comes home from dinner in evening, I ask forgiveness out on lawn. His gentle answer: "You know you always have that. I never remember these things."

Tues., Sept. 29

Day of Swami's Departure for Boston

In late afternoon, on reminder of Sister Achala, he promises to give Alice, Jessie, and me our long promised moments we had almost despaired of getting. Sees each of us about 5 minutes in his temple quarters.

"Lillian, I have been thinking of you and loving you more than you know these last few weeks. I have had you much on my mind and heart, though it may not have seemed so. Do you know that, Lillian? The other evening, when I asked you if you were well, I wanted to give you the offering flower. I was moved by a tremendous impetus and that flower was charged. I wanted you to smell it and just drink it in. Well, I could not give you the flower, but your improvement began after that. You got the impetus.

"I love you, do you know that? That should be enough. Keep yourself charged with a lofty spirit. If you cannot do it for your own sake, do it for my sake. That has carried you before; I have seen it. It will do so again."

For years Lillian had been asking Paramananda to send her to India so that she could apply her pediatric nursing to India's needy children, and thus give meaning to her life. Paramananda promised he would send her when she was emotionally stable enough. Her importunings became increasingly hard to resist as word came from Charushila of the drastic need in India.

Charu herself was seriously ill, and with the Depression in India the funds she had hoped to raise for the new ashrama were not forthcoming. Trying to make the ashrama self-sufficient, the girls worked long hours manufacturing matches and cooking confections to sell. Still, only massive infusions of capital from Paramananda enabled them to scrape by. Charu begged Paramananda to come to India to give impetus to the ashrama of which, as all their literature proclaimed, he was considered the founder. But, as Daya wrote, "He has a very strong feeling that he must not leave till he gets that clear inner command or urge."

Meanwhile, Concorde stepped up her campaign to wreck Paramananda's work. She began circulating the libel that so many were willing to believe about any Oriental teacher (or indeed, any particularly handsome public figure): that Paramananda was having sexual relations with the sisters. She maintained that they were practicing *tantra*, an esoteric system, one part of which directs the aspirant to ritually use otherwise forbidden things, such as wine and coitus, in order to ultimately transcend attraction and aversion. (Sri Ramakrishna had emphatically condemned such practices, long discredited in India, as being more likely to ensnare practitioners than to free them.) Concorde claimed that the West Adams Street house had been the scene for such clandestine rites, and she unabashedly offered herself as witness. After all, had she not lived in the inner circle of the community for six years?

Typically, Paramananda issued no denials or disclaimers to Concorde's allegations. He was stunned that one whom he had accepted as his own could so betray him, and that there were others who would believe her, but he felt strong and confident in the protecting power of the Divine:

> It is not in wealth or in friends that we have the greatest comfort, but in our sense of being in God's protecting care. Yes, the material things bring us certain comfort, but nothing can compare with the security a devotee, a lover of Truth, has in God. It is not that sometimes he has it, but always; always it is his, except when his own mind brings the shadow of doubt.

Many of Paramananda's followers believed that light centers, such as the ashrama, galled the forces of darkness, which hovered at their perimeter just waiting for an inroad to breach the fortification of purity. In her betrayal, Concorde had allied herself with those evil forces; she was the agent for a power mightier than her own petty vengeance.

As for Paramananda, he believed that no negative power could touch them as long as they did not give it access through their own negative thoughts and feelings. Prayer and love were the armor invincible. From Boston in November he wrote to the ashrama:

> The only way to remedy such evils is to fortify ourselves with strong spiritual forces. I have been praying for you all and I know that there is no force that can ever touch any of you personally or the Ashrama Holy Ground, so I shall ask that you all lift your mind and heart, and pray as you have never prayed before. Ask the Divine Power to shield and protect even the least at the Ashrama. Those who stoop to evil cannot touch us if we keep our hearts free from all malicious contact. With God in our hearts, we lack for nothing, and nothing evil can ever touch us.

Concorde was sending a barrage of messages and threats to the community through Edwin Phillips, the elderly man who, with his wife Melissa, had lived at the ashrama cottage since 1926. Succumbing to Concorde's influence, Mr. Phillips gradually became suspicious of the evident love between the swami and the sisters. He began staying away from the ashrama services, and took a job outside, while his doubts of the community's chastity grew more insidious. Finally, late in 1931, Paramananda told him that if he felt that way about the community, then the ashrama was not the place for him. In November, Paramananda wrote to Daya:

> Evil never can survive, though for a time it may seem to triumph. It is only a question of our endurance and patience. I am hoping and praying there may be some way that we can entirely shut out every contact, actual or even mental with Concorde, Khagen, and all who bring un-wholesome atmosphere to us. . . . We must be strong about it as we cannot afford to open our doors to anyone who comes for the purpose of spying or any other underhanded

motive. I think we are justified in taking a drastic step in order to keep our house clean. I know I myself am oversoft in such matters, but I am now certain that the time has come for us to be strong and take a stand toward keeping the house of the Lord clean and sweet. . . .

I have no ill will toward any creature and I try as far as possible to follow Blessed Lord Buddha's teaching that the more ill that comes from others, the more good is called forth from me. But I am very strong and zealous when anything touches the minds and hearts of the people who come to the Ashrama for shelter. There is a line which comes to me very strongly now. It is that I shall always give my last drop of life's blood to keep in safety those who have allied themselves with my life.

While some of the ashrama workers chafed to retaliate against Concorde, Paramananda exhorted them that such negative reactions on their part were the greatest victory Concorde could win. He reminded them of the anecdote of the Buddha: A man came to the Buddha and hurled a barrage of insults at him. When he finished, the Buddha asked quietly, "If you give someone a gift, and the recipient refuses it, what happens to the gift?"

"Why, it comes back to the giver," the man replied.

"Even so," returned the Buddha, "I refuse to accept what you have given me."

On Thanksgiving morning, Paramananda returned to California from Boston. Arriving at the station at 7:40, he raced to the ashrama, showered, conducted the public service, and then cooked the Thanksgiving dinner for thirty or more. After dinner he told the family:

When people try to do evil to you, if they can arouse evil in you, then they are successful. But if they cannot arouse evil in you, then the evil they would do turns back upon themselves. If the sword is brought against you and you do not resist, it turns back upon the wielder and destroys. That is the law. That is why great men do not resist; they do not have to. The evil intention of the evil doer turns back upon himself and destroys the evil doer. You will see.

His own spirits were exuberant, buoyed by an optimism that could not be shaken. From the train returning to Boston, he wrote the ashrama in the mock form of a radio announcement: "All is well! Are you listening? You better listen. All is going to be well! . . . You better tune in. Are you listening? Are you?" He signed it: "Your announcer is/ Basantaraj of V.D.M. [Victory to Divine Mother]."

Even during the worst of the scandal, his mood was exultant, charged with a bliss that he could not have extracted from his external life. "I hope you are all well and happy," he wrote to his workers. "No one should be anything else at the Ananda Ashrama. I hope and pray that Mother will inspire you all with Her great spirit, and that you will all rise above the petty and small. How grand and glorious that experience will be for every one of you. Strive for it with all your heart. Nothing else seems worthwhile after you get a taste of this bliss."

His dedicated workers rose to the occasion, showing the endurance and nonretaliation he had begged of them.

The Depression, of course, still hung like a cloud over his field of play. Notes were falling due, banks were harassing him for payments on the principal of both Boston and California mortgages, the new Dacca ashrama desperately needed funds. . . . One Wednesday in December, Paramananda spoke with great feeling to the community:

> This came to me today in the shrine: I have not lost anything; I never had anything. Likewise, when I go to the platform and feel I have nothing to say, That which came through me before is still there. Why worry? Mother gave me a fortune—Her will. Have I squandered it? Also Her

will. I have nothing. She has all.

Your prayers—I ask for them now. I don't want material help from any of you, but I do ask for your prayers.
Some of you are disappointed in me. I have made mistakes,
etc. All right, I have been giving all these years. Now is
your time. Now *you* reinstate me.

More and more during those days he was climbing down
from the pedestal where they had insisted on placing him. "No
guru, master business!" he would exclaim. "I am here to play a
part, a companion, a friend." At one Vedanta Centre celebration,
after listening to a string of tributes praising him as a great pioneer of Vedanta in America, Paramananda rose and told them:
"Whatever good has been accomplished through my humble
instrumentality, I am certain that a very large portion of it is due
to your unfailing devotion and loyalty. . . . I am no pioneer, and
I do not wish to be placed upon a pedestal even by you." To the
ashrama community, whose staunchness and forbearance during that challenging period had deeply gratified him, he wrote:
"I love you all, and I trust you all. I even consider myself blessed
that such as you are my friends and helpers."

Yet sometimes his vitality and inspiration waned. When he
was dragged down from his exalted moods, it was like stepping
out of the sea, and realizing the weight of the burden he was
carrying. One day Gayatri was praising the sisters to him, admir-
ing their spiritual stature, their strength in the face of the current
onslaught. Paramananda retorted, "Why shouldn't they be? I
have squandered—physically, mentally, and spiritually, I have
lavished upon all Divine power. No wonder they are so strong,
cured of illness and everything."

December 23, 1931, marked twenty-five years since the young
sannyasin first docked in New York harbor. Gathered with the
household that evening, he was caught up in his realization of
the omnipotence of the Divine will which had worked through

all his successes and failures, and which now inextricably bound him to this group of "brave souls":

> It is not through accident that I was brought here twenty-five years ago and set on this line of action which has gone on in spite of my short-comings. Also there has not been any accident in connection with your coming into my life, and these thoughts naturally open, oh, deep, very deep thoughts for reflection: that we are bound together, all of us, for a Divine purpose. A Divine Being has brought you to me and bound my life to yours for a definite plan and mission. I have felt this many times today, and for some reason or other it has given me a new sense of happiness. And I have felt some inward joy which has always been my companion throughout all these years, even through my childhood, and today I have felt it in a new way coming into another phase of my activity. . . . Think of it! Here we are through Divine Mother's will, who has always watched over us.

He was breathing freely, resting in the Divine will, banishing all trials and problems with the magic word, "transitory." "A great many things have confronted me since my arrival," he wrote to Gayatri in 1932, "and some of them were hurled upon me quite unexpectedly, but Mother is ever with me and sustains me through everything, even when I do not know how to meet or handle the problems which come to me. So there is nothing to worry about. All things pass away. Mother alone shall stay."

Charged with energy and enthusiasm, he would be up with the dawn and out in his knickers and cap to survey the ashrama and paint it with his dreams: a lookout tower from where the view of the vast panorama would induce meditation; a re-landscaping of the stately pine grove; and here, there, and everywhere more trees — acacia, eucalyptus, pepper trees. Transplanting trees became his daily sport. When he could find no more trees to move from obscure corners of their property, he went out and bought 150 saplings and planted them with his own hands. Calling them his "nurslings," every morning before service he would water them, stake them, and jubilate over their extraordinary growth. He learned to drive the tractor (despite George's conviction that he could not) and to use the power saw. From then on, only the shrine could draw him indoors. "I do not think I have ever been more active in my life than I have been the last seven weeks," he wrote to Boston in April, 1932.

And three months later:

> It is difficult for me to stay indoors any time. My legs always want to carry me here and there, and this morning I went over the whole row of trees that we planted along the road, and am planning at the present time a front entrance gate. . . . At the conclusion of a five minutes' talk I had with Mr. Kissam this morning, he remarked to Sister Satya Prana that, "Well, Swami has laid out plans for a year and a half." So you see how this brain produces jobs for the jobless. I think the United States Government may in its last desperate effort turn to me to create employment for those who are begging for jobs. I do not guarantee any payment, but I will keep them busy.

He was more than ever in love with the ashrama, and kept exclaiming that it had never looked so beautiful, so green, so lush. Unable, as usual, to contain his enthusiasm, he wrote to Boston: "I wish you could all be here and enjoy the beauty, the sunshine, the health that is permeating every nook and corner of the Ashrama. It is a veritable paradise."

Nor was his activity confined to the ashrama. He was still crisscrossing the continent at frequent intervals, stopping to lecture in Louisville, Cincinnati, Dayton, and other Midwestern cities. A new weekly class was instituted in Altadena, fifteen miles from the ashrama, at the home of Mr. and Mrs. Atckison. When he was in Boston, the pervasive sanctity of the Cohasset ashrama ignited his enthusiasm. He encouraged guests to come there for weekend and weeklong retreats, and brought George east to make the place suitable for them. Paramananda found, to his satisfaction, that all he himself needed was five hours of sleep a night.

Music was now taking a prominent place in their programs. Almost every celebration at the ashrama featured Mrs. Dunn on the harp, Mr. Starick or Mr. Gegna on the violin, and two or three accomplished vocalists. The Boston Centre too with, among others, Einar Hansen, first violinist of the Boston Symphony, and Florence Colby on the cello, could boast enough musical talent not only for their regular services, but to hold a benefit concert for Charushila's work.

By April, 1932, the ashrama was beginning to feel the pangs of Concorde's calumny. Many whom they had considered faithful friends were swayed by her stories, and attendance at the ashrama services took a sharp drop. From Boston Paramananda replied to the sisters' letters:

> Some of your reports have wounded me to the core, but the life and purpose of the Ashrama goes deeper and must not be forgotten. Keep on with your path of devotion and staunchness, and the end will justify what you now find lacking. Remember, we are nothing but stewards and servants and we must keep right on doing our part. There is One who watches over us and we want to make ourselves plastic to that One, first, last and always. This fills the gap that is made by the unthinking, unfeeling public. When our mind is filled with this understanding, there cannot be any loss.

The slander which continued to be hurled was a formidable challenge for the man who had vowed never to let anything but love occupy his mind. He had to charge himself anew, as the following poem, written that April, reveals:

My soul, be thou gracious still!
In distress and pain
In sorrow and in anguish,
Be thou gracious still.
If perchance thou art slandered
And insults hurled upon thee,
Thy heart torn and bleeding,
Yet be not ungracious
Nor think harsh thoughts.
If proud world hurts thee
And man shuns thee,
Still be thou gracious in thy thought.
Remember, my soul,
Remember life within!

"Life within" was the keynote of Paramananda's own spiritual practice. He would wake up at 3:00 or 3:30 in the morning and meditate, then would go back to sleep. Sometimes he would keep silence for a day. For the most part, however, his inner life was precisely that, the cultivation of an inner state rather than any external practice. As Gayatri Devi described it years later: "He did not meditate so much as he *was* meditative. When he would walk through the ashrama hills, he would be in a meditative state. . . . Sometimes I had the feeling that there was a kind of armor about him, that you couldn't draw near." Hindu literature often refers to the "cave of the heart" where the Lord abides. That was the only secluded spot which Paramananda was to find in his people-thronged life, and he retreated there often.

During the trials of 1931 and 1932, Paramananda gave most of his time and attention to California. Eventually this redounded on the Boston work. Upon her return from Europe in October, 1930, Gayatri Devi had been put in charge of the services at the Vedanta Centre. As Daya described Gayatri in a letter to her: "You are like a pure, white flame, blessed child, and there is in you a profound strength." Paramananda was proud of the spirit she instilled into the Vedanta Centre by her fervor and one-pointed dedication to "the life." During one visit to Boston he wrote to the ashrama: "The spirit of the house here is very lovely. I have not felt such warmth and spiritual atmosphere since Queensberry Street days." In September, 1931, Daya could write to Gayatri: "Swamiji feels so relieved of the responsibility at that end of the continent as far as the spirit, dignity, and prestige of the work are concerned."

Gayatri herself was not as satisfied. Relentless in her own zeal for inner perfection, she complained that Boston had "too much indulgence, too much freedom, too much pull from the outside." Indeed, the 32 Fenway house was occupied mostly by working women who, while committed to Vedanta, had one foot—and most of their heart—in the world. The only "consecrated workers" there were Gayatri and Mary Lacy, who, for all her unswerving loyalty and selfless service, could never turn down a theater party or social outing. Some of the women, like Belle Barnard and Anna Johnson, did not have sufficient respect for the twenty-five-year-old Gayatri, especially when her ideas threatened to interfere with their worldly amusements.

The community often used Paramananda's playfulness as the rationale for their own frivolity. The swami himself clearly distinguished between the two in a letter to Gayatri:

> You see, my child, I lead a very spontaneous life. I give expression to my moods, and most often that mood expresses itself through joyousness, but can anybody imitate that without making himself ridiculous or losing his principal aim? If the bliss of God comes out of the inner depth, it will have soul quality, and if it is a pretended thing it leads to fickleness and frivolity.

By July, 1932, reports that some of the Boston household were missing the daily shrine services, although they had time enough for personal pastimes, prompted Paramananda to take a stern stand in a letter to the Vedanta Centre:

> It is quite important for us to keep up the spirit of the work for which it is consecrated. . . . It is not a place for worldly atmosphere, pleasure seeking, rendezvous, or any such notions. It is to help people who need help spiritually, and in order to give that abiding help and solace, we must possess it and radiate it even in the atmosphere. This has always been the characteristic note of the Vedanta Centre of Boston. Of course, I admit that since moving the major portion of the consecrated workers, it has somewhat lacked this quality. Some of you have lost your objective and you naturally seek your pleasure in moving pictures, ice cream treats, and other diversions, and I blame myself for it greatly because your spiritual life has not been filled adequately. If you had something bigger in your life, you naturally would not stoop down to these small and trivial interests.
>
> I am a hundred percent for strength — moral strength, spiritual strength, and strength of character, and those who exhibit these, they are closest to me; the others will only find passing contact with my real purpose.

He decided to send Sister Daya to Boston. He felt she needed the change in any case, for she was suffering from "tired nerves." Despite the swami's pleas not to strain or feel hurried, Daya worked under the constant pressure of one whose heart was bigger than her day was long. She would spend hours visiting sick friends, taking ailing cats to the veterinarian, and doing favors for anyone who asked her, then would rush back late to the ashrama to prepare the shrine for vespers, amidst the scowls of the rest of the community who were waiting in the temple. To make up for her daytime missions of mercy, she would have to spend half the night editing the *Message of the East* for its deadline, and at 5:30 would wake up to prepare the morning shrine, exhausted.

The stock market crash and onset of the Depression had left

Daya the heiress with only a meagre remainder of her father's legacy. For a couple of years, the family struggled to salvage their real estate holdings. By 1931, her older brother, who managed the family's finances, wrote that they were on the verge of being wiped out. Although Daya herself had never cared to have more money than what was needed for her own modest living expenses, always giving away and loaning more than she spent, her new dilemma of how to make ends meet and the distress of watching her family in turmoil must have added to her strain.

Ever prone to self-depreciation, Daya referred to herself as "a poor, blundering instrument." To Gayatri she wrote, "I beg you to pray for me that I may be washed clean of all but the vast and the unbounded. I need your prayers. I am sickened sometimes at the things which rise up in me and call themselves 'me'—Egotism, brooding, pride, resentment, a whole flock. Pray that they may be shriveled up in the dazzling light of Pure Beauty—my God."

Daya's transfer to Boston in August meant that Gayatri would have to go west to conduct the ashrama services during Paramananda's absences. While plans for her trip were being made, Paramananda received an anonymous letter warning him not to let Gayatri travel alone, for someone was planning to harm her. As a matter of fact, Paramananda had always arranged for someone—one of the sisters, George, or himself—to accompany Gayatri on her cross-country journeys. This time he was adamant that she would travel alone. "Do not be afraid of anything or anybody," he had written Gayatri earlier that year. "Fear is a terrible obstacle. . . . We are in His hands, therefore always safe." Gayatri departed Boston on September 14, and four days later arrived in California, without incident.

Paramananda, who deeply admired Daya's spirituality, despite her own disavowals, hoped that it would likewise inspire the Boston household. "Your spirit is so noble and consecrated,"

he wrote to her shortly after her arrival there. "I hope that the
Boston people will feel more and more the value of truly spiritual life as they come in contact with you."

Lax habits, however, are not so easily relinquished. Two
months after Daya's arrival in Boston she wrote to Gayatri
facetiously: " 'Let not the flame die out!' That is in my heart
constantly. But here the only flame that is not allowed to die out
is the furnace flame."

Paramananda, who could tolerate anything but a lack of
consecration, decided on a "house cleaning" and named at least
three people whom he wanted to leave the Centre. With unprecedented severity, he wrote to Daya:

> The spirit of renunciation and holiness must dominate,
> and I am quite ready now to face the consequences, be-
> cause there was a time when I was afraid to hurt anyone,
> and that should not be the standard of a spiritual community.
> It is better to hurt a little, than to let the wrong prevail for
> fear of hurting anyone.
>   . . . I have felt so heavy-hearted and really sick, that
> after all these years of aspiration such things should
> prevail. . . . I am not going to reprimand anyone, because
> who am I to do it, but nevertheless there is a heart that
> bleeds. Here everyone, especially the Sisters, are denying
> themselves. They do not even hear the word "cream," and
> I understand from Gayatri's description that there are eight
> half-pints used for the weekends, and everybody is gaining
> weight. This does not make for spiritual life. I was never
> austere, and I do not expect to go to any extreme, but life
> is stern now, because I see without strength there is no
> happiness and there is no hope for spiritual life.

Such a severe stance, especially when it came to hurting
other people, was hard for Paramananda to maintain. By his
own admission he was "soft." Indeed, one of the three whom he

wanted out managed to stay comfortably ensconced at the Vedanta Centre for the rest of her life.

In California the cast of characters was constantly shifting. Melissa Phillips missed her husband greatly, despite her devotion to Paramananda, whom she credited with her speedy and almost complete recovery from a major stroke in 1929. The swami, loath to stand between a married couple, urged Melissa to join Mr. Phillips. She left in September, 1932, the same time that Willie Verbeck embarked on a trip to his native Holland to visit his mother.

Such exits were always balanced by entrances. Recommended by Mrs. Dunn, a destitute young couple, Joe and Yvonne Rubles, and their infant daughter, came to live and work at the ashrama. Then in August a Mr. Walter took up residence there.

After a year of entreaties by Charushila, Paramananda decided to go to India in December, 1932. He would be accompanied by Dr. Peter Boike, a long-time devotee from Cincinnati, who was eager to introduce chiropractics to India; Miss Edwina Post, an elderly New York society lady who was one of the swami's faithful followers; Sister Satya Prana, who would remain in Dacca to help Charushila; and Lillian, the nurse, who, ready or not, could no longer be put off.

Ten days before their scheduled departure, Paramananda received a letter from Concorde bidding him to meet her at her Los Angeles house to discuss "several points which concern you most." She warned that "otherwise the press here and abroad might be greatly interested in the life story of consecrated workers of Ananda Ashrama." She gave him a deadline of the following Sunday, "after which the matter will be in other hands."

Paramananda made no response. He and his party sailed, as scheduled, on December 26. The December issue of the *Message of the East* published the swami's prayer, which was his real answer to Concorde:

Tonight, as I prayed before Thee, O Lord!
I was more conscious of those
Who have hurt me and caused me great pain.
My heart was full of love for them,
As I prayed and implored Thee to give them peace.
Oh, what a sweet solace filled my whole being!
I found a new delight,
As Thy light burst upon my soul.
I saw, as never before,
What it is to love one's enemies, —
To bless them that bring a curse upon us;
And do good to them that turn their hate upon us;
And to be able to pray from the depth of our being —
    fervently —
For those who abuse and persecute us.
O Lord, giver of all true blessing,
Keep this vision with me —
Though I be stripped of all earthly goods!
    Amen.

16

Betrayal

"WE ARE A CHOICE BUNCH to say the least," Paramananda wrote of his travelling party aboard the *Chichibu Maru*. "Sister Satya Prana in her habit and stern bearing, and Dr. Boike with his artistic necktie and broad grin, and Lillian with her evident missionary and somewhat antiseptic outlook, and Miss Post with her girlish enthusiasm to go round and round the promenade deck to outdo the speedy *Chichibu Maru*, and myself as a mysterious magician disguised as a lad, make a very enviable group."

Despite the crisis which was climaxing at the ashrama, Paramananda was in a jovial mood. During this Pacific voyage, he wrote some of his most amusing letters:

> Well, I must not forget to share with you some of the funny conjectures about my age. Some of them were absolutely sure that I was 65. Heavens and hurricanes help us. One elderly gentleman told me that a certain Sarat Chandra Guha Thakurta told him that he was my classmate and that I was 3 or 4 years older than himself and that he was now 56. Well, can you beat it! He must have studied with my ghost. That is the only part in me that ever studied. . . .

It was a time of reflection for him; he discerned changes in himself, a mellowing in his personality and a growing realism in

413

his passion to help people:

> In some way I think I am changed this time. My heart
> is full of mellowness specially for those who think that
> they are on a lower rank. I used to be shy of people,
> retiring, and sometimes aloof. All this made them feel that
> I was unapproachable. This time I go down anywhere and
> make even advances to those who are afraid to come near me.
>   . . . I fervently hope that Lillian will find herself in
> India. We make our heaven and its opposite. I am begin-
> ning to realize what hold destiny has upon human life. . . .
> There was a time when I disregarded all personal fitness
> and karma and tried to force happiness upon others, but
> it did not work in most cases. People must earn their rights
> by renunciation and selfless consecration.

Docking in Japan, the swami had to stave off newspapermen
who pursued him into his cabin, one even posing as the Chief of
Police in order to get an interview. They made brief, triumphal
stops in Singapore, Penang, and Rangoon. In each city, Paramananda lectured to appreciative thousands at meetings presided over by dignitaries such as the Lord Mayor of Rangoon.
On February 5, 1933, they reached Calcutta.

With Paramananda's departure, it was as if a protective shield
surrounding the ashrama fell. On Sunday, January 22, 1933,
Concorde and Khagen appeared at the Cloister. Entering through
the rear courtyard gate before the three o'clock public service,
they demanded to see Sister Devamata alone. Devamata, who
had trained herself to retain the swami's spontaneous discourses,
later dictated a verbatim transcript of the conversation which
followed. This was typed and sent to Paramananda.

In the scathing interview, Concorde accused Paramananda
of slandering her, pursuing her, trying to kill her, and using "all
kinds of evil, occult forces" on her. Sister Devamata, without
ever sacrificing her composure, countered each allegation, and
asserted, "Swami does not know anything about those forces.

How could he use them?"

Finally Concorde announced: "I have in my pocket a letter to the Ramakrishna Mission which I am going to mail tomorrow. It tells the whole story. Swami will have to stand the consequences, for they will put him out of the Mission when they read it. Would you like to see it?"

"No," Devamata answered nonchalantly. "I have no curiosity to see it at all."

"Well, I have come to warn you." Concorde's tone changed from ominous to solicitous. "I love you, the work is going to crash, and I want to save you. It has gone out of my hand into more powerful hands. I have no power to stop it now and there is going to be a terrific attack made on the work here."

Devamata was unruffled. "Sri Ramakrishna's work cannot be injured. His power is greater than any power of evil you can turn against it. I am not afraid to stand with it. . . ."

When Khagen insinuated that the ashrama was corrupted by "sexual perversion and prostitution," Sister Devamata had had enough of the conversation. She summarily closed it, but the intruders were not so easily ousted. Three times the senior sister had to declare that the conversation was ended.

"You have our address," Khagen told her. "Any time you need us, you know how to reach us."

With all the grand hauteur with which she was endowed, Devamata replied, "I shall have no need of it."

It was time for the public service in commemoration of the birthday of Swami Vivekananda. Concorde and Khagen walked quickly to the Guest House where they accosted Ida. They told her that they had come to warn her of the imminent crash of the work. Ida replied that she did not want to hear anything that they had to say. Then, while Khagen paced the parking lot, Concorde took her seat in the temple for the service conducted by Gayatri. The community felt that Concorde was trying to unsettle Gayatri by her presence, but the young woman was unaffected. "Gayatri was inspired and everyone felt tremendous power," wrote Achala. "Sri Ramakrishna was right there, and I am sure Concorde never felt more powerless."

After the service, Concorde and Khagen and two women they had brought circulated among the congregation, speaking to whomever would listen to them. Khagen approached Jessie and asked her if she knew what had been going on in the West Adams Street house, painting for her a lurid picture of profligate rites. Jessie, fiercely loyal, told Khagen to get out, that she wanted nothing to do with him. "I am so thankful it was Jessie to whom he made these remarks," wrote Achala to Daya, "for I am afraid some of us might have been violent, and he would have liked that. I don't know what George would have done, for when he heard of it afterwards, he was so mad he said if he had known it before he would have kicked him off the Ashrama. I think Khagen would have been lucky to get no more than that from George."

They must have left disappointed, for they had not managed to create a scene or any major disruptions. But they told Ida that not a week went by that there were not spies at the ashrama, and that soon there would be a civil investigation and arrest. "Her hatred for Swamiji is something terrific," marvelled Achala.

Many in the community were surprised and impressed by Sister Devamata's performance that day. They need not have been. They tended to sell her short, cognizant of her obvious foibles, unaware of her spiritual stature or of her inner growth in those years since she had been snatched from death.

This was partly due to Devamata's own aloofness. More than anyone else in the community, she was a person alone, always present at community gatherings (every evening, like a ritual, she sat in the Cloister living room until nine o'clock to encourage "togetherness"), but rarely revealing the woman behind the veil. As one of her poems describes her attitude:

As the red Indian moves through lonely forests,
Erect, silent, grave and fearless of his foe;
So do men move through this human life
Enveloped by a silence none can penetrate
Wrapped in an aloneness none can tear aside or lift;
Single file, silent and apart they march through
    the days and years.
Let them walk erect and fearless, to eternal ends.

It was those "eternal ends" which most absorbed Devamata during the years of her physical infirmity. Feeling more comfortable with God than with humans, she would spend long hours in meditation, going up to the temple shrine at night after the others had retired. Shortly before her death, she recorded the mystical experiences which were periodically vouchsafed to her, unbeknown to the community which considered her merely a fretful old woman. Once, kneeling in the shrine at night, she saw the wall behind the altar roll back and high in the hills behind, amidst a blazing light, the figure of Sri Ramakrishna. Moving on a trail of light, he descended into the temple, and stood on the right side of the altar, with his hand resting on it. Smiling at Devamata, whose fear and awe were melted by his tenderness, he spoke to her, a message that she did not divulge.

She had several such visions, one coming to reassure her when she was troubled by the criticisms of the community. They were not simply psychic phenomena, but always conveyed a deep spiritual impetus, leaving her with a heightened sense of the Divine presence. Her scientific, rational mind had no trouble accepting these experiences, which are uniformly reported in all religions. As she put it: "The Divine is present in every human heart. It is the eternal part of man. . . . Why then could it not take form as a living Presence and become the daily companion of the devotee, who through intensity of devotion calls it forth? It may appear in different forms, it may bear different names, . . . but that it comes there can be no doubt."

One evening, she went up to the shrine before the evening worship. As she described what happened.:

> I knelt before the altar and had been there for some time when suddenly I experienced a sense of strange lightness. I looked down and saw with open eyes that my body was gone. Only the heart remained and on it, as on a throne, sat Sri Ramakrishna. The seated figure was small, but unmistakably living.
>
> From the body on all sides shot forth leaping flames of different colors. . . . Something made me understand that it was these flames which had burned away my body. How it gathered again substance and form I do not know. The glow and the exaltation that came with it continued for many days. The flames died down, but the figure has never gone.

She suffered from Parkinson's Disease, as if the rigidity of her personality had been transferred to her body. Parkinson's concomitant syndrome of worry and anxiety belied her spiritual state. It made her difficult to live with, for the swami as well as the community, who were often impatient with her carping fears. Her sisters had no idea of her inner consolation.

Her personality would always be austere, but she had changed since the days of Queensberry Street. Paramananda's gentle example and teaching, and her devotion to it and to him, had indeed wrought a transformation which is obvious in this poem of those later years:

> A towering snow-veiled mountain
> Lifting its head to heights immeasurable;
> Sharp ledges and sharper crags
> Down its rock-hewn sides,
> Tearing the climber's slipping seeking feet;
> No tree, no bush, no root to hold to—
> So seems the Ideal to the soul aspiring.

A peaceful sun-bathed meadow,
Sweet with fragrant bloom and waving grasses
Freshened by soft rain-scented breezes
Blowing from distant blue-green hilltops;
Everywhere blossoming and brightness —
Such is the Ideal to the soul attaining.

———————◆———————

Concorde did indeed mail her letter to the Ramakrishna Mission headquarters at Belur. She also took her story to Swami Prabhavananda, the head of the nearby Hollywood Vedanta Society, and to Swami Ashokananda, the new head of the San Francisco Society. Pointing out to them that sensational publicity about one swami would inevitably ruin the reputation of Vedanta in America, she promised that no action would be taken if Paramananda remained permanently in India. As soon as he made any effort to return to the United States, however, an investigation and the ensuing publicity would be let loose.

Swami Prabhavananda telephoned Sister Devamata twice that day, the second time asking her if their work could continue for a time without its leader. Then he cabled the Belur Math, relaying Concorde's allegations and advising that Paramananda be kept in India. He also cabled Paramananda not to return, for the sake of the whole American work.

The sisters were irate. Achala wrote to Paramananda:

We have felt simply stunned to think that Swami Prabhavananda should have cabled you, without informing us, especially as he had talked with Sister twice on the Saturday when he must have sent his cable to the Math. . . . It is inconceivable that he should take such an attitude and allow himself to be so frightened. He has it in his power to disarm Concorde, and everyone feels he is nothing but a tool in her hands. He should never have listened to all she had to say.

They were shocked to realize that Swami Prabhavananda might actually have believed Concorde's tales.

Concorde had one more card which she threatened to play. If all other efforts to keep Paramananda away failed, she promised to go to Washington and convince the immigration authority to deny his re-entry. The influx of Oriental charlatans during the last decade had made a large sector of the establishment suspicious of all swamis, and Concorde hoped to play on this antipathy. "Since you left," a frightened Achala wrote to Paramananda, "the Government has become more and more strict with immigration, and has been very drastic about sending out 'aliens'. . . . Of course, we have not forgotten you have your re-entry permit, but Sister [Devamata] and Sister Seva seem to think that may not count for anything, if anyone chooses to make trouble."

By this time Concorde's slander campaign had percolated through the public, and gossip was rampant. "There is no doubt but that the work has sustained a very severe blow," Achala lamented. People who had never even been to the ashrama were now whispering about its private life. One devotee who had just begun attending the services was listening to a lecture in Los Angeles, when the gentleman next to her commented on the speaker. She agreed that he was absorbing, but explained that her real interest was the Ananda Ashrama and the swami there. "Oh, you mean Swami Paramananda," the man replied. "He is in India now, and he will never be allowed to return."

In Calcutta, Paramananda responded to the storm with characteristic forbearance. "When I pray," he once remarked, "it is never to minimize my burden, but that I may be given wisdom to meet it." He was determined to use every crisis to approach closer to God.

One day at the Belur Math, Swami Shivananda noticed that Paramananda looked uncustomarily glum. When he asked him where his usual smile was, Paramananda referred to news of problems at home. "Why do you worry?" Swami Shivananda replied. "Truth alone conquers."

Paramananda tenaciously believed that it would. While the other, younger swamis who directed the Order were urging him to stay longer in India until this whole scandal should "blow over," Paramananda held firmly to his April 10th sailing date. Some of these swamis, who had sided with Akhilananda five years before, actually wondered whether the stories related in letters by Concorde and Swami Prabhavananda were true. Sister Satya Prana wrote to the ashrama: "The whole situation in America cannot be appreciated. I do not mean that Swamiji has not spoken, but he has not been fully understood and feels, as always, he must move according to his own light and not be directed by others."

Meanwhile, India kept him spinning between private audiences and mass lectures. Invitations poured in from different cities, and individuals exclaimed how much they were inspired by his presence. "India has gripped me this time," he wrote, "not with mere sensational receptions and ovations, but never did I find such point of contact, and such openness of Spirit as this time. Its genuineness is very living."

He arrived in Dacca in time to celebrate the second anniversary of the Ananda Ashrama there, much to the elation of the exhausted Charushila Devi, the now sixty ashrama residents, and the two hundred and fifty students in the school. They greeted him with the blowing of conch shells, singing, and loud shouts of "Jai Swami Paramananda Ki Jai" (Victory to Swami Paramananda). He stayed with them for over two weeks.

As more reports of Concorde's threats were received from America, Paramananda become more resolute to return there as scheduled. "His fighting spirit is roused," Sister Satya Prana wrote, "and he wishes to 'face the brutes'!"*

---

*"Face the brutes" in Vedantic circles refers to Swami Vivekananda's story of his once being chased by vicious monkeys. An onlooker called to him: "Don't run away. Face the brutes." As soon as he turned and faced them, the monkeys fled.

In mid-March, he left Calcutta for Puri, Mysore, Bangalore, and Madras. It was his first trip to South India since his fateful 1911 trip, when he had arrived too late to see his beloved mentor, Swami Ramakrishnananda. The cities which had known him as a youth now hailed him as "the messenger of peace, love and good will—the standardbearer of your illustrious Master Swami Vivekananda." They held mass meetings in his honor and presented him with lavish addresses of welcome. "You have held aloft the ideal and striven to keep us on the Godward path," proclaimed the printed Mysore address. "You have been a living poem of Harmony and Love." His books, especially his poetry, had circulated throughout the subcontinent, some of them in vernacular translation. He was known, and loved, wherever he went.

One by one, he was leaving his original travelling companions behind. Miss Post, finding India beyond her power or inclination to adjust, had already left for Europe and America. Dr. Boike was staying in Calcutta to implement his dream of helping India through chiropractics. Paramananda arranged for Lillian to serve as a nurse at the Ramakrishna Mission's clinic for infants, the Sishu Mangal Pratisthan in Calcutta, established only the year before by Swami Dayananda. She would be working with another American woman, Miss Pfeffer from San Francisco. Sister Satya Prana, amazingly adaptable despite her age, accompanied Paramananda as far as Colombo, then returned to Dacca to live at the Ananda Ashrama for two years, to lend support to Charushila Devi.

Paramananda was taking back to America two young people from his family. Bibhu Charan's second son Kanai had refused to apply himself to his studies. His father felt (accurately as it turned out) that a change of environment would stimulate Kanai's motivation, and he begged Paramananda to take him back to Boston for college. Paramananda's younger sister, Labanya, was a widow struggling to raise her four children. She appealed to Paramananda to take charge of her daughter Sumita, without informing him that she was a temperamental and unruly girl whom she simply could not handle. The swami, who had seen the diffident Gayatri and the burdened Charushila transformed into shining credits to India, decided to take these greater challenges. On April 10, 1933, Paramananda, Kanai, and Sumita sailed from Colombo via Europe to America.

On May 8, they docked in Boston. After all of Concorde's schemes and contrivances, Paramananda descended the gangplank to his adopted home without the least obstruction.

In mid-May Daya could write from Boston, "Swamiji is beautiful and well. The joyous, surrendered child who knows that Mother is watching—and yet what deep pain in his heart!" Three weeks later she described how she came upon Paramananda unawares in the library and found him singing and dancing for Fluff, their pet parrot, "who was all aflutter with excitement and was dancing too in time with Swami's teasing finger. It was a real picture."

Paramananda stayed in Boston two months, waiting for Divine direction before proceeding to California, where the ashrama seemed to be bearing blow after blow. Gayatri was hospitalized for a heart murmur for the third time since March, causing Paramananda to suggest suspending the public services temporarily, unless Sister Achala was willing to read for them. (She was.) Several members of the community abruptly left that summer: Ida and Jackie McCarthy, Joe and Yvonne Rubles, Victor Peterson, and Lester Flint (for the nth time), leaving the Community House so vacant that they considered closing it. Some of the intimate householder followers who lived outside the ashrama, too, were suddenly acting cold and distant.

The anvil does not shatter, but it shakes. Paramananda withdrew into his periodic state of quiet detachment. The Boston work was thriving, but in this mood he could relish none of it. At the end of June he wrote the ashrama:

I feel tonight a strange apathy which I cannot account
for in any way except perhaps that the public work no
longer seems to appeal to me. It is not that I do not like my
work, for instance, tonight's class was a great inspiration to
me as well as to all those who came. It was a very large
class, and I felt grateful that so many received help and
fresh inspiration through it. If it were not for the feeling
that others derive benefit from it, I think I would drop it
in a moment.

Life is like a book; every chapter has its own special
significance. I think some of you are puzzled to know why
my mind is withdrawn from the Ashrama. It is not from the
Ashrama or those of you who are closer to me than life itself,
but circumstances have given a strange turn to my mind.

I gave myself as completely as I knew how to create,
through His grace, a beautiful spot, fragrant with spiritual
atmosphere. And also, without hesitation, I have given
what is best in me in the way of love and service. And it
seems to me very strange that some of the very people
whom these hands have served and even fed should consider me a blockade in their path. . . .

One of the particular objectives in my mind was to
make a home for you all, and if some good has been
accomplished, why should I ever feel even a moment's
disappointment? My home is the whole world, not in a
figurative way, but in the most real way. You see, I am
almost afraid to write these thoughts because some of you
would feel deeply my mood and would grieve and weep
and that would only make my heart sadder. I only want
you to understand that my mind is greatly changed in
regard to public activity. It does not mean that I want to be
inactive or give up that which is best and highest, but
nevertheless, a change.

The sisters were less distressed about the work than about
the effect Concorde's betrayal and the subsequent defections

might have on their ingenuous leader. Only the previous year he had written in his Thanksgiving Message: "Most specially, I feel thankfulness in my heart for the great blessing of having devoted and loyal hearts as my friends and as friends of the work. Of all blessings, I consider this the most precious." Now that very blessing had been harshly wrested from him. In reply to a concerned letter from one of the sisters, he wrote this reassuring response:

> I appreciate greatly your staunchness of spirit and your loyalty. Do not feel distressed over whatever disappointments I have received through those whom I have trusted. In no life is it known that one can achieve anything without meeting with upheaval and disappointment. My one solace is I have always tried to do my best for those who have come to me. It is better to be hurt than to hurt anyone. Hatred is never conquered by hatred; evil is never overcome by evil; nor is treachery overcome by treachery. There is only one cure for these ills, and that is unalloyed love and the spirit of Truth. Those who are armed with Truth, they need nothing.
>
> I am indeed glad that you are trying to help Norma, and I hope that you may succeed. There is nothing nobler than helping others, especially when we can be instrumental in lifting the clouds from their minds. These experiences of human unreliability have done me an enormous amount of good, and I think I am better and stronger in every way to carry on the work God has placed before me. . . .
>
> Wherever He keeps me, in whatever circumstance, may I only sing to the Glory of the Highest without looking to the right or to the left. . . .
>
> I go on with a faith and a hope and a trust not only in the Divine, but in humanity. You know I do not believe in a faith that discards the human.

No more was heard of Concorde's doings. The threatened investigation never took place. The ashrama household, united

by the external onslaught, was more harmonious than perhaps it
had ever been. Gayatri's ill health was finally, gradually, recovering.
When Paramananda returned to the ashrama in July, he wrote
exultingly: "The Ashrama seems more beautiful than it has ever
been, in every sense of the word. . . . I have never enjoyed it in
recent years as I am doing now."

His old friend Katherine Sherwood wrote of Paramananda
that summer: "It seemed as if India had given him a great strength
and an indefinable something he had never had before. Everyone felt it and I realized as never before the privilege of being
near him."

It was only a lull. The next year, and periodically during the
rest of Paramananda's life, Concorde tried to stir up trouble and
made threats. These later efforts created barely ripples. She never
succeeded in destroying Paramananda or his work; like the saying
of the Buddha which Paramananda often quoted, it was like
spitting at heaven. But she never gave up. Even in 1973, a couple of ashrama devotees reported that they met an old woman in
Santa Monica who insisted that Swami Paramananda had practiced black magic on her. That was the same year that Ananda
Ashrama jubilantly celebrated its fiftieth anniversary.

17

Fire And Flood

NOVEMBER 21, 1933, was a quiet Tuesday evening at the ashrama. Most of the community were relaxing in the Cloister living room, some listening to the radio, some putting together a jigsaw puzzle. Gayatri was curled up at one end of the sofa writing to Paramananda, who was in Boston. Sister Seva was avidly pouring through a Ferry-Morse catalogue for annual seeds to start in the new hothouse constructed by Mr. Walter, which was already the incubator for many new flower gardens throughout the ashrama. Sister Devamata, still recuperating from a fall that August which had broken her collar bone, was propped up in her chair reading letters typed up for her by Alice.

George was particularly tired, having spent all day splitting and stacking the last cord of firewood. For many weeks men had been cutting trees and hauling wood from different properties in the valley to supply the ashrama's twenty wood stoves, installed early that year for their cooking and heating needs. The men could now proudly point to a three-year supply of firewood stacked neatly behind the Cloister and the Guest House, while Sister Achala equally proudly pointed to a 75 percent reduction in their electricity bill.

At 8:30, George, yawning and stretching, decided to go to bed. He walked into the kitchen, picked up an apple from a

427

boxful that he had just bought wholesale, and headed toward his cabin. Just as he reached the bridge between the parking lot and the orchard, a red-gold glow over the ridge to the east caught his eye. In moments he was back in the living room announcing, "There's a big fire, and it looks close."

He and Sister Seva jumped into the Beverly and drove down to the clearing by the entrance to get a better view. The blaze was alarmingly close: the Bissell property adjoining the ashrama. A strong northeast wind was blowing, and the flames were spreading rapidly, both toward the valley and deeper into the canyons.

A few minutes after nine, they wired Paramananda: "TERRIFIC FIRE ON BISSELL PROPERTY GOING UP MOUNTAIN NORTHEAST WIND PRAY." At one o'clock in the morning Boston time, Sister Daya received the message by telephone. The swami was sleeping, having retired early after conducting the Tuesday night class. Daya knocked on his door with a heavy heart. How do you tell a man that his dream-child is in mortal peril? He had her repeat the message twice, then very quietly said, "All right." Daya withdrew, feeling, as she later described, "that his whole soul had retreated inward, even to the Feet of that One who alone can answer prayer."

Three thousand miles away the community watched in dread as the ravaging flames, propelled by their inexorable ally, the wind, advanced on their beloved ashrama. Sister Seva, first with one group then another, kept driving back and forth to the public road to get a clearer view. They saw the Bissell property with its ornamental trees and gardens laid waste, a bed of smouldering cinders illumined by the vanquishing blaze. Their eyes were on the fire break between the Bissell property and their own. Only when the fire reached that point, they felt, could they truly gauge their danger. "But," recalled Sister Achala, "when we saw how those flames jumped fifty to one hundred feet, over the fire break, we knew we could depend on nothing that man had made."

Great patches of flame broke out all along Ward Canyon, then in Cold Canyon behind the temple. Teams of fire fighters raced to the scene, and began battling the blaze on this new front. A second telegram was sent to Paramananda.

The community was advised to be prepared to evacuate if the flames threatened the buildings. George backed the Pierce-Arrow up to the kitchen door, and into it they packed Sister Devamata together with some of their holy things. Others threw their most precious belongings into suitcases and piled them into the truck. They were actuated by practicality, not fear. When Sister Achala ordered Gayatri to go pack her clothes, the young woman replied, "My clothes? The whole ashrama is burning! How can I think about clothes?" "Don't argue! Come Sunday, you'll have to conduct the service, and where am I going to buy you new saris?" snapped the ever-pragmatic Achala.

They did not dismantle the shrine. As the blaze raged toward it, one or another of the sisters sat there in prayer throughout the night. Sister Seva avowed that she would not disturb anything in the shrine until the flames actually licked the temple.

It was morning in Boston when the second telegram arrived, informing Paramananda that Oak, Ward, and Cold Canyons were in flames. Swami Nikhilananda, the head of the Ramakrishna-Vivekananda Centre of New York, had arrived at 6:30 A.M. to spend a few days at the Vedanta Centre, and to be guest speaker at a dinner to be held on Thursday night to benefit Charushila's work. Paramananda was self-contained, solicitous for the comfort of his guest, quietly attending to the duties of the day. Inside, however, he was racked with apprehension. He was remembering a fire of a few years before which had come to the boundaries of the ashrama. While he was outside directing the men, some of the anxious household had dismantled the shrine in preparation to flee. When Paramananda heard of it, he chided them for their lack of faith, reminding them that the shrine represented the heart of the ashrama and should be maintained in the face of such danger. Now he wondered in dread whether they would take his admonition to the extreme and, standing in guard of the shrine, be consumed in the encircling inferno. He wired them to take no chances with their own safety, but his heart quivered with foreboding.

He rightly gauged his workers' spirit, for as the flames crept down the mountainside, none of them consented to abandon the hallowed grounds. When Sister Devamata told George to collect his things, he replied, "Sister, I once promised Swami that if anything happened to the Ashrama, I would stay with it." With that he stalked out to direct the fire engines through the canyons and to check the thousands of feet of pipeline supplying the ashrama from the spring.

Even the frail Devamata, who had been seated in the car expressly for that purpose, refused to evacuate. One by one during the night, the community approached and vainly begged her to go to a place of safety. At four o'clock George came to the car window and pleaded with her. She replied that she was captain of the ship and nothing could induce her to leave it. "If it sinks, I go down with it," she vowed simply.

Scores of fire fighters heroically fought the conflagration, imperiling their own lives in the contest. The deputy sheriff come up to the Pierce-Arrow and spoke to Sister Devamata. As she later recollected, deeply moved: "He said they had all decided to give up their lives rather than lose ours."

The critical spot was a pocket in the canyon behind the temple. As a fifty-mile-per-hour wind drove the flames to that point, the assistant fire chief sent twenty-five men around to the east of it and twenty-five around to the west, and took his ten best men right up to the face of the sheet of fire. There, just before dawn, they quelled it.

At 11 A.M. Boston time, Paramananda received the message: "DANGER ABATING BUILDINGS FAMILY SAFE HEARTS COURAGEOUS GRATEFUL YOUR WIRE." He could breathe again.

While the sisters unpacked their suitcases sighing their gratitude to God, the firemen warily surveyed the smouldering terrain.
Warning that if the wind came up again at eventide the forty or
fifty burned acres could ignite again in a flash, they laid over a
mile of firehose around the property, attaching it to the big
hydrants on Pennsylvania Avenue. Among the regiments stationed throughout the widespread Angeles Forest, almost two
hundred firemen had been dispatched to the ashrama, including boys from the New Deal's Civilian Conservation Corps camp
and a large crew from Oregon which had just fought a 125,000
acre blaze for seventeen days.

One fireman came into the Cloister dining room and asked
for something to drink. Hilda offered him coffee. Soon he returned with his brigade, and Hilda, Jessie, and Alice found themselves pouring gallons of strong coffee and throwing together
sandwiches with whatever they had on hand. As a steady stream
of firemen filed in, their faces blackened, their eyes bloodshot,
and their lungs full of smoke, the women passed out coffee,
fruit, eggs, fried potatoes, and two-thirds of the box of George's
apples. In between shifts they washed stacks of dishes.

That morning the *Los Angeles Examiner* published an "un-
confirmed report" that the Ananda Ashrama had been destroyed.
Agitated friends kept the telephone ringing incessantly. Swami
Prabhavananda and Swami Ashokananda kept in close touch,
and others drove up with hose and provisions. Two ardent new
devotees, Philip and Ruth Reihl, heard the report of the fire on
the radio in the early morning. Leaving their own home in the
La Crescenta valley unprotected, they rushed up to the ashrama
and forced their way through the police barricade. Mrs. Reihl
immediately set to work in the kitchen, cooking up a huge pot of
potato soup, while Mr. Reihl joined the brothers who had been
working side by side with the firemen.

Wednesday afternoon, Achala sat down at her typewriter
and wrote a letter to Paramananda. "I feel so utterly incapable of

giving you an idea of the terrifying experience that we went
through," she told him. "It truly was the closest call the Ashrama
has ever had, and I hope and pray that never again will we have
to witness such a scene."

An hour after she mailed the letter, the scene of the night
before faded into a mere dress rehearsal. At sunset the much
feared wind came up at fifty miles an hour. Oak Canyon burst
into a brilliant conflagration. The flames, leaping fifty feet in the
air, devoured their way to Quail Canyon. The roof of the reservoir caught and caved in, while the fire jumped to the unburned
part of Ward Canyon, advancing toward the temple and Cloister.

At that point, Paramananda placed his very first long-distance
telephone call. He told his community: "Never mind if the whole
ashrama is wiped out. Take no risk! Your safety is paramount."
As soon as he had hung up, he was seized by a great restlessness,
and wanted to call them back and admonish them again. But
even as they spoke, the telephone poles were burning, and soon
after the first call, they crashed to the ground, leaving the ashrama
without electricity or any means of contacting the outside world.
When Paramananda dialed again, the wires were silent.

His last word from the endangered community was a telegram,
sent shortly before his telephone call. It is a great piece of religious literature (if a telegram can be called literature), bespeaking
a faith immune to outer conditions. It read: "NEW OUTBREAK OAK
AND QUAIL CANYONS GONE VALLEY IN FLAMES FEEL SAFE." Paramananda
smiled at the anomaly, but his face was ashen, his eyes anguished.

The Central Operator informed him that the house had
been abandoned and the people had all left, but he knew in his
heart it was not true. Keeping vigil by the radio, he heard Lowell
Thomas report that the "Hindu colony" in the La Crescenta hills
was trapped and unable to evacuate. His mind revolved to a
recent tragedy in Hollywood, when twenty people had been
trapped by a similar forest fire and had burned to death. He was
tortured as he had never been. Had he brought them to his

"veritable paradise" only to perish? Had he built the temple and Cloister only to be the funeral pyres of his own spiritual children? Paramananda went to the shrine and prostrated himself before the altar. He implored God to take everything, the whole ashrama, its verdant hills and cherished canyons, its fragrant trees and luxuriant gardens, its hallowed open-air sanctuaries, its stately buildings, even the Temple of the Universal Spirit, but—and this he begged with his whole soul—let not a single life be lost.

Sister Devamata was in the temple praying when Amala burst through the side door and announced that there was time to escape from the ashrama if she came at once. Devamata refused to go until Sister Seva could come up to guard the sacred relics. Those few minutes cut off all chance of fleeing; the flames closed around the ashrama in a lethal circle, a fiery wall with no exits. When Seva reached the temple, Devamata and Amala retreated to the Cloister. The firemen told them that their best hope of survival was to close themselves up tight in the stone and stucco Cloister, and hope that the leaping flames would skip over them.

The firemen were steadily dousing the buildings with water. Mr. Kissam was lookout for the Community House and lower cabins; Mr. Carlson (whom they called "Lama") guarded the upper cabins and garage; Philip Reihl was standing on the arcade roof, hosing down the library and the burning brush just beyond. When the heat of the flames scorched his face, he started to move away. One of the firemen shouted, "Get back on your job! What are you doing?" Mr. Reihl stayed and kept spraying.

George, dashing from place to place acting as foreman, let the cows, goats, and chickens loose from the barn, chasing them toward the apparent safety of the vineyard. The animals headed for the temple, instead, and huddled there by the front doors. There Mr. Walter found them, led them back to the barn, and kept a hose trained on the building.

The stone house, which had come with the property and was

used for storing books and bee supplies, was burning. One carefully stacked woodpile was completely devoured. The new greenhouse went up in flames, showering sparks around the temple.

Inside, Sister Seva knelt in prayer. When the firemen discovered she was there, they insisted she come down to the Cloister, for they doubted they could save the temple, surrounded as it was by burning brush. Calmly, she gathered up the relics. A deluge of fiery sparks was raining down around the Cloister. One of the firemen took Seva in his car from the upper terrace around through the parking lot, fifty feet from the Cloister door. While two firemen held their asbestos coats over her, she dashed between the flames, clutching the holy relics to her breast.

Inside the Cloister, the community was praying and chanting the Lord's name. The firemen, who had expected to find a group of frantic and hysterical women, exclaimed that they had never seen such poise and calm courage. Some even evinced interest in the philosophy which could produce such character. As the weary fire fighters trailed in for coffee and food, Hilda, Ruth Reihl, Jessie, Amala, Achala, and Alice served them as graciously as if it were a leisurely afternoon tea party, instead of possibly the last night of their lives.

When the sheet of flame roared to the very edge of the Cloister terrace, the fire chief entered the living room and said quietly, "The fire is going to strike us, but we will do our best to save you." As soon as he left, they heard a roar, and a shower of flaming cinders poured over the Cloister. The interior, which had been dark except for candles and kerosene lamps, suddenly lit up like daylight with a ghastly red glow. The heat was terrific, and the smoke, issuing around the closed windows, was stifling. The community sat and repeated the Lord's name in unison until the whole flame-engulfed house seemed to vibrate with it. A woman watching the conflagration from beyond the barricade exclaimed that they must be praying, for she could feel the throbbing power of their prayer.

Outside, amidst twenty-five-foot-high flames, twenty specially picked men lay on their faces and kept steady streams of water trained on the house and the surrounding vegetation. "They seemed determined to save us at all costs," declared Devamata. Nor did these men flinch when the bushes at the edge of the terrace caught fire and went up like rockets right at their backs.

After a short time, the fire chief again appeared at the living room door. The chanting died down. He announced in a trembling voice, "The fire has gone over you and your lives are saved."

But the inferno continued to rampage the ashrama, roaring its way down to the Community House. It jumped across the driveway and ignited the second woodpile, shooting flames a hundred feet into the air. "It seemed as if the Ashrama could not escape," Devamata's memoir records, "that the garage and cottage and everything would go." The women in the Cloister, still praying and chanting for the safety of the fire fighters, were told that the Community house was in flames. They redoubled their fervor.

By 3:00 A.M. the worst was over. Men staggering from smoke and fatigue still came in to be fed, until the last apple was gone. George lay down in front of the fireplace in the living room and slept for the first time in forty-five hours. "We all slept about an hour," recalled Devamata, "Gayatri in her long chair, Alice on the wood-box, Jessie on the floor. We felt we could not bear to go far — we belonged together. You cannot imagine the unity of love and life that was in our hearts." She added: "I never was so proud of people in my life as I was of the family on those two nights."

When dawn broke, the community emerged from the Cloister to view what was left of the ashrama. The grounds were a scene of waste and desolation. The sage-covered hills were denuded. Where sprawling sycamores and twisted manzanita and century-old oaks had flourished, only charred stubble remained.

The precious, lush growth of fragrant mountain lilac and buck-wheat had disappeared, leaving a ghostly carpet of smouldering ash. In a single night the ashrama had been stripped of its pristine beauty.

But the Temple of the Universal Spirit still towered above them. The Community House, belying the reports, was untouched; the eucalyptus trees surrounding it were barely scorched. Except for the stone house, all of the buildings were intact: the cottage, the garage, the bee house, even the barn, which was filled with hay, although the flames had come within fifteen feet of it. The charred ground in front of the wooden cabins, the most combus-tible of all the structures, testified that the fire had come up to their very steps, then stopped. The bee hives were unscathed. The beloved pine grove, the orchard, the shrubbery and large trees around the houses, and most of the swami's nurslings were all green and vibrant.

The view from the valley was even more awe-inspiring. In a desert of ashes that stretched for miles in all directions, there stood only one green spot: the inner precincts of the Ananda Ashrama. Incredulous firemen whispered to the sisters, "You have been saved by the hand of God," and the word "miracle" spread around the ashrama as the fire had done the night before.

But for Paramananda the fiery ordeal was not over. He had received two brief reassuring telegrams in the early hours of Thursday morning, but he was still unconvinced. Had not Wednesday morning's wire assured him that danger was past, only to be repudiated by a worse onslaught? The ashrama lines were still mute. As the swami waited for a word of confirmation, a Boston friend telephoned to say that she had just seen a news-paper headlining the California fire. It said that one hundred and seventy men were trapped by the flames, unable to get out. Paramananda was silent, his heart a cauldron of agony.

Almost one hundred people had accepted invitations for the benefit dinner to be held at the Vedanta Centre that evening. It could not be cancelled. Paramananda directed the setting up of the tables and the preparation of the food with his customary efficiency and attention to every detail. Daya, knowing his inner anguish, marvelled at his self-mastery. Swami Nikhilananda, observing the scene, later commented that Paramananda exemplified the great ideal of the Bhagavad Gita: equal-mindedness in pain and pleasure. His heart, nevertheless, was raw with pain. If his workers had left the ashrama, as Western Union had informed him, and if even one of them were conscious, why did they not send him word?

The afternoon dragged on in suspense. A kitchen full of people sat cutting vegetables while Paramananda sprinkled in the cumin, coriander, and ginger, and stirred the huge cooking pots. At four o'clock the doorbell rang. It was the longed-for telegram, confirming their safety and giving details of their condition. As Daya read the wire aloud, Paramananda's face lighted up with a great exaltation. He exclaimed: "I always told you that they were golden souls, and now the fire has proved it."

An hour and a half later, Paramananda received a telephone call from Mrs. Bowers, a friend of the ashrama who, recuperating from an illness, heard of the fire on the radio, threw on her bathrobe, and drove up there. "They were the center of an inferno, yet there was not a scream or a cry. . . . Not only that, they fed hundreds of people to whom the authorities could not get food and they did not eat themselves at all. I expected to find them faint and weary, but found all brave and cheerful and busy. . . . I am proud to feel that I even in part belong to such a band of noble souls." Throughout the ordeal, the daily shrine services, morning and evening, were faithfully held, except for Wednesday evening, when Devamata prayed in the shrine alone.

Paramananda was overwhelmed, not by the tragedy of what had been lost, nor by the miracle of what had been saved, but by the inner victory of his disciples. They had proven their unflinching faith, their strength of devotion, and in the midst of the holocaust they had spent themselves in serving others. In this, Paramananda felt, his whole life's effort was vindicated. Compared to this inner triumph, the loss of the precious beauty of his ashrama was an insignificant detail.

Later that evening, while the dinner guests waited, Paramananda telephoned the ashrama again. The lines were reconnected, and he could personally give them his message which he had carefully written out: "Your unearthly devotion has proved your golden spirit, tested by fire only to bring forth more shining qualities. My heart is dumb with feelings that cannot be expressed in words. This, your selfless victory, is my crowning blessing. If nothing further I'm able to achieve in life, this will remain indelible."

The following Sunday, the swami gave his address at the Vedanta Centre on, "Miracle of Faith." He told them:

> I think miracles do happen. But they do not imply any confusion or accident or anarchy; they are an expression of the Highest. Suppose we do not call them miracles, but the fulfillment of the Higher Law. I do not pretend to be wise enough to know all about this Law of Miracles — nobody does — but I believe that when we place our hand in the Divine Hand, without thought of self, the impossible becomes possible.
>
> Nor do I feel that these people were different from others, chosen by Divine Providence to play a spectacular part. Their faith had been nurtured by their thoughts and at the hour of test it did not fail them, that was all.

For days after the fire, sight-seers and ashrama friends jammed the parking lot. Gayatri wrote to Paramananda: "Those who came [to the Sunday services] were moved to tears both times. We can never fully know what feeling many bear toward this holy place. There have been sufficient tears to extinguish several fires." Her compulsion for cleanliness frustrated by the layer of soot that covered everything, inside and out, she added: "We hope and pray there will be a good soaking rain before your return." She did not realize that with 6,000 acres of watershed destroyed, rain was now a more fatal enemy than fire.

On December 5, after his most enthusiastic reception ever in Louisville and Cincinnati, Paramananda arrived at the ashrama. The sight that greeted him pulled heavily on his buoyant spirit. He wrote to the Vedanta Centre:

> It is heart-rending to see the beautiful hills stripped beyond absolute recognition. . . . However, time will heal it, as it always heals all our wounds, and in spite of all the devastation, last night Ashrama with its star strewn canopy overhead, as I stood in the Temple patio after the Service, was a picture of great beauty and sanctity. . . .
>
> I smell even now the smoke as I walk over the grounds, and how it pains me to see some of our beautiful trees scorched and devastated. . . .
>
> I do not like to dwell on it, as something inside hurts, and I must take all these things philosophically, with understanding and spirit of resignation. I feel that if the Ashrama had escaped from this devastation completely, it would have brought upon it envy and wrath of the people, and I do not believe it would have been as great a miracle as it is now, because no one can see it without being awestruck. How close the flames came and how horrible they were in their devastation, and yet the Ashrama stands as a monument.

The ashrama's manpower had been severely depleted with the exit of three men the previous summer. Two days after the fire, Mr. Kissam, suffering from a swollen hernia, moved out. The devastation of the beloved ashrama hills left Brother George grief-stricken. Paramananda, as if to make up for them all, kept busy planting new pepper trees in the temple patio and pruning the charred wood from trees that were already beginning to send forth new shoots. "The ashrama is short of workers," he wrote, "so I rather enjoy doing things myself." Meanwhile, crews from the Forest Reservation Department worked in Ward Canyon every day building new check dams against the threat of floods.

On Friday evening, December 29, Paramananda and Gayatri Devi were invited to dine at the Hollywood Vedanta Society with Swami Prabhavananda and Swami Ashokananda. After dinner, they all went to see "Little Women" at Grauman's Chinese Theater. When they emerged from the movie house, a light, steady rain was falling.

Showers continued intermittently throughout the night and all day Saturday. The community was busy preparing for the traditional New Year's Eve service to be held at 11:15 Sunday night, when the congregation would usher in the New Year with prayer in the solemn dignity of the candlelit temple. The Guest House was almost booked full with devotees who planned to come for the weekend, but cancellations came in all day Saturday as people shied from the danger of the eroding hills, which were already slashed with furrows and running rivulets.

Sunday morning the community awoke to the gurgle of newborn brooks on every side. Despite the increasing downpour, twenty-five people drove up the hill through flooding roads for the eleven o'clock service. While Paramananda spoke with feeling to this small congregation, Brother George was digging ditches in back of the temple to divert the growing flow of water cascading down toward the temple wall.

After the service, the Reihls, Mr. Nelson, and other devotees went home, leaving Mrs. Bowers, Miss Sheppard, and Craig Garman, who had resolved to spend the night at the Guest House.

By the time for the three o'clock service, the rain was falling in torrents. The roads from the valley were all but impassable. Sister Achala was answering all telephone inquiries by telling people not even to try to come up.

Brother George ventured down the hill to fetch Evelyn MacMinn at her home for the service. The handful of guests sat scattered throughout the temple listening to Alice and Lama sing introductory hymns. Swami Paramananda sat in the Cloister living room deciding whether he dared wear his orange silk robe up to the temple. Suddenly Amala darted in and announced that the flood water was about to burst through George's dike and threaten the temple and book room (in which thousands of books were stored). Paramananda pulled on his hiking boots and raced up to the temple complex. In his own words:

> When I arrived there I found the situation perilous. . . . I started to make outlets for the water, but the effort was almost impossible, as the tide was so very strong. Also I realized that the water should be diverted from an upper source, so I began to battle with it in the canyon above the book room. The book room was really threatened, as this great volume of water was beating against the wall, and rocks and debris of every description were piled up against it. It did not take long before everyone came to my aid. Sister Seva was one of the first ones; then George, Mr. Walter, Lama, Mr. Craig Garman, Mrs. MacMinn, Amala, Jessie, Hilda, Gayatri, Miss Houghton. Practically the whole Ashrama force was there.

Amidst the downpour, they shovelled, desperately trying to divert the water around the temple; but as fast as they worked the steady onrush of water refilled their excavations with mud. Finally George called for gunny sacks, which they filled with silt, building a wall of sandbags. The sandbags held.

Trying to rescue other trouble spots, the crew dug channels where currents broke through safety ditches, threw up dams with sacks of dirt, and piled up benches and burlap, as sheets of water continued to fall. The swami had to change his garments from the skin out four times, and providing dry clothes for the guests became a difficult problem. The upper and lower dams in Ward Canyon, filled with burned wood, charred brush, mud, and debris, were overflowing. The force of the rushing water was rapidly carving the canyon deeper and wider. As darkness was descending and Paramananda felt that they had done as much as they could, he sent his workers to dry out and rest.

After the household service and dinner, several of the community lingered in the living room waiting for the midnight New Year's Eve service. Mrs. MacMinn asked Paramananda to read some of his poems. As he did so, Amala stole out to check the temple situation. She came running back with the report that the temple patio was a lake and the library was again threatened. Paramananda put on his heavy boots, dashed up there, waded through the current, and found the library floor covered with slimy water and mud. He and George rolled up the muddied Oriental rug and lodged it against the outside of the door to serve as a barricade. They did the same with the swami's study at the other end of the library arcade.

Then Paramananda, Sister Seva, Jessie, and Amala walked through the blinding rain to check the lower dam. Ward Canyon had become a roaring river. Paramananda told the women to stand back from the dam; the wall could go at any moment.

When they returned, Paramananda decided to inspect the patio again. He reached the temple steps to find it a flowing waterfall. Holding onto the railing, he made his way up. Suddenly there was a deafening roar from Dunsmore Canyon, adjoining the ashrama, as a maddened flood wave catapulted down towards the valley. Moments later streaks of light, resembling lightning, flashed across the sky, as the high-tension electric towers crashed to the ground. The ashrama and surrounding areas were plunged into darkness.

Water was already seeping into the temple. The flood stream was pouring through the temple arcade like a raging river, depositing charred branches, silt, and debris which began to block the water's escape. Unable to find a shovel, Paramananda tried kicking the debris away with his feet. Then he grabbed the longest pipe of the temple chimes and with it cleared a channel.

When the cloudburst abated, Paramananda and Brother George went behind the temple arcade to inspect the book room and Nature's Sanctuary, the site of their outdoor services. Scanning the scene with their flashlights, they found it buried in four feet of mud. The only thing visible above the mire was the top of the outdoor altar, shining with its inscription, "Thee I Love in All."

After checking on the animals, Paramananda and George walked toward Dunsmore Canyon, picking their way carefully over fallen wires, possibly live, and broken, twisted pipes, the remnant of the ashrama's demolished water system. The canyon was a terrifying sight, a rapacious river carrying in its thunderous current huge trees and giant boulders and hurling them onto New York Avenue. "What we saw made our hearts sink," Paramananda recalled. "The little brown house that stood at the head of New York Avenue, occupied by Professor MacIntyre, his wife and little baby, was gone. All that was left was a portion of the chimney. Of course we could not see very much at night, and as it was very dangerous, I felt the responsibility of the safety for everyone, so I rushed to the Cloister."

At least with the fire they could see when it was coming and could battle it face to face. But the flood waters struck from behind without warning, mocking their sandbags and check dams. They never knew when a canyon wall would give way, or an avalanche of boulders would come smashing down. There was no way to fight the flood.

The new year had stolen in an hour before, the only noise-maker to greet it the roar of the death-dealing flood current. The swami, soaked to the skin, called everyone into the Cloister living room for an impromptu service. There, in the dim candlelight, sitting by the fireplace in his dripping clothes, Paramananda chanted invocations to the beneficent Divine Being and asked everyone to join him in praying for the people of the valley.

O, Great Mother Heart, may always Thy will be fulfilled in everything, and may we never, never will anything but Thy will. May we learn to see Thy Divine hand through the beautiful and through the terrible. Under all circumstances may we never forget that Thou dost make us strong, as we require strength, to meet every situation. Grant unto us not only our desires and wishes, but strength, staunchness of spirit, unshakable faith in the face of all difficulties and dangers. Put us through anything, but grant us unshakable faith, gladness of spirit, surrender unto Thee under all circumstances.

At the conclusion, Paramananda declared that he had a peculiar feeling of depression about the valley, as if he heard a cry of distress.

After the service, Paramananda insisted on personally escorting the guests to the Community House through the darkness and deafening roar. "Nothing seemed safe," he asserted. The floodwater had carved a crater into the road near the Cloister twelve feet deep, ten feet wide, and thirty feet long. On the way back from the Guest House, George almost stepped into it. Paramananda shuddered whenever he looked at the dangerous cavern, marvelling that none of the community, in all their dashing about that night, had fallen in. "One can only be silent and thankful," he sighed. At 2:30 A.M., everyone retired.

The first day of 1934 dawned grayly amidst the diminishing drizzle. At six o'clock, Paramananda rose and went up to inspect the temple complex. "When I got up there it was indeed a strange sight. Everything seemed altered. The contour of the hills, the levels of the temple grounds, were unbelievably changed." As Amala recorded, "It seemed that mountains had been moved during a few hours of the night."

The fire had stripped the ashrama; the flood mangled its body. The familiar terrain was lacerated beyond recognition, terraces swept away, canyons widened and deepened, hills melted like the ruins of a child's sandcastle when the tide sweeps in. Giant trees and boulders were strewn across the landscape like so many sticks and stones. Many trees had been pounded into pulp. All the sisters proclaimed that the flood, while not as terrifying as the fire, was far more devastating. Paramananda walked to the edge of the ashrama property and saw New York and Pennsylvania Avenues, once pleasant streets, now cratered riverbeds. Houses had been crushed to splinters. Looking over the edge of Dunsmore Canyon, where dancing boulders had dug holes forty feet deep, he was appalled to see that just that one wall of earth had kept the terrific torrent from sweeping over the ashrama and tearing it to pieces. He was even more overcome when he noticed that the opposite bank, over which the torrent had flowed, was higher.

They were anxious about the welfare of the people in the valley, but driving down there was impossible, for the washed-out roads were perilous with unseen chasms and buried rocks. Even walking was treacherous, for one either sank into deep mud holes or slipped on loose rocks. Gradually, however, they heard the grim tale of the valley's fate. Just as midnight had struck, and New Year's Eve revellers had shouted and hugged each other "Happy New Year," the savage floodwaters, like a tidal wave, smashed into the valley, decimating homes and sweeping up automobiles and human bodies. In the morning, party hats and paper streamers lay strewn among the flotsam of the flood.

Shortly after 10:00 A.M., a distraught Philip Reihl telephoned the swami. He told him how, just after he and his wife had exchanged a New Year's embrace, the floodwater broke through the walls of their home and tore Mrs. Reihl from his arms. He himself was swept along on the current, battered against furniture, nails, and rocks, and finally thrown up onto the porch of a house three blocks away. He was so encrusted with mud that the inhabitant could not recognize whether a human or an animal lay at his doorstep. Now Philip was desperately searching for Mrs. Reihl.

"He was beside himself," Paramananda recounted, "and we did not realize until later how terribly bruised and battered he was. It was more than I could really bear when I realized the agony of his devoted soul. I went into the Shrine and I could hardly contain my tears."

Early in the afternoon, Mr. Reihl telephoned again from the Montrose Red Cross. He had found his wife, dead, her body pinned under the wreckage of their own house. Now, in shock and practically hysterical, he insisted that he would go nowhere except to the ashrama.

Paramananda resolved that he would go down and get him. Taking with him George to drive, and also Sister Seva, Gayatri, Jessie, and her brother Ralph, who heroically had climbed the hill to bring dry clothes to the brothers, he set off on what proved to be "probably the most hazardous trip I ever took in my life." George maneuvered around chasms and over rocks, first trying one washed-out street, then another. They drove around uprooted trees and boulders weighing thirty tons or more, which had bounced down from the mountains like ping-pong balls. One boulder that had rolled along Briggs Terrace weighed 180,000 pounds. They finally reached the main thoroughfare, Foothill Boulevard, only to discover "there was no Foothill Boulevard left."

"It was like a war experience," Jessie recorded, "gullys and chasms and hills where streets and hollows had been. Unrecognizable country. Homes demolished and others with earth to their windows."

After seeing scores of buried automobiles, some of them with only their roofs showing above the mud, Paramananda later wrote: "We could not help but shudder to think how many lives might be locked up in automobiles and also buried under the debris."

They found Mr. Reihl at the coroner's office, suffering from bruises and abrasions, a torn ligament, and eyes scratched by the branches hurled against him as he was swept along on the current. Yet his mind was in greater agony than his body.

By that time darkness was falling and the rain was coming down heavily. Everyone was nervously expecting a repetition of the previous night. When they asked one of the relief workers which would be the best way to get to the ashrama, he replied, "Leave your car and walk." With Mr. Reihl's condition, that was impossible, so, as Paramananda put it, "We prayed and we held fast with faith, and finally we went over the dangerous places and reached the Ashrama safely."

They helped Mr. Reihl into the living room and put him in a chair by the warm fireside. He wept pitifully, telling them the tragic story of the night before. Then the brothers led him to the cottage to sleep and Mrs. Bowers, a registered nurse, dressed his wounds.

On January 6, Swami Paramananda conducted Mrs. Reihl's memorial service. "I know that every heart has bled," he told them. "Everyone of us has felt so much that we have not even wanted to talk about it at times." Then he gave them the most precious thing he had to share, his own concept of and trust in the Divine:

> The Great God, the Almighty, the Infinite Spirit, is ever bestowing upon us His tender blessings. Do not ever let us think anything else. We sometimes do not understand the purpose of life. Often we cry out in agony like little children. We think that there is tragedy; we think sometimes that He is punishing us. No. That beneficent, that all-tender Being, who is more affectionate, more tender than the most tender mother—let us never think that of Him. There is always a Divine purpose, and we must always fall in line, with surrender in our spirit, with love in our heart, with spiritual devotion in our soul.

As for Ruth Reihl, in line with the Vedantic teaching that death is merely the soul's abandonment of the body for a different realm of being, Paramananda summoned everyone to pray that her transition would be unimpeded either by her pang of separation or their sorrow of sudden loss. "So let us make her passage full of love. . . . Let us ask that Great Spirit to give us strength that the bond of love we bear toward her may bring her only good, and that the All-beneficent Spirit may take her into His ministration. He knows how to protect, He knows how to give solace . . . and may we not interfere with our grief and misunderstanding."

The fire had left exaltation in its wake, but the flood left only sorrow and depression. Each day the death toll grew as cars and bodies were unearthed. The newspapers eventually reported one hundred dead, but Paramananda and others believed there were two or three times that. Six days after the catastrophe, he wrote to Boston: "I cannot tell you how choked at times I feel with the depression that comes up from the valley. What a calamity! What a tragedy! What a heart-rending experience for the people."

Two days later he recounted a chilling experience:

> I cannot tell you what weight has been thrown upon my heart each time I have been down in the stricken area. Yesterday morning when Sister and several of the others accompanied me, desirous of seeing some of the happenings which they had only heard about, I was so overcome by something which I cannot describe in words, that I had to ask George to turn back quickly. My breathing was almost stopping. It was not any ordinary psychic experience, but I felt as if many, many drowning souls were just reaching onto something which might steady them.

These outer sights battled with Paramananda's inner vision to gain control over his mind and heart. Often during those weeks following the disaster, he would be overcome by the sorrow of what he had seen and sensed. Then he would remind himself that it all came from the one Divine Beloved, so it must somehow, somehow, be right. He would quote Vivekananda's verse, "Who are Thou, Beneficent Spirit, doer of good? Thou dost bestow with one hand happiness, and with the other misery."

Alluding to the myriad reconstruction problems the ashrama now faced, he wrote:

> Well, One Who has led me thus far, will lead me further. How is that for a slogan always to carry in our hearts? I smile as I always have, and yet deep down in my heart there is a weight for the people who have suffered through it, and my prayers are constant and full of appeal for the solace and safekeeping of everyone who may be related to us and who may not be in any way connected with us.

When the fire chief offered to send up a tank of water for their drinking and washing needs, Paramananda declined it, saying to give it to the people in the valley, who needed it more. A few days later, he wrote: "We have been having intensive prayers in the Temple and the atmosphere seems to be lifted."

He was struggling to maintain the cheerfulness which he considered indispensable even, or especially, in such harrowing situations. In one note to Boston, in which he ludicrously compared the fallen boulders to the pyramids, he explained, "Of course, you know I cannot help but have a little streak of humor. If I did not, it would be more difficult to bear."

None of the ashrama buildings had been damaged in the flood; not even a drop of water had entered the endangered book room. Part of the foundation of Jessie's cabin, which stood on the very edge of Ward Canyon, had been washed away; but the cabin, amazingly enough, still stood, its contents unharmed. Nevertheless, the work necessary to restore the ashrama justifiably overwhelmed Paramananda. The water system had sustained $25,000 worth of damage. Thousands of feet of two-inch pipe were snapped, wrapped around tree trunks, and twisted into

bowknots as if they were thin-gauge wire. The two tunnels leading into the ashrama's spring had caved in, forcing the sisters to
put out all their cooking pots during the storm to collect rain
water for drinking and washing. The roads were pock-marked
with trenches eight to ten feet deep, in addition to the crater by
the Cloister large enough to hold two cars. Five feet of mud
filled the temple patio. The two dams were completely stuffed
with mud and debris. Even to bring the tractor up to the reservoir to start the reconstruction there would require building a
new road, for the old one had been totally washed out. For all
this work they had exactly six men, including the swami and the
limping Mr. Reihl.

"To give you a picture of the enormity of the task," Paramananda wrote, referring to tapping the main tunnel's water,
"George says that each length of pipe—this is, twenty feet each—
weighs about 160 pounds. How on earth can all this material be
carried to these heights, especially when there are no trails left?"

They started industriously, first hooking up a temporary pipeline to tap the water still flowing from the flood. Then they filled
in the dangerous gullies in the road. They planted black mus-
tard over the barren, washed-out hills. They had, of course, no
money to hire helpers. By the middle of January, when they
began to tackle the tons of dirt filling the temple patio, Paramananda was feeling discouraged. As he himself described:

> Sunday night I felt peculiarly indrawn, not merely
> weighted down, but greatly puzzled by the whole condition.
> I think I spent a great deal of time in prayer and indrawnness
> even all through the night. One thing I remember distinctly,
> sending forth thoughts and pleadings that if this work had
> in any way evolved through my misguided zeal, or per-
> sonal ambition, to have everything completely taken away
> and not even stay a single day, but if it were to serve any
> Divine purpose, then I must have assurance of how to
> carry it on.

The next morning, as Paramananda and the other men were clearing a tractor trail up to the reservoir, Mr. Keck, one of the swami's most devoted students, appeared. He told Paramananda he had lain awake all night wondering how he could help him and the ashrama. He decided to seek assistance from one of the government agencies, if Paramananda approved. The swami consented, and Mr. Keck went off to requisition the authorities.

The next day they were again on the trail when Amala conducted the fire chief to the spot. Paramananda showed him some of the work to be done, and he at once offered them twenty men, although Mr. Keck had asked for only a dozen. Then the swami showed him the temple grounds and explained what had happened there. "Well," the fire chief declared, "I think you need fifty men here and a truck. I'll send them tomorrow morning."

As if this were not boon enough, an hour later the engineer assigned to the job appeared: the ashrama's friend Mr. Chapman. After looking over the grounds, Mr. Chapman declared, "Swami, we are coming here not merely to clean up this mess, but to render service, and you are to tell us what is to be done and the way it is to be done."

In chronicling this turn of events, Paramananda summed up, "Well, if this were not heaven-sent, what may we call it?"

The next morning, Paramananda called the special shrine service in honor of Swami Brahmananda's birthday for 6:30, so as to be finished by the time the crew arrived at 7:30. "We got through in breathless state, and I was on deck, all dressed in knickerbockers and boots to receive the foreman and the gang. . . . They introduced me as the 'main boss.' It was amusing."

The "main boss" distributed the men among different spots, and for the next five days they worked steadily. They cleaned up the temple patio and other areas, laid a new pipeline to the main tunnel, and dug as far as it was safe into the tunnel. Just as they began clearing out the dams, the C.W.A. funds ran out.

Paramananda was not disappointed. The crucial projects had
been completed, and he was relieved to have the ashrama quiet
and secluded again. Besides, when he drove down to the valley
and saw the pathetic conditions still existing there, he decided,
"We have no right to take anything until these poor people have
been cleaned up and their homes restored."

Philip Reihl made a remarkable recovery. By mid-January,
Achala could write to Mary Lacy: "I really think that man would
have lost his mind if Swamiji had not been here. You can't
imagine the picture he was when they brought him here—almost a wreck mentally, not to say anything of his physical
condition—and today he is happy, cheerful and normal. Last
evening when he came in the house, he was singing!" Asserting
again and again, "It is Swamiji's strength that has sustained me,"
Philip Reihl determined to stay and give his life to the ashrama.
Eventually, the new Brother Philip undertook to singlehandedly
dig a 150-foot tunnel through the granite hill behind the temple,
which would divert any flow which could again endanger the
temple complex.

By early February, Paramananda had regained his perspective.
From Boston he wrote to the ashrama: "I feel that I must share
with you the most glowing thought in my mind and heart—that
whatever comes through Him is full of sweetness and whatever
causes us sorrow or suffering is because we have broken contact
and do not feel that it comes from Him. . . . I realize more and
more, without inner life there can be nothing but chaos, unhappiness and lack of peace."

When someone asked him how tragedies like wars, earth-
quakes, and floods could really be the Divine will, he replied:

> "What we ordinarily call tragedy brings us face to face
> with the deeper realities of existence, and thus quickens
> in us a truer sense of spiritual values. . . .When we see
> such a great transformation, which rarely comes except

through great sorrow, suffering or pain, shall we still continue to be embittered, and speak of Divine injustice? Shall we not rather bend our knees before the Omnipotent Will for His great mercy toward us? He never abandons any creature, but is ever working through joy and sorrow, . . . through good fortune and misfortune, through infinite tenderness and tragic blows, to awaken the soul from its slumber of self-delusion, and call it to the shelter of the Divine Bosom of unfailing compassion.

———————————◆◆———————————

Boston was undergoing the worst winter in its history, the temperature dropping to sixteen degrees below zero and staying sub-zero for days on end. Despite the blizzards and virulent cold, Paramananda was feeling spry and lighthearted, jesting with his community more than ever. On February 5, they celebrated his fiftieth birthday. He wrote: "Well, I am no worse for these things. On the contrary, I think I feel I am just getting started. It takes about half a century for anyone to make up his mind what is to be done, and what should be done. And the next fifty years one might be able to accomplish something. . . ."

When Paramananda returned to his scorched and flood-ravaged ashrama in March, he wrote with upturned spirit: "I know you are all anxious to hear about my impression of the Ashrama since all these disasters. To me the Ashrama looks quite as beautiful as it has ever looked. I was going to say more beautiful than ever, but that may not be quite true. The new growth has practically covered the whole area and gives a sense of delicate green."

The public work had suffered a major setback, as the roads leading up to the ashrama took many weeks to restore. In addition, every cloudy day now aroused fear of venturing into that area. "People are mortally afraid to come to these hills when the weather is not favorable," the swami wrote Daya in March.

By Easter the roads and the ashrama were in top condition, and the community worked frenziedly to prepare for the outdoor Easter Sunrise service, always the biggest occasion of the year. Many benches that had been damaged in the fire and flood had to be repaired, and George had to build a new outdoor platform to replace the one that had burned.

Easter morning, however, turned out to be almost symbolic of the whole catastrophic period. After a clear, moonlit night, they awoke before dawn Sunday to find the ashrama enveloped in clouds and fog, a fine drizzle falling. One of the sisters greeted Paramananda by exclaiming, "What a terrible disappointment!"

Paramananda replied: "There is not going to be any disappointment. Whatever is ordained by the Divine Hand cannot be a disappointment."

As the sisters busily wiped the chairs and benches, two hundred people drove up the hill, half the number they had expected. Paramananda began the service by telling them that there was no need for any disappointment at the failure to see the sunrise, for what is ordained by the Divine Providence is the very best thing that could come to them. In this case, the mist was just what was needed by the tender new foliage trying to redeem the charred hills. He went on to give what many considered to be his most elevating Easter service. At the conclusion, he asked Gayatri Devi to sing the chant of immortality from the Upanishads:

> Hear ye, all ye children of the Immortal One,
> I have known that indestructible, all-glorious Being;
> He is beyond darkness, like the radiant sun.
> By knowing Him alone, mortals overcome death.
>   There is no other way!
>   There is no other way!
>   There is no other way!

18

Disappointment In Friends

MANY PEOPLE MURMURED that a New Year's as inauspicious as the flood of 1934 augured a bad year ahead. Indeed, it proved a bleakly grim period not only for Paramananda's work and its members, but for the whole planet. As the Depression tightened its stranglehold on the globe, the world was letting out a war cry. The Nazis had come to power in Germany. Japan, which had already invaded Manchuria, in 1934 renounced its treaties with Washington. The King of Yugoslavia and the Chancellor of Austria were assassinated. A Stalinist purge in the U.S.S.R., a bloodbath in Germany, and a revolution in Austria symptomized a world gone haywire. As Winston Churchhill warned the British Parliament of the German air menace, nations frantically armed, as they maintained, for peace.

"These are strenuous times," wrote Paramananda, who would sit by his radio and listen to the nightly news broadcast with increasing dismay. "The only counteracting remedy we can bring is not through our own calculation and power, but through prayer and faith and staunchness of spirit." Giving an address over Radio KNX, he declared: "We are living today under disturbing conditions, and therefore our hearts must reach out for that One who is Father, Mother, Friend, and Protector of all living beings. . . .

There may be harrowing conditions, but we can always rise above them, knowing He stands behind us."

One morning in February, Sister Devamata was offering flowers before a picture of Sri Ramakrishna on a shelf to the left of the temple platform. Stepping back, she stumbled on a corner of the oriental rug and fell, fracturing her leg. Her body would not permit her to get up, and her relentless scruples would not permit her to desecrate the solemn silence of the shrine, only a few feet away, by shouting for help. Stoically she tried to roll herself toward the door, until Sister Achala, wondering why the ever-punctual Sister Devamata was late for breakfast, sent Hilda up to check.

In the hospital, they sealed her in a cast from above her waist to her right foot and left knee. Until the rigid enclosure was removed three months later, she had to lie flat in bed, unable even to sit up or bend. She had to be fed and waited on throughout the day.

Paramananda, in Boston at the time, was ardently concerned for her welfare. Lola Haynes in a letter to Sister Devamata described "how tender and full of feeling his eyes are" as he read news of her suffering. The swami himself wrote to the ashrama community: "I want you all unitedly, prayerfully and with all the exalted feeling you possess to do everything you can that will bring relief to Sister."

Devamata was determined to "keep on top" of her trial. While imprisoned in the cast, she dictated a booklet, "The Companionship of Pain," in which she asserted: "Physical ailments are not a misfortune. They are often remedies,— remedies for deeper sicknesses of mind or heart or character. They cure by chastening. They make us brave, strong and enduring. Pain allied with spirit heals and exalts. It makes heroes of men."

Providentially, the most qualified nurse for Sister Devamata appeared just three days after the accident when Lillian returned to the ashrama from India. Her curtailed term of service there had unfolded like an allegory of what happens when one tries to flee from one's problems: run away from a lizard and end up facing an alligator. Less than a year before, Paramananda had left her in what seemed to all like the ideal situation, the Ramakrishna Mission's newly established and well-equipped hospital for children, assisting another English-speaking woman, Miss Pfeffer. Within a month, however, an aggravated Lillian was accusing Miss Pfeffer of the exact same transgressions she had found intolerable in her co-workers at Ananda Ashrama: that she was "inefficient," did not perform her duties with high enough standard, and was "bossy." Swami Dayananda, just as Paramananda had done, tried to placate Lillian by giving her her own domain of authority, a new ward for infants within the hospital, but Lillian reacted just as she had at the ashrama, by panicking at the responsibility. For months she writhed in depression and inner turmoil, no doubt exacerbated by India's stifling heat and physical hardships. In early December, Miss Pfeffer returned to America; on December 29, Lillian boarded a Japanese ship bound for California. It was a year to the day since she had sailed from the shores of America in search of a better place to serve.

From Calcutta she had written to Paramananda that more than ever she wanted to live a retired life. Paramananda responded that he would give her her own secluded quarters in the ashrama cottage. Devamata's accident, however, obliterated all such plans. The day Lillian returned to the ashrama, Paramananda wrote from Boston charging her with Devamata's care: "Anything you can do to relieve her suffering and cheer her spirit will be a tremendous service to me personally. . . . These are strange times and we must all keep our mind focused on the Ideal and on our objective and keep on repeating His Name and meditating on His grace."

The year tumbled on in its hapless way. On February 20, Swami Shivananda, the beloved head of the Ramakrishna Math and Mission, died. In March, defective wiring ignited a fire in the Vedanta Centre, which destroyed the laundry room before the firemen succeeded in quelling it. At the same time, heavy rains in California were washing away most of the reconstruction work done since the flood.

While the public work at Ananda Ashrama was floundering, attributed to the post-flood conditions, Louisville, New York, and Boston were receiving Paramananda with glowing enthusiasm. The Truth Center led by Mrs. Georgiana Tree West gratefully hosted the swami whenever he managed to stop in Louisville, and overflowing crowds invariably came to hear him. Collections were taken at these gatherings, and his half of these, together with the sale of his books, were a precious source of income during those days.

New York City also became a frequent stop on Paramananda's cross-country jaunts. The brilliant young Swami Nikhilananda, who, after a falling-out with Swami Bodhananda, had founded his own center on New York's East Side the year before, felt profound admiration for Paramananda, and prevailed on him to address his congregation whenever possible. Paramananda in turn often invited Nikhilananda to speak at the Boston Vedanta Centre. "This interchange is good," Lola wrote enthusiastically, "and it brings joy to our Swamiji's heart when his brothers show the least warmth or love for him."

She went on to describe how the swami's spirit was flourishing in consonance with the Boston work: "He looks so radiant as he gives his inspired addresses to appreciative audiences. Never has he given more and never has Boston seemed more thirsty for the Highest."

Whenever he returned to California, however, a battery of ills besieged him. In April, a boil on his thigh, refusing to heal, kept him bedridden for days and housebound for two frustrating weeks. "My boil is practically healed up," he wrote to Daya, "but I must confess that physically I have been greatly run down because one thing or another seems to have given me a set-back.

Just sort of 'broken rhythm' is the thing which will convey the whole situation."

Brother George was suffering from lumbago, Sister Seva was afflicted with sudden headaches and bouts of nausea, and Amala frequently consigned herself to bed with one complaint or another. The unity born of the fire and flood was punctured by petty squabbles, for as they had risen to the great crisis, so they now sank to the less dramatic challenges of day-to-day community life. Their golden hour quickly tarnished.

Lillian accused Sister Devamata of being uncooperative and disobedient to the doctor's orders, while Devamata complained that Lillian's nervousness, clumsiness, and depression were harder to bear than her own injury. Although her cast came off on May 25, the frail Devamata could not even take her first steps until autumn, and did not succeed in walking alone until the following spring. Meanwhile, the two women grated on each other's nerves until they both petitioned Paramananda for a new attendant. A young woman was hired to take care of Sister Devamata, and Lillian became Brother Philip's assistant flower gardener, a job which suited her perfectly until the goats got out and ate up her prize annuals.

For Paramananda such problems were like mosquito bites on a typhoid patient. His real burden was his stifling financial quandary, which grew worse with the years. The banks were pressing him for payments of loans, as well as the mortgage and interest on the still unsold 875 Beacon Street house. It was all Paramananda could do to keep up the mortgages on the ashrama and 32 Fenway, plus the operating expenses of the two establishments. He had overextended himself, and now his response was to retreat within. After touring a huge Roman Catholic estate outside Chicago, he wrote to his old friend Miss Sherwood:

> Does the world need these things to make it better? Do we
> need to create things which invariably must look neglected,
> with paths overgrown? My mood at the present moment

is to get away from these things and learn to worship the God of the interior, the innermost, and keep away from all the vain pomp and glory of the outside.

I may have been guilty of some of these things myself, but it is never too late to be quickened and I am honest enough to confess my guilt even now. . . .

Now, a few words in regard to this modest little grand Ashrama. I wish it were really modest, but Nature has made it gorgeous, and we through our misguided zeal and folly have made it extensive.

In the same vein he wrote to the ashrama community: "May the Mother make me more simple and take away from me all thoughts that are of the world and even desire and ambition for spiritual propaganda. If we live close to the Divine Heart, there is nothing else that matters."

Despite this recoiling from outer involvements, the debts already incurred had to be paid off, and Paramananda's correspondence of this year is full of complicated business transactions with banks, investment counsellors, and stock brokers, at least two of whom tried to take advantage of what they considered the swami's simplicity.

Moonan, the dishonest broker who had swindled him and been sent to jail in the late twenties, called on Paramananda again. Understandably, he was having trouble enlisting clients, and appealed to the swami for another chance. To the sisters' horror, Paramananda gave him a small sum to invest. "Somebody has to have faith in him," Paramananda plaintively declared. Moonan vindicated the sisters' fears by again cheating the swami out of his money. Paramananda showed no remorse. Instead he told them a story about a holy man who kept rescuing a drowning scorpion from a well. Again and again, the holy man lifted the scorpion out and held it against the warmth of his chest, only to be stung once more. When he was ridiculed for his credulity and told to leave the wretched creature to drown, the holy man replied: "It is not a wretched creature. When it stings me, it is simply acting according to its nature, and when I save it, I am acting according to mine."

Nevertheless, the continual entanglement in business affairs took its toll on Paramananda's spirit. In choosing to become a monk, he had renounced the world with all its personal and material encumbrances. Yet, as Swami Shivananada had said to him upon hearing about the many responsibilities Paramananda carried, "Why, Paramananda, your position is worse than a householder's."

"For some reason or other," Gayatri wrote from California, "Swamiji has not been his vibrant vital self this time. We have to coax him about his eating, etc. I know that mental worries are responsible for his physical depletion."

He spoke of pulling in, but in fact he was incapable of rejecting others' importunings or his own dreams of endless possibilities. Gayatri recounted how he used to visualize and "speak of a community, an army of young workers, devoid of pettiness, jealousy, and all the lesser traits, whom he desired to prepare for India and her service." Again, she wrote: "Ah! How he dreams to do for others, to give all his children opportunities, to enhance their happiness and peace. If only Mother would free him from material burdens, and grant him his natural happy and carefree spirit. He has spent long hours thinking and looked very grave at times."

In India, Bibhu Charan was having trouble with his nineteen-year-old daughter Ranu. A rebel and a nonconformist, she was bursting with artistic drives which could find no respectable outlet in Dacca's restrictive, Muslim-dominated society. When Bibhu Charan approached the local saint, Anandamoyee-ma (later to become the most revered holy woman in modern India) and asked her what he should do with Ranu, she replied, "Don't you already have one daughter in America with your brother?" Bibhu Charan took this as Divinely inspired guidance, and immediately wrote to Paramananda, asking him to give Ranu a chance in his American community. Of course, Paramananda was not due to come to India for a while, but Bibhu Charan proposed that Ranu could make the trip accompanied by her younger sister Chokanu, a bright but physically frail girl who could also benefit from American education and climate.

The ashrama workers were aghast at the possibility of undertaking such an expense. The swami had already had to borrow money in India to bring Kanai and Sumita the year before. Now, in addition to two more steamer tickets as well as the required bond, the girls would have to be enrolled in an American college in order to procure visas. That meant not only tuition, but the cost of books, school supplies, and countless other details, which Paramananda was already paying out for Kanai and Sumita. Soon after Sumita's arrival, she had had to undergo an emergency appendectomy, which meant unexpected hospital and doctor bills, too.

Besides, the responsibility of taking care of these youngsters might be worse than the expense. Sumita had proved difficult and temperamental. The swami had arranged her admission to Boston's Simmons College, but, not qualifying for the academic courses she had anticipated taking, Sumita balked at enrolling there at all. It took three months of altercations, searching out alternatives, and Paramananda's coming from California before a school was found that suited the immigration requirements, the swami's pocketbook, and Sumita's tastes: the rather unlikely Miss Harrison's "Out-of-Door School" in Sarasota, Florida.

Paramananda overruled all objections and wrote Bibhu Charan to send Ranu and Chokanu at once. After all, the funds came not from the ashrama coffers, but from his own pocket, money given to him personally or from outside speaking engagements or returns on his own assets.

Why did he further entangle himself, especially when such patronage of his family provoked bitter criticism of him in India?

Paramananda was a speculator, and these young people were an investment too promising for him to resist. He had high hopes that they would eventually render India the service she so desperately needed, probably in conjunction with Charushila's noble venture. As he clearly wrote about Sumita: "The object of her coming is not merely the secular training. It is to get something fundamental which will enable her to work in India. Her mother is expecting it, Charu is counting on it, and in fact everyone is more interested in that than any degrees or diplomas she may receive."

But why were all those he brought over for training from his own family? Once Gayatri, annoyed at the demands and ingratitude of some of their family, threw this question up to him. He replied weightily, "I take material where I can find it." Indeed, when other Indian families occasionally offered their progeny for Paramananda's American work, he enthusiastically encouraged them, but in the end the Guha Thakurtas were the only ones who entrusted their children to him.

On July 19, 1934, Ranu and Chokanu docked in San Francisco. Swami Paramananda, Brother George, and Kanai, who was visiting the ashrama during his summer recess from M.I.T., made the 450-mile drive to fetch them, returning to the ashrama after midnight that night. Paramananda was weary from the inevitable wrestling with the immigration authorities and the long drive. When Gayatri, after putting her sisters to bed, came in to see Paramananda privately, he broke his brooding silence only to say, "They are not like you."

Indeed, they were not like her. The ten years of India's modernization which separated them had bred a demeanor quite different from the obedient and long-suffering paradigm of traditional India. Gayatri had never talked back to any of the ashrama sisters, had obeyed their every direction even unto how many layers of undergarments she should wear, and had undertaken to please them as a religious responsibility, writing in her diary,

"My Lord resides in all; to please His devotees is also to please Him, then how can I neglect it?" Ranu, Chokanu, and Sumita, who after one year in Florida joined them at the ashrama to study at nearby Glendale College, were a new generation of Indian youth, independent and outspoken, often to the point of impertinence. When they did not make their beds, argued with the other ashrama residents, and rebelled at the swami's and the sisters' doting, Paramananda had to reassess his dreams. Ranu was proud, self-willed, and short-tempered, Sumita was emotionally erratic, temperamental, and moody, and Chokanu succumbed to a string of ailments which kept her bedridden for long stretches and often in the hospital, so that the sisters' worst fears of extra expenses were far surpassed.

Yet Paramananda kept his faith in them, not that they would fulfill his expectations, but that they would fulfill their own highest potential. While others complained about Ranu, Paramananda would tell her, "Be yourself. Be your best self." Even though Gayatri mothered the girls until they told her plainly that they could manage very well without her, she refused to listen to their complaints, expecting them to endure and transcend as she had. Paramananda, on the other hand, was always ready to hear them out without rebuke. Sometimes he would help them to try to see the other person's side; sometimes he would try to satisfy their demand for justice by saying soothingly, "I will talk to that person." Realizing that they were not meant for the religious life, he did not exact from them the high standard he expected from the other ashrama workers. But his nature could not bear to give up on them, or on his own ability to quicken them. Two years after their arrival, he wrote to Gayatri:

> I want you to make an impression on them, especially Sumita, that I desire nothing for myself. I want them to succeed, to make good in whatever they may undertake. My attitude is always to inspire people. Without that, my

life would be inconceivable. . . . Please make the girls feel my love and try to understand me a little. I think of them so much, I feel such great and overwhelming love for them. It pains me to think that I am not able to inspire them and make them happy.

All those entrusted to his care Paramananda sought to satisfy on every level, spiritually, materially, and socially. Just as he took financial responsibility for the ashrama workers, he also played ping-pong and roller ball with them, entertained them by dancing and telling jokes, and doted over their health. His multifaceted role as guru/father/friend was particularly evident with the young Kanai. He would take the boy to the beach, engage him in swimming races, treat him to his favorite Italian restaurant, play ping-pong tournaments with him on the basement's wide laundry table, teach him how to tie a Western necktie, counsel him to develop his intuition rather than just his intellect, train his tastes by outings to the symphony and the theater, and encourage him in his schoolwork when Kanai felt overwhelmed by M.I.T., telling him, "Have faith and you will pass." Recognizing that the boy needed to experiment with the gamut of college experiences, however they differed from the standard he upheld at the Vedanta Centre, Paramananda did not bind him with a long list of "Do's" and "Don't's," requesting only that he not drink. But he did not let Kanai forget the ideal toward which he was rearing him. "I have brought you here," Paramananda told him. "Do something for India when you go back."

The ubiquitous financial burdens continued to drag after him like a lead shadow. To keep the work and the workers afloat, he juggled their finances so skillfully that few realized he had only one ball. He borrowed from one party to pay off another, gauged which creditors could be put off and which could not, and managed to scrape by on one-digit balances. Contending with the sisters' anxieties was often the hardest part of the routine.

Sister Devamata, who had lent him a large part of the funds he invested for the ashrama's income, worried continually, while Sister Achala, the ashrama's tight-fisted bookkeeper, distrusted Paramananda's extravagant nature. Sometimes when he would ask Achala to show him the accounts, she would demur, saying the figures were not tallied. When, after two weeks of waiting, he would ask again, she would cry indignantly, "Don't you trust me?" Once he suddenly decided that he had to go back to Boston to supervise some matters there. When he asked Achala for his train fare, she replied that there was not enough in the ashrama account to pay for it. "Just think," he remarked plaintively to Gayatri, "when I come, I see the money pour in, in collections and offerings, but when I ask for my train fare, she says there's no money." He ended up paying his passage from his own pocket.

The world situation, with its growing belligerence and mutual hostility, deeply disturbed him. Repeatedly he lectured on peace — peace through spiritual evolution.

> Modern man is restless and full of intrigue and aggressiveness, yet he is trying to organize movements which will bring peace into the world. Impossible! No precept can ever succeed unless there is an example behind it. We hear men talk about peace when all the time we know that they are thinking in terms of war. I have heard such type of eloquent addresses given over the radio. Not very long ago, for example, a man spoke on the necessity of preserving peace through armaments. If we were really well armed, he said, then we could give a slap to Japan, and she would at once come to terms. As if peace could ever be brought about that way!
>
> . . . The more we study the question of peace, the more we become convinced there is only one way to find it, and that is the spiritual way. Our material preparations, our shrewdness, cunning, and clever diplomacy — these will never make for permanent peace. The spiritual way is

the only sure way to find peace and hold it.

We who have no great power or position in world affairs can only withdraw within our inner sanctuary and pray to the Supreme with sincere yearning and wholeness of spirit for the peace and protection of our fellow-man.

A small incident recorded in the autobiography of Laurel Keyes gives a glimpse of Paramananda's own state of consciousness about that time. Miss Keyes, now a metaphysical teacher, was then a young seeker spending her first day at the ashrama. It was Easter, when the swami always gave three public services and served both breakfast and dinner to the congregation. Miss Keyes recounts:

> When I returned through the Temple courtyard, Paramananda was going to his study. On the sun-warmed stones a flower had been dropped from a bouquet for the altar. He stooped to pick it up. He handed it to me.
>
> "Please take this down and put it on the grass. A flower should not die in the heat."
>
> I took the wilting blossom and carried it to the shrubbery where I placed it on shaded, moist earth.
>
> It was a small incident yet it touched me deeply. This man, with so many things to attend to on a festive day, took time to notice a flower lying in the sun. It was out of place. Anything out of place was out of harmony. That gesture revealed the depth of the Teachings which were a part of his nature. Oneness with all life was not something outside but was ourselves. The flower was a part of his consciousness, therefore a part of himself. To leave it to wilt on a hot walk, where it might be stepped on by unobserving people, was to leave a part of one's self vulnerable and neglected. . . .

Elsewhere in her autobiography, Laurel Keyes describes the swami, who had profound influence on her inner development,

although she did not remain a devotee of the ashrama: "Paramananda was the mystic—the example, the ideal human, devoted to his God, practical, adaptable, blending prayers and
gardening, building and wise counseling all together."

———————————◆◆———————————

By autumn, 1934, the disheartening decline of the ashrama's
public work could no longer be blamed on post-flood conditions.
The widespread rumors that the ashrama had been closed after
the fire and inaccessible after the flood had finally been quelled,
but still, Sunday after Sunday, Paramananda poured out his
heart to a partly empty temple. As Jessie wrote in September,
"There haven't been so many coming as usual—and no one
knows why, whether it's just the trend of the times or what." For
Durga Puja (the Divine Mother's Festival), the most elaborate
event of the year, they planned a large banquet and a dramatic
presentation of a tale of the Buddha in the temple patio, with
Ranu and Sumita dancing Indian classical dances. Heavy rains
that night spoiled the performance and the swami served the
lavish dinner he had cooked to a meagre fifty guests.

Despite Paramananda's oft-repeated wish to reduce the public work, its vitality sparked his own enthusiasm even as its lassi-
tude depressed him. Ironically, while his contentment was so
often marred by the demands of public lecturing, that very contentment was contingent on the benefit which souls received
from such lecturing. Paramananda often declared, "As long as I
am able to do any particle of good to others, I am content." But
when the languishing of the public work that autumn made him
doubt that very particle, he plummeted into despondency.

The sisters, looking on sorrowfully, whispered that it was
"the dark night of the soul" for the swami. As he went about his
duties swathed in an indrawn, pensive silence, Gayatri and others would plead with him to share the cause of his despondency.
Paramananda would shake his head and reply, "I never want to

cast my burden on anyone."

They surmised that the foundering of the public work had triggered his depression, unaware that it was caused not by the number of empty seats in the temple, but by the particular people who might have filled them. What had happened to the Dobles, to Ruth Norton, to the Cleveland sisters, to John and Polly Verbeck, to Ida McCarthy, and to the score of others whose souls he had fed with the milk of his own heart? Through what failing of his had they left him, sometimes bitterly, casting harsh glances at the ashrama as they left, sometimes causally, as if leaving a restaurant after finishing their meal, with a respectable tip for the waiter?

The nucleus of dedicated workers from Queensberry Street, plus George and Gayatri, had remained loyal through all the years; but hardly any of those who had enthusiastically joined the ashrama community or congregation since its founding were still with him in 1934. Many, of course, had drifted in from curiosity or were looking for the keys to longevity and material gain rather than self-development. Others were genuinely interested in the Vedanta philosophy, but not its hard-won application. Still others were disillusioned when they discovered that the sisters were not saints, or that the swami liked ice cream. But there were some who sincerely responded to Paramananda's invitation to enter the inner sanctuary and feast on his essence. Why then did they run away before dessert, taking the silverware with them?

"It is not the personal loss or suffering which grieves the great soul," Paramananda once declared. "Rather is it when his life, his motive, his love fail to reach the hearts of men."

Daya, from 3,000 miles away, intuited his despair and self-doubt. She was truly his kindred spirit, and shared his dreams and disappointments. "Everybody loves me," he sometimes remarked, "but so few understand me." Daya understood him, and now let her heart spill over into a letter:

You have planted an eternal seed in my heart. I know it now. What are a few short years, even a few lives? If you are the gardener it should not trouble your heart too much if for some little time you have to spade and dig and cultivate barren ground. It is not barren. The miracle has already been performed. The seeds are safe even though the gardener has to toil and suffer in the great heat. Perhaps people even say, "You are a dreamer. You will get nothing for your pains." But in his dreams he sees the beds glorious with beauty. He sees great shade trees and, underneath, roses and lilies, forget-me-nots and lilies of the valley. He smells the fragrance. . . .

Then there are times when he blames his own lack of skill, thinks that he may have killed the little seeds instead of helping them to birth, and these are the worst times of all. Dear Gardener, he cannot see into the depths of the earth and what is happening there. . . .*

Someday you will be amazed to be shown the vision of the joy and renewal that you have brought. It cannot be measured now.

Daya's letter and her penetration into his spirit caused Paramananda to break his silence with an unusually revealing response. He wrote to her:

The hardest thing that I have to endure is the disappointment in friends. You know how completely I rely on people, place my faith and give my heart's best devotion, and when without any apparent rhyme or reason they

---

*Even Daya could not have guessed how long some of those seeds would remain dormant. Forty years after Paramananda's passing, a ninety-two-year-old lady, with clear mind and sharp faculties, came to visit the Vedanta Centre. She told them that although she had steadily attended the swami's services, she did not have the capacity to fully appreciate him or his teachings, until, only eight years before, at the age of eighty-four, in the darkness following the death of her daughter, she rediscovered Paramananda's message and it transformed her life.

turn their faces away, you can imagine how hurtful these experiences are. And yet I know that the Mother wants me to go through these and is preparing me for something greater. There is no experience which is devoid of blessing.

In spite of the strange problems that confront us, I feel confident that the dawn is quite close. I do not ask for material advantages, but I do ask for peace, freedom, and power to serve without restriction. Certainly such prayers cannot remain unfulfilled. I have learned through recent experiences the complete emptiness of all material desires. Only the life, character, true unselfishness, and purity of vision contain the whole of spiritual exaltation, and nothing else matters.

One line from the "Path of Devotion" is constantly before me now, although it was written over twenty-seven years ago: "Human friends and foes are nothing. Divine Mother is everything." How true it is, and how nice it is to be able to remember and feel an inner strength.

Remind me always, yourself, and others like you, whenever I forget my big vision, because that is the main thing in life. Other things come and go; people and appreciation and adulation and promises, they come and they go, but Mother alone forever stays, and Her protecting arms seem stronger as life goes on.

. . . She has given me to sing, and I keep on singing, or rather I hear Her sing through me, and while She does so, there is nothing that can stop it.

Paramananda considered it his purpose in life to inspire souls. "Without that, my life would be inconceivable," he had written. But the Indian youth who had had to surrender even his noble desire for austerity was now having to learn the ultimate surrender: to surrender his very meaning for living. If, by Divine dispensation, he could not quicken souls, could not lift them out of their darkness and delusions, then that too would have to be accepted.

He wrote in his letter to Daya, "This is one of the hardest times I am passing through, and naturally my mind is indrawn, my heart filled with holier things, which take me off from all the entanglements of this material world." There, in the stillness of his depths, he found his answers and his strength. That is why he was so often described as "buoyant"; he went deep and got his breath, then came bobbing up again.

Paramananda was a man whose dreams outlived his disillusionments. On the train to Boston at the end of October, with his spirit rallied once more, he wrote to the ashrama: "Thinking of you most constantly and dreaming my dreams of perfection. Perfection, beauty, peace and harmony in everyone's personal life. Nothing is impossible for those who seek shelter in Him."

In Boston, Sister Daya had a chance to speak to him personally. She told him that she was afraid that he would forget his past wounds and again expose himself and get hurt. "I hope I *will* forget," he replied zealously. "Times that I have borne insult, have felt crushed and saddened, I have prayed that these experiences would not make me so wise that I would ever lose my faith in people. I would rather be fooled and betrayed again and again in the same way than lose the power of loving. Many would think me a fool, but that is how I feel about it."

The Boston work was flourishing, "the whole atmosphere charged with freshness and new strength," as Paramananda put it. Even such rare species (in Vedanta habitats) as young people and men were frequenting the Vedanta Centre. The Christmas Bazaar, their major fundraiser, which featured ashrama handicrafts and honey, baked goods, and donated items, netted $100 on its first day, an impressive figure in those times. With Willie Verbeck, who had returned from Holland, and Mr. Kissam, who had left California to get married and instead turned up in Boston, the Vedanta Centre for the first time had an excess of manpower. Paramananda was thrilled with the work's vitality, and gave abundant credit to Sister Daya, who was in charge during his absences.

Daya needed that bolstering, for she, too, had been going through a long period of struggle. It tortured her to be away from her beloved California during the crises of fire and flood. Paramananda, knowing her acute sensitivity to every suffering being, warned her not to "go to pieces over" the catastrophes. Nevertheless, as she wrote ten days after the flood, "When I think of the valley, the transformation there, and all the agony of heart, I feel such waves of depression that I almost go down under them."

Truly, it was a gruelling period of transition for Daya. The year before, Robert Walton, her former husband and still good friend, had died prematurely; her mother had been stricken with her final, long illness; and Daya herself was going through menopause with its concomitant traumas. In a letter to Gayatri, thanking her for her prayers, Daya wrote: "This past year I have needed them more than you will ever know. There comes a time when we can no longer live in the outworn world of old viewpoints, tendencies and habits, when we must step into the new world or die. But what that step costs one, and how many times we fall back!"

The inevitable conflicts within the Boston community also took their toll, for as Paramananda said of her, Daya was "most often not appreciated by those who live with her constantly." Though her own health was never vigorous, she would not protect herself from the constant importunities that leeched away her energies. When, earlier that year, Anna, a woman who lived at the Centre, was going through a mental crisis, Daya depleted herself in giving Anna a constant transfusion of morale. Paramananda, sensing this, wrote to Mary Lacy about Daya, "I hope she is not overdoing in connection with Anna. One must use discrimination, and there is such a thing as giving, giving, giving, but our life and strength do not belong wholly to ourselves. We also have to bear that in mind."

Most of all, Daya was tormented by her own self-doubt. All

her life, she had tended to belittle herself, blind to the merits that everyone else admired in her. In India, describing his community, Paramananda had referred to Sister Daya as "a great soul." Nevertheless, seeing the others with their practical and domestic talents, she felt that she was incompetent, valueless to the swami's work. Although she was an eloquent speaker and an excellent assistant editor of the *Message of the East*, she felt herself unequal to her assignments. Once she wrote to Sister Devamata, "How often, how often I have wished that I could be equipped as you are (save for your physical condition) to do the tasks that are given me." Nor could the oft-expressed love and appreciation of the swami and the other ashrama members convince her of her own worth. "Humility is all right," Gayatri once wrote to her, "but you must not belittle yourself. . . . Such one-pointedness, such flame of devotion . . . all these and many more qualities have found their root in your big soul."

One can visualize Paramananda and the two most prominent American women in his life, Devamata and Daya, lined up as in a medieval morality play: on one side Devamata, battling with pride; on the other side Daya, battling with its converse, self-depreciation; between them the swami, representing true humility, where one knows oneself to be a mere drop, yet part of the great ocean. As Paramananda used to teach: "When real humility dawns in our heart, through the realization of the infinitude of God, we realize our relation to that infinitude, and our finite nature fades into insignificance." To concentrate on one's virtues or to concentrate on one's faults were both pastimes of the ego; to lose even one's smallness in the magnitude of God was true humility.

The goal of life, according to Paramananda, was to become an instrument, a channel for the Divine power to work through one. Just as egotism clogged the channel, so self-depreciation constricted it. Devamata had illustrated the danger of the former; now Daya, swirling into the vortex of her own mental fabrications, was about to illustrate the danger of the latter.

Meanwhile, young Gayatri was playing an ever larger role in the swami's life. Often she took over the cooking for the weekly shrine offerings and the special celebrations. After one such dinner, Paramananda told her, "Your cooking suits me." Gayatri took this as the highest possible commendation. Again, when Paramananda's health and vitality flagged, he sometimes let Gayatri relieve him of conducting the shrine worship of Sri Ramakrishna, Swami Vivekananda, and Holy Mother. "They are pleased when you worship," he told her with a smile.

Her influence on his life during this trying period went deeper than helping with outer duties. "I want you to know, my child," he wrote to her, "that your spontaneous outpouring of soul qualities is a great solace to me, as there are moments when I really want to give up all contact with the public, but you have a peculiar influence in reviving my zeal for serving more and more, for more and more giving."

Once Gayatri, in a flush of spiritual ardor, exclaimed to the swami how much she wanted to please him. He replied, "Why try to please me? Be one with me." That became the thrust of her whole spiritual endeavor. From then on she strove to forge such an inner union that like St. Paul she might be able to say, "Now it is not I who live, but he lives in me."

Sister Daya, whose love for Gayatri had not dwindled during all their years of separation on opposite coasts, often wrote to her of the leadership role for which she knew Paramananda was priming the girl. To this Gayatri replied:

> Lately you have often mentioned that I shall be given some work to do. Sometimes I too have little similar feeling. I ask you to pray for me that I may learn to live the life first with wholeness of consecration. More I read about great lives, better do I understand how far I am from the sublime attributes of spiritual life, and more ardent grows my longing to offer my all for the attainment of purity and

selflessness. I know Mother will grant me all my desires, for She had roused in me such passion.

Paramananda, effusing pride and satisfaction at Gayatri's unfoldment, once wrote to her: "You are the product of some of my highest dreams and aspirations."

Suddenly, at the very end of 1934, Paramananda announced that he was going to India. "I do not know why I am going to India," he wrote, "but there is an impelling power pulling me there."

Some of that pull must have come from Charushila's work. Sister Satya Prana, who was stalwartly lending her support there, declared that Paramananda's presence was needed if that work was to continue. The school was the first of its kind in East Bengal, where free public education was unheard of; and indigent girls were enrolling in large numbers. A branch for vocational training had been started in an outlying village. The whole burden rested on the self-sacrificing Charushila Devi, who was collapsing under the strain. The doctors' one remedy for her, complete rest, was a sheer impossibility. The news of Paramananda's coming acted on her like a tonic.

Paramananda also announced that he was taking with him Gayatri, who had not seen her motherland in nine years, and Amala, who everyone hoped could fit into Charu's work. In addition to Sister Satya Prana, Lois Houghton from Boston had taken up residence at the Dacca Ananda Ashrama that autumn, and was helping in whatever way the language barrier would permit. Such interchange between Eastern and Western women was one of Paramananda's cherished dreams, and he fervently hoped that Amala would find her place there too. On December 29, they sailed from San Francisco, leaving behind American shores and a year that no one would miss.

19

The Great Reassurer

MUCH TO SWAMI PARAMANANDA's astonishment, they travelled through a world which knew him. He was recognized in places he had never been, was enthusiastically greeted by people he had never met. In Hong Kong, where they were unexpectedly delayed for two days awaiting their steamer connection and where Paramananda knew not a single person, several Hindu men hastily arranged a lecture for him which drew a large crowd of Europeans, Americans, and Orientals. Paramananda was introduced as "the intellectual, philosophical, and spiritual ambassador of India to the world." A Chinese gentleman rose to say how much he appreciated meeting the swami whose books had inspired him for the last eight years. As Paramananda remarked, "It seems my point of contact is no more dependent upon my personal presence." The swami, who since 1930 had been listed in *Who's Who in America*, had become an international figure.

Indeed, his books and the monthly magazine the *Message of the East*, which always carried reports of the Ananda Ashrama and the Boston Vedanta Centre, had circulated far and wide. Entering its twenty-third year, the *Message* files included subscriptions and enquiries from virtually every major city in the United States, Canada, Mexico, South America, England, Russia, Germany, Norway, France, Italy, Switzerland, China, the Malay States, Japan, and Hawaii.

During this 1935 voyage to India, Paramananda lectured four times in Singapore and twice in Rangoon. But the swami's most moving reception was given him in Penang, Malaya, where they spent only four hours. As Gayatri Devi described the visit:

> Swamiji was taken from one home to another (altogether six, I believe) where wives, sons, daughters, children, all performed their acts of oblation with garlands, flowers, and money. Swamiji's face grew more tender, more illumined as the fragrant garlands rose higher and higher around his neck. He was obliged to remove them several times so that there would be room for more. What impressed me most was, there in a setting of this kind, amongst simple, devout people, Swamiji's work was not dependent on lectures and public approval. They recognized what he was and derived blessings from his presence although many of them could neither speak nor understand English. . . . After all, his mission is not to establish institutions and be chained by them, but rather to inspire in human hearts love, faith and understanding.

Paramananda himself recorded his response to this adulation: "The reaction on me was very similar to what I experienced at the outset of my spiritual life in Madras in 1901. I felt that I must not fail them and that my life must be made worthy of such love, trust and devotion. I cannot describe to you how deeply stirred I was by their love and faith." As for institutions, the incorrigible dreamer could not resist adding, "I have already planted the seed for an International Ashrama somewhere in the Malay States. If it is the Divine will, it will come to pass."

On February 10, 1935, Paramananda, Gayatri Devi, and Amala arrived in India. Paramananda spent the next two and a half months lecturing at public receptions, schools, colleges, and different branches of the Ramakrishna Mission. During four weeks at the Dacca Ananda Ashrama, he grappled with its problems, gave classes and private interviews, presided over special functions, and infused into a worn-out Charushila Devi renewed vigor and faith.

He was greeted with love and adulation by many. Swami Akhandananda, one of the last surviving disciples of Sri Ramakrishna and the new President of the Math and Mission, lavished affection on him. After Paramananda visited the senior swami at his Murshidabad ashrama, Swami Akhandananda wrote to Sister Devamata: "How humble, sweet and loving was he by nature! Every one of the Ashrama was simply charmed." And Paramananda, equally charmed by the visit, wrote Swami Akhandananda: "I am still under the spell of your love. . . . I have not seen such a beautiful, alive ashrama anywhere. When I come to India after retiring, may I have a little place there?"

A new generation of monks was being initiated. These young men had heard of Paramananda and were eager to meet him. Forty years later they would give their recollections of him as "the personification of purity," "princely, affectionate," "the sweetest person I have ever met." Swami Nityaswarupananda in 1979 could still enthusiastically quote the first line of Paramananda's address on Swami Vivekananda which had so stirred him as a young college student. Paramananda had begun, "The swami, the great swami at whose feet I sat, whose fire I caught, whose sparks I have the privilege to scatter. . . ."

Yet, the intermediate generation of swamis, those contemporaries of Swami Akhilananda and Swami Prabhavananda, continued to regard Paramananda with disapproval. Their suspicion had only festered since last he left them at the height of the Concorde scandal, and it now broke out in an open confrontation. The issue this time was Gayatri Devi.

Paramananda took Gayatri with him wherever he went, and had her sit beside him on the podium at all non-Mission functions. Whenever someone would approach and invite him to speak before their group, Paramananda would gesture toward his young companion and ask, "Have you met Gayatri Devi? Why don't you ask her to speak, too?" Thus, Gayatri lectured in Singapore, Rangoon, Calcutta, and Dacca, much to Paramananda's pride and satisfaction, for he was Pygmalion and this deep, poised young speaker was the product of nine years of his loving tutelage.

To be sure, he had taken a diffident, young widow with no future in her native society, and turned her into a teacher of Vedanta and a noble representative of India. But his pride stemmed more from her inner unfoldment than her outer accomplishments. By the development of her character, she epitomized the very ideal of discipleship. As Paramananda once explained:

> Primarily people must have character, . . . and, as I have said, discipleship makes for character. It is like moulding raw material. The Teacher with no ulterior motive, who desires only to see a fine thing produced, moulds this unformed clay in the form of the student. If the clay is brittle, it will not mould. That is, if we come with brittle mind, rigid and unyielding, even the greatest Teacher can do nothing for us.

Gayatri had proved herself a fit disciple, strong yet pliable. Moreover, it was Paramananda's conviction that most Indian women had hidden potential, if they could only be freed to express it. For years he had been identified with the cause of India's oppressed women, a cause cherished by Swami Vivekananda and forgotten by most of his followers. In speeches throughout Asia, Paramananda often aroused his audiences to the urgent need of women for opportunity and social and spiritual equality. The Dacca ashrama for underprivileged women was founded in his name and sustained by his funds. At its fourth anniversary that March, Paramananda fervently addressed a crowd of one thousand. "Swamiji gave the men a real blast of eloquence in English," wrote Lois Houghton, "telling them to

Gayatri Devi and Paramananda.
Ananda Ashrama, December, 1927.

Sister Devamata. c. 1928.

Sister Daya. September, 1929.

Paramananda. New Year's Day, 1927.

Aboard ship, en route to India, December, 1932. Standing: Lillian, Dr. Boike. Seated: Edwinna Post, Paramananda, Sister Satya Prana.

Outdoor class at Dacca Ananda Ashrama, 1931. Charushila Devi in center, her mother to her right.

Dacca, 1935. Left to right, rear row: Lois Houghton, unknown, Amala, Sister Satya Prana, Kadumbini (Paramananda's older sister). Second row: Sati, Charushila Devi's mother (Paramananda's oldest sister), Charuprava, Paramananda, Gayatri Devi, Bibhu Charan, Hemmalini (Paramananda's older sister). Front row: Khana, Parabi, Arundhuti, Charushila Devi, Gopal, Badal, Nitai, Bolai.

Chapel of the Vedanta Centre, 420 Beacon Street, Boston, 1939. Gayatri Devi and Swami Paramananda. On left, bas relief of Jesus Christ, Buddha, Krishna. On right, bas relief of Vivekananda, Sri Ramakrishna, Holy Mother.

Boulder tossed down by flood, Ananda Ashrama, January, 1934. Sister Achala, Paramananda, Gayatri Devi.

Gayatri Devi, Ranu, Paramananda, Sumita, Chokanu, Kanai. Ananda Ashrama, c. 1937.

Paramananda with Cincinnati students. July, 1933.

Last picture taken of Paramananda, with Miss Sherwood at her 80th birthday party, June 5, 1940, Ananda Ashrama.

Swami Paramananda. Cohasset ashrama, 1939.

wake up to their responsibility for the training of women."

Now this champion of opportunity for women had with him a living example of what Indian women could become once they were released from the drudgery of being household chattels. That example was Gayatri Devi. After her lecture to a group of Indian men in Singapore, Paramananda rose and gave his usual admonition that India could not rise as long as it stifled its women. Then he pointed out Gayatri Devi as an illustration of what opportunity could produce. He told how her fine, latent qualities had blossomed in the United States and how she was inspiring scores of Americans. To Paramananda, Gayatri Devi was a model of the practical and spiritual possibilities of Indian womanhood, and he lost no opportunity to show her off, though she was often mortified in the role.

Paramananda's critics at the Belur Math, who by then had assumed positions of considerable authority, could not countenance one of their monks travelling about in the company of an attractive, young woman. Ironically, while Paramananda saw Gayatri as a glowing example of discipleship and spiritual unfoldment, his critics saw only her sex. As a general rule, considering certain age-old principles of monasticism, they had a compelling point, but Paramananda was never one for general rules.

Finally, they accosted Paramananda and censured him for taking Gayatri Devi everywhere with him. Paramananda listened to their accusations, then replied simply. "If you don't like what I'm doing, I don't have to stay at the Math." With that, he went to his room to pack. Swami Virajananda, also a disciple of Vivekananda, and Paramananda's beloved friend, who as Secretary of the Math was really its chief executive, heard of the encounter, and rushed to Paramananda's quarters. He pleaded with him to stay and ignore the insult. Paramananda consented, but the situation remained strained.

He found himself repeatedly at odds with certain younger swamis. Once he heard the outspoken Swami Vijayananda, who had recently founded a center in Buenos Aires, calling the American people "dollar-worshippers." Paramananda, staunchly loyal to his adopted countrymen, spoke up in their defense. "Have you ever been to America?" he asked the younger swami.

"No," Vijayananda replied.

"Then how can you say those things?" Paramananda upbraided him. "I have lived with them all these many years, and I have not found them so materialistic."

Five years later, at the Ananda Ashrama, this exchange would have its consequences.

The old accusation, that Paramananda associated too much with his family, flared up again. His brother Bibhu Charan, utterly devoted to the swami, whom he considered a saint, managed to come to Calcutta whenever Paramananda was there, and followed him about whenever possible. When Paramananda was in Dacca, Bibhu Charan's wife Charuprava would cook special dishes and bring them to the Ananda Ashrama for him. Bibhu Charan's children (those of the sixteen still residing at home) would be roused at four o'clock each morning to collect flowers and make garlands for their esteemed uncle. Especially with their beloved Gayatri present, the family swarmed around without respite. Nor was the flow of criticism one-sided. Bibhu Charan, too, was critical of what he considered lethargy at the Belur Math. A relentlessly active man despite his frail health, he was appalled to see some of the swamis of the intermediate generation spending hours leisurely sipping tea in the afternoons.

An entry in Amala's diary of that April gives a glimpse of the acrimony which Paramananda faced, not only from the other monks, but from some of his own followers (Amala always always referred to herself in the third person as "A"):

> A's heart feels sad that Gayatri's family has so completely absorbed Swamiji and caused just criticism and indignation of Math and others. Swamiji is a sadhu and sannyasin

and renouncer—pure, gentle and loving and Mr. Guha
has no right to absorb Swamiji so much for Mr. Guha's
selfish ends. Mr. G. absorbs to the point where S. is feeding,
clothing and educating Mr. G's children. Which is not right.
& Mr. G. is trying to turn S.'s mind against the Math. A.A.
in La Crescenta is become a Guha Thakurta clan. A. told
all this to Swamiji this morning. . . .

Amala herself was proving to be one of Paramananda's most
embarrassing, if predictable, problems. Strong-willed and contrary, with sweet voice and smiling face she did the opposite of
whatever was asked of her. Paramananda explained to her that
in India men and women sit separately at public meetings, and
asked her to take her seat with the women. When he rose to face
his audience, he found Amala smiling attentively at him from
the middle of the men's section. Swami Vijnanananda, one of
the three remaining disciples of Sri Ramakrishna, asked Amala
not to salute him with elaborate displays of devotion, such as
touching her head to his feet. Giggling as if the request were an
amusing joke, she prostrated before him and laid her forehead
abjectly on his feet.

The combined strains began to take their toll on Paramananda's nerves. When he saw his sister Labanya, Sumita's mother,
he sternly upbraided her for coaxing him to take Sumita without
telling him of the girl's deficiencies. Later Labanya declared that
it was the first time in her life she had ever seen him angry. Yet, a
new strength was issuing from him, a decisiveness and self-
assurance which was the fruit of his years of trial and maturation.
He was coming into the fullness of his power, and it startled
many who were used to only the meek and tender Paramananda.
It was reflected in his public speeches, for while he had never
been a dynamic speaker, his appeal being rather his ethereal
spirituality and pervasive serenity, now he was thundering his
message with the force of a Vivekananda. Lois Houghton wrote

after one such address: "His audience listened without moving. He sent out a clarion call to the people of India to remember their glorious spiritual inheritance and bring it out of the dust of ages. It was one of the strongest and most powerful speeches I have ever heard Swamiji make anywhere."

On April 25, Paramananda and Gayatri Devi sailed from Colombo via Europe for America. They were accompanied by Sister Satya Prana, who had given India two years and twenty pounds of her attenuated frame. Amala had been left in Dacca to help Charushila, despite the misgivings of most of the swamis and her own fluctuating health. Paramananda reaffirmed his faith in her higher nature, and crossed his fingers.

The party landed in Boston on May 25, to find a thriving Vedanta Centre and a haggard Sister Daya, her one remaining kidney threatened by infection. While she recuperated, Paramananda remained in Boston for three months, luxuriating in the hours of solitude which Ananda Ashrama could never give. On Saturdays they enjoyed idyllic outings to Cohasset, with the afternoon service under the pines, the supper served from the upper house, and the favorite sunset meditation on the high rock.

Only once did Paramananda venture out, for a one-week lecture tour to Cincinnati and Louisville. The Louisville Truth Centre received him with much fervor, too much for Paramananda's taste. As overflow crowds thronged into the meagre 300-seat hall, he complained that it was "too crowded." From Ohio he wrote, "I was very ill on the train after leaving Boston. I am realizing that I cannot lead any more this race-horse existence. The body has not the same resistance. Perhaps the Mother has other plans for me."

During his brief passage through Europe, he had felt again the atmosphere of a continent preparing for war, and it sickened him. Italy was invading Ethiopia. Germany had repudiated the Versailles Treaty and had reintroduced compulsory military service. Paramananda's talks during the next few years were a frequent indictment of the state the modern world had "progressed to."

Today, instead of boasting of our present civilization and the strides it is supposed to have made toward progress, would it not be better to ask ourselves why the world is rent asunder through hate and distrust? Travelling today is a nightmare. You cannot leave the country without obtaining complicated documents; and though you may go all around the world, it will be difficult to find one single person who believes in another. . . . In place of advancement, we have created a condition which entangles the minds of men. That cannot be right. There must be a raising of the mind of man and an illumination in the soul of man, in order again to simplify the order of humanity. We must follow the path of faith and love — the path that leads to God, instead of to ever greater and greater confusion. . . .

Let a man cleanse his heart from egotism! What is this ego which he asserts every day as he clashes with his fellows? There would be no war in this world, there would be no conflict in our social life, were it not for the prevalence of this colossal egotistic tendency in man, which has been increased by his wrong, detrimental training. Man wants everything for himself, and in his blindness even grasps for those things which bring disaster and death. . . .

More cleverness — for a long time this has been our standard. Where has it brought us and what has man obtained through his cleverness — tell me that? Today I can speak very frankly because you are thinking along these same lines. Man has set his own traps, has created entanglements, mental worries and unhappiness for himself and for the world, yet now he does not know how to get free from them; he is unable to find any solution. He might turn within, but unfortunately he has been nurtured with the thought that the idea of submission to the Divine Will is a weak, old-fashioned idea, and is not for the practical province of mankind. . . .

Why not look to Him? Why not try to find some definite point of contact through our faith and feeling, that we may discover what He really want us to do? It is not a thing that is impractical, my friends, but we make it so through our doubt, through our constant critical attitude. Oh, how we drive God away from us! And yet we say, "We need Thee every hour." We sing hymns and talk glibly of many wonderful things, but when the test comes we fail to apply them. No wonder we lose our faith in the Divine, the world loses faith in itself.

The remedy Paramananda offered, as always, was all-conquering love. "You may wonder what new idea or thought I may express in regard to our passage to God," he proclaimed. "There is only one idea both new and old, for all times. Love!" In the face of those who derided such an ideal as quixotic, Paramananda held up the example of Mahatma Gandhi, who was bringing the mighty British Empire to heel with his practice of nonviolence and *satyagraha*, soul-force. Paramananda often quoted Gandhi: "War will only be stopped when the conscience of mankind has become sufficiently elevated to recognize the undisputed supremacy of the law of love in all the walks of life."

Paramananda began every service, as he had for almost thirty years, with a Peace Invocation. Like Gandhi, he believed that two things must never be sacrificed: peace and one's principles. An uncompromising pacifist, he maintained that love was the only weapon worth wielding, and the only one that ever produced an effective result. Yet always his words broke against the wall of resistance called "practicality."

The way is open to us all, but the trouble is, we have convinced ourselves that it is not practical. Even ministers have said, "For this age it cannot be made true." An unfortunate attitude of mind, especially if we dismiss the subject before we have tried it. We must admit that that is not fair. We find thousands who will undertake a hazardous

adventure on hearing tales of a gold mine, but when someone comes to us and says, "I will show you the way to God,
Peace, and Beatitude," sad to say, there is nowhere any
response. . . .

The practical thing is to educate humanity one by one.
Man must advance by means of the individual. It may
sound like a gigantic task, but is it not better than continuing always in the wrong way, without making any effort to
change our direction?

. . . When individuals, groups of men and women
everywhere, in this country, abroad, in the distant places
of the earth, learn to think along these lines, projecting
thoughts of unifying influence for the healing of the hearts
of humanity — these thoughts will be like a beautiful
canopy, a dome of white light, going from West, North,
South, and East, and peace will pervade it. . . . Perhaps I
have spoken like a madman. Conditions in the world as
we know them do not seem to call for such a vision. But I
have faith.

On August 28, 1935, Paramananda returned to California
after an absence of eight months. As he described the conditions
there in a letter to Gayatri: "All you need to do is to visualize the
Ashrama life and add at least 25% more confusion and difficulties."
The community, dreadfully shorthanded, had become demoral-
ized. The public services, with Daya in Boston and Gayatri in
India, had consisted of readings by Sister Achala, which predictably had drawn few people. The only element which had remained at a consistent level were the community tussles. Brother
George, the keeper of the livestock after Mr. Walter's abrupt
departure, insisted on letting the animals graze freely on the
ashrama hills, proclaiming their need for freedom, but no doubt
equally motivated by the high cost of feed. When Brother Philip,
the hard-working gardener, found the cows trampling his flower
beds or the goats nibbling on his newly set-out plantings, he
would fly into a rage, which did not affect George in the least.

And so it went.

Yet this time Paramananda seemed beyond it all. He was emanating a power many sensed with awe. A week after his arrival, Evelyn MacMinn wrote to Boston:

> There were only about forty-odd people (outsiders) at each of the Sunday services. Attendance has been practically nil for too long. But never have I heard such a talk as Swamiji gave in the morning. So brilliant, so electric; a verbal flood of the Water of Life. The afternoon talk simply continued the effect. It was all one. I feel as if we who are privileged to hear and come close to him are truly the elect of the world. Then the evening meditation and chanting in the temple. All so high and other-worldly. It seemed as if currents of electricity were shooting and shooting through our bodies, cleansing, purifying, filling them with Life.

Others echoed her observations. They declared that they had only to come into his presence to be bathed in peace and purified. One person who had just begun to attend the Vedanta Centre services wrote to the swami: "What a rare and beautiful power to arouse in one such deep feeling by the utterance of a few simple words so eloquently spoken, and I am filled with wonder and amazement that one fellow-being can impart to another such a feeling of restfulness and genuine pleasure. If I say to you that it is my wish that you may continue to so unconsciously delight people wherever you go, would it be as silly as my suggesting to the sun that it continue to shine?"

A young girl who used to attend the ashrama services with her parents was recuperating from a serious illness. One Sunday she determined to go and see the swami. In her memoir she recounts how he was standing at the top of the long flight of stairs that led to the temple. Slowly she made her way up, her eyes riveted on his encouraging smile. When she reached the top, he held out his arms to her and gently seated her on a nearby bench. She was too breathless to speak, but Paramananda sat beside her and laid her head on his chest. He spoke not a word, but she felt that he was praying. "I felt the power of his healing rays flooding over me, and I experienced that peace which passeth all understanding."

Another time, an inmate of a nearby mental hospital was brought to a Sunday service by her attendant, who thought that the atmosphere of the temple would be salutary for this seriously disturbed patient. At first she sat there quietly, but manifestly on the defensive, armed against the people around her. During the swami's talk, however, she became increasingly restless, until the nurse had to take her away.

Once outside, the woman refused to go farther, and lay down on one of the wooden benches under the library arcade. When the attendant tried to force her to go to the car, she tried to bite him, struggled and fought like an animal at bay, and shrieked wildly. She was still in that frenzied state when the service ended. Many people gathered around, at a safe distance, no one daring to go near her. Then Paramananda emerged from the temple. As he walked directly toward the crazed woman, Hilda grabbed his arm and insisted that he keep away, for the woman was violent. Releasing Hilda's grip, and ignoring the others who called to him not to go too close and not to touch her, Paramananda walked right up to the woman and stood beside her. Suddenly her frenzy subsided; the lines on her face relaxed and tears started to roll down her cheeks. When Paramananda reached out his hand to her, she clasped it in both her hands and kissed it. Then, sitting up, she spoke to him quite rationally, saying that she thought he could help her. When he finally told her that she had better go, she went quietly, without a word of protest. Daya, who witnessed and recorded the scene, compared it to New Testament incidents of the "casting out of devils."

A unique published description of Paramananda and his effect on people by someone entirely outside the Vedanta movement is given in the autobiography of Josephine Whitney Duveneck, California's well-known humanitarian and champion of social causes. She eventually joined the Society of Friends, but in the 1930s she was casting about for spiritual guidance, while her instinct for social service was being paralyzed by her own sense of unworthiness. Her spiritual quest led her to visit the Ananda Ashrama:

> The presiding genius of the Ananda Ashram was, of course, Swami Paramananda. When you first met him he appeared like a young boy, tall, slim, moving with the grace of a deer or a panther. His face was unlined and the warm smile on his lips and in his eyes seemed to envelop the stranger with an encompassing welcome. He was in reality no longer very young for he had been active in the Ramakrishna Mission for at least thirty years. He was one of those people who seem timeless, who do not age, but live in a perpetual springtime of love and service. . . .
>
> I talked alone with him twice. He knew exactly where I stood, without my telling him. I felt that it was not so much what the Swami said but the validity of his whole being that had meaning. Tagore said in one of his poems, "He who opens the flower, does it so simply." To be totally immersed in the Divine Presence results in simplicity — there can be no barriers to the flow of love from that source and he who has become part of this Reality becomes an instrument for its fulfillment. . . . From the Swami I learned the joy of the sacrificial life, and that I should not worry about unworthiness and shortcomings, but just go ahead and really renounce the world, the flesh, and the devil by becoming a child of God, rejoicing in His manifold appearances and revelations. He suggested a prelude of recollection by which I could quickly enter the threshold of communion, and negative considerations of past shortcomings melted away in the positive sunlight of adoration. . . .

Swami Paramananda was the most joyous and simple person I ever met. He said to me, "No single soul has ever found happiness or peace or lasting contentment in the outer world, but after one has found it within, one can carry it to the outside. . . ."

It was a lull in Paramananda's life, perhaps brought on by his own inner state of passivity. The tribulations were still there, the human conflicts, the financial harassments. In August the bank had attached his savings account for the unpaid interest on the 875 Beacon Street house. But Paramananda was sitting back and watching it all with the air of a well-seasoned spectator. He had seen the play before, so it no longer gripped him. In October he wrote to Boston:

It is patience, and patience alone, which will clear our way and bring to us the fulfillment of our great dreams. This thought is taking hold of me more and more and seems to hold me back from quick action, although people who live with me think I am strenuously active; but still there is a definite change in my attitude toward life, that with patience, perseverance and love that does not fluctuate, everything can be conquered. In spiritual life there is no other alternative.

At such quiet times we can see Paramananda in his favorite roles, as teacher, counsellor, comforter. Observing that people blocked their own access to the Divine within themselves by their self-doubt and low opinions of their true worth, he acted as the Great Reassurer. The God he knew was a beneficent, all-loving Deity, a Mother with Her arms ever outstretched toward Her children. Once Gayatri accidentally spilled some holy water on her feet, a horrifying desecration by Hindu standards. When she ran distraught to Paramananda, he consoled her, "Don't be upset. Mother never takes offense at what the children do."

Ananda Ashrama, for all its internal squabbles, was regarded as an island of peace by those outside. They came there with their troubles and tragedies — unfaithful husbands, delinquent children, financial failures — seeking help. Paramananda gave them no pat answers. He was not a physician who dispensed aspirin to cover up the symptoms. He believed that people were tormented by material conditions because they made material realities fundamental in their lives. He counselled them to look up and look in, to leave the petty behind in the realization of the vast.

Once Mrs. Amy Russell, an ardent new devotee who came with her two children to spend every weekend at the Guest House, was feeling weighted by a seemingly insolvable problem. That night after dinner at the Cloister, while everyone was busily engaged cleaning up, she slipped out to the terrace. She stood there for a while, mulling over her alternatives or lack of them, when suddenly she saw Paramananda standing beside her. "Look up to the immortal stars," he whispered.

When people came to him buffeted by conflicting opinions and advice, he declined to add his own judgement to the melee. Instead he would tell them, "Why not consult your inner voice?" Eager to help people, he nevertheless did not want them to become dependent on him to solve their problems, find their answers, be their intermediary with God. God was within them too; they would have to make their own contact. That was the essence of spiritual life. As he once told his congregation: "Occasionally I am asked, 'Won't you please pray for me? I know that your prayers will be heard.' That can be true for all of us. I do not believe that it is the will of the Divine Providence that a few personages are appointed to bring us saving grace. Great souls show us the way, but it is the individual alone who must attain perfection."

One evening as the community stood in the Cloister living room before bedtime, the swami vocalized this idea which was dominating his consciousness:

Let us always seek to draw from within. I want to impress this upon your minds. Whenever perplexities, problems, or distressing conditions arise, try to solve everything from within. Go to the shrine, the temple, wherever you can get your adjustment, and retire within yourself.

. . . Let us never try to solve anything in the ordinary way. This thought has come to me very strongly, and I hope I may always remember it myself. . . . To turn within, to draw from within—that is the only cure for all ills, the only sustaining power that we may depend upon. There is nothing, no tragedy too great, no malady so incurable, that we cannot find something to counteract it if we but do not forget to go within.

Once, seeing Sister Daya dejected, he handed her a scrap of paper on which he had pencilled this note: "As our understanding deepens, we realize more and more that the whole secret of life consists in learning to go within, way within the very depth of our inner being where no storm of emotion or stress of depression can find access. This inner kingdom of man, the goal of religion, free from all dual conflicts, holds for every world-weary soul unbroken harmony and abounding peace."

Perhaps the earmark of saints is that, because they are not absorbed in themselves, they have plenty of attention to give to others. Paramananda carried the most responsibility of anyone at the ashrama, yet he always managed to remember each one's favorite dish, to recognize even people who came only once a year, to write encouraging notes to those whose despondency he intuited across the miles, and to minister to the ashrama saplings. From the platform he would notice that a newcomer at the back of the congregation, feeling chilly, was putting on her coat. He would ask for the windows to be closed. Rushing to a crucial business appointment, he would notice Sister Devamata seated in a corner of the Cloister patio, looking worried. He would stop and, stooping beside her wheelchair, take her hand between his two fingers in his characteristic gesture that meant, "Everything will by all right." Those who were easily irritated by Sister Devamata's fretting marvelled at Paramananda's unending patience with and concern for her.

His teaching methods had not changed since Queensberry Street. As Gayatri described them in her diary:

> With everyone his attitude is the same. He sees in all the same — the manifestations of the Mother, therefore he finds fault with no one. He never condemns anyone, nor even disciplines or points out that we have blundered or failed. For this all of us jab him, express our disapproval, saying he indulges and encourages people's misconduct. One night we had a discussion about this. . . . I cannot recall his exact words, but remember the gist of his remarks: "I have extraordinary faith in all. I see everyone's divinity. I believe that in each one there are unlimited qualities, such as unselfishness, nobility, magnanimity; therefore by reminding them of these I try to lift their mind high. Otherwise my method of teaching would become ordinary. Faultfinding, scolding, correcting are not my ways, so how can I change my own nature?"

One day, standing by her corner room, Gayatri heard Paramananda say, "Whom shall we discipline? Sometimes one feels like whipping, but it does no good. My part is to inspire and I want to go on inspiring."

In the evenings, before the bedtime meditation, the ashrama community would gather in the living room. Paramananda would read poetry or Shakespeare to them, or he and Ranu would sing, or he would get Ranu and Sumita to dance by gliding through a few steps and asking, "Am I doing it right? Show me how you would do this dance." Sometimes, while the rest of the community conversed, Paramananda would tune in the radio to his favorite comedians, and chuckle and chuckle. When the community's discussions and debates began to intrude on his listening, he would turn up the volume and drown them out with an Eddie Cantor soliloquy.

Paramananda enjoyed going to movies. He liked Clark Gable, Fred Astaire, and Robert Montgomery. The Indian girls used to tease him that he had a crush on Joan Crawford. He would come home after taking them all to see *Top Hat*, and, donning his own hat, dance through one of the movie's numbers with Ranu playing Ginger Rogers to his Fred Astaire, as he crooned along, "Cheek to cheek."

He sometimes quoted from the Rule of St. Francis: "Let the Brothers take care not to appear long-faced, gloomy, or overpious; but let them be joyous about their faith in God, laughing and agreeable companions." Everyone acknowledged that the swami was the most agreeable companion, and laughed the most of them all. He loved to tell jokes. He would ask Sumita, Chokanu, and Ranu to stock his repertoire by telling him jokes they had heard at school. But even when his supply ran low, he was capable of telling the same joke for the tenth time and still laughing heartily at the punch line. A few members of his congregation were more smitten by his merry laughter than by his preaching.

And he loved to tease. That year Kanai graduated from M.I.T. and got his first engineering job with the International Nickel Company in Bayonne, New Jersey. After a month, Paramananda drove down from Boston to see him. Kanai proudly displayed his first monthly paycheck of $250. To the boy's horror, Paramananda asked him to sign the check over to him. Kanai hesitated but, fully cognizant how much he owed the swami, he finally complied. With crestfallen mien, he showed Paramananda and his companions back to their car. Paramananda turned on the ignition, then reached into his pocket, and handed Kanai $300 in cash.

Yet, for his community, the swami's joking and teasing was not a break from the spiritual life, but an integral part of it. As

Gayatri noted in her diary:

> When every night we gather around him to say "goodnight,"
> sometimes he laughs like a boy or he dances or cracks
> jokes; again being absorbed, he sings or, remaining totally
> silent and detached, listens to our idle prattle. Under all
> conditions his divine mood is the same. Like our very own
> intimate relation he mingles with us and shares our joy
> and pain; yet no matter how we partake of his comradeship,
> his ways, moods, conversation, playfulness, everything re-
> minds one of the world beyond the senses.

In October, 1935, Paramananda left the ashrama for Boston.
A few days later, Sister Seva fell critically ill. She was hospitalized with an acute kidney infection, the culmination of a long
series of symptoms which no one had been able to diagnose.

Sister Seva was a unique figure among Paramananda's
disciples. Amidst a community of avid diary keepers and letter
writers, she alone never put pen to paper. We have not a single
sentence by her, a void which inevitably conceals her importance in the community. In fact, Seva, while not cultivating personal friendships with others, was one of the pillars of the ashrama
in her unflagging service and her selfless spirituality. When Ida
McCarthy moved out two years before, leaving the swami at a
loss for someone to take care of the Guest House, Seva volunteered
to move down there, thus accepting a lifelong exile from the
center of activity where the other sisters got to live in close
proximity to the swami. Yet, greatness in routine matters is easy
not to notice. As Gayatri Devi wrote to Paramananda in 1933,
when Victor was suffering from influenza: "This brings to my
mind how wonderful Sister Seva is. She entirely took charge of
him in spite of all the important duties that keep her occupied
every moment of the day. I am just beginning to realize what a
great source of strength she is. Her concern for each and every
one of us, the mother love she bestows on all your children, is a
real blessing." The fiery-tempered Mrs. Gladwell had turned

into what Paramananda himself termed "a saint." Once he testified of her, "I have never seen another soul so selfless, so full
of service and saintliness." Her attainment must have gratified
him immensely.

It was harrowing for Paramananda to be physically distant
when one of his children was sick. After less than three weeks, he
cut short his stay in Boston and returned to California with Sister
Satya Prana. By the time he arrived, Seva was on the upswing.

Yet other problems cropped up to be handled. Within a
week, the irascible, but hard-working, Hilda and the woman
who took care of Sister Devamata both announced they were
leaving. At the same time, Evelyn MacMinn, who rendered service to the sisters and to the ashrama in a half dozen different
capacities, was called to Boston to tend to a sick uncle. That left
an indoor working force of Sister Achala, Alice, Sister Satya Prana,
and the convalescing Sisters Devamata and Seva, plus Jessie and
Mangala, who showed up periodically. Hardly a robust crew.

No matter. Paramananda resolved to train the Indian girls
"to do something in the line of domestic science and housekeeping during the weekends when they are free." Sister Achala,
staunchly transcending her own physical frailties, stepped forward to shoulder the cooking and shopping. Paramananda was
determined to be unsettled by nothing. "These are times of real
readjustment," he wrote that November, "and we must take
things as they come. As I am sitting here out-of-doors in the sun,
it seems most heavenly, and all the difficulties and unpleasant
realities fade away completely from the mind." Lillian noted in
her diary that she felt in the swami an "ever-increasing mellowness
and relaxed attitude."

Again, when Daya sent him disappointing news about the
Message of the East, he replied: "Do not feel distressed. . . . It is
not worth being disturbed about anything. If this work were
only a momentary thing, we might be perturbed over small
matters, but it goes on steadily, and just as it is true of a river
stream, it has its ebb and flow."

The year 1936 marked the birth centenary of Sri Ramakrishna. The event was celebrated with great éclat at the Ramakrishna Mission centers throughout India, Asia, and America. For the American centers, it was a chance to flex their very new muscle. For almost thirty years after Vivekananda left America, the only new centers in the United States were those founded by Swami Paramananda. Then, around 1930, a new crop of centers sprang up: Swami Akhilananda's in Providence; Swami Prabhavananda's in Portland and Hollywood; Swami Gnaneswarananda's in Chicago; and Swami Nikhilananda's on New York's East Side. In addition, short-lived attempts were made in Washington, D.C., Philadelphia, and Denver. In the late thirties, three more centers would be founded in St. Louis, Seattle, and Berkeley. What for decades had centered around one man had finally become a movement.

The timing was perfect, for Paramananda was pulling in. His body could no longer take the arduous train trips and rushing to meet connections. Even the necessary journeys between Boston and La Crescenta had become gruelling for him. "These trips should be taken only once in a great while," he wrote from the "California Limited" speeding its way across the continent. "However my destiny calls me forth to such ventures and I must follow my course. . . ." His friend Swami Virajananda wrote to him from India. "The relentless activities are too much for your advancing age with its unavoidable limitations." Paramananda, at fifty-two, could only agree.

The Centenary year, however, was not arranged to be restful. In the three weeks between February 22 and March 15, public meetings, banquets, receptions, colloquia, and special services were held in New York, Providence, Boston, Washington, and Chicago. Paramananda spoke at all of them, as well as being the host for the Boston ceremonies. On March 29, the Centenary celebration at Ananda Ashrama drew five hundred people to the Temple of the Universal Spirit. Paramananda cooked a feast for two hundred that afternoon. The following Sunday the ashrama celebrated the birthday of Lord Buddha. The Sunday after that was Easter, with its three services and public breakfast and luncheon. On April 23, Paramananda wrote to Boston, "My physical body rebels a little at this constant drudgery of routine without cessation." Three days later, they celebrated the ashrama's thirteenth anniversary.

Shortly after Paramananda's return to Boston, Concorde sent messages threatening the three Indian college girls. While Paramananda's policy was to ignore all Concorde's provocations, the safety of the girls prompted him to write reluctantly to Gayatri, suggesting she take certain steps for their protection if, after prayer and meditation, that seemed advisable. However, he added: "I hope we need do nothing and that the whole matter will be taken care of through a Higher Power." Paraphrasing Richelieu, again and again he declared, "I draw the awful circle around the Ashrama." And to all of them he asserted: "As long as you stay within the circle of protection, not a hair of your head will be touched."

As news arrived from India, the community's relief at Amala's resettlement turned into apprehension, then horror. Four months after taking up residence at the Dacca ashrama, Amala was complaining against Charushila, who she felt did not understand her, and the ashrama, which she claimed lacked the spiritual presence of La Crescenta. As Amala herself ingenuously wrote, her "childlikeness and outspoken frankness" provoked antagonism. In fact, the very traits which had alienated her in La Crescenta and Boston were now wreaking havoc in Dacca. Some forces transcend the language barrier.

In reply to Amala's letters of distress and complaint, Paramananda wrote to her from Boston:

> . . . No matter what the situation is, patience, humility
> and spirit of service will not only overcome the obstacle
> for us, but will give us added strength to serve His cause.

With all my love, I am asking you to get hold of your inner life more and more, and get over the emotional difficulties which have always been your great drawback. Because, you will recall, the same difficulties were prevalent here and at the Ashrama, and how I tried to shield you with all my love. Please do not feel hurt or depressed because I am telling you this.

I have always tried to show you your inner qualities and how high above all these petty things you are. I pray you will be triumphant, and small things will not drag you down and shatter your health. . . . You must know how much Swami Shivananadaji loved and extolled the work Charu-ma is doing and what it means to me, so if you do not find any spiritual presence there . . . , it is perhaps because you do not open yourself with harmony, sympathy and loving spirit.

Even her unwavering devotion to Paramananda could not rescue her from the vortex of her own nature. By September, Amala was suffering from depression and a variety of digestive and nervous ailments. Early in February, 1936, fearing cancer, she was hospitalized. The doctors administered opium, a common enough sedative in those days, but the dosage was possibly too high, for Amala became deranged. She wrote to the Belur swamis to come immediately because Charushila Devi was trying to poison her. After transferring her to a Calcutta hospital, when Swami Virajananda and others from the Belur Math would come to look after her, she would greet them with a stream of sexual obscenities. In Boston, Paramananda received a barrage of cables and letters reporting that Amala was running naked through the wards, had thrown her arms around and kissed Swami Virajananda, and other alarming incidents. It seemed that all of Bengal knew that Paramananda's disciple had gone mad. Swami Virajananda warned Paramananda: "When she is cured, she has to be returned to her mother, or else your work here and in

America will get a very bad name. Our Mission will also get a bad name. Not only that, the whole American work will get a bad name."

Paramananda received the news with equanimity. He would not send Amala away from his community in order to save his reputation in India or America. He wrote to Gayatri: "Please do not let your mind be disturbed over what has happened in India. Time will straighten out everything, and I am learning to take everything philosophically through His grace. When so very much has happened in these recent years, a little more does not matter."

The siege lasted less than three weeks. By the end of February Amala was moved to the home of Dr. Peter Boike, Paramananda's Cincinnati devotee, who was living in Calcutta with his wife. Amala wrote to Paramananda, assuring him that it was a temporary delirium caused by an allergic reaction to opium, but she refused to return to Dacca.

Paramananda cabled her, encouraging her to come home to America, or at least go to Germany, where her sister lived. But Amala was intent on remaining in India to witness the dedication of the grand temple to Sri Ramakrishna being raised at the Belur Math. The dedication was scheduled to take place during that Centenary year, but in true Indian fashion the construction dragged on for two additional years. In April, Amala was befriended by an Indian gentleman named Mr. Mallik, who invited her to move in with his wife and children in their comfortable home north of Calcutta. For the most part, that is where she stayed until Paramananda came to India to retrieve her.

It was a burden Paramananda did not need just then, either mentally or financially. Naturally, he had to pay all the bills connected with her illness and hospitalization, as well as her return passage. As he wrote to her in May, "I am willing to do everything I am capable of doing, but just now I am not in a position to incur a large amount of financial expenditure." The banks were closing in on him. He needed $8,500 to clear the mortgage, unpaid taxes, etc., on the 875 Beacon Street house, and was carrying a $30,000 mortgage on 32 Fenway, without the means to pay the interest on either. By mid-1936, he was desperately trying to sell both houses, and having no success.

That summer a dissatisfied Brother Philip decided to go to India to receive the formal vows of *brahmacharya* (preliminary renunciation) from Swami Akhandananda, and to stay and render service at his Murshidabad ashrama. Philip's departure in August left only Brother George and Lama (Mr. Carlson) to maintain the extensive grounds, which, in addition to all else, needed daily watering in that hot, arid climate.

George himself was feeling restless. A Socialist much longer than he had been a Vedantist, he talked of going to Russia to participate in the great Communist experiment. The very possibility of the blow this would be to Paramananda tormented Gayatri. She wrote in her diary:

> Nothing is more painful to bear than to see one's own fall away from Mother's lap through discontent and broken rhythm. So many have come to Swamiji and gone away, even after coming very close to him personally. They have wounded his tender heart, and we have seen him suffer. Today we are just a handful of people living at the Ashrama. May we not leave him, may Mother take away from us the power to pain him.

Paramananda, sensing George's discontent, wrote to him:

> You are in my thoughts often. I think of all the selfless and heroic service you have given the Ashrama. Such things can never be without great good. I personally may not have succeeded in bringing you comfort and solace in recent months, but my faith in you ever remains unchanged. . . . You know in your heart of hearts my real feeling for you without my having to speak in so many words.

Apparently George did know. He abandoned his idea of going to Russia, dedicating himself instead to the swami's great Vedanta experiment, obeying Paramananda's injunction to "take care of the ashrama and the children," for another thirty years.

In the face of all that year's upheavals, Paramananda was proving amazingly resilient. "Swamiji seems very well and buoyant," Daya wrote that autumn. "His spirit is a constant miracle."

Rather than feeling oppressed by his misfortunes, Paramananda was feeling singularly blessed. From one cross-continental train ride, he wrote to the ashrama: "Where can you find such a collection of staunch hearts. That is the way I see you all. Am I blessed! Let me be so more and more. To see everything with the eye of love is bliss. It is God's very own blessing. For He is Love and nothing else."

Even his financial quandary, which was growing more critical every week, seemed to him relatively unimportant. The money given to him for his birthday he sent to India for Charu's works, writing to California:

> When I see people who are in actual want and in struggle, I am reminded how blessed we must all feel for our safety and shelter, especially for the boon of spiritual outlook. Only this afternoon as I sat at a counter to take coffee and doughnuts with others, I could not help observing people who were really hungry. Food meant a great deal more to them than to any one of us. At such moments, we cannot help realizing that to complain over our own destiny is to forget our spiritual blessings. I am writing this that you may all feel in your heart of hearts what is indelible in your life and forget altogether the passing, momentary trials and struggles.

His continuing concern was that he really be able to render service. He elucidated this yearning in a letter to the ashrama: "I cannot expect everyone to understand me, but my prayer is that

I may not fail toward any of you. . . . I am always offering my prayer that whatever usefulness I may have left will be for the good of many and the happiness of many, and this work to which I have dedicated my life for so many years may really be of some lasting service."

Paramananda was making it increasingly obvious that he considered Gayatri a central factor in that future service. As Gayatri's inner life was unfolding, his relationship with her was growing deeper and more complete. He believed in the Divinity inherent in everyone, but he could see and feel the Divinity manifesting in Gayatri, and he exulted in it. As Gayatri recorded in her diary:

> Swamiji sees me with his supersight. What divine faith and love! It cannot be compared with anything. The other night when I saw him alone for a few seconds, what beautiful things he said: "All think that I am partial to you. This is not possible through calculation. . . . Baba [little son], you are such a great comfort to me. I specially depend on you. There is nothing greater than this, baba. In this fleeting world, what can one depend upon? So many are devoted to me; can I depend on them all?"

On September 16, Paramananda left California for Boston. Gayatri recorded the scene:

> The picture of this parting is vividly on my mind. The confusion with Ranu in the kitchen was for the moment about to crush my spirit. So in that state of mind, when I went to offer him goodbye *pranam* [salutations], tears came to the eyes. Placing both his hands on my forehead, he blessed me. Then he gave me that indescribable, the tenderest, the sweetest, the most compassionate look, filled with love which no one else possesses. He said, "You are feeling the pang of this departure, baba. Maybe, I will return for Durga Puja; everything is possible." Then seeing

my moist eyes, he gestured that I control the tears. Again I heard those words which he had uttered hundreds of times: "I depend on you *terribly.*" By the look of his two eyes he made me understand the inner meaning of that remark. . . . Then at the last moment, holding my hands by both of his, he said, "I give myself to you, wholly. Here, take me." . . . The disciple receives everything through Sri Guru's grace, this is what I am experiencing all the time.

Paramananda maintained that he gave to each in the measure that he or she could receive. Nevertheless, his doting concern for Gayatri was bound to arouse jealousy. One morning Gayatri was serving him breakfast, a task at which all of them took turns. Each time she would bring him his toast or jam from the kitchen, he would coax her, "Gayatri, please sit down and eat yourself." Gayatri, of course, had been trained in India never to sit down until the person she was serving had finished. When Paramananda continued to coax her, Sumita flared up, "Why don't you just get up and serve *her* breakfast!"

Once Gayatri herself asked him, "Why don't you give me more discipline?" Paramananda turned grave and replied, "Life will give you plenty of discipline." Again, when one of the sisters complained that he indulged Gayatri, as if sobered by a distant vision, he murmured, "You see, she will have so much to bear."

He was hinting at a future which he only obliquely disclosed. When Annie Payson Call, the New Thought leader, asked him if he had made any provisions for a successor, he answered, "Well, everybody says Gayatri Devi is so much like me." After coming in from a hike through the ashrama hills one day, Paramananda sat down in his room while Gayatri helped him pull off his boots. Suddenly he looked up at her thoughtfully and remarked, "Someday you too will be the refuge for many souls."

In the spiritual tight-rope walk required for sainthood, Gayatri balanced herself between deep humility and daring aspirations.

"So small a disciple for so great a master," she described herself. Yet, her own self-effacement was itself effaced by her towering faith in her guru's power. As a typical entry in her diary records:

> I see too plainly how far I am from any form of perfection, but I also know none of my yearnings are in vain. Swamiji has told me many times that the least of my desires, my unspoken longing, my hiddenmost prayers will find their fruition. Placing my whole-hearted trust in my Swamiji's words, I go on aspiring for greater and ever greater treasures.

Both communities were witnessing important shifts during 1936. Katherine Sherwood, Boston's perennial supporter, had fallen in love with Ananda Ashrama during her spring visit to California, and decided to build a home there. Her two-story stucco house was constructed below the pine grove, between the orchard and the Guest House garage. Miss Sherwood moved there in December. Just before that, Lola Haynes, Paramananda's devoted secretary and patroness, separated from her husband and moved into the Vedanta Centre. Even though she continued to give her time to the management of the Boston office of the William S. Haynes Flute Company, her mere presence, as well as financial support, were a vital boon to the Centre.

During the final month of the Centenary year, Paramananda's house problems suddenly snapped into resolution. On the third day of the Divine Mother's Festival, one of his students told Paramananda of a magnificent house at 420 Beacon Street, overlooking the Charles River, which, in that Depression economy, was on sale for a fraction of its worth, and much less than what they had paid for 32 Fenway. By a strange set of circumstances, the key was left with the swami. As soon as he saw the house, he was enraptured. Its large, enclosed stained-glass dome seemed meant to crown a temple. The great, grilled entrance door, nine feet high and five feet wide, opened onto white marble steps which led to the domed reception hall. Around the staircase beneath the dome were five arched, pillared panels, currently decorated with Baroque paintings, but oh! how he could see inscriptions from the various religions lettered on those panels! A temple truly worthy of Sri Ramakrishna! The marble mantels and fireplaces had been imported from Italy, the walls of the chapel were paneled with burled walnut, and the walls of the reception hall were handpainted with golden cherubs. "Not the outer only," the swami wrote, "but there is a vital impressiveness which is difficult to describe." The house, which had cost a quarter of a million dollars to build in 1894, was selling for $16,000.

Paramananda stunned everyone by announcing that he was going to buy it. "The sisters will think I am crazy," he remarked, his eyes twinkling. Much to his frustration, however, no bank would give him a mortgage. Banks were losing a lot of money on churches during the Depression, and none of his connections could squeeze out even a loan.

Meanwhile, he sold the 875 Beacon Street house for $7,000, glad to take the $1,500 loss in order finally to be rid of the responsibility. On December 1, he returned the deed of 32 Fenway back to its original owner. The $30,000 mortgage was torn up. "Now we are homeless," Belle Barnard whined. Paramananda fairly cheered with relief, "But what a blessed sensation to be *so* homeless!"

The 420 Beacon Street house seemed almost beyond their hope. Real estate sharks had come in and matched the swami's offer. Then Florence Fain, a devotee from the South who had long been devoted to Paramananda, heard of it, and offered to give him her estate of $9,000 if he would pay her 4% interest (compared to 2½% she was receiving from the bank). Still $7,000 short, Paramananda decided to go ahead and make a cash offer. His agent got their deposit down minutes ahead of the speculators.

That week marked the thirtieth anniversary of Paramananda's arrival in America. On two successive days, he was handed a gift check of $1,000. Lola teasingly called him the "$1,000-a-day-man." The rest of the money to purchase 420 Beacon Street would come from other devotees.

A jubilant Paramananda wrote to California:

> The more we learn about the new house, the more strange everything seems in connection with this episode. If I waited even one-half hour more to decide, perhaps it might not have been ours. Everyone was very much startled when I said *we would pay cash*. But an inner urge led me on, and the last few days' happenings have surprised everyone. . . . I feel that Divine Mother truly is working and She will make this thing possible.
>
> . . . It seems more like a fairy-tale than anything I have ever read in modern fiction. In this year of our Master's Centenary, I have had many heartaches and sad thoughts about how unworthy I was not to be able to do my part in expressing my homage to Him. Mother undoubtedly heard my inner yearnings, and this has come out of a clear sky.

Thus, by the time the momentous year had closed, the Vedanta Centre had acquired its next "permanent home," and for the first time in a decade, Paramananda was mortgage free.

20

Sister Daya

THE WOUNDS of Paramananda's life were like concentric circles, each cut successively closer to his core. At the beginning of his career, he was attacked by conservative Christians whom he did not even know. During the Akhilananda controversy, some of his own monastic brothers were ranged against him. With Concorde's betrayal, a member of his own community hurled the blow. The bull's-eye gash was yet to be inflicted.

Sister Daya was buckling under the accumulated weight of lifelong paradoxes and frustrations. She was a robust spirit trapped in a sickly body, a romantic whose marriage had failed, an eager mother whose sole pregnancy had ended in miscarriage, an emotional personality who had committed herself to even-mindedness and nonattachment, an altruist whose acts of mercy conflicted with shrine schedules and *Message* deadlines, a mystic who had renounced the world and had not yet realized God.

She was the surrogate mother to all the Indian girls, who called her Mâm (pronounced Mom). But her "Baby," Gayatri, to whom she was closest, she seldom saw, for their identical roles as Paramananda's platform assistants kept them assigned to opposite coasts. She had loved Charushila Devi like a daughter, but Charu soon was whisked back to India. Sumita, Ranu, and

Chokanu wrote frequent and affectionate letters to their Mâm, but the latter two Daya had never once seen, nor hugged. "Children of my heart," she wrote to the four girls in 1936. "Not many mothers have to wait so long to gaze upon their own."

There was in Daya an element which found no place in Paramananda's ethereal world. The swami's delicate nature loved all beings, but handled some of them gingerly, preferring to salute them from a distance. Daya, on the other hand, could embrace mangy mongrels and drunken derelicts who had not bathed for weeks. Feeling that the holes in her clothes and the clutter in her room offended Paramananda's sensibilities, she strove to live up to the swami's meticulous standard. Yet, despite her unremitting efforts to master the practical skills in which the other sisters excelled, she remained basically impractical and disorderly. The feeling that she had let Paramananda down reinforced Daya's innate tendency to self-depreciation. This, coupled with her lingering menopausal depression, left Daya at fifty-four enshrouded in a sense of failure.

Daya herself had prophetically identified the cause of her pain in a passage on her idea of discipleship which she wrote during her first years in the community:

> When the teacher comes, shall we be ready to live with our Ideal? Oh, yes, we shall find it easy to live for it, perhaps to die for it, but to live with it? For the first time all that is not pure spirit in us will be thrown into continual and sharp relief by the white light of his presence. . . . Therein lies our pain. All that is not in tune with him will suffer and bleed, and bleed and suffer till the agony forces us either to leave our ideal or become it.

By late 1936, Daya was beginning to despair of ever becoming her ideal. After seventeen years in the community, she told Paramananda that she doubted whether she had a genuine vocation as a monastic. Shaken as he may have been, Paramananda's response was firm: "Why don't you have a little faith in me? Do you think I can be so mistaken in you all?

This was Daya's precarious state when she met Gladys Stuart, a short, stocky, robust baker in her thirties from New Hampshire, who began to attend the Vedanta Centre services. Daya was immediately drawn into a warm, personal friendship with Gladys, such as she had not experienced with any of the members of the community. Struggling in her dark night, she gave Gladys the name "Dawn." Daya and her Dawn quickly became inseparable. When Mrs. Georgina Jones passed away in December, 1936, it was Dawn who drove Daya to her mother's deathbed.

The year 1937 began like a cyclone. Within a single month, Paramananda made a one-week visit to California, supervised the move to the 420 Beacon Street house, conducted three dedication services for the new chapel with distinguished guest speakers, cooked and served a banquet to one hundred guests, and sailed off for India.

The Ramakrishna Mission was holding a Parliament of Religions in March to commemorate the 101st birthday of Sri Ramakrishna, the official conclusion of the Centenary. Paramananda had received his invitation the previous October, when he was steeped in negotiations over three houses. He tendered his apologies, explaining that his responsibilities in Boston made a trip to India at that time utterly impossible. Besides, he was not in a financial position to make another trip around the world.

Early in January, he received an emphatic reply from Swami Sambudhananda, the chairman of the Centenary activities:

> I do not find words adequate to convince you that your presence on this occasion, particularly to represent our North American centers, is a necessity. Nor do I find a man who can better represent our ideas and activities in the West on such an august occasion than you. Considering the great importance of the occasion which is expected to be unique of its kind in India, I earnestly request you to

make it convenient to attend the Parliament of Religions without fail.

He added: "I have great pleasure in informing you that the Lloyd Triestino Company, a well-known shipping concern of Italy, has granted a 50% reduction over a passage of all Asiatic, European and American delegates embarking from any Italian port to an Indian port." He also intimated that the Math would help finance the rest of his passage. Paramananda had no choice. He sailed from New York on February 6.

Before leaving, he made vital transfers in the personnel of both centers. He had brought Gayatri and Sister Satya Prana east for the dedication, and Jessie to do the lettering of the inscriptions from the various religions on the panels beneath the dome. He also called on Hilda to come from Cincinnati to help them move. This naturally left Sister Achala in a state of nervous prostration over the already depleted ashrama. Hilda, somewhat mellowed in disposition, agreed to go back there. After five years in the east to be near her ailing mother, Daya too was now free to return to her native California. Paramananda was anxious to send her back, away from the harsh climate and emotional attachments of Boston. When Daya returned to Ananda Ashrama that February, however, Gladys Stuart accompanied her and took up residence in the Guest House.

The voyage to India proved to be the fastest—eighteen days from New York to Bombay—that Paramananda had ever taken, and the most uncomfortable. During the first leg of the journey, he absorbed the rest which his whole system craved, despite the rough sea and the scores of letters and postcards which he had to write to his "special friends." Making his connection in Naples, however, he found that the Lloyd Triestino shipping firm would not give the promised 50% reduction. He had only enough money to pay for a third-class room. It was the first time in his life that he was travelling third-class, and he resolved to take it as "an

adventure," repeatedly reminding himself of the philosophical
challenge:

> Teaching of the Gita is the greatest thing in practical life.
> Luxury and wants, praise and blame, gain and loss, etc.
> — all have their influence in moulding our lives. Blessed is
> the man who can take all experiences with calm dignity.
>   . . . I do not want any of you to worry about me. I
> am really having an interesting time. You all know that I
> like changes, and this is one of the biggest I am having in
> many years. I noticed that my body was getting altogether
> too delicate.

The Parliament of Religions began three days after Paramananda arrived in Calcutta. During its week of sessions, 110 papers were read and lectures given. The Parliament was attended
by delegates from all over the world, including such personages
as Colonel Charles Lindbergh and Rabindranath Tagore (who
took the opportunity to ask Paramananda, "When are you returning Gayatri to India?"). Not one of the Christian Churches
of the West, however, sent a delegate. The tolerance which Sri
Ramakrishna expounded was still far from being realized. Christianity was represented by the head of the local Y.M.C.A. and several
liberal European professors, thus adding to the Parliament's distinctly intellectual cast.

Swami Paramananda was elected to preside over one of the
sessions, and gave several addresses, sometimes taking less than
a third of the time allotted to him. Amala wrote: "I noticed that
the audience had been a bit lax during the reading of some
addresses, and it was most interesting to see when Swami
Paramananda arose to speak, all the newspapermen suddenly
sat up in rapt attention, and Dr. Tagore with animated face turned
to watch the Swami. There was complete silence and attention."

Such imposing colloquia, with their long, erudite presenta-
tions, invariably bored Paramananda. He distrusted oratory that

analyzed without inspiring, words that were not borne out in action. Once when he was called upon to speak, he proclaimed:

> Instead of theorizing, let us do something constructive, as did Sri Ramakrishna. We are tired of theories. Who wants to be reminded that the world is a bad place? If you are lovers of humanity, instead of repeating such words, come and give your helping hand.
>
> Let us hope that the fundamental principles which we discuss during these sittings shall be lived. Those of us who know something of the life of Sri Ramakrishna know it is not through politics, not through science, not through any of these ingenious methods that he attained spiritual vision. Through love, the golden thread that ties humanity, he realized Truth.

Paramananda must have felt somewhat like St. Francis, who denounced scholarship because he felt it deflected the simplicity and humility of the true religious life. When, returning from a long absence in the Holy Land, St. Francis discovered that his own Order had constructed a library and college, he climbed to the roof of the building and began to dismember it tile by tile. Paramananda took no such remedial actions; he simply accepted that his own viewpoint diverged from the mainstream of his Order, which that very year was stipulating academic prerequisites for the admission of its monks, which, had they been in effect in 1901, would have disqualified Paramananda (and Ramakrishna, too, for that matter).

He keenly felt the absence of Swami Akhandananda, who had suddenly passed away just three weeks before Paramananda arrived in Calcutta. As his dear friend Swami Virajananda, who the following year was to become President of the Math and Mission, confided to Paramananda in a letter, "The old Math ways of Swamiji's and Maharajji's days have changed so much that I feel myself a misfit at every turn. I am almost ignored and looked upon with mistrust; my ideas, opinions and advice have no value, except as one vote among the rest." Paramananda shared that sense of alienation.

The hardships of his voyage had only presaged the adversities to come. Amala, of course, accompanied him wherever he went. His visit was overshadowed by the embarrassing memory of her illness, which was known everywhere, and by his own fatigue and failing health. In conjunction with the fifteen actual sessions of the Parliament, he had to attend endless receptions, dinners, tea parties, and secondary meetings.

On March 20, Paramananda was asked to preside over the Howrah Town Hall Meeting in honor of the Centenary. "Thousands greeted the Swami on his arrival with music and cheering," Amala reported. "On departing from the Hall, one hundred conch shells were blown in honor of Swami Paramanandaji." During the Parliament, too, Paramananda's speeches were received with "enthusiastic and almost deafening applause." He had become a popular hero.

As always, he went to Dacca to administer to the needs of Charushila Devi's ashrama, which was gaining in scope and recognition. There he fell sick. His two-week visit stretched into a month as he succumbed to one relapse after another, all of which he blamed on the "excessive heat." Day and night, people swarmed around him with their requests, demands, and ceaseless importunings.

Back at Belur, Paramananda was seated in meditation in the shrine room of the Math when he suffered a heart attack. Feeling the presence of Sri Ramakrishna's great disciples, he opened his eyes and in a vision saw their hands outstretched to take him.

He did not go. Years before in Madras, Swami Ramakrishnananda had told him that he would give up his body at will. If he actually had the choice, why did he not accept this auspicious chance, in the sanctum sanctorum of his Order? Perhaps because his symphony had several bars yet to be played, and the rest of his orchestra was in America.

He recovered, and borrowed five hundred rupees from the Math to secure his passage back to Boston. In spite of the promises, he had to bear the full cost of his journey in both directions. Amala, Brother Philip, who, having received the vows of *brahmacharya*, was more than ready to return, and Paramananda travelled south to Madras, where he received what Swami Virajananda called "a right royal reception." Appropriately enough, from Madras, where Basanta's spiritual life was launched, he took his final leave of India. He would never see his motherland again.

They sailed form Colombo on May 3, with Paramananda heaving from fever and cold. The voyage was hardly restful, with two such gregarious companions as Amala and Philip. Stopping in Italy, they saw signs of militarism everywhere: soldiers, battleships, submarines. Their ship had to make a four-hundred-mile detour to avoid the coast of Spain, where the Spanish Civil War was raging.

On June 3, 1937, they docked in New York City. Swami Nikhilananda, Sister Satya Prana, and Jessie met their ship. Paramananda immediately boarded a train to Boston. When Gayatri Devi opened the door of 420 Beacon Street to receive him, she stepped back, stunned. His hair had turned white.

Later, when they were alone, he declared, "I have been sapped—body, mind, and spirit."

After less than two weeks in Boston, Paramananda crossed the continent for an eleven-day visit in California. Seated in the Cloister living room one evening, he appealed to the community, "Please forgive all my shortcomings." Sister Daya shot back, "It isn't your shortcomings that bother us, but your short-stayings."

Lola had accompanied him, her first visit to the ashrama. Overwhelmed by the natural and architectural beauty of the place, far beyond her expectations, she quoted Queen Sheba's exclamation when she was shown the glories of Solomon's court, "The half had not been told me." Pronouncing Ananda Ashrama a "paradise on earth," Lola paid tribute to Paramananda's success in making his dream a reality. She was particularly impressed with "the sweet good humor, efficiency and ordered rhythm, with which the work of the Ashrama is performed. There is love, harmony, and oneness of purpose among the members of the household and above all, deep devotion to a common Ideal." The ashrama community was finally registering Paramananda's maxim: "God loves those who love each other."

But perfect peace is not the setting for spiritual growth. The nettle in paradise this time was the presence of Gladys Stuart. Shortly after their arrival early that year, Daya had written that Dawn was making herself indispensable with her tireless energy and service. In truth, many members would have dispensed with her. They looked askance at this interloper to whom their Sister Daya had given her heart. They found Miss Stuart (as they invariably called her) aggressive, and her dog Laksa, who had been given the run of the ashrama, a nuisance. Unable to fathom what Daya saw in Miss Stuart, most of the community deduced that the pair must have been together in a previous lifetime, and left an unfinished relationship. The community's bafflement and disapproval are revealed in a letter which Lola wrote from the ashrama: "Sister Daya has been nice, but has that silent, faraway look in her face and at times looks completely distraught. . . . When Miss S. works in the bee yard, Sister Daya carries her ice water but never thinks of giving Sister Seva a drink. Strange! Passing strange — and yet she is fine and good — and I know it is only her 'compassion run riot' as Miss Sherwood says."

Daya was not well, physically, mentally, or spiritually. She was disappointed in the community's aloofness toward Dawn, knowing full well how they could shower affection on one whom they considered their own. (Lola, upon her arrival, was virtually swamped in hugs and caresses.) Dawn, who lived and ate at the Guest House, was rarely invited to dine with the swami and community in the Cloister. Even Paramananda, the epitome of love and affection, showed little warmth to Daya's friend. As Lola wrote in a "Private" note to Gayatri: "All is not going so well with Miss Stuart. There was a real blow up today about which I will tell you. Swamiji seems to be actually stirring things up. Sister Daya is no different. In fact, she defends her 'son' against her ashrama sisters."

The situation was harrowing for both Paramananda and Daya. Once, finding Daya weeping over something he felt he had caused, Paramananda said to her: "You don't know what pain it gives me, what deep pain, to feel that I have even unconsciously made anyone suffer, even a little bit." But Daya was no longer tuned to his wavelength; she could not hear the messages he transmitted.

On June 28, bedlam broke out in the Cloister when Laksa ruined a whole pound of butter by slobbering over it. A trifling incident, to be sure, but great wars have been started over less. Accusation led to accusation, and the unspoken grievances of months flared up with fury. When the smoke had cleared, Gladys Stuart was packing her bags. She left for San Francisco, and ultimately New Hampshire, where she resumed her baking business. The community's relief at her going was marred by the tense question: "Will Daya follow her?"

The next day Paramananda, Lola, and Sumita left for Boston. Sumita and Ranu had just graduated from junior college. (Chokanu was a semester behind, due to illness.) The girls were finally making a valuable contribution by giving impressive Indian dance recitals both at special occasions at the ashrama and at outside engagements for clubs and churches around Los Angeles. While Ranu and Sumita danced, Chokanu (when she was well enough) gave the interpretations. "It is a great credit to the ashrama and to India," Paramananda proudly exclaimed after one such performance.

Nevertheless, Sumita, with her peevish personality, continued to pose problems. Paramananda was bringing her to Boston in hopes of enrolling her in an art school there. Two months after her arrival, Sister Satya Prana wrote to Paramananda that he should definitely send Sumita back to India. Finally conceding that he could only help people if they were willing to help themselves, he responded in a letter to Gayatri:

> I can readily see her reasons, but also I feel sad hearted to think what might be the destiny of Sumita if she should return to India now. . . . If she is not capable of having any mental resolutions, . . . I am afraid there is very little that I can do for her. It has caused me no little unhappiness and uneasiness, but as you know, I am always full of optimism and never like to give up anything. I have already showered upon her all the lovingness that I am capable of giving, but she seems to have peculiar complexes, which I am afraid no one else can remove from her mind and heart but herself.

Eventually, Sumita matriculated at Leland Powers School of Drama, winning a $200 scholarship, much to the swami's relief and gratitude.

In mid-July, Paramananda received a cable telling him to send Gayatri to India immediately. Both her parents were seriously ill. Five days later, another cable arrived. Bibhu Charan was gone.

Paramananda mourned for his brother, that gentle and affectionate man who had wanted everything for his children but little for himself. He had been the instrumental cause of scathing criticism that Paramananda had to bear, but Bibhu Charan had been devoted and loyal, qualities that Paramananda was appreciating more and more. When he saw that Gayatri had been weeping, Paramananda, his own eyes moist, remarked sadly, "I knew him longer than you did."

A month after settling at the Vedanta Centre, Amala was

clashing with Sumita, then with Belle and Jennie Reymond. The swami had no choice but to take her back to the ashrama when he went in August. It was her last move. She would stay there the rest of her life, a thorn in the side of successive ashrama generations, for by a smirking dispensation of fate, she would live longer than all the rest of Paramananda's American community, except for Lillian, who ever desired the "blessed extinction" and who lived to be ninety.

The California work was still sluggish, the attendance usually poor, the community understaffed and listless, despite the occasional excitement of a visit from Greta Garbo or Stokowski. Paramananda was maintaining his hard-won detachment. When he heard that Willie Verbeck had turned his back on the work, he wrote to Boston, "The news about William is indeed a surprise, but let people live and act according to their light. Destiny is a strange thing. 'Oh, unhappy fate that leads the weary travellers from light to dark.' "

More than William was on his mind. On September 17, Daya left the ashrama to visit Gladys Stuart in New Hampshire.

Paramananda came east a week later. One Sunday early in October, the household returned from an outing in Cohasset to find Sister Daya waiting. She had come to tell Paramananda she had decided to leave the work for an indefinite period and make her home with Dawn in New Hampshire. She would try to earn her living as a writer.

Daya remained at the Vedanta Centre three days to clear up her loose ends, eighteen years' worth of them. During that time, Paramananda tried every conceivable means to persuade her to stay. He appealed that he needed her. He asked her to wait before making her move, warning her that a precipitous decision might be regretted later. He pointed out to her the importance of steadfastness, stability, and persistence in the spiritual life. He asserted that a mind in turmoil could not make a wise decision. Daya was deaf to his pleas.

On Tuesday afternoon, leaving her suitcase at the foot of the stairs, Daya approached Paramananda in the hall beneath the dome to say goodbye. Paramananda clasped both her hands between his own and implored, "Daya, these hands have touched the feet of Holy Mother; these hands have touched the feet of Swamiji, who was inseparable from Sri Ramakrishna, and now, Daya, these hands are begging you not to go."

She looked away, silent. Then she extricated her hands from his grasp, picked up her suitcase, and ran out of the great, grilled door, back into the world.

Paramananda stood there and watched the door close behind her. Then he noticed Gayatri, who had witnessed the scene from a corner of the hall. He did not speak to her. He made no comment about what had happened, then or ever. It was a wound sealed deep inside him, as if a bullet had penetrated but not exploded. No gushing blood on the surface, hardly a scratch perceivable to anyone as he went about his days and months, but unseen a deep, internal hemorrhage, his vital force seeping from his heart but never spilling to the ground.

"How could she have done it?" was the pulsating question of everyone in the community. Was her love for him so fleeting? Was she oblivious to the pain she was causing the one whom she had regarded as her redeemer?

From Tamworth, New Hampshire, Daya revealed her inner state in a letter to Lillian, written in response to an affectionate note she had received from her:

> There are times in life when only love and deep understanding make it possible to go on. These came to me through your written words and helped me immeasurably.
>
> I am feeling, Oh, very much better, and if only there can be understanding, then I will be with you again as I want to be. Perhaps I ask for too much. I am not asking, only desperately hoping. . . .
>
> There is so little I can say. I have never wanted to hurt

anyone. I have never wanted to fail in my love or service, but for a time my universe crumbled . . . and I was left crushed and broken. There were certain stands I took which I would still take, for I could do no other. But I love you all, and my heart is ever suffering. . . . I have taken cod liver oil and will take more of it. Under the quiet conditions here in this primitive country I have gained very much physically and nervously; but frankly if inner pressure is put on me again, I do not know how I will stand up under it, for there are areas of thought and consciousness that I still cannot approach without terrible physical and mental reaction, a sort of terror in the night, as it were. . . .

She threw herself into writing, mostly children's poems and tales, a couple of adult short stories, witty and romantic. Under the pen name "Frances Stuart," she submitted them to publishers ranging from the *Saturday Evening Post* to American Baptist Publications. All of them were rejected, with the exception of a single poem, for which she received one dollar. She spent each day minding the bakery and waiting on customers, while Dawn did the baking or rested from all-night bread production. There, living among ordinary people in the unspoiled woods of New Hampshire, Daya's yen for the earth was being fulfilled. But it is doubtful that she enjoyed a single day's inner peace from the moment beneath the dome when she tore herself from Paramananda's clasp.

For the Sunday service two weeks after her leaving, Paramananda chose as his theme, "Crossroad of Life:"

During our earthly pilgrimage, we often come upon crossroads; and in spite of our secular education and training, we cannot help feeling baffled and perplexed. It is not that these roads can be labeled as altogether good or altogether bad, but they lead to different destinations. Our wise selection not only saves us from unnecessary turning back, disappointments, heartaches and endless regrets, but it gives us added capacity to fulfill our specific aim and thus become instrumental in helping others. . . . If we are fearful of disappointments and failures, we cannot choose wisely. If we are influenced by public opinion, we also cannot choose wisely. There is only one way by which we may be helped to find our definite course out of endless confusion and bewilderment, and that is by cultivating serenity of spirit, spiritual intuition, and a regard for the voice from within. In the *Mahabharata*, the great Indian epic scripture, we read, "One who is not possessed of clear vision does wrong even when he wishes to do right."

Those close to the swami knew he was speaking to Daya, but she was well out of earshot.

On October 27, three weeks after Daya's departure, the swami's attention was dramatically diverted to another cataclysm. That morning, Evelyn MacMinn was driving Ranu to school when an optical illusion made the car approaching in the opposite lane appear to be heading straight for them. Evelyn swerved to the right, accidentally slamming her foot not on the brake, but on the accelerator. The car smashed into a concrete abutment, flinging Ranu through the window. When the police arrived on the scene, they sent for an ambulance for Evelyn, who was badly, but not critically, injured and, for Ranu, finding no sign of life in the tiny, smashed body, they called the morgue.

However, she was alive, but just barely. Countless bones were broken, her jaw was crushed, and her neck was broken in two places. Even when they realized she was alive, they were afraid to move her, for the slightest shift could snap her spinal cord. When they finally got her to the hospital, for the same reason the doctors declined to operate, or even to wash the blood off her body.

Paramananda had just finished a lecture series in Louisville. As he was boarding the train to take him west, a porter dashed up with the urgent message that Western Union wanted him. The swami rushed to the telephone, but the connection was unclear, so he asked them to send the message to the next station. Waiting to receive the actual news, Paramananda was in torment, which was not abated when the message finally came through. From the train speeding its way to California, he wrote the Centre: "Prayers & more prayers, miracles do happen. Nothing is impossible unto Him."

He reached California three days after the accident. When he arrived at the hospital, the attending physician told him, "There is no reason for the little girl to be alive, but she is." He explained that people had survived with broken necks before, but not with the particular vertebrae that Ranu had broken.

Paramananda, her legal guardian, gave them authorization to operate. They drilled four holes in her skull through which they attached traction. It was a novel procedure at that time, and it took many days of trial and error to get the weights just right. Three weeks passed before it was definite that she would live. When she did, even the doctors called it miraculous. Her case was written up in two medical journals, and many surgeons attending a convention in Los Angeles in January came to examine her for themselves.

Paramananda claimed that he had not prayed she should live, only that she not go out of this world in confusion, as often attends such violent accidents. Nevertheless, Ranu gave all the credit for her recovery to Paramananda. On the very first day that he saw her, when she could not even speak, with her jaw shattered and every tooth in her mouth loose, she wrote with her left hand on a pad of paper: "You have made me all well." Again and again in the weeks that followed, she told him, "I get my life and strength from you." Filled with spiritual exaltation despite her agonizing pain, she kept on saying, "I am the most fortunate person in the whole world." Paramananda, marvelling at her spiritual state, exclaimed that she had been literally reborn. Ranu dated that rebirth to the day that Paramananda had arrived on the scene. After all, he himself had once remarked to Gayatri: "I interfere with people's destinies. Aren't I daring?"

During that first week, Ranu was moving in and out between worlds. She reported visions to Paramananda which he at first doubted. But, when she told him secrets of the Order which she could not possibly have known by any ordinary channel, he began to accept her experiences as genuine. One day she said to him, "Tell the sisters, why do they worry? I saw. . . . I saw the ashrama sitting on Sri Ramakrishna's lap."

Another time, she reported seeing Sri Ramakrishna with Swami Vivekananda on his right and Paramananda on his left. This dismayed Paramananda, for Holy Mother was normally represented on Ramakrishna's left. The next day Ranu told him that she saw Holy Mother seated on a high pedestal, and Paramananda was worshipping her with hibiscus flowers. The swami felt relieved.

Physically, however, Ranu was in excruciating pain, which neither the doctors nor nurses could alleviate. As Paramananda described one incident in a letter:

> Last evening she was in very great pain. Doctors and nurses could not do anything for her, and as you know, it is not easy for them to make her comfortable under the circumstances. I went there a little after half past seven and found her in great agony, and crying like a helpless child, and feeling desperate. Chokanu was with me. . . . After I had been with her for a few minutes, she quieted down, and the whole atmosphere of her room changed greatly. Then she asked me to sing, and as I sang softly, within a minute she became so very quiet that Chokanu was a little bit afraid. So I called her three or four times before she woke up, and then she said, "Why did you awaken me? I was sleeping so soundly." Then she said, "When you come, all my pain leaves me, and I feel such power coming from

you when you hold my hand, that it is not only enough for me, but I could give it to the whole world."

Once, as Paramananda was sitting beside her singing, Ranu leaned forward, reaching upward with her good hand. She repeated this motion several times, until Paramananda interrupted his song to ask her if she wanted something. "When you sing," she replied, "the Mother comes. I was trying to touch Her feet."

Although she was less critically hurt than Ranu, Evelyn had a severely injured leg. As she related her experience:

> The doctor was convinced that amputation would have to take place. He made visits to my bedside even at midnight and many times during the day. Then Swami came to me. He said: "Are you suffering greatly?" I told him, "Yes," and he said: "Just where is the worst pain?" I indicated the exact place, as nearly as I could, and he closed his eyes and gently laid his hand there. Instantly I felt that healing power flow into me. I knew what had happened definitely and distinctly. From then on, there was no more talk of amputation. The crisis was past.

Paramananda was bearing the burden emotionally, spiritually, and financially. "It is needless to say what I feel, and how I feel," he wrote when Ranu's life still hung in the balance. "I have been able to keep up through all this strain only through Divine Grace. Little Ranu so desperately clings to me, and there is nothing that I would not do for her."

In addition to doctor and hospital bills for Ranu's private room for the three and half months she was there, the swami paid for round-the-clock private nurses for the first five weeks. None of the ashrama residents was covered by insurance, nor did Evelyn's auto insurance cover Ranu's treatment. Everything came out of Paramananda's pocket.

At that time his busy schedule included cooking a large offering for the shrine each Saturday and afterwards serving it to a party of twenty or thirty, as well as cooking the Sunday luncheon for the public. Nevertheless, every day he took time to drive down to Glendale to visit Ranu, usually twice a day. It could not help but tax his own strength.'

He had planned to return to Boston at the end of November, but Ranu begged him not to leave her. "You see," she cried, "I may sink again if you are not here." He stayed more than another month, as Ranu steadily improved.

Her recovery was to be complete. The doctors warned that she would have to wear a brace for the rest of her life, but a year after the accident she danced in the temple patio, her movements fluid and graceful, the only trace of her ordeal a tiny scar under her chin.

By late 1937, a regeneration in the California work was noticeable. Paramananda pronounced the birthday celebration of Vivekananda in January, 1938, "the most beautiful day that we ever had in the annals of the Ashrama history." The Guest House was full of weekend guests, the temple was packed for the morning service, the swami served 150 people at the banquet in the Cloister patio, and well over 200 came for the afternoon service, at which two Christian ministers spoke (one of them from the Episcopal church). "Although we have had many occasions with great multitudes gathered here," Paramananda effused, "none has ever gone so smoothly and successfully."

This momentum was abruptly interrupted on March 2, when the worst storm in California's history flooded the ashrama, unleashing avalanches of mud and rocks, destroying the water system, sweeping away one of the lower cabins, and depositing tons of silt in the temple patio again. According to Sister Achala's letter to Boston:

> Swamiji was out and working with the men all during the worst of the storm, but all their efforts were to no avail. He had a very narrow escape of being struck by a huge yucca as it was washed down. How divinely pro-

tected he was, for just at the instant when this thing was
washed down, he stepped aside. He has been constantly
out, guiding and advising, first one place, and then another.
He is in hardly long enough to get something to eat.

Several men volunteered their services, and the ashrama
was presentable again by early April, in time for the celebration
of its fifteenth anniversary. Few people, however, hazarded the
Ramsdell Avenue detour to attend the service. The main banquet table, which was set for a modest sixty, was barely filled,
and the side tables remained neatly untouched.

Paramananda expressed neither disappointment nor discouragement. He was taking things as they came. His body
was not well. "Since I left Boston," he wrote to the Vedanta
Centre, "physically I have not been quite up to the mark. I
kept up through past habit and momentum, but really my body
needed rest."

It never got it. With Easter, two weeks later, the work rallied
and surged ahead. Each Sunday the temple would be full, and
sometimes crowded. On weekends the Guest House had barely
an empty room. One successful celebration followed another in
a phase that would last the rest of Paramananda's life. It was as if
the ashrama had emerged from a season of hibernation, and was
suddenly faced with the pandemonium of spring. Paramananda,
"the spring bird," shuttled across the continent fourteen times
that year, also the next.

Sister Devamata, too, was not well. During those last three
years of her life, her crippled body became increasingly restricted,
while her spirit became more and more free. Many people in the
congregation admired her as a valiant, holy person. Wrote Maud
Keck in a foreword to Devamata's booklet, "The Companionship
of Pain": "Ten years of pain lie behind all that Sister Devamata
writes, years heroically spent. Every one of them seems to have
dug deep; to have wrung something wiser and sweeter from her.
As if the Divine Artificer could not be satisfied with anything

less than a spirit very finely wrought."

Devamata, however, encouraged no canonizations. She used to enter the temple for Sunday service just before it was time to begin, and make her way slowly up the aisle to her seat in the front. Before sitting down, she would stand there briefly, benignly looking around. An admirer once asked her, "Sister, you look so holy when you stand there like that. Are you praying?" "No," Devamata replied, laughing, "I'm counting the congregation."

For a woman confined for long periods to bed and wheel-chair, her last poem reveals a life and movement unseen:

> I sway in glad cosmic dance,
> The stars are my companions
> The sky is my floating veil
> The moon I wear in my hair.
> The earth far below my feet
> Is lost in limitless space.
> Pain, pleasure melt into one.
> Favour of man counts as naught—
> Great suns are my companions.
> I sway in exultant dance,
> The stars of heaven turn with me.

An advantage of humble people is that it costs them nothing to humble themselves. On April 29, 1938, Paramananda telephoned Daya from Boston and asked her to come back. Daya refused.

Several hours later she sat down and wrote him the following letter:

> Swamiji, always loved and revered:
> Ever since I heard your voice over the telephone, I have been torn inwardly more than I can possibly express.

Never before have I ever refused to come to you when
you have directly requested me and to do so now is great
suffering, and I know that it will cause you renewed pain.

   I have thought and pondered and inwardly questioned.
I have taken the train and gone to you mentally a hundred
times. I have gone to you with flowers in my hand and
love in my heart, but always that mental picture has been
shattered by an inward barrier, deep differences, conditions inward and outward that *are* and which I know will
cause again the terrible tearing, wounding deadlock that
has caused before such heartache on both sides. Swamiji,
I cannot go through this again.

   I know as I look inward that I cannot go back into the
work (even if you should want it) in the spirit and with the
outlook that would be helpful. Not that I would bring
unlovingness or an evil atmosphere — there would be no
cause for the latter (no matter what has been thought or
said), but I would not fit. I would be restless and out of
rhythm with much that is inherent in your work. It must
be that I have to work this out in myself and in the world. I
feel that it is so. In the meantime, you and your ideal —
beauty, purity, truth — stand as always for me synonymous
and enshrined in my heart.

   I could not bear to cross swords with you again, for I
do love you with a love that does not change, in spite of
what you may feel or anyone may think.

   . . . Swamiji, if I did not love you as I do, if there were
not the unbreakable ties binding me to the Centre and all
there, this would not be so hard to write. As it is, it is
almost agonizing.

   I am very well, Swamiji, and I try never to forget the
beauty and the grandeur of the Ideal. You perhaps will
laugh when you read this, for you feel very differently
about me, but I can only try to tell you what is in my
heart. . . . I think of you constantly, of each and every
one, and always will.

Despite her decision, she could not resist the pull. Four days later Daya showed up at the Vedanta Centre.

To the household she was a jarring sight. She had taken off her habit and was wearing a knee-length dress. Her crown of golden braids, normally tucked beneath her long veil, stood bare for all the world to see. Those who for eighteen years had seen Daya only in her ample, flowing vestments must have felt like they were spying a bird stripped of its feathers.

Daya stayed at the Vedanta Centre for four days, spending much time in conference with Paramananda. Then she returned to New Hampshire just long enough to fetch her belongings, and moved back into the house at 420 Beacon Street. Paramananda wrote to California that he would probably bring Sister Daya with him when he crossed the continent on May 16.

Instead, he brought Gayatri, who was physically run down after carrying the charge of the Centre for over a year. Daya stayed in Boston to resume her duties and conduct the public services.

When Paramananda returned to Boston on June 12, Daya moved back to New Hampshire. Three weeks later the swami wrote, "The work here was in very great chaos when I arrived. Sister Daya's presence here instead of helping the work proved most disastrous. I do not think it was intentional on her part, but the reaction was very sad. . . ." Near the end of July, having heard no word from Daya in the meantime, he reported to California, "The work here is going on as well as can be expected under the circumstances, and recently it has shown signs of a definite rebounding."

After weeks of silence, Daya finally wrote to Paramananda: "All through this time of silence, there has been a constant turning to you as of old, a very great longing for you, and not only for you, for all who are and will forever remain dear to me." Then, after several pages of small talk about Dawn's bakery and her own strawberry picking and cookie baking and news about some common acquaintances, she continued:

I have become very vitally aware of two worlds, one a
surface world, in many ways a pleasant world where there
are all the personal relations, and the other is the inner
world where one's life is nourished. I am living in the
surface world. I am enjoying many things that it has to
offer and that in a strange way I was hungry for, but my
roots are in the inner world, and I never can let go of that
or really live apart from it. . . . In my inner world you
reign supreme. I have not changed, nor the hunger in my
heart. Be patient with me a little while more. I do not
forget, and in my heart there is always that love that originally drew me to your feet. I have said all this very
stupidly — and my actions must seem to belie my words. I
regret this with all my heart, but I have to do as I am doing
now. There are many elements and my actions, though
they may appear wrong and misguided and no doubt are,
are yet not based on purely selfish motives. . . .

You were so beautiful and tender to me that last time
in Boston. Such memories are as strong as steel.

. . . My life has been blessed in that I have known a
few truly great human beings and one that is more than
human. Even yet I may be able to redeem some of the
pain I have caused and prove myself not altogether despic-
able, at least in the sight of God.

. . . I know indeed that you are truly my best friend
and unfailing shelter.

She had asked him to be patient a little while more. Patient
he was, as she gathered wild raspberries and blackberries that
summer, and grapes that autumn, and sat contemplating the
snow-covered mountains that winter, and exulted in New Hampshire's profusion of wildflowers the following spring, and again
the berries in summer, and the autumn grapes. . . . A year after
Daya's departure, Gayatri wrote of Paramananda in her diary:
"Mâm is on his mind and he suffers terribly. He loves her as he
alone could love, and will never cease missing her."

21

The End Of Spring

THE LAST TWO YEARS of Paramananda's life were more strenuous than the others. Instead of slowing down like a man with a heart condition, he speeded up his pace like a man who knows his time is running out. As he wrote to Amala in 1938, "There is so much to be done in His name."

During one eighteen-day period in 1938, Paramananda held fifteen public functions at Ananda Ashrama. In addition to the regular classes and two Sunday services and the Sunday luncheons cooked by the swami, their calendar now included Upanishads classes held at a devotee's home in Alhambra and "Moonlight Festivals" in the temple patio, which might feature performances of Eastern or Western classical music, a ballet recital by a local devotee, an *esraj* solo and songs by Gayatri Devi, or an address by a distinguished guest. Transforming even the most secular holidays into religious observances, the afternoons of Memorial Day, the 4th of July, and Labor Day were designated as public periods of silence and meditation in the temple, followed by a banquet prepared by Paramananda. As if the year were not crowded enough with a rapid succession of Christian, Hindu, and Buddhist holidays, Paramananda, anxious to spread himself between the two centers, sometimes held a major celebration like Durga Puja or Sri Ramakrishna's birthday a week early and then duplicated the whole elaborate festival a week later on the other coast. His outside speaking engagements at clubs and churches, which he had reduced since 1930, were again proliferating. He crossed the continent practically every three weeks. As Alice, the musician, described his coming: "We were at once caught up in this great output of energy. I told Swamiji that each time, his tempo seems to be more and more accelerated." Paramananda's finale was all allegro.

Upon Daya's departure, the whole responsibility of the *Message of the East* was cast on him. Even several months before that, with Daya depleted physically and emotionally, Paramananda had made a rare concession to the limitations of time and human energy: he reduced the publication of the *Message* to four times yearly. However, as he assured his readers when announcing the change, each new quarterly issue would be three times longer than the former monthlies. Thus, while the number of harrowing deadlines was reduced, the work necessary to write articles, edit Paramananda's talks for publication, and select edifying excerpts from ancient pagan writings, Buddhist canons, medieval Christian treatises, Taoist reflections, Talmudic injunctions, and modern homilies remained the same. After Daya left, Paramananda trained Gayatri and Lola as assistant editors, but he still spent untold hours editing and writing. Sometimes he toyed with giving up the magazine entirely. It had never been financially solvent, due mainly to the swami's 1912 promise not to cheapen it with advertisements, so it was one more drain on his limited resources. All it took, however, was a few appreciative letters from different parts of the country to convince him to continue. "When I see how much it means to others," he wrote, "I have not the heart to give it up as yet."

Naturally, his "relentless activity," as Paramananda himself termed it, taxed his strength to the utmost. Sometimes after giving the last service of a particularly strenuous weekend, he would collapse into bed at 6:30, unable to stay on his feet a moment longer. He suffered frequent angina pains, particularly in his arms and legs. Still, he was loath to go to doctors; he was unwilling to submit to the one remedy they were sure to prescribe, complete rest. By mid-1939, he was often walking with the aid of a cane. He was fifty-five years old.

One day he was lying very still in bed, suffering from a severe angina attack, with beads of perspiration covering his agonized face. Gayatri, who was waiting on him, silently watched his suffering for a few minutes, then asked hopefully, "Are you feeling any better?" Paramananda, almost voiceless from the excruciating pain, smilingly replied, "I'm trying to."

The community was, of course, anxious for his health, and often appealed to him to cut back. He stated his position in a letter in 1940, three months before his death: "Now, in regard to myself. I deeply appreciate your feeling of concern for my physical well being. But my real attitude is that as long as I am sustained by One who has placed me in this role of service, nothing matters but His work."

On May 8, 1938, a bas-relief portraying Jesus Christ, Buddha, and Krishna side by side was dedicated at the Vedanta Centre chapel. Paramananda had commissioned Christina Meade, an aspiring young sculptress, to execute the piece, to be enshrined on one side of their altar, balancing an earlier bas-relief of Sri Ramakrishna, Holy Mother, and Swami Vivekananda.

"On this special occasion," Paramananda addressed the congregation, "as we dedicate a symbol which represents the ideal of unity and oneness of all world Teachers, one of my great dreams for many long years comes to fruition. . . . For more than a quarter of a century this is what we have tried to accomplish: to place before the people of this country the wisdom and truth from all lands, classics, and scriptures, in fact from the whole world, showing their underlying unity and harmony."

The swami went on to point out how the times were bringing the fulfillment of such ideals, that fifty years ago it would

have been impossible to execute such a graphic portrayal without arousing fanatical denunciations. Still, he was acutely aware
that the ideal of universal tolerance was far from being realized.
In a letter to the ashrama, he confided, "The more I think about
this new bas-relief, the more greatly amazed I am at the daring
thing we have done, in putting before the public the idea of
unity in concrete form. For, in spite of all education and scientific
advancement, the average person is far from being really tolerant.
So this was an epoch-making event."

Indeed, at that very time Paramananda was facing his most
direct confrontation with religious prejudice. It was a contest he
was determined to win.

The taxes on the palatial 420 Beacon Street house far
exceeded the Vedanta Centre's meagre income. As a church, of
course, it was entitled to tax exemption, but Boston's Irish-
Catholic bureaucracy refused to recognize the Vedanta Centre
as a genuine religious institution. Granting tax exemptions to
synagogues was about the limit of their religious tolerance. While
Paramananda avoided legal confrontations whenever possible,
this was an issue he simply could not afford to concede. He had
not even been able to pay the bank loans which had come due
that summer, and was bailed out only by a hidden reserve of
Florence Fain. Now, the swami figured, the Centre could manage its operating expenses and the interest to Florence Fain, if it
were not encumbered by heavy taxes. The financial future of
the Centre depended on winning tax exemption.

The legal battle lasted two years. The Centre's lawyer, Mr.
Raphael Boruchoff, submitted to Mr. Downing, the Chairman of
the Board of Assessors, piles of the swami's books and lectures,
as well as letters from Christian ministers who respected Paramananda. Mr. Downing wrote to the Belur Math to ascertain if
Paramananda really belonged to a genuine religious Order. At
one point, two city assessors attended a Sunday service at the
Vedanta Centre to see what actually went on there. At the con-

clusion of the service, when the swami asked everyone to rise for the final benediction, addressed to "the Father in Heaven of the Christians, Allah of the Muslims, Jehovah of the Jews, Buddha of the Buddhists, Tao of the Chinese," etc., the two men stayed pointedly planted in their seats. They were not about to take part in any heathen rite.

When the case finally came to court, Paramananda was summoned to testify. On cross-examination, he was challenged, "What do you worship? The sun? The moon? The stars?" Paramananda maintained silence. Afterwards Lola described the scene: "He was like Christ before Pilate."

Mr. Boruchoff himself, the son of a long line of rabbis, was so impressed with his client's "calmness, his understanding of the others' point of view, his sympathetic approach to problems, and the entire lack of antagonism that you generally find in those who have a dispute, whether it be with the authorities or anybody else," that he began attending the Vedanta Centre services and eventually became a member of its Board of Directors. A scrupulously ethical man himself, the attorney marvelled at the swami's adherence to his ideals even when he had to take economic loss because of them. "In every matter his ethical approach was paramount to the economic question," Mr. Boruchoff recalled years later. "In other words, he would not allow the practical, material matters to dominate his attitude or in any way cause diminution in his ethical approach."

The lingering prejudice against Oriental religions exerted itself also on some of the individuals who attended the Vedanta Centre. Mildred Prendergast, who came from a well-to-do Catholic family, began coming to the Centre in 1938. She describes her family's reaction:

> I was disowned actually, absolutely persecuted, and told I couldn't come, by my husband. My parents felt that the thousands of dollars they had spent on Mildred was just thrown away, and that I was just running around with the

worst kind of people. My husband in his wrath said that I would never get any money to go to Vedanta. In fact, he would never give me any, and it was the most awful embarrassment to me. I would have to put only the little bit of coins I had in the collection basket, and there was nothing I could do about it. You know, they never noticed that at all.

Paramananda had seen it all before. Once he told his congregation:

You may say: "When I follow this path I have to stand alone; my friends all leave me." Let them leave you! They will not leave for long. Eventually they will turn to you again. I have seen this in my own life and experience these years of my stay in America. I have known people to be opposed by their families, but they have held to their ideal, and in the end the family has sought from them the help and consolation which the world could not give.

So it turned out with Mrs. Prendergast. Eventually Paramananda's teaching of love and calm endurance so mellowed her nature, ameliorating her fierce temper and turning her into the peacemaker of a discordant household, that first her children and then her husband began to wonder what had effected the change. Mr. Prendergast remarked to his friends, "Mildred has found something. I don't know what it is, but it is far above anything I ever heard of in a church." Finally he too came to the Centre, at a time when he was engaged in some immoral activities. Paramananda told Mildred and the community: "Be kind to Michael. He is in hell." Ironically, just at the height of the tax exemption case, Michael Prendergast, who was a lawyer, offered the Centre his help. Paramananda gratefully accepted, for, as he astutely pointed out to his community, Mr. Prendergast was an Irish Catholic.

In September, 1938, Paramananda was invited to speak at

the Sunday morning service of the Zion Lutheran Church in Wooster, Ohio. The engagement was a watershed in his career, after a lifetime of addressing avant-garde groups and Unitarians, with an occasional foray into the folds of Congregationalism. While Paramananda was esteemed by many individual ministers of different denominations, this was the first time that he delivered a sermon from the pulpit of an orthodox Protestant church during its worship service. He had come a long way from Covington, Kentucky in 1921, when he was barred from addressing a New Thought meeting in an Episcopal church because "he was not a Christian."

The next morning the swami addressed the Cleric Club of Wooster, a group of twenty ministers representing various denominations in the area. Reverend Kelly, the Lutheran pastor, knowing the narrow-mindedness of some of his colleagues, feared the question-and-answer period would turn into a bitter debate. When it came off without a single note of antagonism, he walked away jubilant, and later wrote to Paramananda: "The fact that all acrimony was absent from the discussion which followed is a tribute to your own fine spirit."

Paramananda's method and victory were aptly described by a Congregational minister who had been invited to address a banquet at the Boston Vedanta Centre. He quoted Edwin Markham's poem:

> He drew a circle that shut me out —
> Heretic, rebel, a thing to flout.
> But love and I had the wit to win:
> We drew a circle that took him in.

The minister concluded, "You have drawn a circle that takes me in. Thank you."

Ananda Ashrama remained the same, "breath-taking" in its

beauty as Paramananda described it, yet "not without many responsibilities and a sense of burden." In July, 1939, he wrote from the ashrama:

> Although I have been here only a few days, there have been no end of problems of one kind or another. We cannot have an extensive work such as this without being confronted with human complications and material entanglements. I only hope and pray that the big ideals which we hold in our heart may triumph over all these. . . . I know that what we have to offer will bring healing and solace to all souls who come in contact, and may we do it with conviction and real humility of purpose.

Although the individual members had developed spiritually, and would continue to grow, the "human complications" would never disappear, just as individual basketball players may improve, but the game remains the same.

Paramananda the dreamer also remained the same. "I roam over the Ashrama grounds," he wrote late that year, "and conceive in my mind more and more beautifying expansions."

Many of those dreams had come true. The ashrama was an oasis of peace for many world-weary souls. Practically every day visitors drove through the new arch which Amala had illuminated with "PEACE BE UNTO ALL." Every evening the community held a fireside meditation in the Cloister living room. By request, on Tuesday nights Paramananda concluded with a talk on meditation. Friends from outside began to attend these talks, and they became so popular that they had to be moved to the temple, and, when that overflowed, to the temple patio. The ashrama had become a center of pilgrimage for people from all over the country. As Paramananda described the visit of Mr. Starick from Cincinnati in a letter to Boston:

> I think Mr. Starick was in the seventh heaven especially after I gave the morning household service. Twice he

could hardly speak, and said he would have gone the whole way around the world just for one of these occasions. I am sharing this with you, as I know you will get some real satisfaction out of it — that there are those who really care, and yet there are some who leave this place, hoping that they might find more satisfaction outside. So the world goes.

Daya, of course, was on his mind. The pain of her leaving had not dulled with time. No one spoke of her; no one could bear to speak of her. Paramananda wore his hidden anguish like a hairshirt under his silken garb. One Saturday in Boston, as the community and a group of devotees prepared to drive to Cohasset, Gayatri entered Paramananda's room and found him standing transfixed in front of his tie rack, fingering one of the ties. "Are you ready?" she queried. He kept staring at the tie in his hand, as if he had not heard her. Then he remarked abstractedly, "Your Mâm gave me this tie."

A new set of faces was frequenting the ashrama: the Hesses, the Kopps, the Belchers, Mr. Belaiff, Mr. Seelig, Audrey Myland, Franchon Mowers, Mrs. Overholt, Mr. Hamilton. Two newcomers would play a significant role in the ashrama's future. John Quick became the ashrama's third lifelong brother. The nonconformist in a family of prosperous professional people, John had been a prize fighter, an institutional cook, and a hobo before coming to the ashrama late in 1938. He had learned life's lessons well. A person of volatile temper, he once became so enraged in a fight with another man that he later realized he could have killed him. He vowed never again to yield to anger. The ashrama knew him as the cheerful, hearty, gentle, easygoing, and hardworking Brother John, a delight to Paramananda.

Alice Loeb, who was later to become Sister Anjali, was too shy even to speak to the swami at first. He took the initiative. After only her second service, he invited her for Saturday dinner and to stay overnight in the Guest House. The young woman was ecstatic. Walking around the ashrama that Sunday morning, she met Paramananda. "Are you happy?" he asked her.

She replied, "I've never been more happy in my life."

"You know, you've come home," he told her. "Know that nothing happens by accident."

After that, she came every weekend. Having had a stint as a dancer in the movies, she now worked as a bookkeeper. She lived with her mother and had little money to contribute, but Paramananda assured her that she should come whether or not she could make an offering. Like the young people then frequenting the Boston Centre, sometimes she had barely enough for busfare. When Alice did not show up one Saturday, he telephoned her to offer money if she needed it. Alice soon became friends with Chokanu and Franchon. One Sunday afternoon, the three girls were about to leave the Cloister living room to go to Alice's house in Los Angeles. Paramananda playfully reached into his pocket and exclaimed, "Oh, look what I found!" He handed them a five-dollar bill, saying, "Go have a good time."

Several months later, Alice had a severe attack of appendicitis. Her appendix was on the point of bursting, but she refused to go to the hospital. She had a foreboding that she would not live through the operation. Chokanu told Paramananda, and he came to Alice's house. Entering her room wearing a new camel's hair coat, he spun around like a little boy, asking, "How do you like it?" He was carrying a small bouquet of flowers. He came up to the bed and handed them to her. Then he asked tenderly, "What is it, my child? Why are you afraid to go to the hospital?" Alice replied desperately, "But I am afraid." With his finger, Paramananda wrote something on her forehead, then asked her to open her mouth, and wrote something on her tongue. According to Alice, "All the fear just vanished." When he asked her, "Will you go to the hospital now?" she gave a resounding, "Yes." The operation proved more complicated than expected. Her appendix had become entwined with her colon, and she was on the operating table for hours. Afterwards, she was in a coma for three days.

Every day Paramananda would send her a rose with Chokanu. Alice attributed her recovery to Paramananda's intercession.

In May, 1939, Bill Rodman, a young engineer who had been attending the ashrama services for two years, proposed marriage to Ranu. This stirred up a storm among the sisters, not that they had expected Ranu to be a monastic, but they doubted Bill's maturity and the couple's stability. Sister Achala fumed, "She could have a half-dozen children, and we would have to take care of them." (A prophecy that proved partly true.) Achala told Paramananda to send Ranu back to India, Miss Sherwood recommended sending her to Boston, and amidst all the commotion, Paramananda let Ranu make her own decision.

His policy in most matters was, "Hands off!" People had to be free to work out their own destinies, even to make their own mistakes and profit by them. As he had written a few years earlier to Gayatri, when she was worried that a pool she had taken the initiative to create at the Cohasset ashrama might not meet with his approval:

> I have no doubt in my mind of its being pleasing to me. . . . You have known through all these years that I give utter freedom to everyone who comes in contact with me, because I believe that is the way people can express themselves in their fullest measure, and I hope all the workers will realize it and not interfere with each other. Sometimes slight errors can be remedied, but when we thwart at the outset, we thwart the whole scheme of self-expression. This is not a vague and visionary dream on my part. It is so ingrained that I cannot live without it.

He warned Ranu, however, that her life would not be easy, that she would live many lives in this one life. She and Bill were married in Mexico in July.

It was a time for settling destinies, or finalizing them. The year before, Paramananda had brought Mary Lacy to California, where on September 3, in the shrine, he conferred the veil on her and on Alice Affsprung, giving them the names "Shanta" and "Vimala" respectively. On July 29, 1939, he gave Amala a special blessing in the shrine, telling her that Sri Ramakrishna was really giving her the blessing through him. Afterwards, exhausted, he said it was like giving birth to a child.

As Paramananda's schedule intensified, he increasingly begrudged the precious three days it took him to cross the continent by train. On August 2, 1939, in happy defiance of the sister's misgivings, he took his first cross-country airplane flight. The Los Angeles—Boston trip now takes five hours by nonstop jet, but on T.W.A.'s vintage "Sky Queen" in 1939, it took twenty-four hours, requiring six stops and two changes. Nevertheless, Paramananda loved it, not only for the two days it saved, but for the exhilarating sense of rising up and leaving all the paraphernalia of earth behind. During the next year, he took five more cross-country flights. After his fatal heart attack, his community blamed the flying (well before pressurized compartments) for wreaking havoc on his heart.

———————————— ⬥ ————————————

It was a cataclysmic period for mankind. At the beginning of the decade, fathers had mourned that the fortunes they had earned for their sons had been wrested from them. Within ten years, the sons themselves would be wrested from them. The bitterness of penury would give way to the agony of war and death.

Paramananda had no sons to lose, or rather, he had millions of sons to lose. He who for years had taught that all humanity was one family now had to face that family, his family, destroying each other. Like a Kentucky mother during the Civil War, living in dread that her sons in the Union army might kill her other sons in the Confederate army, Paramananda's heart was caught in an excruciating vise; the movement of either side tortured and crushed him. His very spirituality, while giving him invincible inner fortifications, had stripped him of outer defenses. Indian lore tells of a saint who screamed agonizingly in the presence of a bull being beaten. The marks of the lash were found upon his own back. This was Paramananda's state as the world plummeted to self-massacre. "It is needless to say," he wrote after Easter, 1939, "that my heart has been very heavy over the world situation, especially during Good Friday. I am naturally very susceptible to any depressing condition anywhere."

During the last two years of his life, Paramananda's resounding cry was, "Peace!" Sunday after Sunday, whatever his chosen theme, he invariably brought in the issue of peace. In an address on, "If Christ Came Today," delivered before a Rosicrucian meeting in 1938, he articulated his passionate message:

> One of Christ's greatest sayings in "The Sermon on the Mount" is, "Blessed are the peace-makers." After two thousands years, might He not reasonably expect some tangible result in that direction? What would be His reaction to a world feverishly engaged in preparation for war—and what a war! Bursting bombs, poison gas, and wholesale destruction of defenseless men, women and children! If He came today and found these existing conditions would He give up His dream of peace-making as an impractical visionary idea, and surrender to the inevitable?
>
> . . . What would happen if He came today? Would He reform us, or would we try to reform Him? Can you not hear men say, "Who is He with His old-fashioned, impractical and visionary ideas? We cannot follow His plan of life. What we need is strong defenses and more powerful weapons than those of our enemies, or we shall be destroyed!" And he who once said, "Blessed are the peace-makers," what would He say to the war-makers and to those who believe in preparedness for war?

Earlier that year, Paramananda had been the guest of honor at a meeting of the International Peace Association held in Los

Angeles. He had been introduced as "one of the world's out-standing exponents of peace," and found a predictably receptive audience. Among the various pacifist organizations then prevalent, he took keen interest in the Moral Rearmament Oxford Group Movement. But both his Order and his own temperament barred him from any direct political involvement. He believed that the solution to war, like all humanity's problems, lay not in politics but in spirituality.

Despite the tragic world situation, Paramananda's optimistic spirit would not be routed. Even when, in autumn, 1939, the dark stormcloud hanging over Europe broke, drenching and drowning hundreds of thousands of human beings, Paramananda would not concede the defeat of his ideals. He looked ahead, to an era beyond the storm, when peace would prevail and seeds would germinate in the flood-soaked fields, covering the world with new blossoms:

> I cannot help feeling that we are on the threshold of a new and better era, wherein we shall experience a glorious awakening into the real prosperity of the soul. It must be so. We are growing through suffering. After we have gone through a period of darkness, uncertainty, and spiritual blindness, we shall gain a new sense of values. We shall look for a spiritual dawn and begin to hunger for it. . . .
>
> Let us not be disheartened because of the prevailing conditions of the day. Humanity has gone through such experiences before, and has survived. Truth will triumph again. Let us not lose sight of that. If suffering purifies the heart of mankind and brings the beautiful realization of humility and surrender to the Divine Will, then indeed it will be our greatest blessing.

Paramananda himself took refuge in that Divine Will. The Hasidic masters said that it is God alone who determines how many times the dry leaf will turn in the dust before it comes to rest, or as the Hindu scriptures put it, "Not a blade of grass moves but by His will." During a question and answer period at the Vedanta Centre, an ardent young Socialist named Richard Creesy (later to become the Cohasset ashrama's Brother Richard) asked Paramananda point blank: "Do you go along with the maxim, 'Whatever is, is right'?" Paramananda replied simply, "Yes, I do."

It was not an easy stance for him to maintain, for his heart rebelled at human suffering, even though he believed that it eventually could lead to the greatest of all boons, spiritual awakening. As he said once to Lillian, who was always lamenting her fate, "Things would not be as they are if the Lord did not will it so. I, too, feel sometimes like 'busting up' everything, but it is all right. It is as it should be, or it would not be."

That conviction had to include even the war, no matter how he had resisted its onslaught. He had to believe that wars are fought not with swords, but with scissors, a single Hand moving both blades.

"This morning at the end of the service, I spoke," he wrote to the Vedanta Centre late in 1939, "And as I did so, I felt so close to the Great Spirit, and realized that nothing really happens without His will. If we can always keep ourselves fastened to this consciousness, then nothing can really go wrong with ourselves or with the world."

One evening at supper, the ashrama community engaged in a vociferous discussion about the war. After the fireside meditation that night, Paramananda said to them, "I give freedom, but expressions of hate, even in talk of world affairs, are out of place here. This place is a place of peace. Don't get entangled in the net of strong feeling. . . . A prayerful attitude is the only solution for such times." Paramananda recognized no enemy but war itself.

While the world reeled in sorrow, Paramananda's one consolation was Gayatri. Once he said to her, "If I didn't have you, I would have been very lonely." In her diary of 1939, she wrote:

With a light heart I went to wait on my Swamiji this morning. He too was in a serene state of mind, expressive and tender. He told me, "You make me happy, supremely happy." O, how grateful I am, Mother allows me to bring him even a flicker of solace! How alone he is in this world with his pure exalted consciousness, and so few understand him! I would like to be a true comrade and disciple. He loves me in so many ways. It is a love far above all earthiness and self. This morning our communion was complete. He raised me to a higher plane, to his own plane of pure, unalloyed love. . . . What can be better compliment than this, that I do not drag him down to an earthly plane, but he lifts me with him to the Great Mother's Feet?

One afternoon the community was eating lunch outdoors. Gayatri went into the kitchen to get Paramananda's dessert. When she came out again, she found the swami standing over her tray, fanning the flies away from her food with his napkin. "Who ever shows such tender concern for any of us?" she queried in her diary. "At breakfast time he insisted on carrying a chair to the right place for me. We carried it together. It embarrasses me to receive such service from him. To set us the example he does these things. May Mother help us to learn the higher ways from him."

According to all testimonies, Paramananda showed tender concern for all his children, even for general members of the congregation. Once, in Boston, he received word that a devotee of the ashrama had had a nervous breakdown. Gayatri, watching his withdrawn mood throughout the day, obviously absorbed in prayer for the woman, exclaimed, "Why, he is like a mother with her only child!"

At one banquet at the Vedanta Centre, the tenor who had been asked to sing arrived drunk, and sang two "highly inappropriate" numbers. As eyebrows raised and some men rose to escort the man out, the swami took hold of the situation. He spread the word not to embarrass the man or make him conscious of his *faux pas*, but to let him sit down and have supper with the rest of them. Much to everyone's consternation, the man behaved himself admirably for the rest of the evening.

Still, Paramananda's concern for Gayatri was more than this. She was his stock in the future. Once, in Boston, Gayatri went alone to shop for groceries at the North End's open market, and did not come home promptly. Paramananda kept coming out of his room to check if she had returned yet. When he finally saw her, he exclaimed, "When I think that something might happen to you, my blood turns to water."

One of the greatest disappointments in Paramananda's life was that his Order refused to recognize Gayatri Devi as a legitimate pulpit speaker. One evening the swami, Gayatri, Sister Shanta, and Lola drove down to the Providence Vedanta Society for a special service at which several ministers, a rabbi, and Paramananda were to speak. Paramananda secretly hoped that Swami Akhilananda would ask Gayatri to say a few words too, but he did not. On the way home that night, Paramananda was grimly silent. The next day, too, driving to Cohasset, he was distant and laconic. Finally Gayatri cornered him in the lower field and demanded, "What *is* the matter? Won't you tell me?" He stared at her a few moments, then blurted out. "Just think! You are the only Indian woman doing something in this country, and not one of them will recognize it." Then he added, "Swamiji would have understood."

When the Ramakrishna-Vivekananda Center of New York moved into its new home on East 94th Street in October, 1939, a three-day celebration was held, with several of the swamis as guest speakers. At Paramananda's earnest request, Swami Nikhilananda asked Gayatri Devi to say a few words at the banquet on Thursday night, and to give a full address at the service on Friday night. At Thursday's banquet, Paramananda was seated at the middle of the head table, and Gayatri at the end. When

Paramananda, Miss Josephine MacLeod, Swami Visvananda, Swami Akhilananda, Gayatri Devi, and Swami Nikhilananda finished speaking, everyone got up to rearrange the room for moving pictures. Suddenly Gayatri felt Paramananda at her elbow. "You stole the show," he whispered proudly.

The triumph was short-lived. The next evening, just before the service at which she was to be one of the two principal speakers, Gayatri was waiting in the parlor for her cue to go downstairs to the chapel. Swami Nikhilananda entered the room, peered out the window, and saw that it had started to rain, a factor which could seriously deter the large audience he was expecting. He turned to Gayatri and declared, "You have brought me bad luck." She was crushed. Mortified, she managed to go downstairs, sing and play on the *esraj,* and deliver her speech on Holy Mother, "the worst talk I ever gave in my life," she later recalled. Thirty-five years would pass before she would again be asked to speak at a Ramakrishna Mission function.

On Thanksgiving Day, 1939, Paramananda arrived in Boston from California. No sooner had Gayatri, bursting with excitement, opened the door for him than she announced, "A letter from Mâm is waiting on your desk. It came yesterday." Paramananda bounded up the stairs to his study and opened the letter. It read:

> Blessed Swamiji:
>
> Now I can speak! May I come home to stay? I am asking this not because there has been any break in friendship here, but because there is no real life or peace or happiness away from you.
>
> I have knowledge enough of conditions and imagination enough to realize a little the pain I have caused and the harm I have done. I ask the chance to try to redeem my actions, so far as in me lies. . . .
>
> I have suffered til often it has seemed to me my heart would stop beating, and this longing for you is nothing new. Though you may not believe it, and though my ac-

tions seem to deny it, I have loved you and love you beyond all other love. My words I know may mean nothing to you, so I ask the privilege of trying to prove by the rest of my life what I now am trying to say to you.

I know that my road ahead may not be easy, but I shall try to meet bravely whatever comes as the result of my own actions.

What is past is past, what is done is done, but there is always left courage and the Unfailing One.

My heart is and has been warm for all my brothers and sisters and I pray that before I die, they may learn to love and trust me again a little.

May I sign myself, as always,

Your child,
Daya

P.S. Please answer this by letter, not by phone or wire.

Paramananda's answer was brief and all in capitals: "YES, A THOUSAND TIMES YES."

A week later Daya moved back to the Vedanta Centre, then to the ashrama for good. Her love for her guru had superseded her own failures and self-doubt. Two years and two months of suffering and learning had reinstated her faith in his faith in her. Her prayers and his faith were both to be fulfilled. By the time of her death in 1955, no one in the community was more loved and admired than Sister Daya. Ananda Ashrama's exalted and inspiring platform speaker for fifteen years after Paramananda's passing, her congregation testified that she became transfigured while speaking. Generally regarded as a saint and sought out by many for spiritual guidance, Daya did prove by the rest of her life that she loved her guru beyond all other love.

Early in 1940, Paramananda's impasse with his monastic brothers erupted in a scathing scene. The founder of the Vedanta Society of Buenos Aires, Swami Vijayananda, who had been corrected by Paramananda for calling Americans "dollar-worshippers" in 1935, was touring the United States for the first time. Paramananda held a reception for him at the Vedanta Centre, and invited him to a private dinner beforehand. As Lola described the occasion:

> Immediately after dinner, they all went up to my sitting room which Swami Vijayananda, blissfully unconscious of our dislike for it, filled with clouds of smoke. Swamiji let him do exactly as he liked without rebuke of any sort, so he had a wonderful time and seemed to reverse his opinions completely and warm up to the Boston Centre to the extent of fairly beaming upon it. . . . There is no doubt he is doing fine work in South America and our people really loved his talk to them.

Swami Vijayananda was on his way to California, where he planned to stay with Swami Prabhavananda in Hollywood and visit the Ananda Ashrama. Paramananda decided to go to California to receive him. The ever-touchy relations with Prabhavananda had been especially strained since July, 1938. At that time, the Hollywood Vedanta Society had dedicated its new temple. Paramananda was supposed to be present, as he had been for the laying of the cornerstone in January. That was the month, however, when Paramananda arrived in Boston to find the Vedanta Centre in chaos following Daya's brief sojourn. Paramananda felt it essential to stay in Boston long enough to repair the work. Also, the 4th of July celebration coming the day after a busy Sunday had left him fatigued, and he would have had to catch the train that very night to arrive in time for the Thursday service, a sacrifice that he did not feel obliged to make. In his naive way he wired Prabhavananda that he deeply regretted being unable to be with him for the dedication, but if Prabhavananda considered his presence vitally important, he could still be with him on Sunday. Prabhavananda's assessment of the senior swami's vanity must have been aggravated by this

allusion to his presence being "vitally important." He wired back
sarcastically: "If you feel the importance of joining your brothers
when they meet to rejoice in the name of the Lord, please come,
it would make us happy."

"You can imagine how surprised I was," Paramananda wrote
to the ashrama. "I do not need to make any further comment
about the telegram." He stayed in Boston another four weeks.

Paramananda was due to arrive in California early in the
afternoon of Saturday, January 27, 1940, the day that Swamis
Vijayananda and Prabhavananda had been invited to dinner.
Vijayananda was also scheduled to speak at the ashrama's afternoon service the following day. After a crowded and cold journey,
Paramananda's train arrived two hours late. In order to give him
time to cook the evening dinner, Miss Sherwood invited the two
other swamis to take tea with her. Arriving at the ashrama,
Paramananda bathed and began cooking. It was to be a big
dinner, for many guests were invited, some of them new people.

Apparently, Vijayananda and Prabhavananda were offended
that Miss Sherwood, rather than Paramananda, had received
them, and took it as an example of Paramananda's alleged superiority complex. At five o'clock, Paramananda, still in his cooking smock, greeted them and had someone show Vijayananda
the temple.

After the household's evening service, when dinner started,
Swami Vijayananda was in a terrible temper. He yelled at Miss
Sherwood that she had spoiled everything for him, that she was
nothing but a big "I," "I," "I," and other insulting remarks. The
seventy-nine-year-old Miss Sherwood made no reply, and Paramananda tried to calm him down, saying that it was nothing but
a misunderstanding and that he (Paramananda) would take the
whole blame. But Vijayananda was not about to be placated. He
told Miss Sherwood that she had better watch out, that she was a
troublemaker, etc. When he stormed that he had come to the
ashrama to find peace, Brother George told him to have some

peace then, and not talk that way, to which the irate swami replied that George had better stay out of this.

George was seething to throw Vijayananda out, but was quickly restrained. He left the table exclaiming that even though he himself had had no education and was no gentleman, yet he would never speak to a lady the way Swami Vijayananda had spoken to Miss Sherwood. Amidst insults to Amala and Ranu, and snubs to Daya, Vijayananda continued his dinner. When Miss Sherwood tried to explain the situation to him, he retorted, "Will you shut up and let me eat." Paramananda prevailed on them all just to be quiet. Even before the meal was finished, the visiting swamis wanted to leave.

A half hour after their departure, Swami Vijayananda telephoned Paramananda to inform him that he would not come to speak at the Sunday afternoon service. When Paramananda asked him to sleep over the matter, suggesting that the Lord might change his mind, he replied that neither the Lord nor he saw fit for him to come to that benighted ashrama.

Paramananda termed the episode, "the most incredible situation that I have ever encountered in all the years of my public career. . . . Of course, all through it I could sense that Prabhavananda had poisoned his mind wholly and completely, and this had to happen." He continued to describe his reaction in a letter to the Vedanta Centre:

> For some reason or another, this did not distress me greatly, and I think I saw very clearly how useless it is on my part to make friendly gestures to Prabhavananda. I do not feel any blame towards Vijayananda, except that he was absolutely uncontrolled, and certainly he does not represent himself as a gentleman.
>
> . . . I feel that the best thing is to forget the whole matter, and hereafter my attitude is going to be that of aloofness. I am not at all upset over this episode; on the contrary, I feel a strange calm within.

Not all reactions to the episode were as calm. When Swami Virajananda, the President of the Mission, heard of it, he admitted to being shocked, and wrote to Paramananda:

> It was most contemptible for Pashupati [Vijayananda] to make a beast of himself by his mischievous trick towards a venerable Brother like you who was his host and a venerable lady like Miss Sherwood, in the presence of strangers!!! We all have been humiliated by this action. Nirmal, Paresh, and Prabhu [Swami Vireswarananda] read your letter and expressed real pain, and have been greatly displeased with him. However, the devotees from outside must have appreciated your greatness, because you and the ashramites showed surprising and praise-worthy self-control and endured it. It shows your great-heartedness. . . . Abani [Prabhavananda] certainly poisoned him. He has always been vindictive and bearing ill-will toward you. Let it go, brother. What can you do? Such things are beneath your dignity. The youngsters treat the old ones as fools. Laugh and shake off these things. They know not what they do.

In fact, this too was a resolution, however negative. All issues were being resolved, one way or another. Paramananda left behind him no question marks.

At the Vedanta Centre on March 10, Paramananda gave Sri Ramakrishna a birthday present that he thought the great prophet of religious tolerance would enjoy. "Harmony of Religions" was a convocation, spread over three services that Sunday, of Christian ministers from various denominations, a Chinese follower of Confucius, the leaders of two New Thought centers, and, of course, the Hindu swami, all addressing themselves to "the oneness of all religion behind its varied forms."

The event was probably the grandest occasion in the Centre's history. A total of seven hundred people crowded into 420 Beacon Street for the three services, packing the entire first floor and even using the imposing staircase beneath the dome as bleachers to seat the overflow. All the Boston newspapers covered "Harmony of Religions," some of them quoting at length from the speeches given. The reporters commented that it was the first time anything like it had happened in Boston.

Several of the Protestant representatives came from Boston's conservative Christian establishment. Indeed, during the week preceding the convocation, Paramananda was invited to address such bastions of Boston orthodoxy as the congregations of the Old South Church, Union Church, and Mt. Vernon Church, and Tufts Divinity School. As Lola, who attended one such occasion, described it: "He spoke so tenderly of those following other faiths and creeds. His religion sounded so big, so noble and charitable, so all-inclusive and free from bias and intolerance." Then, after telling how impressed the other ministers were with the swami, she added, exultantly, "A new era has dawned."

It was not the dawning, but the culmination of an era, the fruit of a mission that had begun thirty years before when a young Hindu monk first came to Boston amidst the jeers and denunciations of a one-religion society. Paramananda never took the city by storm, but as one person put it, "he conditioned Boston," he prepared it to accept the validity of non-Christian faiths, he let them know that, whether they agreed with it or not, universality was a force to be reckoned with. As the eminent Rev. Harry Emerson Fosdick, Pastor of New York's Riverside Church, had declared a few years before: "Christianity is at work in India and Hinduism is at work in the United States. There is no possibility of Indian religion escaping the influence of Jesus Christ, and there is no possibility of American religion escaping the influence of the great Indian faiths."

At the end of March, Paramananda held a "Harmony of Religions" at Ananda Ashrama, with a Moslem, a Buddhist, and Christian speakers. An incessant downpour marred the occasion, reducing the attendance considerably. Paramananda had envisioned a great crowd of between 500 and 750 people filling the temple patio. That was not to be until three months later, at his memorial service.

His days at the ashrama were filled, as usual, with people and problems, the ubiquitous financial burdens and personality disputes, services, public functions, outside engagements, thrice weekly cooking, supervising the men in repairing the roads, and always, always, planting and transplanting trees.

One day he started off on a walk through the ashrama hills. Amala followed him. He turned around, and explained that he felt the need to be alone, and asked her to please not accompany him. Amala laughed and kept on following. Again he turned and asked her to let him have some solitude. Again she laughed and kept on following. Finally he turned and shouted, "Please, Amala!" Later he confessed that he had felt like throwing a bucket of water on her. Then he added, "I am losing my patience. It is time for me to go."

The prospect of leaving this world seemed to be much on his mind those days. He asked Amala, "Will you look after my little trees when I am gone?" Once, after an exchange with the swami, Sister Achala burst into tears. Paramananda watched her help-lessly, and then said, "I think I could help you all more when I am no longer here."

The motive that had kept him there, his yearning to help souls, now seemed to be pulling him away. Vedanta teaches that the soul is immortal, and when it sheds the body at "death," it simply proceeds to another plane. There "free souls," those who have been spiritually liberated during this life, can succor beings on that plane or on earth, without the limitations of the physical body or the personality. Just as the Catholics pray to their saints, so people can appeal to such free souls even after they have left the body. In the years since Paramananda's passing, many peo-ple have claimed to have been physically cured or emotionally helped through his intercession. Some of his followers felt that he left when he did, at the beginning of the great European inferno, so that he would be on hand to receive and comfort the millions of souls who would be violently hurled to the other side by the war.

During those final months, his message shifted somewhat. He still trumpeted peace, despite warnings that it was impolitic to do so, explaining that the peace he advocated was an inner state and had nothing to do "with the ever-changing social, political or racial conditions." Yet primarily his subjects now harkened back to his favorite theme, the individual's relationship with God:

> Let us lift our inmost thoughts and prayers to that One Who is our all-abiding shelter. Let us come close to Him Who is unchanging love and compassion. Let us try to comprehend His all-enfolding love in our heart of hearts. Let us cling to Him in the midst of all the fleeting, unstable conditions of life, that we may place our feet upon an unshakable, immovable rock, and there find shelter from the uncertainties of life. May we learn to know that His guidance is always ours if we know how to reach out for it. Let us be still and find our inmost sanctuary in Him, and let us abide there in joy, exaltation and peace. May the Supreme Being of the universe, Who is our Father, Mother, and Eternal Friend, bestow upon us His grace and His tender blessings.
>
> . . . In these troubled times I realize more than ever how essential it is for us to live close to the Divine heart and cling humbly to His beneficent protection. I can offer you no new theories, but I do and I can offer with my whole heart my prayer that we may be sustained by higher motives and that we may be helped to lift our gaze above the turmoil and the transitory upsets of life.
>
> Sometimes when I speak it seems almost like crying in the wilderness. But who can blame me for bringing these things before you. I see so many people who are sick, so many who are burdened with the weight of their own

thoughts! To them I say, "Do not carry this burden. Lift your mind from hatred and worry and fear, and all that is destructive. By doing so you will help infinitely in clarifying the world's disaster.

I am pleading with every one of you with all that is best in me, with all that has been given by Christ Jesus of Nazareth and in the name of all the holy ones who have dwelt on earth, that you try to live by these great principles.

. . . Set aside some time each day for communion with Him. Give yourself to Him wholeheartedly; and He, the all-loving, all-wise will feel the response of your heart, the call of your soul, and will come to you and abide with you.

After big celebrations, like the Memorial Day silence and dinner, Paramananda looked faint and fatigued. He went to bed early, and sometimes stayed in bed all the next day. But the day following he again plunged into his schedule of work. Amala noted in her diary on June 1, "Swamiji is extraordinary the way he rebounds and goes on carrying on without defeat. So many look to him for inspiration and blessing." As one Boston devotee put it, "We were living off him. Jesus said, 'Eat me and drink me.' We were doing just that."

On June 5, the ashrama was planning to give Miss Sherwood an eightieth birthday party. Sumita was appearing in a play at her drama school in Boston on June 6, and requested Paramananda to be there. In order to attend both functions, he decided to fly to Boston the night of the 5th. It was a hectic day. Paramananda acted as host at the party, posing for photographs with Miss Sherwood, who was wearing her mother's wedding gown, and mingling among the many guests. At six o'clock he conducted the evening worship in the shrine, then left for Burbank Airport to catch the nine o'clock "Skymaster."

A large crowd from the party came to see him off, but a few, including Ranu and Bill Rodman, got caught in traffic. Nine o'clock came, the plane was warming up, the propellers were whirling, and the attendants wanted to roll the stairs away, but Paramananda refused to board. He told them that he had to say goodbye to some people. A few minutes later the latecomers arrived, running across the airfield. Paramananda smiled and called out to them, "I held the airplane. I didn't want to go without saying goodbye to you." They did not realize how final this goodbye would be.

When he arrived in Boston the next evening, Lola later commented, "He was so deadly tired that it wrings my heart to think of it." Sumita described the subsequent activities:

> Somehow he got dressed and came to see my play. He was late for the first curtain rise, although the school, out of great courtesy toward him, held the curtain twenty minutes or so. . . . That night when we gathered at Sandy's, as Sandy had especially prepared some refreshments and, as you know, he never disappointed anybody, he went out of his way to please her, but looked shockingly tired and worn. There he tried to get our attention almost by begging. He told us, "Don't you want to hear what I have to say?" Then he continued, "I had two warnings. I may not be here long." Of course, we never believed it.

That was Thursday. On Saturday morning, as Sumita was hurrying to prepare the shrine before her graduation, she heard Paramananda calling her name. She ran to his room, and found that he had had another attack. He was crawling toward his couch to lie down. She helped him and called the others, who hovered over him, looking anguished and distraught. Paramananda chastised them for their attitude: What good was their philosophy if they could not use it to cope with such situations? Soon the pain passed. Paramananda overrode all protests, and went to Sumita's graduation.

For the next two weeks he threw himself into the regular activities of the Centre. One day he declared to Gayatri: "I have become so involved. I am asking Divine Mother to take me out of it whole."

France was falling, Holland and Belgium were already in the hands of the Nazis. At night Paramananda could not sleep. He heard cries of people in anguish.

Gayatri noticed that he was moving slower, was stopping frequently to lie down between duties, and his mind was withdrawn, reflective. Once he startled her with the question, "Have I been a good shepherd?"

On Thursday, June 20, at three o'clock in the morning, Paramananda had a bad angina attack. He said that the pain was all over him. At five o'clock, another attack came. Gayatri, trying her best to make him comfortable, told him, "When I see you like this, I wish Divine Mother would take you at the prime of your life." He beamed at her. "I am very proud of you," he whispered to her later, "but don't tell the others. They won't understand."

That final week Mr. Boruchoff came to announce that the tax exemption case for the 420 Beacon Street house had finally been decided, in their favor. Everyone was jubilant. Now the financial security of the Vedanta Centre was assured. Paramananda looked relieved. In every way, he was being freed.

On Friday, June 21, 1940, Paramananda woke up not feeling well. From his room he could hear Gayatri wheezing from hay fever. In order to relieve her, he insisted on conducting the morning worship. Afterwards they offered to bring him breakfast in his room but he did not want to create extra work. The household was shorthanded with Shanta and Jennie Reymond in Cohasset preparing for the little ashrama's eleventh anniversary, to be held the following day. Gayatri had her hands full cooking the anniversary banquet, and Sumita was busy preparing the dinner for that night. He came downstairs and ate breakfast with them.

Afterwards he went up to his study and worked for hours on the *Message of the East*, which had to go to press as soon as possible. For the front page of that issue, he wrote an editorial which turned out to be his last message, and plea:

> What is the most constructive principle we can offer to disillusioned humanity? What solace can we give to those who are plunged into the depth of darkest misery? Our high ethics, theological doctrines and crystallized dogmas can hardly suffice at this time of crisis. Is it possible for us in this hour of great need to make untried, lofty principles living in our thought, our conduct and our actions? Most often, people are only found on their knees when they are face to face with death and disaster. The present situation is one of the direst.
>
> Can we not somehow out of all this seemingly hopeless chaos find our way back to God—having learned the great lesson of humility—without which man never really asks for divine aid? Cunning, cleverness and human ingenuity have brought upon mankind this great calamity. Can we not abandon our evil ways and seek the divine dispensation simply, with childlike faith and unflinching trust?
>
> There is not a day nor a night nor even an hour that does not throw upon my heart and many like mine the weight of suffering that our brothers and sisters are undergoing in many parts of the world. Therefore, humbly and fervently, we offer our inmost prayers that He who knoweth all, He who giveth all, He whom we call the Compassionate may find our prayers acceptable, and shed His beneficence upon this wounded, desolate, helpless, homeless and suffering humanity.

When he finished with the magazine, he came downstairs to eat lunch. Gayatri served him some chicken casserole she had prepared and some eggplant which Sumita had baked especially for him. When he heard this, he went over to Sumita and patted her shoulders, evidently pleased. He was, as Sumita put it, "so easily pleased." He said to her, "How much you all do for me, and I cannot do much for all of you." He fed them both some of his chicken, and went upstairs to rest.

A while later Sumita came to his room with a letter which had just arrived from Sister Daya. As she read it to him, he kept hunting around for his coin purse. When he could not find it, he lamented, "Well, I cannot give you any ice cream cones today." They both laughed.

Someone had to drive down to Cohasset that afternoon to bring back Shanta, Jennie, and Brother Philip. Gayatri was too busy and everyone else was unavailable, so Paramananda volunteered to make the trip, taking Lola along. At quarter to four, he came waltzing down the wide staircase, humming and singing the Bengali song, "Love all! Love everyone! Give, give away the best in you, as the flower gives its fragrance!"

It was like a refrain of the song the boy Basanta, transfixed, had heard his guru sing on the bank of the Ganges so long ago:

> Give, give all—whoever asks return,
> His ocean full of gifts dwindles to a drop. . . .
> Love, love alone is the only one treasure.

With the words, "Love all! Love everyone!" on his lips, Paramananda danced his way through the great door and out of the Vedanta Centre for the last time.

At the Cohasset ashrama, shortly after five o'clock, he was walking from the upper house to the cottage along the woodland road when he passed Lola, who was gathering greenery for the altar. He said to her, "Lola, I have been in another world." Twenty yards further on, he stopped, turned, and suddenly collapsed on the bare earth. Lola and Philip came running, and turned him over. A few minutes later, Basanta Kokhile, the spring bird, flew away.

Among the piles of condolences, tributes, and expressions of grief which flooded the Vedanta Centre and the Ananda Ashrama in the weeks which followed, there was a note from a twelve-year-old Boston boy. He wrote: "I was distressed to hear that Swami passed away last night. I know that wherever he is, he shall still love us." It was a wise appraisal of Paramananda, who had once described himself: "I'm not a teacher; I'm a lover."

EPILOGUE

IN THE WAKE of Paramananda's passing, his centers faced obstacles greater than any during his lifetime. The other Ramakrishna Mission swamis were eager to replace him with another swami. Paramananda's community, distrusting the attitude of some swamis toward women, refused to accept any new swami. They applied to the Belur Math authorities to be allowed to continue as a Sisterhood, with Sister Daya and Gayatri Devi conducting the public services as they had done in Paramananda's lifetime. The Ramakrishna Math and Mission had no provisions for such a Sisterhood. The Sarada Math, their women's counterpart, would not be founded until 1953. The Order's constitution stipulated that every branch center must have a swami at its head, and neither Gayatri Devi nor Sister Daya, being women, could ever fulfill that requirement. When, after much soul-searching, Paramananda's two centers chose not to accept a new swami as their leader, they were severed from their parent Order. Swami Yatiswarananda and Swami Nikhilananda warned them that, without the backing of a larger organization or the leadership of a swami, they would not last more than a year or two.

They underestimated the strength and dedication of Paramananda's community. Every one of them rose to the challenge, determined, as Paramananda had once implored them, "to unite in one holy resolve and banish all petty interests." For the rest of their lives they maintained the ashrama and the Boston Centre (which relocated in Cohasset in 1952), gave the public services and classes, conducted the daily shrine worship, served the many seekers who continued to come for spiritual retreat, kept up the publication of Paramananda's books and the *Message of the East* (until 1963), and strove to actualize the ideals and teachings of their leader. Every one of Paramananda's monastic disciples zealously served the ashrama and the Centre until her or his death.

At the time of this writing, forty-four years after Paramananda's passing, both centers are thriving, carried on by a vital, young community under the leadership of Gayatri Devi. The dreams outlived the dreamer and were fulfilled.

SELECTED BIBLIOGRAPHY
Of Works Quoted and Consulted

GENERAL
The following works have been referred to throughout the book. They have not necessarily been re-cited in the chapter bibliographies.

BOOKS
Daya, Sister. *The Guru and the Disciple*. Cohasset: Vedanta Centre Publishers. 1976.

Devamata, Sister. *Swami Paramananda and His Work*. (2 vols.) California: Ananda Ashrama, 1926 and 1941.

Gospel of Sri Ramakrishna, The. Trans. Swami Nikhilananda. New York: Ramakrishna-Vivekananda Centre, 1952.

Hinduism Comes to America. Chicago: The Vedanta Society, 1933.

Jackson, Carl Thomas. *The Swami in America: A History of the Ramakrishna Movement in the United States, 1893-1960*. Ph.D. Thesis, University of California, Los Angeles, 1964 (Ann Arbor: University Microfilms International, 1978).

Paramananda, Swami. *Book of Daily Thoughts and Prayers*. Boston: Vedanta Centre Publishers, 1926.

_____. *My Creed*. Boston: Vedanta Centre Publishers, 1929.

_____. *Rhythm of Life*. Boston: Vedanta Centre Publishers, 1925.

_____. *Soul's Secret Door*. Boston: Vedanta Centre Publishers, 1922.

_____. *The Path of Devotion*. 8th ed. Cohasset: Vedanta Centre Publishers, 1980.

_____. *The Vigil*. Boston: Vedanta Centre Publishers, 1923.

Thomas, Wendell. *Hinduism Invades America*. New York: Beacon Press, 1930.

Vivekananda, Swami. *The Complete Works*. 8 vols. 11th ed. Calcutta: Advaita Ashrama, 1962.

_____.*Letters of Swami Vivekananda*. 3rd ed. Calcutta: Advaita Ashrama, 1970.

PERIODICALS
Message of the East, vols. I-LIII (1912-1964).

MANUSCRIPTS

Amala, Sister. Unpublished diaries, 1920-1941. Courtesy of Mrs. Paul Spain.

Interviews with Srimata Gayatri Devi, 1975-1981.

Private Collection. Sara Chapman Bull Papers. Letters written to Mrs. Ole Bull by Sister Nivedita, Swami Saradananda, Swami Abhedananda, Swami Paramananda, Josephine MacLeod, and others. Also, copies of letters written by Mrs. Bull to Swamis Abhedananda and Paramananda, and copy of letter written by Swami Abhedananda to Francis Leggett. This collection was made available to the author through the kindness of Mrs. Nelson G. Curtis.

Vedanta Centre Archives and Ananda Ashrama Archives. Letters and telegrams to and from Swami Paramananda, Swami Rama-krishnananda, Swami Brahmananda, Sri Sarada Devi (the Holy Mother), Swami Shivananda, Swami Akhandananda, Mahendra Nath Gupta (M.), Swami Saradananda, Swami Premananda, Swami Virajananda, and other swamis of the Ramakrishna Order, Josephine MacLeod, Sister Devamata, Sister Daya, Sri-mata Gayatri Devi, Miss Katherine Sherwood, Sister Achala, and other members of Swami Paramananda's community and his family; diaries of Swami Paramananda, Sister Lillian, Sri-mata Gayatri Devi, Sister Vimala; memoirs of Swami Parama-nanda; brochures, circulars, and notices of the Vedanta Centre and Ananda Ashrama; notes of Swami Paramananda's sponta-neous talks to the community recorded by Sister Achala and Sister Daya; Sister Daya's notebook of her experiences with Swami Paramananda; Sister Devamata's notebooks of extracts from letters to her by Swami Paramananda; jottings of Swami Paramananda.

Chapter 1 — YOUTH IN THE INDIAN VILLAGE

Gambhirananda, Swami. *History of the Ramakrishna Math and Mis-sion.* Calcutta: Advaita Ashrama, 1957.

Interview with Bimala Guha Thakurta, wife of one of Paramananda's nephews. Calcutta, November, 1979. (Mrs. Guha Thakurta, who was only four years Paramananda's junior, lived in the ancestral household at Banaripara during Paramananda's teen-age years.)

Interview with Bupendranath Ghosh, nephew of Swami Paramananda. Calcutta, November, 1979. (Mr. Ghosh, who was a childhood playmate of Paramananda, was 89 years old at the time of
the interview.)

Paramananda, Swami. Unpublished memoirs of 1929. Vedanta
Centre archives. (During the preparaton of this book, an edited
version of part of these memoirs was published in *Vedanta for
East and West*.)

_____.Unpublished notebook, circa 1898-1906. Vedanta Centre
archives.

Chapter 2 — WITH SWAMI VIVEKANANDA

Interview with Amita Tagore, niece of Swami Paramananda. Calcutta, Nov., 1979.

Paramananda, Swami. Unpublished memoirs of 1929. Vedanta
Centre archives.

The Story of a Dedicated Life. 2nd ed. Madras: Sri Ramakrishna
Math, 1959.

Tapasyananda, Swami. *Swami Ramakrishnananda: The Apostle of
Sri Ramakrishna to the South*. Madras: Sri Ramakrishna Math,
1972.

Chapter 3 — THE MADRAS MATH

Interview with Clifford Ross, Swami Paramananda's stockbroker in
the 1930s, who assured the author that Swami Paramananda
had been educated at Cambridge University.

Paramananda, Swami. *Christ and Oriental Ideals*. 4th ed. Boston:
Vedanta Centre Publishers, 1968.

_____. "Freedom." *Udbodhan*, autumn, 1903. (Translated from Ben-
gali by Atreyee Mazumder.) A handwritten copy of this article
was provided through the courtesy of the *Udbodhan*.

_____. "Love." *Udbodhan*, No. 18 (1903). (Translated from Bengali
by Shuma Chakravarty.) A handwritten copy of this article was
provided through the courtesy of the *Udbodhan*.

_____. *Right Resolutions*. Boston: Vedanta Centre Publishers, 1930.

Rangam, Dr. P. Venketa. Unpublished recollections of Swami Paramananda in South India in 1906. Vedanta Centre archives.

The Story of a Dedicated Life. 2nd ed. Madras: Sri Ramakrishna
Math, 1959.

Tapasyananda, Swami. *Swami Ramakrishnananda: The Apostle of Sri Ramakrishna to the South*. Madras: Sri Ramakrishna Math, 1972.

Vivekananda, Swami. *Letters of Swami Vivekananda*. 3rd ed. Calcutta: Advaita Ashrama, 1970

Chapter 4 — NEW YORK TEMPEST

Abhedananda, Swami. *Complete Works of Swami Abhedananda*. Vol. X. Calcutta: Ramakrishna Vedanta Math, 1970.

Atulananda, Swami. "My first Contacts with Vedanta." *Prabuddha Bharata*, Vol. LIX.

Burke, Marie Louise. *Swami Vivekananda: His Second Visit to the West*. Calcutta: Advaita Ashrama, 1973.

_____. *Swami Vivekananda in America: New Discoveries*. Calcutta: Advaita Ashrama, 1966.

Devamata, Sister. "The Living Presence." Manuscript in the Vedanta Centre Archives. Later published in *Vedanta Kesari*.

Jagadiswarananda, Swami. *Hinduism Outside India*. Rajkot: Sri Ramakrishna Ashram, 1945.

Shivani, Sister. [Mary LePage]. *An Apostle of Monism*. Calcutta: Ramakrishna Vedanta Math, 1947.

Smith, Mortimer. *The Life of Ole Bull*. New York: Princeton University Press, 1943.

Vedanta Centre Archives, Cohasset. Brochures and circulars of the New York Vedanta Society, 1907-1912. Letter from Mrs. C.G. Kelley, Secretary of the New York Vedanta Society, to Swami Paramananda, Sept. 26, 1908.

Vedanta Magazine of the New York Vedanta Society, 1909.

Vedanta Monthly Bulletin of the New York Vedanta Society, 1907-1908. Xeroxed copies made available to the author through the kindness of the New York Vedanta Society.

Western Disciple, A. [Br. Gurudasa, later Swami Atulananda]. *With the Swamis in America*. 1st ed. Mayavati, Almora, Himalayas: Advaita Ashrama, 1938.

Chapter 5 — BOSTON BEGINNINGS

Alexander, Mrs. Gross. "Hinduism in America." *Methodist Quarterly Review*. July, 1912.

Boston Globe, Feb. 6, 1909; June 27, 1911; June 28, 1911; July 18, 1911. Microfilms of the Boston Public Library.

Boston Herald, Jan. 2, 1909; Feb. 7, 1909; Feb. 13, 1909. Microfilms of the Boston Pubic Library.

Boston Transcript, Jan. 2, 1909; Jan. 23, 1909; Jan. 30, 1909; Feb. 6, 1909; Feb. 13, 1909; Feb. 20, 1909; Feb. 27, 1909. Microfilms of the Boston Public Library.

Burke, Marie Louise. *Swami Vivekananda in America: New Discoveries*. Calcutta: Advaita Ashrama, 1966.

Chase, Frank. "A Religious Census of Boston." S.T.B. Dissertation, Boston University School of Theology, 1901.

Daggett, M.P. "The Heathen Invasion." *Missionary Review*, Vol. XXXV, 538-540.

_____. "The Heathen Invasion of America." *Hampton-Columbian*, Vol. XXVII, 399-411. Also *Current Literature*, Vol. LI (1912), 538-540.

Dwight, Phoebe. "Swami, Mystic, Explains Age Long Life Problems." *The Boston Traveler*, Nov. 7, 1910.

Ellinwood, F.F. "Vedantism in America." *Current Literature*, Vol. XXXI (July, 1901), 102.

Foxe, Barbara. *Long Journey Home*. London: Rider and Co., 1975.

Interview with Katherine Weld, niece of Katherine Sherwood, Massachusetts, 1979.

Miner, Frank. "Christian Science as An American Form of Hinduism." S.T.B. Dissertation, Boston University School of Theology, 1902.

Paramananda, Swami. *Right Resolutions*. Boston: Vedanta Centre Publishers, 1930.

Shaw, Mark Ravell Sadler. "The Social and Ethical Teachings of Brahmanism, Buddhism and Confucianism studied in the Light of the Social and Moral Dynamic of the Gospel of Jesus Christ." S.T.B. Dissertation, Boston University School of Theology, 1920.

"Strange Gods of American Women." *The Literary Digest*, Vol. XLV (1912), 64.

Swami Vivekananda and His Guru. Christian Literature Society: London, 1897.

Udy, James Stuart. "Attitudes within the Protestant Churches of the Occident towards the Propagation of Christianity in the Orient: An Historical Survey to 1914." Ph.D. Thesis, Boston University, 1952.

Chapter 6 — WASHINGTON

Devamata, Sister. *Days in an Indian Monastery*. 3rd ed. Cohasset: Vedanta Centre Publishers, 1975.

_____. "Memories of India and Indians." *Prabuddha Bharata*, Vol. 37: April, June, Nov. (1932).

"Indian Swami In Washington Teaches Universal Brotherhood of Man." *Washington Sunday Star*, Jan. 16, 1910.

Chapter 7 — "TO INFUSE THE SPIRIT"

Atkins, G.G. *Modern Religious Cults and Movements*. New York: Revell, 1923.

_____.*Religion in our Times*. New York: Round Table Press, Inc., 1932.

Boston Globe, June 27, June 28, July 18, 1911 (Mrs. Bull's will trial). Microfilms of the Boston Public Library.

"From East to West." *London T.P.'s Weekly*, Aug. 18, 1911.

Ingersoll, Anna Josephine. "The Swamis in America." *The Arena*, Vol. XXII (1899), 482-488.

Interview with Leela (Ranu) Thakurta, niece of Swami Paramananda, Cohasset, Sept., 1977.

"Public Letter Box." *Boston Herald*, c. June 10, 1911.

Reymond, Lizelle. *The Dedicated*. New York: The John Day Co., 1953.

"Swamis and Others." *Boston Herald*, June 2, 1911. Microfilms of Boston Public Library.

"Swami Paramananda Makes Boston Vedanta Centre." *Boston Post*, Mar. 28, 1909.

Tapasyananda, Swami. *Swami Ramakrishnananda: The Apostle of Sri Ramakrishna to the South*. Madras: Sri Ramakrishna Math, 1972.

Warne, Sybil. "Sister Devamata is Here to Work." *Boston Transcript*, c. Aug. 6, 1910.

Woodman, Isabel. " 'Outside' Spell Held Mrs. Bull." Unidentified Boston newspaper, c. June 4, 1911.

Chapter 8 — "THE HEATHEN INVASION"

Atkins, G.G. *Religion in our Times*. New York: Round Table Press. Inc., 1932.

"Bomb Slays, and Wrecks Hindu Temple." *San Francisco Examiner*, Dec. 28, 1914.

Burke, Marie Louise. *Swami Vivekananda in America: New Discoveries*. Calcutta: Advaita Ashrama, 1966.

Daggett, M.P. "The Heathen Invasion of America." *Hampton-Columbian*, Vol. XXVII, 399-411.

Dresser, Horatio. W. "An Interpretation of the Vedanta." *The Arena*, 498-499.

"Hindu Exposes Swami Fakirs." *Boston Herald*, May 6, 1913. Micro-films of the Boston Public Library.
"India and her Achievements; First Parish Club Hears Swami Parama-nanda of India." *The Quincy* (Mass.) *Daily Ledger*, Dec. 17, 1913.
Interview with Katherine Weld, niece of Katherine Sherwood, Mass-achusetts, 1979.
Reed, E.A. *Hinduism in Europe and America*. New York: Putnam, 1914.
Schultz, Harleigh. "Fenway Temple for Vedantists." *Boston American*, Oct. 25, 1914.
"Strange Gods of American Women." *The Literary Digest*, Vol. XLV (1912), 64.
"Swami Tells of the Message of Vedanta." *Boston Herald*, June 2, 1913.
"Tells Growth of Swami Cult: Boston Representative of Order Re-plies to Recent Criticisms." *Boston Herald*, c. May 9, 1913.
"Thinks Rules Ruin Religion; Swami Paramananda Says All Creeds Are Based on Doctrine of Love." *Boston Herald*, Jan. 19, 1914.

Chapter 9 — THE TIDE TURNS

Devamata, Sister. *The Open Portal*. La Crescenta: Ananada Ashrama, 1929.
_____. *My Song Garden: Child-Poems*. La Crescenta: Ananda Ash-rama, 1930.
Gambhirananda, Swami. *History of the Ramakrishna Math and Mis-sion*. Calcutta: Advaita Ashrama, 1957.
Interview with Cunard Nelson conducted by Ruth Knowlton, Cali-fornia, August, 1979.
Interview with Ruth Knowlton, who related the background infor-mation told to her by Sister Seva, Cohasset, 1979.
St. Denis, Ruth. *Ruth St. Denis: An Unfinished Life*. New York and London: Harper and Brothers Publishers, 1939.
Vedanta Centre Archives, Cohasset. Letters to Swami Paramananda from Swami Sachchidananda, Swami Abhedananda, Swami Prakashananda, Bertha E. Petersen, and C.F. Petersen, President of the San Francisco Vedanta Society.

Chapter 10 — QUEENSBERRY STREET

Achala, Sister. Notebook of Swami Paramananda's spontaneous teachings, originally taken down by her in shorthand. Vedanta Centre Archives.

Daya, Sister. "From a Disciple's Notebook." *Message of the East*, Vols. XXXIV-XLIV (1945-1955). Twenty years after Sister Daya's death, these serialized memoirs, in an edited and abridged form, were published as a book: *The Guru and the Disciple*. Cohasset: Vedanta Centre Publishers, 1975.

Devamata, Sister. *The Companionship of Pain*. La Crescenta: Ananda Ashrama, 1934.

———. *The Open Portal*. La Crescenta: Ananda Ashrama, 1929.

Dictionary of American Biography. New York: Charles Scribner's Sons, 1933. Entry on John Percival Jones.

Interview with Dorothy Hanson, friend of Sister Daya, New Hampshire, 1978.

Interview with Ruth Knowlton, who related the background information told to her by Sister Achala, Cohasset, 1979.

John Percival Jones Collection, Special Collection No.208, University of California, Los Angeles. Letters to and from Sister Daya's family, especially her husband, Robert Walton. This collection was researched through the kind efforts of Viola Carlson.

"L.A. Society Woman Takes Veil of Indian Cult; Sister Daya Must Work as Servant." *Los Angeles Examiner*, May 26, 1923.

"Mr. Hampden's Spectacle." *Wall Street Journal*, Oct. 18, 1928.

Paw Tun, Lady [Elizabeth Jewitt]. "Even to This Day." *Message of the East*, Vol. L (Autumn, 1961), 145-151.

Walton, Georgina. "The Key to the Palace of the Yellow King." *The American Theosophist*, Vol. XIV (March, 1913), 471-479.

———. "The Web of Life," "Moment in Fairyland," "My Spirit Child," and other poems. Unpublished manuscripts prior to 1919, in the Ananda Ashrama Archives. Xeroxed copies made available to the author by the kindness of Viola Carlson.

Chapter 11 — SISTER DEVAMATA

"A New Singer from Old India; Swami Paramananda, A Gifted Oriental Writer, Offers an Exceptionally Fine Book of Verse." *The Cincinnati Commercial Tribune*, Jan. 21, 1923.

"A Swami's Creed." *Boston Transcript*, Mar. 14, 1930.

"Books." *Los Angeles Saturday Night*, Jan. 26, 1924.

"Current Poetry." *The Literary Digest*, Dec. 16, 1922, 36.

Daya, Sister. Notebook of her experiences in the community, 1919-1922. Vedanta Centre archives. This notebook formed the basis of the published serial, "From a Disciple's Notebook," *Message of the East*, 1945-1955; however, there are several private recollections, especially about Sister Devamata's illness, which have not heretofore been published.

Devamata, Sister. "Introductory" to *Swami Paramananda and His Work*, Vol. 1. La Crescenta: Ananda Ashrama, 1926. For her account of her illness.

_____. *The Open Portal*. La Crescenta: Ananda Ashrama, 1929.

_____. *My Song Garden: Child Poems*. La Crescenta: Ananda Ashrama, 1930.

_____. *Sri Ramakrishna and His Disciples*. La Crescenta: Ananda Ashrama, 1928.

"Hindoo Vedanta Exponent Gives View of New Religion." *Louisville Courier Journal*, Nov. 14, 1920.

Interviews with Cunard Nelson, conducted by Ruth Knowlton, September, 1977, and August, 1979.

Letters from Swami Saradananda to Mrs. Sara Bull, relating to her financial help of his family. Sara Chapman Bull collection. Courtesy of Mrs. Nelson Curtis.

"New Thoughtist is Barred; Pastor Resigns." *The Kentucky Post* (Covington), Feb. 14, 1921.

"Pastor Quits in Row Over Lecture." *The Cincinnati Post*, Feb. 14, 1921.

"Poetry." *Methodist Review*, Vol. CIX (Sept., 1926), 723.

Chapter 12 — ANANDA ASHRAMA

Belcher, Stuart. Unpublished recollections of Swami Paramananda, 1979. Vedanta Centre Archives.

"Cult Will Settle in Hills." *Los Angeles Times*, May 27, 1923.

Interview with Cunard Nelson, conducted by Ruth Knowlton, Sept., 1977.

Letters from Swami Paramananda to the Vedanta Centre community and the Ananda Ashrama community. Vedanta Centre Archives. After Ananda Ashrama was founded, Paramananda kept contact with his divided community through weekly or biweekly letters, which form a major resource for the remainder of this book.

Chapter 13 — "LOVE WILL CONQUER"

Boston Herald. Portrait of Swami Paramananda. Feb. 6, 1927.

French, Cara. Unpublished memoirs. Xeroxed excerpts made available to the author through the kindness of Marie Louise Burke.

Gambhirananda, Swami. *History of the Ramakrishna Math and Mis-*

sion. Calcutta: Advaita Ashrama, 1957.

Interview with Raphael Boruchoff, Swami Paramananda's lawyer, Boston, 1977.

Letters from Mrs. Cara French to the Ananda Ashrama Community. Vedanta Centre Archives.

Martin, Alfred W. *The Fellowship of Faiths*. With Forewords by Rabindranath Tagore, Mahatma Gandhi, Swami Paramananda, Channing Pollock, John Haynes Holmes, and Rabbi Rudolph Grossman. New York: Roland Publishing Co., 1925.

Moore, Rev. John. "The Reawakening of Mysticism." *The Methodist Review*, Vol. CIX (Sept., 1926), 713-723.

The Ramakrishna Math and Mission Convention, 1926. Belur, Howrah, Bengal: The Math, 1926.

Chapter 14 — THE SWAMI'S CALAMITY

Amiya, Sister. "Vedanta in Southern California." *Vedanta and the West*, Vol. XIV (Sept.-Oct., 1951), 140-151.

"Ashrama at Cohasset Offers Peace to Weary." *Boston Globe*, c. June, 1929.

Bois, Jules. "The New Religions of America." *The Forum*, Vol. LXXVII (March, 1927), 418-422.

"Dedicate Temple to World Faiths." *Glendale News-Press*, July 23, 1928.

Isherwood, Christopher. *My Guru and His Disciple*. New York: Farrar, Straus & Giroux, 1980.

Pember, John E. "Swami's 'Peace Retreat' Draws Many to the Solitude of Cohasset Woods." *Boston Herald*, Sept. 1, 1929.

Sorabji, Cornelia. "Hindu Swamis and Women of the West." *The Nineteenth Century*, Vol. CXII (Sept., 1932), 365-373.

"Young Brahmin Priestess Expounds Hindu Philosophy in Cohasset Sanctuary." *Boston Sunday Advertiser*, Aug. 9, 1931.

Chapter 15 — CONCORDE AND DISCORD

Ananda Ashrama (India Branch, Dacca), First Annual Report. Dacca: 1932.

Baxter, Elizabeth Perry. Letter to the author (Sept. 11, 1979) describing her coming into contact with Swami Paramananda in Louisville in 1934.

Devi, Charushila. "Ananda Ashrama." Introductory brochure. Dacca: 1931.

John Percival Jones Collection, Special Collection, No. 208, University of California, Los Angeles.

Chapter 16 — BETRAYAL

"American Ramakrishna Mission Leader Here." *Ceylon Independent*, April 8, 1933.

"Commonwealth of Humanity; Swami Paramananda's Address." *The Malaya Tribune*, Jan. 25, 1933.

Devamata, Sister. "The Living Presence." Manuscript in the Vedanta Centre Archives. Later published in *Vedanta Kesari*.

_____. *The Open Portal*. La Crescenta: Ananda Ashrama, 1929.

_____. Transcript of interview with Concorde Brodeur and Khagen, Jan. 22, 1933, dictated to and transcribed by Sister Achala. Vedanta Centre Archives.

"Swami Paramananda's Visit to Singapore." *The Malaya Tribune*, Jan. 26, 1933.

Chapter 17 — FIRE AND FLOOD

Accounts of the fire, written by Sister Devamata, Sister Achala, Amala, Gayatri Devi, Mrs. Ellen Bowers, and Hilda Johanigmann, Nov., 1933. Ananda Ashrama Archives.

Accounts of the flood, written by Swami Paramananda, Jessie Trueworthy, Lois Houghton, and Amala, Jan., 1934. Ananda Ashrama Archives.

"Ashrama Thanks Fire Fighters Here." *The Crescenta Valley Ledger*, Dec. 1, 1933.

"Raging Brush Fire Halted at Foothill Boulevard." *Los Angeles Times*, Nov. 23, 1933.

"Where Red Demon Defies Efforts of Six Hundred Fighters to Stop Its Destructive Onslaught."*Los Angeles Times*, Nov. 24, 1933.

Chapter 18 — DISAPPOINTMENT IN FRIENDS

Devamata, Sister. *The Companionship of Pain*. La Crescenta: Ananda Ashrama, 1934.

Interview with Kanai Guha Thakurta, nephew of Swami Paramananda, Calcutta, November, 1979.

Interview with Leela (Ranu) Thakurta, niece of Swami Paramananda, Cohasset, September, 1977.

Interview with Miriam Leskavich, ninety-two-year-old woman who had attended Paramananda's services in Boston, Cohasset, 1980.

Interview with Raphael Boruchoff, Swami Paramananda's lawyer, Boston, 1977.

Keyes, Laurel. *Sundial*. Denver: Gentle Living Publications, 1979.

Chapter 19 — THE GREAT REASSURER

Anthony, Jeanne [Amy Russell]. "Intimations of Immortality." *Message of the East*. Vol. XXXVI (1947), 16-25.

Brief recollections of Swami Paramananda told to the author by Swami Nirjarananda, Swami Premarupananda, and Swami Lokeswarananda, West Bengal, India, November, 1979.

Bryan, Olive C. Unpublished recollections of Swami Paramananda, 1979. Vedanta Centre Archives.

Descriptive leaflet of 420 Beacon Street building, by its present owner, the New England College of Optometry.

Duveneck, Josephine Whitney. *Life on Two Levels*. New York: William Kaufman, Inc., 1978.

Interview with Arundhoti Sinha, niece of Swami Paramananda, Calcutta, November, 1979.

Interview with Kanai Guha Thakurta, nephew of Swami Paramananda, Calcutta, November, 1979.

Interview with Leela (Ranu) Thakurta, niece of Swami Paramananda, Cohasset, September, 1977.

Interveiw with Shuma Chakravarty, who related the incident told to her by her grandmother, Labanya Chakravarty (Paramananda's sister), Cohasset, 1980.

Interview with Swami Niramoyananda, Calcutta, November, 1979.

Who's Who in America, 1930-1940.

Chapter 20 — SISTER DAYA

Devamata, Sister. *The Open Portal*. La Crescenta: Ananda Ashrama, 1929.

Rules and Regulations of the Ramakrishna Math. Howrah: Belur Math, 1937.

Stuart, Frances [Sister Daya]. "Entanglements," other short stories, and children's poems, written in Tamworth, New Hampshire, 1937-1939. Ananda Ashrama Archives.

"Two Women Gravely Hurt as Auto Hits Concrete Abutment." *La Crescenta Valley Herald*, Oct. 29, 1937.

"Unity of Religion Emphasized at Vedanta Temple Dedication." *Boston Globe*, Jan. 25, 1937.

"Vedanta Centre is in New Home." *Boston Herald*, Jan. 23, 1937.
"Visiting Speakers at Vedanta Center." *Boston Transcript*, Jan. 23, 1937.

Chapter 21 — THE END OF SPRING

Chakravarty, Sumita. Recollections of the last days of Swami Paramananda, June, 1940. Vedanta Centre Archives.
Fosdick, Rev. Harry Emerson. Quoted in "Oriental Solace; Hindu Ritual of Peace and Tolerance Gains U.S. Devotees." *The Literary Digest*, Vol. CXXII (Nov. 14, 1936), 20.
Interview with Brother Richard [Richard Creesy], Cohasset, November, 1980.
Interview with Leela (Ranu) Thakurta, Cohasset, 1977.
Interview with Mildred Prendergast, student of Swami Paramananda, Brookline, Mass., October, 1977.
Interview with Raphael Boruchoff, Boston, 1977.
Interview with Sister Anjali [Alice Loeb], Cohasset, 1979.
"Sri Ramakrishna Memorial Due." *Passadena Star-News*, March 29, 1940.

Index

Bull, Ole, 90
Bull, Sara, 85, 86, 90, 91, 113, 116-19, 120, 121, 127, 128, 135, 138, 154, 165, 175, 176

Call, Annie P., 505
Camerford, Harold, 283, 292
Chakravarty, Sumita, 422, 462, 463, 464, 483, 495, 505, 509, 518, 559, 560-63
Christ and Oriental Ideals (Paramananda), 313
Christian Science, 115, 152, 175
Christians, Camille (see Sister Amala)
Christine, Sister (Greenstidel), 127, 139, 140, 165
Churchill, Winston, 455
Clarke, John Spencer, 215
Cohasset Ashrama, 359-61, 377, 563
Colby, Florence, 405
Concentration and Meditation (Paramananda), 182
Cousins, Dr. James, 352
Creative Power of Silence (Paramananda), 182
Creesy, Richard, 547

Daggett, Mabel Potter, 176
Dawes, Stanley, 351, 353
Daya, Sister, 217-23, 233, 236, 238-42, 245, 246, 249, 251, 256, 275, 276, 286, 322, 323, 437, 469, 472-75, 493, 497, 509, 512, 517, 520, 521, 522, 531, 532, 541, 565
Dayananda, Swami, 316, 457
Days in an Indian Monastery (Devamata), 140, 349
Devamata, Sister, 94, 95, 99, 103-107, 124, 135, 139-41, 146, 148, 149, 155, 156, 158, 159-63, 169, 172, 181, 182, 185, 186, 188, 199, 202-04, 211, 215, 227, 237-39, 256-59, 265-68, 291, 320, 359, 382, 415-19, 427, 430, 435, 456, 459, 466, 497, 528, 529

Devi, Charushila, 260, 340, 348, 350, 351, 362, 363, 387, 397, 405, 411, 421, 422, 429, 463, 476, 479, 484, 499, 503, 509
Devi, Gayatri, 275, 310, 311, 312-15, 317, 324-26, 333, 338, 349, 350, 351, 353, 356, 361, 364, 365, 367, 376, 383, 386, 395, 402, 406, 407, 409, 427, 429, 435, 446, 461, 463, 464, 469, 475, 478, 479-82, 483-84, 496, 504, 505, 509, 512, 519, 521, 547-50, 560, 561, 565, 566
Dobles, 243, 244, 286
Dresser, Horatio, 179
Duveneck, Josephine Whitney, 490
Dyer, Mary 116

Eddy, Mary Bake, 134, 152
Emerson, Ralph Waldo, 134, 152, 214
Engstrand, Lillian, 322, 332, 354, 383, 395-97, 414, 422, 456, 457, 459, 521, 547

Fain, Florence, 507, 536
Faith, 437, 438
Faith as a Constructive Force (Paramananda), 182
Flint, Lester, 229, 258, 283, 292
Francis of Assisi, St., 41, 107, 356, 357, 495, 514
Fraser, Jennie, 362, 363, 563
Freedom, 225, 226, 331, 332, 374, 543
French, Cara, 305, 307, 309, 315, 316, 319, 328

Garbo, Greta, 520
George, Brother (Weigand), 298, 299, 329, 376, 385, 409, 416, 427, 429, 433, 435, 440, 441, 446, 450, 459, 463, 469, 487, 502, 503, 554
Ghose, Navagopal, 77
Ghosh, Girish, 170, 306
Ghoshal, Profulla, 265

581

583

ACKNOWLEDGEMENTS

Appropriately, this book about community was brought about by a collective effort. Various members of the Vedanta Centre and Ananda Ashrama communities spent untold hours sorting through dusty boxes full of letters, pamphlets, handbills, memoirs, newspaper clippings, notes of Paramananda's spontaneous utterances, and the copious scraps of paper on which he jotted down his stray thoughts. Only through such laborious efforts did a massive accumulation of yellowed papers become a valuable archive. All this was possible because of the encouragement and blessing of Srimata (Reverend Mother) Gayatri Devi, Swami Paramananda's successor, whose many anecdotes of her teacher add immeasurably to our view of him.

Primary credit must go to Swami Paramananda's original followers, whose devotion to their teacher prompted them to preserve every scrap of information by or about him. What was kept for the sake of devotion was available to be used for the sake of history. The sisters were especially avid diary-keepers, recording everything from trivial happenings to intimate instructions imparted by the swami, thus portraying a human dimension which might have been ignored by those conscious only of history. Special grateful acknowledgement goes to Sister Amala, whose fifty-seven volumes of diaries record the happenings in the community for every single day from 1920 until her passing in 1977. As a lazy, would-be diary keeper, I am in awe of her contribution. I am also greatly indebted to her sister Mrs. Charlotte Spain for giving me confidential access to those diaries.

I wish to convey my sincere gratitude to the following people, not only for the help they gave, but for the warmth with which they gave it: Marie Louise Burke, who shared with me some of the valuable material her own research had unearthed; Mrs. Nelson G. Curtis, who gave me free access to the papers of her grandmother Mrs. Ole Bull; Mrs. Viola Carlson, who meticulously researched the background data on Sister Daya; Professor Sankari

Prasad Basu, who sent me letters discovered during his research on Sister Nivedita; all of the people who knew Swami Paramananda and allowed me to interview them (interviewees are named in the Bibliography at the back of the book); Dr. Amiya Chakravarty and Dr. Richard Hughes, who read the manuscript and gave me valuable suggestions and encouragement; Brother David Steindl-Rast, who penetrated to the essence of Paramananda and conveyed it in his inspired introduction; the editors at Lindisfarne Press, Christopher Bamford and Will Marsh, who wielded the editing knife with spiritual sensitivity; Francis Lang, who compiled the index and laced the tedious proofreading sessions with laughter; and Rosee Duffy, who typed and retyped and retyped the whole long manuscript with a cheerfulness that awed me.

ABOUT THE AUTHOR

Sara Ann Levinsky is a Phi Beta Kappa graduate of Brandeis University. Since 1970, she has been a member of the Vedanta Centre of Cohasset. She has made four extended trips to India, including a year's study at the Benares Hindu University, and has studied under the personal tutelage of India's foremost pundit, Mahamahopadhyaya Gopinath Kaviraj.

———◆—◆———

Books by Swami Paramananda may be obtained from the swami's two centers:

Vedanta Centre
130 Beechwood Street
Cohasset, Massachusetts 02025
and
Ananda Ashrama
Post Office Box 8555
La Crescenta, California 91214

A NOTE ON THE LINDISFARNE PRESS

The Lindisfarne Press publishes books in many fields, including history, literature, philosophy, science, sacred science, religion and art. It also publishes the *Lindisfarne Letter*, the journal of the Lindisfarne Association, recent issues of which include such themes as: *Celtic Christianity, Homage to Pythagoras, The New Biology* and *The Evolution of Consciousness*. The Lindisfarne Press also provides an extensive mail order catalogue service in order to make available not only its own books and tapes but also hard-to-find publications and 'tools for cultural renewal' in many different areas. For further information, please write: The Lindisfarne Press, Box 127, West Stockbridge, Massachusetts 01266.